A New Politics of Identity

A New Politics of Identity

Political Principles for an Interdependent World

Bhikhu Parekh

First published 2008 by
PALGRAVE MACMILLAN
Houndmills, Basingstoke, Hampshire RG21 6XS and
175 Fifth Avenue, New York, N.Y. 10010
Companies and representatives throughout the world

PALGRAVE MACMILLAN is the global academic imprint of the Palgrave Macmillan division of St. Martin's Press, LLC and of Palgrave Macmillan Ltd. Macmillan® is a registered trademark in the United States, United Kingdom and other countries. Palgrave is a registered trademark in the European Union and other countries.

ISBN-13: 978–1–4039–0646–5   hardback
ISBN-10: 1–4039–0646–7   hardback
ISBN-13: 978–1–4039–0647–2   paperback
ISBN-10: 1–4039–0647–5   paperback

This book is printed on paper suitable for recycling and made from fully managed and sustained forest sources. Logging, pulping and manufacturing processes are expected to conform to the environmental regulations of the country of origin.

A catalogue record for this book is available from the British Library.

A catalog record for this book is available from the Library of Congress.

10   9   8   7   6   5   4   3   2   1
17   16   15   14   13   12   11   10   09   08

Printed and bound in China

Contents

Acknowledgements

This book began as a sequel to my *Rethinking Multiculturalism*. I had raised several important questions there, some of which for various reasons could not be pursued in detail, and advanced views, some of which, on further reflection, required clarification and modification. A book is written when the author feels reasonably certain of what he wants to say. But once he has said it and placed a distance between it and him, he is able to view it with some degree of objectivity and rise above it. As Hegel sapiently observed, self-objectification is a necessary moment in the unending process of self-transcendence. Every book demands another which, while it is a sequel, acquires an identity of its own. This one is no exception.

In the course of thinking about the issues addressed in the book, I have benefited from discussions with several good friends, and I thank them all. They include John Dunn, Jack Hayward, Noel O'Sullivan, Tariq Modood, Upen Baxi, Simon Joss, Ashis Nandy, the late Ramu Gandhi, Jan Nederveen Pieterse, Charles Taylor, Fred Dallmayr, Yasmin Alibhai-Brown, Richard Fries, Rajeev Bhargava, C. B. Patel, John Benyon, Ferran Requejo, David Held, Susan Mendus, John Gray, Anne Phillips, Jayshree Mehta, Suresh Sharma, Usha Thakkar, Narhari Parikh, Thomas Pantham, Ben Barber, David Goodhart, Lakshmi Mal Singhvi, Nick Wheeler, Seyla Benhabib and Sir Peter Newsam. Several long lunches or dinners with Joseph Raz, David McLellan, Stuart Hall and John Keane have been most helpful. The workshop on terrorism that Onora O'Neill and I organized under the auspices of the British Academy clarified its complex origins. One advantage of being in the House of Lords is the opportunity for constant interaction with several old and new friends. I thank Trevor Smith, Onora O'Neill, Tony Giddens, Raymond Plant, Bob Gavron, Meghnad Desai, Ken Morgan and Leslie Griffiths for generously sharing their insights on some of the questions addressed in this book.

Stimulating discussions over two days with Shlomo Avineri, Michael Walzer and Werner Becker on the religious and national identity at Kfar Blum Kibbutz in Upper Galilee were particularly helpful. I must also thank my sons, Dr Raj Parekh, Dr Nitin Parekh and Professor Anant Parekh, for many long hours of discussion over dinner on the nature and problems of identity in an immigrant family. I thank Pramila for her unstinting support and patience, and my brother Chandrakant for his kindness over the years.

I am most grateful to several generous friends who very kindly read various drafts of the book and made most valuable comments. They include Andrew Mason, David McLellan, Jan Pieterse, Tariq Modood, Raymond Plant, Tony Giddens and Varun Uberoi. Several chapters were tried out as papers or inaugural addresses at conferences in Israel, Vienna, York, Maine, Toronto, Vancouver, New Delhi, Yale, Mumbai, Casablanca, Frankfurt, Paris, Leiden, Amsterdam, Oslo, Brussels, Boston and London. I thank the participants for their helpful comments and suggestions. I have benefited from the comments by Amartya Sen, who was a discussant when the second chapter was presented at a conference organized by the University of York.

An earlier and rather different version of the dialogue in Chapter 8 appeared in Parekh (2002) and an earlier version of Chapter 9 as Parekh (2004d). Some sections of Chapters 3, 4, 6 and 12 draw on parts of Parekh (2004a), (1994b), (2006c) and (1997 and 2003a), respectively, while earlier thoughts on the subject matter of Chapter 10 were published as Parekh (2005a).

I would have started the book but might not have continued with, let alone finished it, without the constant encouragement and prodding of my good friend Steven Kennedy. Many of us are prone to deep self-doubt, and are sometimes lucky to have editors who keep us going with the half-believed but nevertheless most welcome reassurance that we are not as inadequate as we imagine in the dark but sometimes also the most illuminating moments of our lives.

During the course of writing this book I lost my parents and three close friends, Leroy Rouner, G. N. Mathrani and Usha Mehta. I dedicate this book to them with all my love and gratitude.

BHIKHU PAREKH

1

Introduction

By common consent, we are entering a new phase in human history. Thanks to globalization brought about by revolutionary changes in the means of transport and communication and expansionist capitalism, far-flung societies are increasingly being locked into a system of interdependence.[1] They face common problems such as regulating the movement of capital and people, climate change, the environment, the spread of disease and terrorism, which require collective solutions. And their interests are intertwined to the extent that events in one country can have profound consequences in others thousands of miles away. The global reach of the media brings to us vivid images of the struggles and suffering of men and women in distant parts of the world, involves us in their lives, heightens our sense of shared humanity, and demands a response. As different societies come together, there is a deepening of diversity between and within them, and we need to find ways of coping with its challenges at both the domestic and the international level.

Globalization also challenges traditional identities, be they ethnic, cultural, religious or national. And as these come under pressure, personal identity too cannot remain stable.[2] Although the state remains important in the lives of its citizens, it is subject to unprecedented pressures from above and below, raising acute questions about the nature and basis of the national identity on which it has traditionally relied to maintain its unity and stability. Cultural communities are constantly exposed to, and having to change in response to, each other, and can no longer define and maintain their identities as they did before. As generally happens in times of great change, people turn to religion for moral certainty, meaning, stability and principles of individual and collective life. Being required to meet new and sometimes unusual demands, and to operate in a new historical context, religion too undergoes important

1

changes, faces a crisis of identity, and takes new and sometimes perverse forms. With these and other changes taking place all around them, and in the institutions in terms of which human beings generally define themselves, the perplexed individuals face the agonizing question of how to organize their lives and define and construct their identities.

If we are to comprehend and respond to the challenges of our age, we need to rethink our traditional assumptions, categories and even questions. Some interesting work is being done in this area, and this book is intended as a modest contribution to it. Like the joke about the tenth speaker at a meeting, I know that everything that needs to be said has been said before, but not everyone has said it! The book is basically concerned to explore the changing nature of different kinds of identity and the political principles that should guide human relations within and between societies. One of my main concerns is to argue that we need to approach our problems in the spirit of human solidarity, and that this requires us to energize and consolidate our shared humanity, or what I call our human identity. Identity politics has so far been defined and conducted in terms of particular collective identities, such as those based on gender, ethnicity and nationality. While this is important, it is just as crucial to affirm our universal human identity, locate particular identities within its framework, and engage in what I call a new politics of identity.

In taking this view, I differ from both the particularists, who think and live within the limited horizon of whatever particular identity or identities they consider central; and the cosmopolitans or abstract universalists, for whom these are all prisons and the only goal worth striving for is an unmediated unity of the individual and the human race as a whole. Hegel is closer to the truth when he argues that the two identities are dialectically related, and that one does not reach the universal in a single leap, but climbs up to it through a series of mediating stages. As Hegel shows, each is incomplete and needs and points to the other as its necessary complement. His profound insight, however, is distorted by his absolutist metaphysics and idealist epistemology, which lead him to think respectively that all identities form part of a harmonious hierarchical whole, and that the conflicts between them arise only from our inadequate understanding of them, and not from the wider socio-political context within which they are defined and located, a point made by Karl Marx with great effect.[3]

Human beings are the bearers of both universal and particular identities. They share common humanity or human identity and are also fathers, mothers, sons, daughters and spouses as well as members of different ethnic, cultural, political and other communities. As sharers of human identity, they are morally equal and make certain claims on each other. As the bearers of particular identities, they are related to some individuals by varying degrees of special ties. While some of these ties and the identities associated with them are relatively marginal, others are central. They give depth and meaning to their lives as well as a sense of rootedness and belonging, and their lives would be unliveable without them.

Our common human identity and particular identities, and the concomitant moralities of impartiality and partiality, are the inescapable and central facts of our life, and need to be integrated in a coherent framework. The human identity remains abstract unless it is anchored in and enriched by our particular identities. The latter, in turn, are embedded in – indeed made possible by – and nurtured and limited by our shared humanity. We are not homogeneous instantiations or specimens of the human species. We are French or American, Hindu or Christian, mothers or fathers, and thus human in our own mediated and unique ways. And we are all these because we have certain distinctive capacities and needs by virtue of being human. We attain glimpses of our universal identity not by abstracting our various differences, but rather by comprehending imaginatively distant millions in their uniqueness, and thus as beings who are at once both similar and different, or rather similar by virtue of being different.

Global interdependence requires us to act in the spirit of human solidarity and activate our human identity. We are also, however, members of different political, cultural and other communities. Since these are rich sources of moral energy and mean a great deal to us, human solidarity cannot be constructed on their ashes or behind their backs. Instead, we should respect these identities but redefine and restructure them in the light of, and bring them into harmony with, the universal human identity. The two are then no longer conflictual but complementary. Particularity or difference is valued, but not particularism, which absolutizes it. The universal is valued, but not universalism, at least not of the kind that sets itself in opposition to and despises the particular.

This broad approach underpins and is developed in greater detail in the following chapters. To avoid misunderstanding, I am not interested in examining the causes, agents and future forms of globalization, or in whether it is irreversible and how to use it for emancipatory rather than hegemonic purposes, as at present, but rather in exploring the nature of global interdependence and the best way to respond to its moral and political challenges.

In Chapter 2 I analyse the concept of identity, and argue that it involves identifying oneself *as* a particular kind of person and, when appropriate, *with* others of that kind. The individual identity, I suggest, has three dimensions: the personal; the social; and the human. The first identifies an individual as a unique person; the second as a member of a particular group or structure of relationship; and the third as a member of the universal human community. The three are closely related, and I explore their connections. In Chapter 3 I concentrate on collective identities, an important subset of social identities, and examine the way in which they are constructed and contested. Collective identities have their strengths and dangers, and I explore how we can benefit from the former while avoiding the latter. In their search for recognition, collective identities challenge and seek to redefine the prevailing norms that marginalize them. Since the resulting politics of recognition can become culturally obsessed, it has rightly been subjected to criticism by the redistributionists. I examine these criticisms and conclude that, when properly understood, the two politics are complementary.

In Chapter 4 I turn to national identity, one of the most dominant forms of collective identity, and explore its nature and internal logic, the reasons why it has become an important part of individual identity, and the kinds of debates it generates when it appears to be under threat. I argue that it is neither given nor a matter of unfettered choice, but is critically constructed out of the inherited structure of beliefs and practices in the light of current circumstances and hopes for the future. National identity raises difficult issues in multicultural societies, which is the theme of Chapter 5. Since different kinds of cultural diversity raise different problems, I concentrate on immigrants, the archetypal strangers, and argue that their successful 'integration' requires appropriate redefinitions of their own and the receiving society's identity. Since many contemporary societies, especially those in Europe, have defined themselves traditionally as nation states, they feel threatened, in a way that the US does not, by deep diversity, particularly that represented by their Muslim immigrants. In Chapter 6 I explore how they can cope with it and argue that, although they are right to be worried about a deeply alienated, small but significant Muslim youth, the bulk of their Muslim population has adjusted reasonably well.

In almost all contemporary societies, religion has acquired considerable salience. Faced with massive changes in their ways of life and fearful of losing their sense of identity, large groups of people in Western and non-Western societies are turning to religion to give them moral stability. This has taken particularly strident forms in some, though by no means all, Muslim societies, especially those with a weak secular culture and poorly developed political and economic institutions. They expect religion to play the role of a secular ideology, and use it to transform society. In Chapter 7 I show why this happens, and with what disastrous results.

Cultural diversity at the global level can become a source of acute conflict if it is not understood properly and related to wider economic, political and other factors. Samuel Huntington (1996) argues that Islam resents the West's power and values, and that a clash between the two is inescapable. In Chapter 8 I critically examine this view, and argue that it is deeply flawed. A dialogue between societies at economic, political and other levels is the only way to deal with their conflicts. The dialogue, however, is not easy, has its limits, and to expect more of it than it can deliver is to invite disappointment. While fostering the necessary conditions for it, we need to devise ways to contain and manage possible clashes.

In Chapter 9 I take a closer look at the impact of globalization on local cultures, and reject the two opposite views that it leads to homogenization and even Americanization, and to resistance and fragmentation. By and large, cultural communities have considerable resilience and ingenuity, and cope with external influences by reconstituting themselves. While some occasionally panic and turn inward, they too, consciously or unconsciously, absorb a good many global influences, partly as a very condition of their survival and partly because of their inherent appeal. The overall result is neither homogenization nor fragmentation but more complex, rather like a conversation between the speakers of different languages who nevertheless share part of their vocabulary, and are pleased to encounter small but growing passages of lucidity in the midst of large areas of incomprehension.

In the remaining four chapters (Chapters 10–13) I cast the net wider and address the moral and political questions raised by global interdependence. Since it requires collective action and some concern for the interests of others, we need a global ethics to guide our choices and forms of relationship. I discuss the nature, basis and contents of such an ethics in Chapter 10. Since our common humanity cannot be detached from our special relations with some individuals and communities, a tension arises between their claims and those of human beings in general, between the moralities of partiality and impartiality. Chapter 11 explores their tension and ways of reducing it. Chapter 12 explores the political implications of the view I develop in the two preceding chapters, and makes a case for globally orientated citizenship, showing how we should balance the claims of our fellow citizens and wider humankind. I argue that our duties to our fellow human beings could involve humanitarian intervention in certain circumstances. This raises the complex question of whether we have a duty to promote democracy in highly repressive societies. In the last chapter I argue that we *do*, provided that certain conditions are met. Since this chapter highlights the basic concerns of the book, it is a good place to end or, as the optimists say, to 'conclude' it.

A few words about the general orientation of the book might be helpful. I have long believed that philosophy benefits greatly from close familiarity with its subject matter.[4] Moral philosophy would be infinitely poorer, lack internal checks, and might not even get off the ground if moral philosophers did not regularly face moral dilemmas, make moral decisions and know what it was to act morally. This is just as true of political philosophy, perhaps even more so, because we are citizens, vote in elections, read daily newspapers, and think that we know political life as well as we should, when in fact it is often quite complex. Activists or those fighting against injustice have their blind spots, but they discover aspects of political life and understand the complex mechanisms of power and domination that others do not.

This book was begun when I was appointed to the House of Lords, and carries the traces of its context. I found myself asking what political philosophy has to contribute to the understanding and conduct of political life, and what insights and skills, if any, I brought to the deliberations on the great issues of the day that others did not. This was brought home to me rather sharply during conversations with several distinguished public figures in Britain and abroad. They said they expected political philosophers to be 'thoughtful and reflective persons' saying 'something important about the world', but generally found them to be interested only in each other or in 'abstract and trivial' questions. They got little out of the philosophers' writings about how to deal with the sorry state of the world and address such serious issues as whether or not to go to war to topple a tyrant, or ask their countrymen to make sacrifices to alleviate poverty and injustice in other parts of the world, how to respond to 'terrorists', whether to allow religion a valued public role, respect the claims of all manner of identity groups, and promote greater equality within and between societies. My usual reply that political philosophers did not meet their flattering description, that their job was to understand the world and not to prescribe or preach, and that they had no special expertise in handling practical political issues cut little ice with them. If the understanding did not lead to illumination and give at least some helpful general perspective on political life, it was, in the public figures' view, 'pointless' and 'self-indulgent'.

They are mistaken, but they do raise an important question about the nature and aims of political philosophy. Although this is not the place to answer it at length, it seems to me that while political philosophy has its own intellectual and moral discipline and mode of working, it needs, at least from time to time, to take its bearings from concrete issues and test itself against them. This does not at all mean that it should aim to guide the world or pontificate on day-to-day issues. If it ever entertained such a hubristic ambition, it would bring itself into ridicule. It does, however, make a significant contribution to political life by clarifying issues, analysing the language in which they are framed, exposing specious arguments and offering better ones, examining and criticizing the political principles in terms of which political actors take and defend their decisions, and articulating a historically relevant and possible vision of a good society. The challenge before it is how to engage with the great issues of the day without betraying its intellectual integrity and rigour.

This book is an attempt to chart this terrain. It is written at the interface of the *vita contemplativa* and the *vita activa*. Its intended audience is both fellow political philosophers and politically concerned individuals. The obvious danger is that it either falls down the cracks between the two and interests neither, or is much more of one than the other and interests one while alienating the other. I hope that, by and large, it strikes a reasonable balance. Even if it does not, it should, I hope, inspire better minds to explore how political philosophy should be practised so that it does justice to both its equally important halves, and in which politics does not merely supply the raw material but also shapes the appropriate mode of philosophizing it.[5]

2

The Concept of Identity

The question of identity arises in different contexts, and each has generated a rich tradition of discourse.[1] We might ask if we are the same persons today as fifty years ago, whether the story of our life from birth onwards is the story of the same person, and, if so, what the sameness consists in. We might also ask if we are the same persons in our different roles, how they can be said to pertain to the same individual, and what is the basis of that sameness. We might wonder if we are anything more than an endless stream of moods, memories, feelings and thoughts and, if not, what holds them all together and makes them ours. We might also ask what individuates us, defines and distinguishes us from others and makes us this person rather than some other. Although these questions are related, they emphasize different aspects of identity and look at it from different angles. In this chapter, and in the rest of the book, I discuss identity in its last sense.[2]

The identity of a thing consists in those constitutive features that define it as this thing or this kind of thing rather than some other, and distinguish it from others. Pointing to mere differences is not enough, however, as everything differs from everything else in countless respects, not all of which can be listed. More importantly, differences might be trivial, and tell us nothing about the entity in question. We need to probe more deeply and identify significant, constitutive or identity-determining features that explain others and without which the entity in question would not be what it is. The fact, for example, that modern states, unlike their predecessors, are large, require passports and visas and have their own flags and national anthems does not of itself tell us why they represent new political formations. Their identity lies in interrelated features such as territoriality, sovereignty, homogeneous legal space and abstraction of political relations from the rest of social relations that give rise to others and make them historically unique.

We may explore the identity of anything, be it capitalism, Western civilization, modernity, the university, liberalism or Christianity, asking in each case what makes it what it is, individuates it, and marks it out from others. This is also the case with the identity of human beings, with the crucial difference that, as self-conscious and self-determining agents, they are able to reflect on who they are and decide what they wish to make of themselves. To explore an individual's identity is to ask what makes him who he is, how he views and relates to himself and the world, and why as a result he is this person and not anyone else. Not every distinguishing feature constitutes his identity, only those that are an integral part of him, matter to him deeply, and in whose absence he would no longer be the same person. Identity involves interpretation and judgement, and is not a matter of mere empirical description. One could be mistaken about what one takes to be one's own or another person's identity.

An individual's identity is three-dimensional, or has three inseparable components. For analytical convenience and at the risk of reification, I shall call them three related but different identities. Human beings are unique individuals, distinct centres of self-consciousness, have different bodies, biographical details, an ineliminable inner life and a sense of selfhood or subjectivity. I shall call this their *personal identity*. Second, they are socially embedded, members of different ethnic, religious, cultural, occupational, national and other groups, and are related to others in countless formal and informal ways. They define and distinguish themselves, and are defined and distinguished by others, in terms of one or more of these. I shall call this their *social identity*. Third, human beings belong, and know that they belong, to a distinct species, define themselves and decide how they should live and conduct themselves as human beings. As I show later, these three dimensions are intertwined and inseparable, each presupposes and makes sense only in relation to the others, and forms part of what I shall call *individual identity* or the *overall identity* of a human being. They are, however, different in their nature, arise in different ways, and can and should be distinguished in order to counter the widespread current tendency to equate individual identity with one of these, usually the personal or social identity.

Personal identity

Human beings grow up being shaped by countless planned and unplanned influences. Their family, school, culture, class, religion and the wider society mould them in certain ways. They are also subject to the influences of their personal experiences, formal and informal encounters with others, chance remarks they have overheard or events they have witnessed, books they have read, films they have seen, and so on and on. All this often leaves deep marks on them and shapes their identity.

As they grow up, they seek to understand and make sense of themselves. They reflect on their beliefs, values, attitudes to life, qualities of character, and approve or disapprove of some of them. They might find that they harbour all manner of irrational prejudices, or that some of their values and beliefs about the world are misguided, and set themselves the task of overcoming these. The beliefs and values in terms of which they define or identify themselves as certain kinds of person constitute their personal identity. It articulates their conception of themselves or their fundamental orientation, and provides a framework within which they view themselves and the world. Self-understanding and self-reflection do not take place in a social vacuum. They occur against the background of, and are structured by, the range of possibilities, ideals of life, forms of thought, and the intellectual and moral resources available in an individual's society. In traditional societies, the individual is defined more or less exhaustively by his/her heavily scripted social positions, and personal identity, although present in the form of bare biographical details, is neither valued nor allowed much space. This is not so in modern society, and I shall concentrate on this.[3]

Although facilitated by others, personal identity in modern society is an individual achievement.[4] It is within the reach of all, but some may fail to achieve it because of poor upbringing, inadequate or confused self-understanding, lack of critical self-reflection, or aversion to or fear of settled preferences and a stable identity encouraged by the consumerist society Such individuals are no one in particular, they are different people depending on the mood they are in, and drift through life without a clear sense of who they are and what they wish to make of themselves. As the saying goes, a man who aims at nothing misses nothing. If we are prepared to stretch the term and like paradoxes, we might say that not having a personal identity is their identity. Personal identity is not a possession which, once achieved, can be cherished passively. It is expressed in and retains its vitality only in so far as it is exercised and affirmed in appropriate choices and actions. It is never a finished product either. New experiences, new insights into oneself, social changes, exposure to other ways of looking at the world, and deeper self-reflection might reveal its ambiguities and limitations, and lead to its revision.

Identity involves choice in the sense that we deliberate and decide whether to define ourselves as, and seek to become, this or that kind of person. We are not determined by our background and are able to reflect on it critically and sometimes even to break with it. We should not, however, ignore the limits of choice, and define it so widely or thinly that it loses all specificity and nothing falls outside it.[5] Some identities might not involve choice, as is now generally taken to be the case with homosexual orientation: one finds oneself irresistibly drawn to persons of the same sex and simply accepts it as a fact about oneself. Even when choice is involved, it might be internally constrained in a manner of which we might not be fully aware, and limit the range of alternatives we entertain or consider seriously. Sometimes we think it is pointless to spend all our life fighting against some of our undesirable but deep-seated tendencies, and reconcile ourselves to them. Or we are powerfully propelled towards a particular course of action or way of life, and surrender to such an 'inner yearning' or 'calling'.[6]

We sometimes even find that we are not what we had thought ourselves to be, as happens when long suppressed or long forgotten aspects of ourselves unexpectedly come to the fore. Tom Hayden, a fully assimilated Irish-American writer and activist, narrates an experience that is not uncommon. While watching African-American civil rights campaigners marching through the streets singing 'We shall overcome', he had an 'epiphany' and felt most intensely that he was 'really Irish, Irish on the inside'. He felt a 'void in my soul that assimilation had caused', and wanted to recover his 'Irish identity' from the 'forced amnesia'.[7] Many Australian aboriginals, who had been given away for adoption to white parents and grew up thinking of themselves as white, have talked of 'sudden' or 'traumatic self-discovery', a sense of recognition and identification, when brought face to face with aboriginal ways of life, music or rituals. At a somewhat different level, we build up a particular kind of character through our choices and, as we do so, the range of choices diminishes and certain things never occur to us or are acceptable as possible alternatives. Spinoza highlighted the paradox of choice when he observed that to have a well-developed character is so to anchor one's identity in certain commitments and values that one has no or only minimal choice in morally significant matters. When my student does not murder me for failing him in his examination, it would be odd to say that he had a choice to do so but did not make it. The thought either did not occur to him, even as a formal possibility or a fantasy, or, if it did, he thought it too ridiculous or crazy for someone like him to contemplate.

Sigmund Freud provides a different angle on the possibility and limits of choice in the formation of identity.[8] He said he was 'completely estranged from the religion of his fathers', did not share their nationalist ideals and deep insecurities, was critical of many of their beliefs and practices, and had not thought of himself as Jewish. As he reflected on himself, he discovered that he was 'in his essential nature a Jew'. This included 'many obscure emotional forces . . . as well as a clear consciousness of inner identity' (*die Klare Bewussheit der innern Identitat*), about which he could do little and which he accepted as an integral part of himself. He also identified two important qualities in himself which he traced to his Jewish background: freedom from many of the prejudices that restricted others in the use of their intellect; and readiness to dissent from the majority. He did not wish to suggest that non-Jews did not possess these qualities, but rather that, in his case, his Jewish upbringing was their source. He acknowledged that he might be able to change them if he tried hard, though only within strict limits, but argued that he had 'no desire' to do so, largely because these were worthwhile qualities. His case highlights situations where what is involved is reflective endorsement rather than choice.

Personal identity plays an indispensable role in human life.[9] It acts as an intellectual and moral compass, guides one's choices and actions, and makes them coherent and consistent. It enables one to plan and structure one's life, give it a direction, and to ensure that one is not merely a reflex of others' expectations or a plaything of internal and external forces. It provides the norms by which one judges oneself, and is the basis of one's integrity. Thanks to it, one would either not dream of doing certain things or would do so with a profound sense of unease. It indicates how one is likely to behave in certain situations, what one is likely to hate and love (for Saint Augustine, a most reliable indicator of identity) and how in general one is likely to lead one's life. One's choices and actions are one's own, not merely in the biographical sense that one is their agent, but in the deeper sense that they spring from and reflect the kind of person one is. The 'I' who makes these choices is not an empty or formal 'I', but one with a definite content or character, and one is or feels not just causally but morally, or rather ontologically, responsible for them.

Personal identity is the source of such powerful and action-guiding emotions as pride, shame, embarrassment and guilt, and is closely bound up with one's sense of self-worth. One thinks that because one is a certain kind of person, one should or should not do certain things, and one's self-esteem is enhanced or diminished when one does or does not do them. One does what is right not only because one should, but because one loves doing what is right; that is, as an expression of the kind of person one is. Identity thus provides a motive and is a source of moral energy. It also provides a vantage point from which to view one's past and construct a meaningful narrative of one's life. Although it is open to revision, it needs to be relatively stable. And given its unifying role in human life, it is necessarily singular, though not monolithic. An individual with several personal identities, or who wants to be several different kinds of person at the same time, is not one person but several. It is because most, or even all of us, are 'multitudes', as Walt Whitman put it, and harbour several undigested fragments of our 'selves' that we strive to impose a substantial measure of order and coherence on our lives by committing ourselves to being certain kinds of people.

The human self is a vast continent inhabited by all kinds of desires, memories, fears, anxieties, phobias, complexes, emotions and passions acquired during the course of one's life. Some of these are too deep for even the most rigorous self-examination, and we either remain wholly unaware or catch only fleeting glimpses of them. We often find ourselves saying, doing, feeling, wanting and dreaming things that surprise us, are ambushed by unimagined thoughts and fears and anxieties, and are as a result unable to anticipate and guard against their influence. The self exceeds our understanding of it, and the latter, not being always coherent or transparent, often exceeds our articulation of it. Since our self-definition or conception of ourselves is embedded in our necessarily limited self-understanding, it always remains somewhat tentative and vulnerable to the destabilizing impact of unexpected influences. While holding on to our self-conception, we need to be alert to its possible reconsideration. Those who freeze their identity, ignore its fragility, and rule out its revision claim more than what any human being can and should.

The process of self-definition is too complex to be captured by such terms as self-discovery, self-creation and self-authorship. All these are involved, but none by itself is adequate. We form our identity on the basis of what we are as a result of early influences mediated by our constant attempts to make sense of them. In some cases we approve of inherited beliefs, values and tendencies; in others, we are embarrassed by and seek to change them. Even when we revise large parts of our identity, we are limited by the fact that much about ourselves remains opaque and that we cannot make of ourselves what we will. If what we seek to make of ourselves is too far out of step with what we are, we set ourselves an impossible or extremely arduous task and burden ourselves with an unsustainable identity. Human beings are not transcendental subjects standing outside their inheritance, and the latter is not a passive material that readily yields to their design. Except in cases where one breaks radically with one's past, and sometimes not even then, self-definition is a slow and organic process marked by varying degrees of continuity and discontinuity.

No personal identity is self-authenticating or beyond criticism, as some advocates of identity politics maintain.[10] The fact that an individual defines herself in a certain way and seeks to be a particular kind of person deserves respect because we should respect her right to self-determination. Our respect, however, cannot be unconditional. We may think that the kind of person she has become, or wants to become, is indefensible or falls foul of what we most value and does not command our respect. This is particularly relevant when her self-definition impinges on others' lives, as it often does. Indeed, since personal identity is based on critical self-evaluation and has a moral core, she is responsible for it and needs to explain to others why she defines herself in this way and why she thinks it deserves their respect. This involves giving reasons, and they are normally drawn from, though not necessarily limited to, the prevailing body of beliefs and practices. She might argue that the latter justify her identity, or that they are narrow, unduly restrictive and unfairly discriminate against valuable identities, including hers. This leads to discussion and debate, even contestation, and the prevailing beliefs and values are either affirmed or revised, and her identity is disallowed or accommodated. We shall return to this later. For the present we only need to note the crucial point that all identity claims are subject to rational scrutiny. While our identity shapes the way we think and the reasons we find persuasive, it is in turn open to critical reflection and intersubjective validation.

Social identity

Human beings are involved in a variety of relationships, occupy different roles, and are members of various organizations, groups and communities. They identify themselves to, and are in turn identified by, others in terms of any of them. The range of social identification and the categories to which it gives rise is virtually limitless, and can be based on almost any human characteristic, trait, practice, relationship and belief. Height, size, weight, colour, shapes of nose, eyes and lips, time of birth, religion, amount of hair on one's body, the number of sexual partners, and the fact that one is a lapsed Catholic, an atheist, Mahatma Gandhi's grandson or the late President Kennedy's mistress can all be made the bases of categorizing individuals.

For all kinds of reasons, including the desire to maintain a particular structure of power, some of these features and relations become socially significant and are used to classify individuals. They are invested with meaning, governed by norms, and related to each other in certain ways. Being a woman in our society, as in most others, is not just a biological but also a socially significant category. Women are expected to cultivate certain qualities, behave in certain ways, refrain from using certain kinds of language, to dress and sit in certain ways, and are judged to be suitable or unsuitable for certain kinds of occupations. In a racially conscious society, black and white are socially significant categories, and those so classified are subjected to certain norms, forms of relationship, stereotypes and modes of treatment. Since socially significant categories identify and define individuals as certain kinds of persons and subject them to certain norms and expectations, I shall call them social identities.

While some social identities are common to most societies, others vary. And even in the same society, identities are in a state of constant change. The 'old widow' was once, but is now no longer, an important social identity in Europe, and was (but is not now) associated with bad luck and evil powers and excluded from important social occasions. The past few decades in the West have seen the emergence of such new social identities as the adolescent, the elderly, the consumer and the taxpayer, more or less in that order. During the last few years, even winning the Nobel Prize, rightly seen as a great achievement since its inception, is being turned into the basis of a new identity, as befits the age of celebrities. Unlike Albert Einstein, Bertrand Russell, Winston Churchill and its other eminent previous winners, its winners today are constantly and exclusively referred to as Nobel Laureates, as if this was the only identity they had or that mattered. These Laureates are expected to be not only brilliant but also wise, guardians of their society's or humankind's conscience, with views on all kinds of subjects that they, singly or collectively, express, and which the grateful world is expected to take on trust because of their source. Some individuals might accept their heavily scripted identity and live up to its demands. Others might wisely refuse to fall into the trap.

Social identity has a gender dimension. In most societies, women have available to them a narrower range of identities than have men. And since they are generally seen as transmitters of the society's culture, their social identities are more heavily scripted. Their identities also generally undergo greater changes, and as a result they are more aware of their contexuality and transience. In many societies, they are expected to leave parental homes after marriage and join their husband's family, and to adopt their husband's surname. Marriage brings changes in the way they are addressed – a 'Miss' becomes a 'Mrs'. Their biological changes are more evident and their entry into adolescence more pronounced, and these too are socially marked and regulated. Thanks to all this, a woman's experience of her social identity and the way she relates to it is often not the same as a man's.

Every society is a more or less well-articulated system of identities, each subject to certain norms, carrying certain privileges or privations, and enforced by formal and informal sanctions that form part of its disciplinary regime. Social identities represent a blend of normativity and power, being legitimized in terms of the prevailing body of beliefs and sustained by the prevailing relations of power. Society often seeks to ensure that its members not only conform to but internalize their social identities; that is, identify themselves with and internalize the norms of these identities. When they not only behave but also define, live and think of themselves as Brahmins, untouchables, middle-class, blacks, women or good Christians, they are firmly embedded in their social identities. This is a profound form of moral engineering, a 'conquest of the soul', through which society sometimes strikes deep roots in its members. We cannot structure our social relations as we please and dispense with social identities, but they can also take us over and become prisons. They are sources of order and predictability, and hence of freedom, but also a constant threat to it. Not surprisingly, a society's system of identities is rarely free from vocal or silent and individual or organized contestation, in particular by two groups of people:

those whose identities are not recognized – that is, accepted as legitimate and respected by it; and those whose identities are recognized but marginalized or inferiorized. Each involves a different discursive strategy and political struggle. I shall return to this later.

Social identities may arise innocently or half-innocently and go on to have unexpectedly profound consequences. Believing that Indians were a deeply religious people and defined their identity accordingly, the British rulers introduced a question on religion in the census. Whatever their intentions, this simple bureaucratic classification had serious long-term consequences, not by itself obviously but in conjunction with other historical factors. Religion, hitherto a personal and social matter, acquired public salience. Although it had not previously been a primary marker of social identity, it now became one. Thanks to India's syncretic tradition, which allowed people to adopt each other's beliefs and practices, many Hindus – and even some Christians and Muslims – who had done so and not hitherto classified themselves as a follower of one or the other, were forced to make a choice, which over time generated its own exclusivist momentum. Different religious communities were enumerated, each knew how many they were, and what their presence in public-sector jobs and legislature should be. Public policies came to be tailored to the needs and demands of each religious group, and further reinforced their differences. Indians came to be identified in their own and the government's eyes in religious terms, such that even when the quarrels between, say, the Hindu landlords and their Muslim farm workers had an entirely economic origin, they came to be described as those between Hindus and Muslims and given a religious gloss. This does not mean that there are no differences between Hindus and Muslims, or that the census should not ask a religious question, but rather that we need to be extremely careful how we categorize people officially, and should leave room for those who wish to identify themselves in terms of more than one category or none at all.

Although society categorizes and defines its members' identities in certain ways and expects them to conduct themselves accordingly, they might themselves take a very different view of them. In a traditional society in which social identities are fixed, rigid and heavily scripted, such dissonance or asymmetry is relatively rare. It is, however, a recurrent feature of modern societies in which consensus on social norms is fairly thin, individuals are mobile, and are encouraged and even required to define their identity themselves. This leads to a great variation in what individuals take to be their social identities, how they define them, and the degree of significance they assign to them. The 'Jew' has been a socially significant category or social identity in the West for two millennia, and more or less remains so today. It is associated with certain stereotypes and attitudes and, in some cases, discriminatory treatment. It may, however, mean nothing to some Jews who have never identified and thought of themselves as Jewish, and made their choices and organized their relations with others on that basis. They do not deny that they are Jews, rather that this is not how they define themselves. It is not a significant social identity for them, but it is for most of the wider society, with the result that they often find themselves in the painful situation of both forgetting it and periodically reminding themselves of it.[11]

Gender is a dominant social identity in modern society, as in many others, but it might mean little to some women. An unmarried woman lawyer, who has spent all her life among male lawyers, might see herself, and be seen by her colleagues, clients and friends primarily as a lawyer. She knows, just as they do, that she is a woman, but it might mean nothing to her or to them. She might never have thought of cultivating 'feminine' qualities or playing a feminine role in male company, and might have organized her life entirely around her profession. Being a lawyer is an identity for her, but not being a woman. Things might, of course, change. One day she might fall in love with a man, and find that her professional identity no longer fulfils her. She begins to enjoy being a woman, over time defines herself as one, wishes to be a mother, cultivates new qualities and habits, and develops new desires and ambitions. Her gender identity now has a meaning and depth for her, and gives her life a new orientation. She might give up being a lawyer, or assign it a subordinate place in her life. She is now a different individual, seeing the world and relating to it in a very different way. Something like this is beginning to happen increasingly to many professional women, and the bewildered men in our sexually charged culture are finding it difficult to adjust to the changes.

Social roles are social identities, but again different individuals define and relate to them differently. For some, they are just that, but for others they have a deeper significance and form part of their individual identities. Take two teachers: for both, teaching is their way of earning their livelihood through a reasonably satisfying job, but beyond that their attitudes might differ. For one of them it is nothing but a job, which she would readily give up if she got a better one. Not that she dislikes the work; rather, it has no deeper meaning for her, is not an integral part of how she defines herself, and its loss would not entail an emotional wrench for her. However, the other person might take a very different view of the job. Perhaps she always wanted to be a teacher; perhaps she wandered from one occupation to another until she found one that clicked. In any case, being a teacher means a great deal to her. She identifies with it, sees it as an integral part of who she is, and would not even dream of giving the job up for another. We could say that being a teacher is a social role for the former, but a social identity for the latter. A better way to conceptualize their difference is to say that, for the former, her social identity as a teacher is external, whereas for the latter it has a deeper personal meaning and significance.

Some occupations have a tendency, or at least the potential, to become part of personal identity for those engaged in them. This is so because of their social reach and status, the required length and kind of training, the way these shape the individual, and the degree of identification they require in order to be done well. This is generally the case with academics, doctors, artists, writers and politicians. Unlike a boiler attendant, a janitor, a secretary or a typist, a doctor or an academic is likely to identify with his/her work, think it a worthwhile activity or way of life, train for it because s/he wants to, see it as a mode of self-expression, and consciously or unconsciously to build his/her life around it.

This also happens in other areas of life. Take citizenship. Some might see it as a purely instrumental relationship: the country means nothing to them, and they obey its laws out of crude or enlightened self-interest. Some might see citizenship as a moral relationship, and conscientiously obey its laws out of gratitude, a sense of fair play, or obligations of reciprocity. They could just as well be in some other country, and their moral relationship to it would remain the same. Yet others might identify with the country, see it as theirs, feel protective and possessive about it, love it and see it as part of their social and personal identity. When their government behaves badly, they are not indifferent to it or show their detached moral disapproval of it as the first two groups respectively do, but feel ashamed of it. Such differences in the way individuals understand their membership characterize all organizations. As long as they discharge their basic obligations, the differences should not arouse concern. For obvious reasons, most organizations tend to insist that their members should identify with them, internalize them, and relate to them in an identical manner. There is no good reason to accept such homogenization, which is not generally needed for effective functioning of the organizations and violates the moral freedom of their members to decide how to relate to their social roles.

Even close interpersonal relations are defined differently by different individuals, and what is a significant social identity for some might not be so for others. A philanderer 'fathers' many children but is a father to none. Society might call him one and make him responsible for his progeny, but for him it is nothing more than an intended or unintended biological fact devoid of meaning and significance. Even when one sees oneself as a father, one might respond to it in quite different ways: one might see it as a social role, valuable and satisfying, but no more than a role that is discharged conscientiously. When the children grow up and move out, his life goes on as before. But for another, being a father might be a significant social identity. He identifies with it, defines himself in terms of it, assigns it profound significance, organizes his life around it, and feels a deep emotional void when his children set up homes of their own.

Some individuals might even see their natural 'infirmities' as part of their social, and even personal, identity. Deafness is a physical fact and can generally be remedied. Some wish to take advantage of this, but others do not. A twenty-year-old junior at Gallaudet University in the US was asked if he would like to have a cochlear implant so that he could hear. He replied, 'Would it be easier? Yeah. I'm not going to lie, it would. But if I were to hear and speak, I wouldn't be deaf any more. That means my identity would be gone, and I would be a completely different person, and I don't want that.'[12] His view is shared by many members of the National Association of the Deaf in the US and several other countries. If they had a choice early in life, they would have welcomed the implant. Since they have now come to define themselves in terms of their deafness, cultivated appropriate qualities to cope with it, organized their lives around it, and built a new community and subculture on its basis, ending it now would in their view involve a radical rupture in their personal and social lives. Many of them are highly critical of those who go for the implant, even accusing them of betrayal and lack of authenticity and integrity. For their part, the latter and many members of the wider society accuse them of a lack of balance, masochistic self-indulgence and even moral perversity. Since people cope with their natural predicaments in different ways, we should not homogenize them, as is done by both the parties to this dispute. Each group has reason on its side, and its decision makes sense within its framework.[13]

A social identity might formally remain the same but undergo a radical change in its content and character. Castes, for example, remain the basis of social identity in contemporary India, but are less and less associated with particular occupations and an ascriptive hierarchical status. They are largely a kind of semi-voluntary associations providing a social network and sometimes a pool of marriage partners. Furthermore individuals, including those belonging to the 'lower' castes, do not relate to their caste in the same way as before. They present themselves as belonging to a particular caste as a badge of iden- tification or to claim the advantages the government policy confers upon it, but they do not define themselves and shape their ambitions and rela- tions to others in terms of it. Since the meaning, and the individual and social significance, of the caste are no longer what they were, to say that castes persist in modern India is to utter a half-truth. This is also the case with other social identities such as class, family and even marriage in the modern West.

In the light of our discussion, the concept of social identity is far more complex than is generally appreciated. What is a social identity for the bulk of society might not be so for some others, as in the case of the woman lawyer mentioned earlier. Individuals who share a social identity might assign different degrees of importance to it in their lives. Some might see it as part of their personal identity, whereas others might see it as something external, a role they play. All or most social identities prescribe a minimum behavioural content, but beyond that, different indi- viduals define their content differently. Some citizens might be content to respect the law: others might be ardent patriots. No social identity can be a blank sheet of paper, but none can be heavily scripted either. If we ignore the diverse ways in which individuals appropriate, define and order their social identities, we violate their integrity and do them an injustice.

Plurality of social identities

Although we have several social identities, they are not all equal in their reach and depth. Some are major sources of our world views and values, and relate to matters of great concern to us. Cultural and religious iden- tities tend to play this role for most human beings. For religious people, for example, religion is the centre of their life and the source of their guiding principles. They see other identities in terms of it and determine their significance and norms accordingly. A devout Christian aims to be a good teacher, neighbour, father, husband, citizen, sportsman or artist, defining 'good' in Christian terms and asking in each case what he or she, as a good Christian, should do.

While the devout Christian's approach to life is understandable, it is open to the danger that his or her religious identity might colonize others. She might think that, as a good Christian teacher, she has a duty to report on the adulterous relations of her colleagues, disapprove of and win over non-believing pupils, take a dim view of those who are sexually active, emphasize the role of religion in all she teaches and so on. As a good Christian cricketer, a man might think he has a duty to throw away his wicket to allow a bowler to get his hat trick, retain his place in the team, or break a world record. It is not inconceivable that the whole cricket team might consist of true believers who publicly pray before the start of each game, see themselves as the servants of God, approach each game as a battle for Him, dedicate every run they make and every wicket they take to Him, and see bad batting, bowling and fielding as letting Him down.

What is wrong with this approach, and how do we convince the Christian teacher or cricketer that s/he is misguided? It is not enough to tell him or her that s/he has multiple identities because s/he knows that, nor that they are all equally important because they are not. We need to show them that different human activities and relations have their characteristic structures, forms of excellence, patterns of behaviour and values, that the identities they involve make autonomous claims, and that ignoring these claims in the name of a religious or some other identity undermines the integrity of the activities involved. Cricket is a game, a sport, with its own rules, spirit, ethos and standards of judgement. If some players threw away their wickets in the spirit of Christian charity, we would not be able to trust the results of the game, admire the skills of players, decide whether a batsman or a bowler was really good, and in general to enjoy the game. Or if a team saw every match as a crusade for God, healthy rivalry would be turned into bitter enmity, non-religious players would not be recruited into the team, bad batting or bowling would incur a deep sense of guilt or even amount to a sin and paralyse the player, better play by the other team would not be appreciated and so on, and the integrity of the game would be undermined. 'It's just not cricket' as lovers of the game would say. Even God, if I read His mind correctly, would not want it played in this way, and would take a dim view of those who do.

The case of the Christian teacher is more complex. Educational institutions can be organized along the lines he or she demands. Teaching can be religiously structured, teachers punished for acts of adultery, pupils re-educated for signs of atheism and so on. However, this is not how most of society wishes to organize its schools. We believe, on good grounds, that the job of education is to teach pupils to think critically and independently, that their personal beliefs deserve respect, and that teachers' private lives are of no concern to the authorities. Anyone who wants to be a teacher must accept this, or this is not the job for them. Since religion cannot be compartmentalized and excluded altogether from a teacher's role, Christian teachers might be accommodated within limits. They might not be required to take sex education classes, time off may be given for prayer, and days off might be allowed on holy days. But on matters considered central to education, it may rightly be insisted that they should scrupulously discharge their socially determined obligations. They might go beyond them by, for example, staying longer at school to help out weaker pupils, show compassion to the disruptive ones, and taking over colleagues' work when they are going through bad times, but they must not fall below their level of performance. They are in the school as a teacher, not as a Christian. The job represents their primary identity in this context, and the latter – while not irrelevant – must be subordinated to and accommodated only when compatible with it.

Since human life is inherently plural in the sense that different areas of life are autonomous to different degrees and make independent claims, different identities cannot be subordinated to any one of them, however far-reaching it might otherwise be. The context decides which identity is relevant, and that identity, as socially defined, largely dictates appropriate behaviour. We capture this better by saying that we have plural rather than several or multiple identities.

A social identity represents the way in which individuals situate and orientate themselves in the world.[14] It offers a point of view, a way of looking at themselves and others, and is, like all points of view, constituted by certain assumptions and categories of thought. To see oneself as a woman is to divide the social world on the basis of gender, and to assume that it is a significant feature of human relationships and illuminates and explains important aspects of human life. To see oneself as black or white is to classify human beings on the basis of colour or race, and to assume that this helps one to understand society and its history better. The world looks different when seen from the standpoint of different social identities. Human beings and social relations appear in different shapes, assume different degrees of significance, and are classified and understood differently.

The importance of plural social identities in individual and social life can hardly be exaggerated. Since every social identity represents a particular way of looking at the world, plural identities mean plural perspectives, each supplementing the insights and correcting the limitations of others, and collectively they all create the possibility of a broader and more nuanced and differentiated view of the world. Identities do not co-exist passively: their interaction pluralizes each of them, and discourages their essentialization and reification. While seeing them as an integral part of us, we retain some degree of independence from our various identities and do not become their helpless bearers. Since every social identity links us to a particular group of people, makes us part of its historical narrative, and gives our lives a meaning and depth, the plurality of them offers us multiple belongings, loyalties and sources of meaning, and enables us to construct several overlapping narratives of our lives. We are able to appreciate that society and humankind in general can be classified on several different axes, and that those falling out of view or appearing hostile from the perspective of one identity might be partners or friends from another. This helps us to grasp and cope with the inescapable complexity of human life and to avoid taking a simplistic view of it. Having plural identities has the additional advantage that one does not, morally and emotionally, overinvest in (or become overwhelmed by) any one of them, and thus get it out of perspective. The need to balance and integrate different identities into a coherent life also cultivates the capacities for judgement, moderation, self-restraint and self-discipline.

The opposite happens when a single identity becomes dominant. Individuals then see themselves, their society and the world from a single perspective, and not only fail to notice several aspects of them, but take a highly skewed and distorted view of those they do. They divide humankind along a single axis, see individuals and groups as friends or foes, and ignore their commonalities and overlapping ties. They lack a vantage point from which to evaluate the demands of the dominant identity and appreciate its limits. Since it is all they have, they become obsessive about it, cling to it desperately, and worry constantly lest its dilution or disappearance should destabilize their lives and deprive them of all meaning. They guard it fiercely against external threats and purge it of 'alien' internal elements, taking an excessively simplistic and ultimately unsustainable view of it. Far from possessing an identity, they are possessed and virtually enslaved by it.

It is unusual for human beings to become obsessed with a single identity. They grow up within religious, ethnic, cultural, political and other communities, which often shape them, and with some of which they generally develop at least some degree of identification. They are also engaged in different occupations, are parents, lovers, sports enthusiasts, keen supporters of national and local teams, and generally have a variety of interests. Obsession with a single identity involves suppressing or marginalizing all this, cutting themselves off from those to whom they are related by virtue of these identities, which is extremely costly and debilitating in both emotional and social terms. Other things being equal, few human beings want to lead such lives. Since the plurality of identities is essential to human freedom and well-being, the good society needs to create its necessary conditions.

Obsession with a single identity, be it religious, national or some other, and the consequent subordination of all loyalties, relations and interests to it, occurs under unusual circumstances. Other identities might not be available, or available only on unacceptable terms, or offer little of value, or might only involve obligations and no rights. Individuals might be hopeless at negotiating the demands of different identities, and decide to simplify their lives by opting for one of them. Their identity might be widely mocked or attacked, and they might feel it to be a matter of elementary self-respect to commit themselves wholeheartedly to it. There might be a bitter civil war in society with all its murderous effects, and those involved might have no choice but to seek security in their ethnic, religious or some other identity. The wider society might undergo rapid and extensive changes, and its deeply disorientated and deracinated members might seek meaning and stability in a readily available and socially useful identity, such as the caste, tribe or religion.

In apartheid South Africa, individuals were classified and all social relations structured in terms of race. Race was everywhere, part of the air one breathed, and it structured and regulated one's personal and social life, with the result that racial identity acquired enormous significance even for those who personally thought little of it. Young Muslim immigrants to Europe often have few ethnic and cultural ties, do not feel fully accepted in their country of settlement, find little to be proud of in the current state of Muslim societies, and turn to Islam as an identity of refuge, the sole basis of their pride. Humiliated by the terms of settlement of the First World War, savaged by spiralling inflation and economic chaos, lacking a strong moral consensus and feeling deeply insecure, many Germans during the inter-war period felt profoundly demoralized and disorientated, and sought meaning and pride in the all-encompassing racialized national identity that was raucously offered to them. They did not have to comply, and some did not, but others found the pressure irresistible. During the genocide in Rwanda, people were judged on the basis of whether they were Hutu or Tutsi. And even if people rejected such a classification, which had some ethnic basis but was largely a result of colonial policy, they were forced to identify themselves in terms of it, sometimes by pretending to be whatever identity brought safety. Except in the case of isolated individuals, widespread obsession with a single identity generally springs from and cannot be tackled without addressing these underlying political and social causes.

Violence is one of the most important factors in accentuating identity consciousness. It threatens one's very survival because of how one is defined by others, and leaves one no choice but to unite with and against others on that basis. This is why the racial, religious and other forms of violence polarize communities and individuals very quickly, and lead both to an obsessive preoccupation with and an exclusive definition of the relevant identity. Wars play the same role in relations to the states. In all these cases one is required to define one's identity not only in terms of what one is not, but also what one is against. One might ordinarily be aware that one is *not a Christian*; one is now led to say that one is a *non-Christian* as a step towards saying that one is an *anti-Christian*. Even when the violence ends, its legacy in the form of a sharpened sense of identity can last a long time. Since identity can lead to violence even as the latter leads to it, the politics of identity is shadowed by the politics of violence.

Human identity

Prima facie, the term 'human identity' appears either strange or banal. In fact it is neither. It is an important aspect of human self-understanding and has a considerable explanatory value. Identity, I have argued, involves identifying or defining oneself as a particular kind of person and organizing one's life appropriately. Human identity is both the most general and the most basic form of self-identification. The fact that human beings differ from the rest of the natural world in their physical and mental constitution, can do things and form relationships that are beyond the reach of even the most developed animals, and thus belong to a different species or rather order of being is an integral part of their self-consciousness from a certain stage of evolution onwards. Human identity emerges when they see this difference not as a mere biological fact but a morally significant feature about them, and make it an integral part of their self-definition. Just as they identify themselves as fathers or citizens, and ask how to live as good fathers or citizens, they also identify themselves as human beings and ask how to live as good human beings, what minimum norms they should respect, and the violation of which in their view is 'inhuman' and places them outside the human pale. Like other identities, what human identity requires is a matter of judgement, based on both the prevailing moral beliefs and critical reflection on it. Different societies and different individuals within them take different views on the subject, and the debate between them constitutes the substance of the history of moral thought and practice. Some notion of human identity is assumed when we talk of human rights, inhuman treatment, humanity, human dignity, human nature or humankind.

The emergence of human identity presupposes two things. First, human beings should be able to distinguish themselves from the rest of the natural world, see themselves as members of a distinct species, and assign moral and ontological significance to it. Second, they should be able to rise above their social roles, status, occupation, religion and place in society, and appreciate that they are not defined exhaustively by these. This does not mean that they should consider their social identities as being unimportant or marginal, but rather that they should recognize their contingency, appreciate that they have certain properties or capacities that they share with all human beings irrespective of their differences, and see themselves as more than the totality of their social roles. In a highly structured and primitive society in which individuals are identified with and defined by their place in society, the sense of human identity is only partially developed. Human beings know that they can speak, participate in rituals, sing, dance, and make demands on each other that the animals cannot. However, the second condition of this, which requires that they should abstract themselves from their social positions and roles, and relate to others as human beings, is absent. In the West, a fully-developed sense of human identity was recognized and articulated by the pre-Socratics, who asked what it was to be human, and how human beings *qua* human beings should live. They introduced the concept of human nature, a radical innovation that implied that humans *qua* humans shared a nature in common and that it was crucial in explaining why they behaved in certain ways and determining how they should behave. Human identity received a fuller articulation at the hands of

Plato, Aristotle and the Stoics. Christianity, the first universal religion that is not a religion of the Jews, the Romans or any particular community, gave the human identity great moral and emotional depth, and made it part of the popular moral vocabulary.

Seeing oneself as a human being does not necessarily mean that one also sees others as full human beings, let alone as one's equals, though, of course, it facilitates the latter. One might define human identity in terms of certain qualities such as narrowly defined rationality or a particular way of life or civilization, and dismiss those who do not display these qualities or live in this way as barbarians, savages, subhuman, inferior, half-human or only potentially human. Human history is a story of such exclusions and struggles against them. Although we have succeeded in breaking down most of these exclusionary mechanisms and defining human identity as encompassing all human beings, the progress remains uneven and fragile. The murderous Nazi treatment of Jews, the new forms of slavery and racism that are beginning to emerge, and the brazen attempts to dominate vulnerable non-Western societies and treat their members as less than human are all witnesses to how much still needs to be done. The increasing human interdependence brought about by our globalizing world has made the cultivation of human identity both possible and necessary to a degree previously unimagined.

Dialectic of identities

I argued above that individual identity has three interrelated dimensions, namely the personal, the social, and the human or universal. Personal identity defines them as unique human beings, distinct, as this person rather than some other. Social identity pertains to their membership of different organizations, communities and structures of relationship, defines them as fathers, mothers, sons, daughters, Christians, Indians, men, women, black, white and so on, and leads to different forms and levels of social belonging. Human identity, the widest and also the shallowest, defines them simply as human beings. Personal identity articulates their defining beliefs and values, the kinds of persons they are, and how they seek to organize their lives. Social identity articulates the way they define and structure their relations with those falling within its ambit. Human identity articulates how they relate to other human beings, and what they demand of themselves and others *qua* human beings.

The three identities are inseparable and flow into each other. We begin our lives shaped by countless formal and informal social influences and construct our personal identity reflectively. We carry it into our various social identities, roles and relationships, and define, interpret and value them appropriately. We are doctors, academics, plumbers, French, Canadians, Hindus, sons and daughters in our own unique ways, and bring to them a distinct personal flavour. The social identities, in turn, flow into our personal identity and shape it in different degrees. When we identify with our social roles and relationships, they become part of us. Our sense of self or our personal identity expands to encompass them, and we cannot define ourselves independently of them. Our human identity has a similar logic. As we define ourselves and others as human beings, we see ourselves not merely as unique persons and bearers of particular social identities, but also as particular kinds of beings who share a common humanity with others and are subject to their claims.

Our identity as individuals includes our values and commitments as well as those individuals and communities with whom or which we identify. Identity is therefore best understood as a world we build and call our own, and is located not in any particular feature or relationship but in the quality and content of that world. The world that each of us builds is relatively stable but not fixed and permanent. It expands and shrinks, takes in new individuals or relationships and drops others, and becomes deeper in some and shallower in other areas. Individual identity has an inescapable historical dimension, and is best accounted for in the form of a story, a narrative, of how one came to construct one's world in this way.[15]

Since our identity involves others, we are also part of their worlds. Jay might be my dearest friend, even my life, and I cannot imagine myself without her; equally, I might be her dearest friend and she cannot, and I know that she cannot, define herself independently of me. Our worlds overlap, as do our identities. The identity of an individual is thus a site of many overlaps and crossings-over. It has its centre which also falls within the ambit of other centres located in other identities. Its story is thus inescapably tied up with the stories of significant others, and cannot be told in isolation from theirs.

Identity has a complex logic. Critical self-reflection plays a vital part in its formation, but it is best enjoyed when it becomes second nature to us and we are no longer self-conscious or constantly worried about it. While remaining ready to revise it, we generally take it for granted and choose, act and live in certain ways because we want or even love to, as an expression of who we are. In this respect identity is like happiness, which eludes us if it is consciously pursued and constantly monitored. Our lives are defined by the way we construct and harmonize the personal, social and human dimensions of our identity, and that depends as much on us as individuals as on the society and the world in which we live.

3

The Politics of Collective Identity

As I observed earlier, every society is distinguished by a dominant body of beliefs and practices concerning the ways in which its members should lead their individual and collective lives. It privileges some forms of life, social relationships and groups, and disapproves of and imposes different kinds of formal and informal sanctions on others. The latter understandably complain that the dominant culture denigrates their identity, requires them to conform to unacceptable norms, oppresses and humiliates them, traps them into a restricted and alien mode of being, and inflicts varying degrees of psychic and other injuries on them. Women argue that the prevailing patriarchal culture views them as sexual objects, inferiorizes them, expects them to live by norms that are set by and favour men, devalues their experiences, and denies them the opportunity to express themselves freely and fully. Homosexuals complain that the prevailing sexual norms devalue their forms of sexual fulfilment, treat these as a kind of physical or mental sickness, and force them to lead shadowy and self-alienated lives. Black people argue that the dominant racist culture reduces them to their colour, 'overdetermines them from without', views them as inferior or not fully human, and expects them to pursue goals and lead lives that conform to norms set by white people as a precondition of equality. Working classes, indigenous peoples, 'lower' castes in India, religious minorities and others express similar views. The groups involved demand not only equal civil, political, economic and other rights but also equal respect and public legitimacy or 'recognition' for their marginalized identities.[1] Their struggle requires them to organize themselves and pursue their objectives collectively. Since their objectives include not just rights and interests but also recognition of identity, their organizations and demands are based on a shared sense of collective identity. What was hitherto a category of classification is now made the basis of unity and gives rise to a more or less self-conscious identity group.

Given its provenance, the politics of collective identity is, unsurprisingly, articulated in two related idioms. Negatively, it invokes the language of liberation, such as 'women's liberation', 'gay liberation' and 'black liberation', implying that the groups involved want to be freed or liberated from others' power to define their identity and the consequent psychological and moral burden of having to live according to 'oppressive' or 'tyrannical' norms; while positively, the politics of collective identity invokes the language of pride, such as 'gay pride', 'black is beautiful', and 'women are not eunuchs or cuddly dolls'. Those involved are not content to be freed from the socially imposed constraints; they also take – and what is no less important – publicly proclaim their pride in the relevant identity. At one level there is nothing to be proud of in being gay, black or a woman, as these are not personal achievements but the inherited and often unalterable facts of human life. Pride comes for two reasons. First, it is intended to reject the sense of inferiority and shame associated with the relevant identity, and to assert its equal legitimacy. Second, it is a way of identifying with others sharing the identity, and seeing their past and present struggles and achievements as those of people like oneself. The pride is publicly proclaimed and not just privately felt as an act of defiance, an assertion of group solidarity, and to generate the pressure needed to change the relevant norm.

Marginalized and inferiorized groups cannot challenge the relevant social norms without challenging the wider vision of the good life from which these derive their legitimacy. Gays question not only the disapproval of homosexuality but also the prevailing ideas on the nature, basis and role of sexuality in human life. Women question not only their discriminatory treatment but also ideas on gender differences, rationality, emotions, human nature and forms of knowledge with which their treatment is closely bound up. Blacks challenge not only their inferiorization and subjugation, but also the wider views on race, rationality, history and progress in terms of which individuals are classified and their hierarchical gradation is justified. Since marginalized identities cannot attain their objective of gaining equal respect without radically changing the dominant culture, their politics, like all radical politics, has a strong cultural focus.

A mixed blessing

Marginalized and inferiorized groups are sometimes criticized for invoking the abstract and quasi-absolutist language of identity rather than pursuing their objectives in the more familiar and manageable universalist language of equal rights and interests. Take the women's demand for equality, for example. Its early advocates, such as J. S. Mill, William Godwin, Mary Wolstonecroft and many others saw no need to talk of women's identity. They argued that, since women shared a common humanity with men and had the same basic capacities and fundamental interests, they should enjoy the same rights, opportunities and respect as men and, since they differed from men in some respects and had different needs, they sometimes required differential treatment. Although such a universalist approach covers some of the same ground as the politics of collective identity, it does not fully capture and exhaust the latter's basic concerns.

To talk of women's identity is to stress that the differences between them and men are not superficial or limited to biology, but go much deeper. The differences extend to their life experiences, ways of relating to their bodies, relationship to children, manners of expressing their emotions, and ways of seeing the world. While sharing a common humanity with men, they express and experience it differently and should not be seen as uniform instantiations of an abstract human universality. Their differences are not secondary to or a superstructure built on an identical base; rather they are part of their identity, of who they are as human beings. This is captured by the language of *gender identity* and not – at least not as clearly and fully – by the homogenizing language of *gender differences* preferred by the traditional universalist view. In the former, gender is the basis of identity, while in the latter it serves only to distinguish otherwise identical human beings. The former has the further advantage that, unlike the latter, it does not take men as its point of reference, seeing women as being different from them as if men were also not different from women, and establishes women as self-defining agents.

The language of identity also shifts the focus of discourse. It implies that women not only have interests and needs, which others might be able to articulate for them, but also their own views on their place in society, and that they should therefore speak for themselves and in their own voice. This establishes them as a distinct and self-determining social subject capable of playing an active role in shaping society and its culture. Their identity gives them a distinct point of reference, perspective, and a sphere of their own. It also provides a common ground where they can meet as women to share their experiences, articulate their common concerns, arrive at a view of the kind of society they want and the best way to promote it, and in these and other ways raise their level of self-consciousness. Their gender identity also enables them to ask how women viewed themselves in the past, link up with the struggles and experiences of those women, and to construct an inspiring historical narrative.

The collective self-consciousness and the sense of solidarity that this generates gives women's identity a historical and cultural depth and reinforces their sense of subjecthood. It recovers their privatized and semi-forgotten experiences, makes these part of the society's shared collective memory, and opens up vistas that would otherwise remain obscure and unexplored. It is hardly surprising that, for the first time in history, the emergence of the identity-based women's movement has spawned a whole new literature devoted to women's studies, fiction, poetry, new approaches to social sciences, ethics, history and philosophy. This has rendered women intellectually visible, and made it both possible and necessary to ask how a given question or situation appears from 'a woman's point of view'. In so doing it has also deepened our understanding not only of women and men but of human life in general, and enabled us to see aspects of it that we otherwise would not.

What is true of women is also true of black people, gay people and others. In each case, the language of identity expresses and facilitates the emergence of a new social subject with a distinct perspective. Those involved meet on common ground, forge ties of solidarity, and feel empowered. They explore their experiences and struggles from new standpoints, develop new areas of inquiry and genres of writing, and offer new insights into human history and life in general. Since their intellectual and political concerns are articulated and pursued by an organized and self-conscious social subject, they command public attention and do not become diffused or absorbed into a wider agenda. Those who were hitherto confined to the margins of society and defined in negative terms now give themselves a positive identity and emerge in their self-chosen shapes. They display new energy and passion, challenge the narrow universalism of the hegemonic culture, and enrich it with new perspectives and sensibilities.

This is not unique to our times. All new radical groups in the past saw or at least presented themselves as bearers of a new vision of human possibilities, and invoked in one form or another the language of identity. The bourgeoisie in the seventeenth century saw themselves not just as an interest group but also as an identity group challenging the hierarchical medieval culture on the basis of liberal rationalism and seeking to recreate the social order on individualist principles. The working classes did the same from the second half of the nineteenth century onwards, and claimed to represent a new civilization, so much so that Karl Marx gave them a new identity as the proletariat. Many writers argue that, when the working classes began to see themselves as an interest group and replaced the transformative politics of class identity with the reformist politics of economic betterment, socialism lost much of its radical energy and passion and was reduced to the advocacy of the welfare state.

While the collective identity has these and other advantages, it also has its dangers. It tends to essentialize identity and impose on the relevant groups a unity of views and experiences they do not, and cannot, have. Not all women, gay people, black people and Muslims take the same view of their identity, or manifest it in the same way. In the nineteenth century, many secular Jews rejected their religion but wanted to preserve their Jewish identity – that is, their identity as a people with a certain history and inheritance. They saw the Bible not as a religious text but as an epic rendition of ancient Jewish history; Hebrew not as a language of rabbinic discourse or a kind of Jewish Latin but as a secular language uniting Jews across time and space; and Israel not as a holy land but as the ancestral land of the Jewish people. While still having much in common, their Jewish identity or 'Jewishness' was defined differently from that of orthodox Jews, but this did not make them less 'authentic' or less of a Jew, let alone the renegades as the orthodox Jews argued. Similar trends occur in almost all ethnic, religious and political communities, and different individuals take different views on what it is to be a Hindu or a Muslim, an Indian or an American.

Faced with this inescapable fact, the champions of the relevant collective identity tend to dismiss nonconformists and dissenters as victims of false consciousness, Uncle Toms, traitors, renegades who corrupt their inheritance, free riders who benefit from the fruits of others' struggles without sharing their inevitable burdens. Although these criticisms might sometimes contain an element of truth, they are often exaggerated and mask a spirit of intolerance and self-righteousness. The result is the familiar paradox of identity. What began as a protest against the 'tyranny' of oppressive norms itself ends up spawning one. The collective identity belongs to all who share it and is not the private property of its self-proclaimed guardians.

The second danger of collective identity is its tendency to create false antinomies between closed wholes. Women and men, blacks and whites, are sharply distinguished and supposed to share little of importance. Since differences are taken to be the basis of identity, they assume an ontological significance. Indeed, since the consciousness of difference is generally accentuated, or at least sustained, by conflict, the politics of identity becomes the politics of conflict, frowning on all attempts to stress commonalities, exaggerating minor differences, and even engineering conflicts where none exist. It also encourages the view that only those sharing an identity are entitled, and even qualified, to speak for it, and conversely to speak for it alone. Men may never speak in the name or on behalf of women. And if they do, they are disowned by some feminists on the grounds that only women know and could know what they really think, feel and want. Each identity group has its territory marked out for it, and no outsider is allowed to transgress this. As a result, society gets broken up into exclusive, hostile and epistemologically closed groups, raising the crucial question of how they are to resolve their differences and conduct their common affairs.

The collective identity is also open to the third danger of freezing or naturalizing a historically acquired identity. Black people often argue that they are different from whites. Unlike the latter, who are labelled calculating, emotionally constipated, self-centred and individualistic, black people see themselves as spontaneous, warm, emotional, close to nature, communally orientated and generous. They fail to appreciate that while this way of defining themselves might contain some element of truth, it is basically the product of a complex historical process. During the colonial period and the decades of slavery, their white masters justified their domination precisely along these lines, and saw to it that black people internalized it. For their part, black people sought to convince themselves that they were innocent victims of white deviousness and power. They ascribed to themselves and their white masters what they took to be positive and negative qualities respectively, and made these the basis of their moral superiority. Their current view of their identity is a product of this dual process. To accept it uncritically and build their lives around it is to remain imprisoned within and perpetuate their history of subordination.

What is true of black people is also true, with appropriate qualification, of women, gay people, indigenous peoples and others. These groups have long been subjected to marginalization and inferiorization, and their current sense of identity carries deep traces of their past and present domination. They need to interrogate it, trace its roots, uncover the politics of which it is a precipitate, and decide freely how they wish to define themselves. Unless they do so, the politics of collective identity generates yet another paradox. The more the groups involved assert their historically inherited identity in the name of authenticity and freedom, the more they express and perpetuate their heteronomy.

Dealing with its dangers

In the light of our discussion, the politics of collective identity is a mixed blessing. It establishes solidarity among marginalized groups, empowers them, gives focus and moral energy to their cause, and challenges and opens up the possibility of pluralizing the dominant culture. It also, however, has a tendency to become narrow, exclusive, authoritarian, positivist and to replace one form of domination by another that is no better and sometimes even worse. Since struggles are crucial for social change and often require organized groups with clear objectives, collective identities are a necessary part of political life. This raises the question of how to retain what is valuable in the politics of collective identity while avoiding its dangers. I identified above its three major dangers and shall examine each in turn.

Collective identity is essentialized for several reasons, of which three are the most common: namely concentration on one identity to the exclusion of others; an objectivist view of identity; and the political pressure for organizational unity. When one identity is given centrality and others are denied or subordinated to it, the constraints that they place on it are ignored, and it appears to follow its own internal logic. If we are to resist essentializing identities, we need to appreciate their plurality and interaction. Human beings have plural identities, and this is not a contingent but a necessary fact about them. Their identities, further, do not co-exist passively but interact and shape each other. Women, for example, belong to different economic, cultural, religious, ethnic and other groups, and have different interests, aspirations and views of their place in society. They articulate their gender identity differently, and give it different kinds and degrees of importance in their self-understanding. There is no inherently 'womanly' or 'feminine' essence that stays the same across religious, economic and other divisions.

Another reason why a collective identity is essentialized has to do with the view, wrongly attributed to Marx, that identity is inherent in one's social being, intimated and even dictated by it, and a matter of discovery. This is a half truth. A collective identity does have a basis in one's experiences, history and place in the social structure, and these are objectively given and not a matter of personal choice. To be an untouchable in the Hindu society, a worker in the capitalist society, or a woman in a patriarchal society is to be related to others in certain ways, to be subject to certain forms of domination, to experience life in certain ways. These experiences and relations, however, need to be interpreted, explained and given a meaning, and that can be done in several different ways. Individuals also differ in the importance they place on their social being and the identity associated with it. Some black women place greater importance on their gender; others on their race. If we are to break the hold of the objectivist view, we need to appreciate that social identity is not given passively but is a product of interpretation and evaluation, and that it has an inescapable personal or subjective dimension.

The political struggle for the recognition of identity and the promotion of interests associated with it generates a pressure for the unity of views and purpose, and encourages its essentialization. Members of marginalized groups do run the risk of being played off against each other, and their dissenting minorities used to discredit the groups' views of their identities and demands. The answer to it, however, does not lie in imposing a false unity. When members of a group genuinely disagree about the nature and implications of their identity, about what it means to be black, gay, a woman or a Muslim, their differences in matters of such importance are strongly felt and cannot long be suppressed. A group that demands this as the basis of its unity is unlikely to last long. More importantly, such suppression defeats the emancipatory goal of the movement, and denies individuals the freedom to define their shared identity as they think proper. It is vitally important that individuals speaking and acting on behalf of others should respect their disagreement and dissent, and aim at no more than a broad and inherently fluid consensus. Whenever possible, the group should be democratically constituted, so that those speaking in its name have the appropriate authority and reflect the consensus. One can form alliances and fight for common concerns without insisting that there is only one 'correct' way to define a particular identity.

Members of an identity group can arrive at a broad consensus as a result of their shared experiences and concerns. If these are absent, the group has nothing in common and lacks a shared collective identity. Whatever their other differences, all women share certain common experiences, such as inferiorization, male domination, discrimination, sexual stereotyping, biased social norms, and differential needs arising out of their biology. These provide the basis on which a shared identity can be developed. The identity is not given, and has to be constructed by means of a careful explanation, articulation and interpretation of these commonalities. Different interpretations clash, and the debate on them forms part of the feminist, or rather women's, movement. Some are shown to be mistaken, while others, for some reason, convince only a few. Yet others stand up to scrutiny, are found to be persuasive by a large body of women, and lead to action. The dominant view is contested, as it should be, but remains effective until it is replaced by another. What is true of gender identity is also true of other identities. In each case, common past and present experiences and aspirations provide a frame of reference, and different views of the collective identity compete for the allegiance of those involved, co-operating at programmatic and practical levels while contesting each other at the theoretical level.

The second danger of the politics of collective identity, I have argued, is its tendency to create a sharp distinction and even opposition between closed identities. This tendency has several sources, of which three are common: namely, essentialization of identity; failure to appreciate overlapping identities, and the oppositional view of identity. We have already seen why the first is misguided and how to deal with it. The second is mistaken because human beings have not only plural but overlapping identities. Blacks and whites differ racially, but might belong to a common religion, class or political community. Separate at one level, they are related at another. Indeed, fiercely opposed in terms of one identity, they might be closely bound together in terms of some other. Given the commonalities at various levels, relations between groups rule out sharp distinctions and polarization.

The oppositional view of identity is based on the belief that identity involves knowing not only what one is *not* but also what one is *against*, and requires a clear awareness of who is one's enemy. Identity, it is argued, remains indeterminate, blurred, lacking a focus, unless it is separated sharply from and contrasted with its opposite. This is also often thought to be strategically necessary to avoid being co-opted by the dominant groups with a vested interest in stressing commonalities. Black people and women are urged to draw a clear line between them on the one hand, and white people and men on the other, and to resist the appeal to their shared humanity or whatever else they are supposed to have in common. They should, it is argued, insist on speaking for themselves and reject white and male participation in their movements, however sincere and well-meaning it appears to be, because it is bound to introduce alien sensibilities, muddy their collective consciousness, dilute or deflect their struggles, or subsume them under a different agenda.

Although one can see why this view of identity is attractive to marginalized groups for both epistemological and political reasons, it is deeply flawed. The allegedly opposed identities are in fact interdependent and products of a common system of social relations. Blacks make no sense without whites, nor women without men. The same social system that identifies some as white also identifies others as black and creates an opposition between them. And the same culture that classifies some qualities as manly classifies others as feminine, and draws a neat boundary between them. The basic opposition therefore is not between whites and blacks or between men and women, but rather between them on the one hand and the wider social and cultural structure on the other, which they both have a common emancipatory interest in changing.

The opposed identities are also interdependent at another level. Since identities seek social recognition and acceptance, they necessarily make demands on others.[2] Women cannot liberate themselves from patriarchy by some kind of unilateral declaration of independence; men too must change their views and attitudes. Blacks cannot challenge racism and negative stereotypes on their own; whites must also co-operate by being willing to reconsider their views of themselves and of blacks. Gay people cannot enjoy equal respect for their sexual identity unless others are persuaded that it is a legitimate form of sexual expression. Marginalized identities therefore need to defend their claims before others. This involves arguing with them, appealing to some shared principles, winning over those they can and neutralizing the opposition of those they cannot, and helping to create a culture that takes a more hospitable view of their identities. Since arguments alone are often not enough, they might need to mount democratic protests, which have little hope of success without wider support. For these and related reasons, the politics of identity needs to go beyond confrontation and polarization, and find ways of forging wider cultural and political alliances.

The third danger besetting the politics of collective identity is related to its tendency to naturalize or accept uncritically a historically inherited view of it. As we saw earlier, some black groups define and distinguish themselves from whites in terms of certain psychological and moral characteristics acquired during the period of slavery or colonialism. They persist with this view of identity out of inertia, lack of imagination, failure to see its historical origins, intellectual indolence or a misguided sense of ancestral loyalty, and perpetuate the legacy of the past system of domination. They need to interrogate such a reactive view of their identity and decide freely how they wish to define themselves. This involves replacing the positivist view of politics, in which it is a vehicle for asserting a pre-existing identity, with a critical, transformative and reflective politics in which marginalized groups challenge their inherited identity and create the conditions conducive to self-determination. In the former view, an allegedly prepolitical identity dictates one's politics; while in the latter, it is constituted in the course of political struggle and is a collective achievement.

An example will clarify the point. In identity-based politics, black people accept uncritically the historically inherited view of their identity, use it to explore black studies, black literature, black curriculum and black perspectives on education, and demand the rights and opportunities needed to express their black identity. While appreciating its historical and political value, an identity-creating politics proceeds differently. It asks why human beings are defined in terms of their colour, how the colour line is drawn, which groups are placed in which category, how colour classification is mapped on to different ways of life, and why and how black and white identities were constructed historically. It also asks why white is taken as the point of reference and subtly deracialized; why blacks are said to be different when the same could be said of whites; and why public discussions and academic conferences on race and ethnicity are often only about blacks. By asking these and related questions, the critical politics of collective identity does two things: it deconstructs, traces the origins of, and challenges the prevailing manner of thinking about the relevant identity; and it also seeks to change the social structure that generates this way of thinking and depends on it for its self-reproduction. The politico-cultural struggle this generates aims to create a society in which individuals freely decide the basis and content of their constantly reconfigurated collective identities.

Recognition and redistribution

I have argued that marginalized and inferiorized groups demand equal respect and treatment for their identities.[3] This implies uniform or identical treatment in matters where their identities are not relevant, and differential treatment where they are. The demand for recognition involves a number of things such as anti-discrimination measures, culturally sensitive interpretations and applications of laws, exemptions from certain rules and practices, group-sensitive application of public policy, additional rights and resources, fostering public respect for marginalized identities, ensuring their adequate representation in public institutions, and when appropriate acknowledging their presence in the definition of national identity. While some of these demands are addressed towards the wider society whose norms, values, and negative images they seek to change, most are addressed towards the state because of its centrality in social life, reach, power and direct and indirect ability to influence private organizations and public attitudes.[4]

At one level, the demand for public recognition of identity is not a recent innovation.[5] Many earlier societies, including the classical and medieval Europe respected the cultural, ethnic and religious differences of their minorities and treated them according to their own customs and practices, which they were expected to carry with them as an integral part of their collective identity, and it was sometimes even required that their members should be included on the juries trying one of them. Nationalism from the nineteenth century onwards was basically about the recognition of the identity of subjugated national groups. The current movement for recognition is new because, among other things, it encompasses a wider variety of groups, articulates its demands in the language of rights and justice, and occurs in a culture that is often inhospitable to group-based claims.

The demand for recognition by marginalized groups, or what is sometimes called the politics of recognition, has come under considerable criticism from conservative, nationalist, liberal and radical writers. Since I cannot examine them all in detail here, I shall concentrate on the last group, both because their criticisms include many of those made by others as well as a few of their own, and cut much deeper.

For radicals, who are also redistributionists, the politics of recognition is open to the following objections. First, the state is concerned primarily with justice, and the latter in turn with the distribution of rights, liberties, opportunities and life chances. Since recognition does not involve redistribution and has nothing to do with justice, it is not the concern of the state. Secondly, preoccupation with identity weakens the much needed struggle for redistribution, both because it shifts attention and energy away from it and because it undermines the sense of social solidarity needed to sustain a redistributionist programme. Third, the politics of recognition plays into the hands of the dominant class, which is only too happy to accommodate cultural and other differences as a way of diverting attention from the inequalities of wealth and power. Fourth, it is centred on group rights, has a collectivist thrust, homogenizes individuals, and breaks up society into self-contained groups. Finally, it judges the state on the basis of its willingness to respect and accommodate cultural and other identities rather than to secure social justice. By shifting the basis of legitimacy in this way, it removes one of the most powerful weapons in the armoury of the critics of an unjust social and political order.[6]

As I have myself argued in the previous section and will argue later, some of these criticisms are well founded, and the politics of recognition ignores them at its peril. The basic question, however, is whether these limitations are inherent in it, whether the two forms of politics are incompatible, and whether recognition can be a matter of justice. I suggest that they are complementary, that each needs the other to give it moral depth and political energy, and that the theory of justice presupposed by the redistributionists needs to be rethought in the light of the criticisms made by the politics of identity.[7]

Complementarity[8]

The redistributionists take a narrow view of justice, and assume that the equality of rights, opportunities and life chances is the only or the most important desideratum in a good society. Imagine a society in which economic and other inequalities are drastically reduced, or even eliminated, and its members lead the lives of their choice, but all prefer the same kind of life, have the same tastes and think along broadly similar lines. It is naïve to think that this cannot happen in an egalitarian society, for there is nothing about such a society that rules out moral and cultural uniformity. Indeed, Alexis de Tocqueville thought this was an endemic danger, and some perceptive critics of modern society have argued that we are already moving in that direction. The epistemological, moral, aesthetic and other advantages of moral and cultural diversity are acknowledged by liberal and other writers and need no reiteration. Unlike the redistributionists, the advocates of recognition appreciate this, and see the recognition of identity as one way of nurturing diversity. While we may disagree with their answer, we cannot deny the importance of their concerns.[9]

The point of this argument is reinforced by looking at our imaginary society from a different angle. Suppose it achieves redistributive justice, but takes demeaning views of gay men, lesbians, women, black people, and religious minorities. It insists on only one correct way to live, behave, marry, conduct political discourse, to find sexual fulfilment and to organize the family, and attaches different forms and degrees of social, legal and other sanctions to deviant behaviour. Its members enjoy economic and social equality, but not the equality to define and express their identities. Some of them are bound to feel oppressed in the sense that they are made to feel ashamed of who and what they are, their lives are fragmented in a way that others' are not, and that they are unable fully to participate in the collective life of society except on the terms dictated by it. Oppression and inequality take many forms. The politics of redistribution focuses on some of these; and that of recognition on others.

If redistribution alone mattered, it would be difficult to see why one should not dismantle the indigenous peoples' ways of life, or those of gypsies and other traditional communities. Indigenous peoples generally live in poverty, and since their way of life is partly responsible for this, one might argue that it should be dismantled, albeit gradually and peacefully. They also generally sit on vast resources of land, minerals, timber and so on, and it might be argued that we should acquire and use these resources to increase the general level of prosperity. The politics of redistribution cannot tell us why this is wrong; that of recognition provides at least a partial answer.

It is because redistribution is not enough, and identity matters to people that many national minorities seek secession or greater autonomy even when this threatens their economic interests, and women, gay people and others are not satisfied with the rights of equal citizenship. The case of Northern Ireland is illustrative of many such situations. While pressing for equal employment and other rights, and a balanced programme of affirmative action, the Catholics there demanded and secured in the 1998 Belfast Agreement provisions for 'parity of esteem' and 'respect for the identity and ethos of both communities'. At one level, this was purely symbolic, though no less important for that. At another, it paved the way for equal recognition of the Irish language, changes in the symbols of the state, the naming of streets, revisions in the curriculum, routing of parades and marches, and the acceptance of the legitimacy of the Irish nationalists.

We might go further and ask why redistribution is a worthwhile goal and inequalities are undesirable, even when the basic needs of all are met. Redistributionists give good reasons: for example, that inequalities breed arrogance and a sense of superiority in some and obsequiousness and inferiority in others; that they break up society into self-contained groups and undermine the sense of community; that they stifle talent, breed resentment and so on. The politics of identity deepens their critique of inequality by giving it a cultural and moral orientation. Great inequalities concentrate cultural and political power in the hands of a few, and enable them to set the moral tone of the wider society. They confer prestige on certain forms of life, encourage certain types of ambition and motivation, privilege certain values, goals and careers and, by means of a complex blend of inducements and sanctions, shape the choices and lives of others. Great inequalities tend to homogenize society, stifle a wide variety of valuable identities, and discourage a diversity of perspectives and ways of life.

In the light of our discussion, distributive justice is not enough. We also need the freedom to explore, reconstitute and express our individual and collective identities in an environment free from obsession with uniformity. And that requires that the state should, under appropriate circumstances, recognize, respect, cherish and support legitimate identities. This does not mean that all identities need or deserve public, or even interpersonal, recognition. Some identities are oppressive, breed a hatred of others, violate human dignity and other universal values (more about this later) and as such do not deserve recognition, as is the case with sexist and racist groups and religious or ideological fanatics. Some identities can flourish or even survive only when protected from the public gaze; others are devalued or remain precarious when privatized. While we may rightly reject an indiscriminate public recognition of all identities, we cannot as a matter of principle remain indifferent to identity-based claims.

Since the good society must aim at both redistributive justice and expressions of legitimate identities, the politics of redistribution and recognition are both important and need to be integrated into a coherent theory of politics. They challenge the hegemony of a particular group – the economic in one case, and the cultural in the other. Both are concerned with equality – that of power and life-chances in the one case, and of self-definition and self-expression in the other. When analysing a state, the politics of redistribution inquires into its class character and the ways in which this is obscured and reproduced by the prevailing structure of beliefs and practices. The politics of recognition analyses its cultural character, the identities it institutionalizes, the groups it excludes or marginalizes, and the subtle ways in which this is veiled and perpetuated. Far from being in conflict, the two forms of politics offer complementary insights into the mechanisms of exclusion and marginalization.

The redistributionists argue that a programme of redistribution requires a strong sense of solidarity or social cohesion. Since the politics of identity is supposed to militate against the latter, they conclude that it stands in the way of redistribution or social justice.[10] John Rawls was one of the first in recent years to articulate this view when he said that his 'difference principle to be effective presupposed a degree of homogeneity . . . and a sense of cohesion and closeness' in society, and that that was why it could not be applied between societies. His view has been reiterated in different forms by Brian Barry, David Miller, David Goodhart and others.

Prima facie, this argument is plausible because, if members of a society were totally indifferent to each other, they would obviously not want to share their resources with the less privileged. But when probed further, it turns out to be problematic. It is not clear what is meant by 'homogeneity' and 'closeness'. No modern society displays these features, and if they were the preconditions of redistribution, the existing welfare states in Europe, Canada and elsewhere would be nothing short of a miracle. Barry, Miller and Goodhart are more realistic when they say that a society should show a sense of solidarity and social cohesion – that is, some sense of common belonging and fellow-feeling. Since no society can last long without it, and yet not all of them are well-disposed to redistribution, they need to specify what kind and degree of solidarity are needed to facilitate it, which they do not. Furthermore, they set up an abstract and false contrast between solidarity and diversity or identity, and ask us to choose one or the other. No society can do without either, and hence the question is how to strike the right balance. If a society privileged solidarity and frowned on diversity, it would either alienate many and thus weaken its solidarity, or severely curtail individual freedoms, and its solidarity would not be worth having.

Another mistake of the redistributionist argument consists in thinking that a sense of solidarity or cohesion necessarily leads or has a strong tendency to lead to fellow-feeling or redistribution. It might remain confined to symbolic collective events or to war, or take the form of a vague or even intense love of one's country or society without translating into that of one's countrymen or even a sense of concern for the way they live. Even in a cohesive society, the privileged groups might blame the poor themselves for their predicament and refuse to make the necessary sacrifices. The US has a fairly strong sense of social cohesion as seen in its vibrant civil society. Yet, thanks to its individualistic spirit of self-help and economic culture, neither its government nor most of its privileged citizens are much troubled by the poverty and wretchedness of millions of their fellow citizens. Again, a hierarchical society has a strong sense of social cohesion, but is hostile to any kind of redistribution. In short, social cohesion and solidarity are not enough to ensure redistribution. Much depends and what they are based upon, and how they are understood and activated.

Even as social cohesion is not sufficient to ensure distribution, it is also not necessary. The European welfare state is a product not so much of a preexisting social solidarity as of the working-class struggle, promises made during the Second World War, fear of social disorder, a relatively strong social conscience in liberal and socialist circles, and the middle class's need for some form of collective insurance. To take another example, at independence, India had a poor sense of social cohesion, yet it embarked upon a historically unprecedented programme of positive discrimination, initially for the erstwhile 'untouchables' and the tribal communities, which was later extended to other 'socially and economically backward' groups. Its reasons included the fear of disorder, a strong sense of shame and guilt at the abominable way in which the 'high-caste' Hindus had treated these groups, electoral considerations, and the need to unite the country and create a cohesive society. Social cohesion was the intended *product* rather than the driving force of redistribution.

The redistributionists treat social solidarity as though it were a given fact of life – that is, as if a society either is or is not cohesive and solidaristic. In fact, its solidarity is a historical achievement resulting from earlier efforts to unite diverse groups. As new forms of diversity and identity emerge, there are inevitable tensions. These need to be negotiated and resolved, as was done in the past, and a new basis of solidarity created with the relevant groups. Social cohesion is not a simple and primordial fact but an ongoing process needing to be nurtured and recreated constantly. The politics of identity does not militate against social cohesion or redistribution; rather, respecting the legitimate claims of the groups involved is an important step towards integrating them into an expanded basis of solidarity.

Interdependence

I have so far argued that the basic concerns of the politics of redistribution and recognition are complementary. One could go further and argue that each necessarily needs the other to give it depth and energy, and to realize its objectives. This would become clear if we examined the two politics closely in that order.[11]

Economic inequalities have many causes. One of them is the low self-esteem and poor motivation, drive and self-discipline of the marginalized or denigrated groups. Their histories and cultures are generally devalued and even treated with contempt. They are told that they have contributed nothing worthwhile to humankind, that they have no great achievements to their credit, and that these limitations reflect their intellectual and moral inferiority. When such negative images become part of society's literature, arts, textbooks and informal conversation, they tend to be internalized by its members, including the victims who develop what W. E. B. Dubois, in a language reminiscent of Hegel, calls a 'double-consciousness', the habit of always looking at oneself through the eyes of others. These groups have poor self-respect, and sometimes even suffer from self-hatred. They aim low, rule out certain careers as not being for people like them, reconcile themselves easily to their failures, and lack inspiring role models and a supportive social network. Predictably, they achieve little, remain trapped in lowly positions, are drawn to antisocial activities, and pose threats to others, all of which further reinforces the wider society's stereotypes and is used by it as a proof of their inferiority. When Malcolm X was in his teens, he told his teacher that he wanted to be a lawyer. The teacher rejoined: 'A lawyer – that's no realistic goal for a nigger. You need to think about something you *can* be. You are good with your hands – making things. Why don't you plan on carpentry?'[12] Malcolm X's experience is repeated in the lives of countless black men, women, and other inferiorized groups. Some like him manage, by sheer will-power, good luck or unexpected stimulus and support, to break out of the vicious cycle, but many do not, and even the former sometimes carry the scars of their struggle.

But it is not enough merely to enjoy equal rights, opportunities and access to requisite resources. One also needs the basic capacities required to make full use of them, as many writers since Aristotle – including J. S. Mill, Karl Marx and, more recently, Amartya Sen – have emphasized. Capacities, however, have a highly complex logic and can only be developed and exercised under certain conditions, which some of these writers ignore. Individuals should have the drive, confidence and ambition to develop them, and a stimulating and supporting environment. They need a sense of self-worth and self-respect if they are to overcome the passivity and self-doubt generated by crippling self-images. They also need to feel that developing certain capacities and pursuing certain careers would not cut them off from their communities or lose them their support and respect, as sometimes happens to talented and ambitious black and other marginalized youth who are ostracized for bring too 'brainy', 'posh' or having 'gone over to the other side'. Individuals should also feel confident that certain areas of life are not closed to people like them, that their presence would not be resented and their lives rendered miserable if they ever got into them, and that they would not be misfits in their organizational environment. Redistribution cannot be achieved and, what is more important, sustained, unless these and other internal and external constraints are overcome and their deep psychological and social causes tackled. Redistributionists generally say little about how this is to be done, and assume either that the relevant capacities would in some way spring up under conditions of equal opportunity, or that little can be done to bring about the deep cultural changes required in the minority communities and the wider society.

Long-oppressed and marginalized groups need to convince themselves that this is not their fate, natural condition or all they are worth, and that it is within their power to change it. In building up their self-confidence and self-worth, the identity-based group often plays an important part. It shelters them against the humiliations of the wider society and offers them the recognition and dignity they seek. It affirms their self-worth so that they do not internalize the wider society's negative images of them or are crushed by its treatment of them. It also provides them with a ready network of support and builds up the solidarity they need to mount an emancipatory struggle. This partly explains why the relentless and centuries-long hostility of the wider society towards the Jews did not destroy their pride and self-worth, or why the brutality and slavery over two centuries did not totally undermine the African-Americans' spirit of defiance and hope of a better future. The history of many other groups, including the working classes and colonized countries, tells a similar story. Rejected by the dominant groups, they turned inwards, nurtured their sense of collective identity, held on to their collective memories and myths, and gave strength and solace to each other.[13]

In order to build up their self-confidence and solidarity, inferiorized groups often turn to their past. In the 1950s and 1960s African-Americans took a considerable interest in their history and culture, highlighted their great historical periods and contributions, and asserted their pride. Indigenous peoples, feminist movements, gays and erstwhile colonial countries have done the same. These are obviously highly complex processes involving some myth-making and distorted history. While such excesses should be exposed and fought in ways discussed earlier, we must not concentrate on them alone. The search for dignity that inspires them has much to be said for it, and its aberrations should be balanced against the considerable psychological and moral benefits accruing from individual and collective pride. After all, the self-confidence and civilizational pride of the Euro-American peoples too was built on much falsehood and distortion, and even today they feel threatened by attempts to expose the darker side of their history, culture and heroes.

Like personal identity, collective identity has its own dialectic. During the early stages of its formation, every group tends to rely on myths and exaggerations, but once it gains self-confidence and pride, it generally feels relaxed enough to see these myths for what they are and take a critical view of them. Social, economic and political equality are not provided on a platter. They have to be fought for and, what is just as difficult, sustained. This calls for a positive identity among the inferiorized groups, and hence a cultural struggle both within the groups and in the wider society. This is what the politics of recognition is really about, which is why it is an indispensable ally of the politics of redistribution.

People value their collective identity for several reasons: it is the basis of their sense of self-worth and social standing; it bonds them to those sharing it, and generates a sense of common belonging and the collective empowerment that accompanies it; and it gives them a moral anchor, a sense of direction, and a body of ideals and values. As the world becomes increasingly globalized, rootless and impersonal, the cultural, religious, ethnic, and other identities become important sources of stability, giving their members the confidence to change with the times without suffering a moral panic. A theory of politics that ignores this has only a limited appeal. The politics of redistribution therefore needs to link up with the politics of recognition, and avail itself of the energy it generates to realize its redistributivist goals. It is partly because it has so far failed to do so that it has alienated important groups. Its advocates are right to warn against excessive preoccupation with identity and recognition, but wrong not to appreciate that ignoring them altogether also has its obvious dangers.

There is also another way in which the politics of redistribution depends on the politics of recognition. Redistribution requires principles of justice to decide who should be entitled to claim what rights, opportunities, resources and so on. Like all moral values, justice is culturally embedded. Questions about who can be the subjects of justice, what matters fall within its ambit, how to determine its basic principles, their justification, the place of justice in moral life and its relation to other great values receive different answers. For many indigenous peoples, the gods and the spirits of the dead make claims based on justice; most of us think differently. For animal liberationists, animals, or rather the more developed among them, are subjects of justice and have rights; others think differently. Since views on the good life differ, those on what falls within the sphere of justice also vary. The Chinese believe that ancestors make justice-based claims to the respect and veneration of their descendants; some other civilizations take a different view. For some tribal and traditional societies, elderly parents should be looked after by their children in their homes as a matter of justice. Following the revival of Confucian values, the Chinese government is debating whether to deny promotion or welfare-related jobs to those neglecting their elderly parents, a policy that arouses deep unease in the West.

Deep differences also obtain about who has a legitimate claim to a particular object. St Thomas Aquinas argues that need is the primary source of claim, and that a starving man has a justice-based claim on the surplus resources of their lawful owner. Confronted with four children quarrelling over a flute, we can say with more or less equal plausibility that it belongs to one who plays it and for whom music is his life, to one who had invested a lot of his time and energy in making it, to one who happens to own it, or to a poor child for whom it is his only toy.[14] For John Locke, the individual owns his body, hence his labour, and has a just claim to its products, whereas for John Ruskin and Mahatma Gandhi the individual owes his talents and so on to his society, is not their owner but merely the trustee, and is not the sole claimant to the products of his labour. John Rawls was naïve to think that principles of justice were unproblematic and easily agreed upon.

Since different groups often hold different views on almost all aspects of justice, and since we are prone to universalizing ones that appear self-evident to us, a theory of justice risks being biased and, in that sense, unjust unless it emerges out of a democratic dialogue between them. The dialogue is justly structured and conducted when the relevant points of view are allowed to speak in their own voices, and heard with respect. Since every dominant group tends to impose the principles of justice that serve to legitimize its domination, we need to counter it by seeking out those it marginalizes or silences and ensuring their adequate representation in deliberative bodies. This is where the politics of recognition becomes relevant. It ensures that all legitimate identities are heard and able to participate as equals in determining the principles of justice. Rawls bypasses this debate and the complex issues it raises by assuming that men and women in the original condition have a liberal identity and are only interested in liberal principles of justice.

I have argued so far that the politics of redistribution requires the politics of recognition to complement and energize it. The reverse is equally true. When individuals and communities languish at the bottom of the social and economic hierarchy, they remain invisible and count for little. Since their poverty and lowly status need to be explained, the usual tendency is to blame their way of life, low ambition, temperament, psychological make-up and poor natural endowment, and to claim that society can do little about these deep-seated cultural and psychological factors. By contrast, when communities are economically successful and occupy important positions in society, their success reflects on their cultural and other identities, and the latter come to be valued and admired. Thanks, for example, to the considerable economic success of Indian immigrants in the West, they and their culture are viewed in a positive light that bears little resemblance to the widespread negative view of them voiced only a few years ago. The apartheid regime in South Africa felt compelled to classify the economically successful Jews and Japanese as honorary whites and to respect their religious and cultural identities.

A similar process has occurred in relation to gender and other identities. Women were devalued and inferiorized when they remained confined to subordinate positions in the relatively invisible domestic realm. As they became economically and politically active and enjoyed an equal opportunity to enter and rise to the highest levels in all areas of life, their self-perception and men's perception of them began to change. They built up the confidence to speak in their own voices, demanded equality in all areas of life, and have challenged successfully the male-dominated norms and languages of discourse. Recognition is closely bound up with success as judged by society's criteria, which in Western societies are largely economic. In some cases, groups have the resources to succeed on their own, and all they need are the absence of discrimination and equal rights. In others, they require positive state action in the form of equal opportunities and resources, and even a judicious programme of affirmative action. Such redistribution breaks the self-reproducing cycle of disadvantage, and creates conditions in which the self-images of marginalized groups and others' perception of them begin to change. Recognition is not given but, if it is given, it remains fragile, grudging and patronizing unless the struggle for it is accompanied by that for redistribution.

As we saw earlier, a highly unequal society has a structural tendency towards homogenization, and discourages moral and cultural diversity. It institutionalizes and throws its weight behind a particular vision of the good society, and generates the pressure to conform and assimilate. If different moral and cultural visions are to flourish in a climate of mutual recognition and respect, we need to counter this tendency by fighting for greater economic, political and social equality. Equality disperses and checks economic and political power, protects valuable identities against homogenization, and nurtures the disposition to express them.

A bifocal theory of justice

In the light of our discussion, there is no inherent conflict between the politics of redistribution and recognition. In some cases, in fact, they share common concerns; while in others they have different but complementary goals. In yet others their emphases are different, but these can be reconciled. The relationship between them is not a zero sum game, and it is naïve to think that the time and energy given to one necessarily reduce those available to the other. In fact, when properly related, each can reinforce and generate energy for the pursuit of the other. The tension arises when their interdependence is ignored. Since much of the traditional discussion of justice has concentrated on how rights, offices, political power, opportunities and resources should be distributed, and has developed its questions, categories and discourse accordingly, it has excluded and feels uncomfortable with questions raised by identity and difference. This has encouraged the recognitionists, who are relatively recent entrants to the debate, to go off on their own and develop an explicit or implicit theory of justice in isolation from the question of redistribution. We need to integrate the two, or at least bring them closer, and develop a richer bifocal theory of justice. Since such a task falls outside my concern, I shall do no more than sketch its four important features.

First, it should provide principles to determine who may claim what rights, resources, opportunities, offices and so on. It should also provide principles to determine what identities merit recognition, how to resolve conflicts, what recognition entails by way of rights, and how to protect individual freedom against the oppression of such group identities as are recognized. Justice encompasses claims to material resources as well as to those based on identity. Injustice is done not only when individuals are exploited or denied the basic material conditions of the good life, but also when they are demeaned, inferiorized, or denied the opportunity to speak in their own voices and define their identities. Recognition and redistribution articulate different forms of equality, and both need to be addressed by a theory of justice.

Second, a bifocal theory of justice should acknowledge that, like individuals, social groups too can be the subjects of justice and make claims on each other and the wider society. They are treated unjustly when their members are humiliated, oppressed, denied equal respect or subjected to unequal treatment because of their shared characteristics. Racism, sexism, homophobia and anti-Semitism are examples of this. These forms of injustice cannot be explained and tackled in individualist terms, because those involved are subjected to them not as individuals but as members of relevant groups. They therefore call for appropriate forms of collective action, including both a collective struggle and collective remedies.

Third, justice concerns not only the state but also society at large and each of its members. In much of the traditional view of justice, the state remains the focus of attention as it alone is in a position to distribute rights, offices, duties and resources. This is not always the case with matters relating to recognition. Self-respect, self-esteem and a sense of identity are socially constituted and depend on confirmation by others. In a racist, sexist, homophobic or anti-Semitic culture, members of the dominant group, in both their formal and informal encounters, treat target groups with disdain, humiliate them, avoid them, make offensive remarks about them, damage their self-respect and in general make their lives a nightmare. There are thus multiple agents of injustice, including not only the state but also the social practices that institutionalize humiliation and contempt of different groups as well as every one of us. The state can certainly help by institutionalizing the equal dignity and rights of its citizens and taking public cognizance of their identities, but its role is limited. It cannot do much about demeaning social practices and individual attitudes and actions. That requires changes in the moral culture and ethos of society, and the attitude and behaviour of its members. In a bifocal theory of justice, the state, although critically important, cannot be the sole focus of attention.

Since individuals and social practices can cause injustice, how we treat and speak about others becomes a matter of justice. This partly explains the emergence of political correctness, or what is better called political decency, in recent years. It represents a protest against stigmatization, intended or unintended humiliation, subtle and crude ways of keeping others in their place, triggering their painful personal and collective memories, and perpetuating inequalities of power and esteem. Forms of expression and modes of address are never politically and culturally innocent. The objection to them can, of course, be taken too far and bring itself into ridicule, because language cannot easily be sanitized, and the dividing line between light-hearted humour and the manipulation of others' insecurity is often fairly thin. However, the basic concern underlying political correctness is valid. All speech is action, and reflects and reproduces a particular way of structuring social relations. There are just and unjust ways of talking about others and laughing at their foibles and idiosyncrasies. Since language is a powerful tool of regulating and determining human behaviour, a just society may rightly subject it to formal and informal checks.

Finally, although redistribution and recognition are closely related, they are different in their nature and logic. Redistribution facilitates recognition, but that is not the only reason to value it, for the equality that inspires and results from it is desirable on other grounds as well. Conversely, the recognition of legitimate identities expands the society's sense of solidarity by including the hitherto marginalized groups into a shared collective identity and assists redistribution, but that is not the only reason to value it, for it also nurtures freedom and diversity. While highlighting the empirical and normative connections between recognition and redistribution, a well-considered theory of justice should avoid giving a reductionist account of them.[15]

4

National Identity

The term 'national identity' is used in two related but different senses. First, it refers to an individual's identity *as* a member of a political community as different from that of other kinds of community. Being French or Swedish is a national identity, just as being a Christian or a Hutu is a religious or an ethnic identity. Second, 'national identity' refers to the identity *of* a political community, as when we ask what makes France or Sweden this community rather than some other. I shall begin with a brief discussion of the former sense and devote the rest of the chapter to the latter.

The importance of national identity

National identity or the membership of a political community is an important and often valued part of individual identity. Members of a political community are likely to have lived in it for generations, and their history and individual memories are bound up with it. It provides a home, a place they call their own, and whose membership of it generally cannot be taken away from them. They grow up and are educated within it, and are deeply shaped by its values and ethos. Being territorially bounded, the political community also creates a structured space that gives intensity and depth to their relations with each other and forges common bonds. Their personal and collective security is also bound up with it, and creates the ties of common interest. Its laws shape and leave an imprint on all aspects of their lives, including marriage, sexuality, structure of the family, property, career, and formal and informal relations with each other. They pay its taxes, receive its welfare benefits, fight in its wars, travel abroad carrying its passport and enjoying its protection, and identify themselves to, and are in turn identified by, others as its members. Sports and other international competitions are organized along national lines and reinforce national identity. The state has its symbols, ceremonies and rituals, and its citizens' participation in these gives their national identity an emotional depth. Their daily involvement in the common life of the state such as voting in elections, forming and expressing opinions on national issues, and feeling angry or proud at what is done in their name, reaffirm their national identity.

Since members of a political community are shaped by it, they see something of it in themselves, and of themselves in it. They therefore tend to identify *with* it and with their similarly shaped fellow members to varying degrees. Since they think it says something important about them, they also identify themselves *in terms of* it. Unless they are referring to their formal citizenship, when they label themselves 'Indian', 'French' or 'Brazilian', they say where they come from, what community matters to them, why they say and do certain things, and, if they feel so inclined, reveal their attachments. Their self-respect too is often inseparable from the respect for their country, and its denigration is felt as denigration of them personally. Identification with the political community is a matter of degree. Some of its members are, for various reasons, more deeply shaped by it than are others. Some might take a dim view of the way it has shaped them, and try to shed some of the habits of thought, beliefs and values that have been acquired from it, whereas others might value and feel intensely proud of their inheritance. Again, ardent nationalists and fervent patriots might, like the Christian cricketer and teacher discussed in Chapter 2, make national identity the centre of their lives and subordinate their other identities to it, while others might assign it a limited place and balance its demands against those of others.

The importance of national identity in the life of the individual is a contingent historical fact. It was not always and need not for ever remain so. In many premodern societies, national identity, such as it was, did not enjoy this degree of importance. The ruler's reach was shallow and limited. He did not control the society's cultural and educational institutions and seek to shape his subjects in a particular way. All he demanded of them was that they should pay their taxes and obey the laws. They largely defined their identity in terms of their religion and ethnicity, whose influence on their lives and claims on their loyalty were greater than those of the ruler. This was the case in most of medieval Europe, and remains so in some contemporary societies. When asked in 1974 if he was a Muslim, a Pakistani or a Pashtun first, Wali Khan, the doyen of

Pashtun nationalism, said he was 'a 6000 year old Pashtun, a 1000 year old Muslim, and a 27 year old Pakistani'.[1] G. M. Syed, the grand old man of Sindhi nationalism, expressed similar sentiments: 'Sindh has always been there, Pakistan is a passing show. Sindh is a fact, Pakistan is a fiction.' In large parts of Africa and the tribal states of India, the tribe is the primary basis of self-identification, and the tribal identity carries greater weight than the national. In some Muslim countries, religion has in recent years acquired enormous significance, and national identity matters less than it once did.

Major changes are taking place even in Western Europe, the historical home of the nation state and strongly developed national identities. Thanks to the twentieth century's two world wars, the imperatives of globalization and the need for economic, political, environmental and military co-operation, European states are coming together and developing a continental identity. With the bitter memories of the country's Nazi past, many Germans fear their nationhood, and want their country to be linked inextricably to a wider democratic community. France thinks it needs a larger and more powerful unit than the nation state to safeguard its civilizational identity, and many in Italy and Spain think that they can retain a modicum of political stability, contain their secessionist movements and integrate their regional units only by becoming part of a wider unit. Even in Britain, where there is a strong resistance to European integration, it is widely recognized that Europe matters greatly, and that its own identity needs to be reconciled with and located within the wider European identity. Since the devolution of power to its subnational units has accentuated the regional and weakened the national identity, the European Union has paradoxically become necessary to preserve some form of British identity.

Although the process involved is exceedingly complex and both weakens the state and gives it a new lease of life, it would seem that European states are moving towards a new kind of political association based on regional decentralization and continental co-ordination, leaving the reconstituted nation state to play its limited but vital role within the space allowed by this. As a result, national identity in several parts of Europe today is less deep, less passionately held, less strident in its demands, and less privileged over other identities than was the case only a few decades ago. The European trend is not reproduced in other parts of the world, particularly in the developing societies, where the main concern is to construct stable political communities out of disparate groups and to foster the kind of national identity that Europeans developed in the heyday of the nation state. Even here, however, national identity is subject to the pressures of globalization, regional integration and internal resistance, and hence is porous and contested.

The identity of the political community

Prima facie, national identity or the identity of a political community seems a dubious concept. A political community is made up of millions of men and women, each of them unique and with an identity of his or her own. Its membership is in constant flux because of births, deaths and the movement of people. One might ask how such a body can ever have an identity of its own. The difficulty is not as acute as might appear at first sight, however. Large organizations such as universities, corporations and cities have identities. New York is not New Delhi, and Harvard University is distinguished by a history, an ethos and a structure of practices, traditions and self-understanding that are quite different from those of, say, Berkeley and Hull. A political community is obviously much larger, more complex, sometimes has a more chequered history, and its members do not have the kind of constant face-to-face contact to be found in other organizations. It has, however, certain advantages that are unique to it. Its members are territorially concentrated, live together for generations, interact with each other, face common problems and share common experiences, which are recorded diligently and form part of their collective memories. A political community also controls the educational, cultural and other institutions through which it shapes its younger members. Different groups struggle for economic and political power, and the dominant ones structure it in certain ways. As a result of all this, over time it develops a distinct form of life, reflected in both its physical and its institutional landscape.

The identity of a political community consists of those constitutive features that define and distinguish it from others and make it this community rather than some other. It includes its territory, which plays a broadly similar role to that of the body in personal identity, language or languages, and formative historical experiences, including those surrounding its origins in terms of which it traces its development. It also includes its traditions, deep-seated tendencies, beliefs, values and ideals that it cherishes and seeks to cultivate in its members; the discursive framework and the style of reasoning that characterize its ways of debating and resolving differences; its legal and political institutions in terms of which it organizes its affairs and relates to other communities; and the collective memories of internal and external struggles, triumphs and defeats. National identity finds its partial but clearest expression in the Constitution of the country, a self-consciously formulated and authoritative public statement in which it tells itself and the world what kind of a community it is and what it stands for.

Members of a political community seek to make sense of it and its history, form a general conception of the kind of community it is, and arrive at some form of self-understanding. Like individual identity, but even more so, national identity is highly complex, multilayered, composed of different and sometimes conflicting strands of thought, patterns of behaviour, values and ideals accumulated over centuries.[2] It is therefore amenable to different interpretations and, while a particular manner of understanding it tends to become dominant, it is rarely free from dispute. Even the widely shared self-understanding remains tentative, as parts of national identity are opaque and inaccessible even to the most searching inquiry, largely because those reflecting on it are themselves too deeply influenced by it to notice their presence. While some forms of self-understanding are more plausible than others, none can claim to be the only one that is correct. It captures some features of national identity, and ignores or marginalizes others. It is therefore necessarily partial and, since every self-understanding is grounded in a particular point of view, also partisan.

National identity is not primordial, a brute and unalterable fact of life and passively inherited by each generation. Such an essentialist or realist view of it, shared by nationalists and many conservative thinkers, makes sense only if it is homogeneous and unchanging, which it is not and can never be. National identity is not a substance but rather a cluster of interrelated tendencies that sometimes pull in different directions, and each generation has to identify them and decide which ones to build on. A community's dominant values and ideals too are never transparent and unambiguous. They are precipitates of different historical experiences and its members' attempts to make sense of them, and are not and cannot be a matter of simple discovery. They require analysis and interpretation, and these vary over time and between individuals. Furthermore, a community's identity is fashioned in the course of its attempt to meet the challenges it faces at different times in its history. Being a product of history, it can and needs to be redefined and revised periodically. To freeze history at a particular point in time is the surest way to render the national identity obsolete and irrelevant.

Although national identity is alterable, it is not infinitely malleable either, a 'project' to be executed by each generation as it pleases and in disregard of the past, as some radicals imagine. It does involve choice, but within certain limits. No political community is a *tabula rasa*, and its members do not confront it as if they were outside it. It has a certain history, traditions, beliefs, qualities of character and historical memories, which delimit the range of alternatives open to it. Furthermore, to say that each generation is free to define the national identity in the light of its circumstances and needs is to ignore the important fact that its very definition of its needs, what it considers acceptable ways of satisfying them, its interpretation of its circumstances and its aspirations are all shaped, though of course not determined, by the inherited way of life.

National identity is both given and periodically reconstituted. Citizens inherit it, reflect on it critically, and redefine and revise it in the light of their circumstances, self-understanding and future aspirations. This requires a deep historical knowledge of the country and a feel for its past as well as a rigorous and realistic assessment of its present challenges and hopes for the future. Reconstitution of national identity is both critical and conservative, rejecting what is obsolete or morally unacceptable and building on what is relevant, serviceable or commendable. This is broadly like Hegel's and Marx's concept of critique, a historically informed evaluation of the prevailing structure of beliefs, practices and values from the perspective of a vision of the future based on the possibilities that are inherent in it.

The identity of a political community, I have argued, consists in its constitutive features that define and distinguish it from others. A political community is different from others because it is a particular kind of community, and not the other way around. Difference is derivative, and not the central defining feature of identity. In many popular and even academic discussions this is often overlooked. National identity is equated with difference, and there is a constant, even obsessive, concern to remain different from others lest one should lose one's identity.[3] Many Germans were and are obsessed with *Sonderweg* (being neither West nor East) and feel deeply worried that their postwar democratic institutions will assimilate them into the West and undermine their identity. Many Canadians ask how they differ from Americans, and how best they can preserve these differences. Quebec nationalists ask how they differ from the rest of Canada, and underplay all that they have in common. The long Japanese preoccupation with national distinctiveness has generated an extensive literature on *nihonjinon* or cultural uniqueness. This is just as true of Algeria, Iran and most developing countries, where the primary concern is to avoid becoming 'Western'. In all these cases, similarity to others is perceived as an ontological threat, and differences from them are given undue importance. Hardly anyone asks why it is important to remain different, whether all differences or only those deemed to be worth preserving are to be retained and, if the latter, what the underlying principles are and how they are arrived at.

Equating national identity with differences leads to paradoxes and is ultimately self-defeating. If a community's identity consisted in its difference from others, we would be led to the absurd conclusion that its identity has changed when others increasingly come to resemble it even though it has itself remained the same. Again, when it defines its identity in terms of difference, others become its constant frame of reference, and it preserves its identity at the expense of its autonomy. This view of identity also fetishizes difference, discourages intercultural borrowing, and encourages people to pay far more attention to how and how much they differ from others than whether or not they are measuring up to their challenges.

Every political community needs to, and as a rule tends to, develop some conception of itself, of the kind of community it is and wishes to be. It facilitates intergenerational continuity, helps its members to unite around a broadly shared self-understanding, and provides a focus to their sense of common belonging. It inspires them to live up to a certain self-image, gives them a sense of purpose and direction, guides their choices, indicates what is or is not likely to take roots, mobilizes their moral energies, and gives their collective life a measure of consistency. It is also a source of such powerful action-guiding emotions as pride, shame, guilt and embarrassment, which they feel when their country conforms, or fails to conform, to it. Indians, for example, have traditionally seen cultural plurality, openness to other civilizations and tolerance as being central to their identity, and many of them felt deeply ashamed when a fanatical group of them destroyed the Babri mosque in 1992. Martin Luther King invoked the US Constitution and the Declaration of Independence to argue that racial inequality went against the country's self-conception. When people in Europe and elsewhere say that theirs is a 'liberal' society and that *therefore* they should or should not enact certain laws or follow certain policies, they clearly appeal to a particular view of its identity.

Every conception of national identity, however, has its dark underside and can easily become a source of conflict and division. A long-established community includes several different strands of thought and visions of the good life. Since a definition of its identity is necessarily selective, it stresses some of these, excludes others and imposes a false sense of unity on the community. It can also become a vehicle for moulding the entire society in its image, giving rise to an intolerant and authoritarian politics. Furthermore, every definition of national identity has a tendency to distinguish the community fairly sharply from others, and to offer a highly distorted account of both. In the hands of those so inclined, and that includes most politicians, it tends to prevent or corrupt political debate by introducing a pseudo-ontological mode of reasoning. Rather than discussing them in terms of their intrinsic merit, public policies might be dismissed on the grounds that they are too incongruent with the national identity to be taken seriously. Their advocates are then either blackmailed into silence or forced to engage in an inherently inconclusive debate about the community's 'true' identity.

An excellent example that highlights most of these dangers was provided by Margaret Thatcher. After she was forced to resign as prime minister in 1990, she summed up her political achievements as follows:[4]

> I always said and believed that the British character is quite different from the character of people on the continent – quite different. There is a great sense of fairness and equity in the British people, a great sense of individuality and initiative. They don't like being pushed around. How else did these really rather small people, from the times of Elizabeth on, go out in the larger world and have such an influence upon it?
>
> I set out to destroy socialism. I feel it was at odds with the character of the people. We were the first country in the world to roll back the frontiers of socialism, then roll forward the frontiers of freedom. We reclaimed our heritage.

No scholarly exegesis is needed to see what she is saying and implying in these extraordinary remarks. In order to define British identity, she contrasts it with that of other countries and sets up a rigid wall between the two. She defines it in exclusive terms in the sense that the British identity lies in what distinguishes Britain from others, not in what it might also share with them. She finds no fault with the British people and takes a wholly uncritical view of them. Her words imply that continental Europeans are gravely deficient in such virtues as individuality, initiative, fairness and equity, and she has little that is good to say about them. She uses British national character to explain British history, as if the latter were nothing more than its phenomenal manifestation. And since British character is used to explain British history, it has of itself no history and is supposed to be inherent in some way in the British people. Thatcher places post-Elizabethan colonial expansion at the centre of British history, sees it as a wholly beneficial influence, and equates the English with British history. Finally, she uses her view of British identity to declare socialism incompatible with it, and thus as ontologically illegitimate. She is not content to defeat socialism; she thinks she must destroy it, as nothing less than the character of the British people is at stake. The language of national identity in her hands as in others' becomes a mischievous attempt to foreclose a wide variety of views and breathes the spirit of intolerance.

We are confronted with a paradox. Every political community needs and invokes some shared view of its collective identity, if not explicitly than implicitly, but the latter can also become exclusivist, authoritarian, repressive and narrowly nationalistic. A view of national identity is a force for both unity and division, a condition of the community's reproduction that can also become a cause of its fragmentation. One might argue, as some republican theorists do, that we should abandon the language of national identity and talk only of citizenship, and the rights and obligations connected with it. For reasons discussed earlier, that is not possible – or at least not enough, because citizens do need a broad view of the general character of their community and what it stands for. The only alternative therefore is to ensure that, as far as possible, their conception of its identity satisfies certain conditions. First, it should be inclusive and respect the prevailing ethnic, religious, cultural and other diversities and visions of the good life. If it dismissed or ignored the diversity, or was biased towards one of these views, it would alienate the rest. Although no definition of national identity can be purely formal and culturally neutral, its content should be as widely acceptable as possible. When Canada and Australia formally declared themselves to be multicultural and built diversity into their self-definition, they gave their various groups a respectable public status. Resistance to such demands in some European states conveys the opposite impression, that diversity is unwelcome or marginal and expected over time to be assimilated.

Second, we should acknowledge that, since no statement of national identity can ever capture the richness and complexity of the community's history and way of life, it is inevitably partial in both the senses of the term. We should not therefore be dogmatic about it, place excessive moral and political weight on it, or treat it as a kind of first principle, as Margaret Thatcher did. It is a necessary shorthand, and we should subject it to critical examination. Third, the rationale behind wanting a clear sense of national identity is domestic – to unite members of the community, to articulate and focus their collective self-understanding, to present them with an inspiring self-image and bring out the best in them. It is not meant to impress foreigners, help corporate interests to promote their products abroad or to attract tourists, as was done a few years ago by some New Labour zealots who 'rebranded' Britain as if the country and its identity were a commodity. Finally, the statement of national identity cannot be given from above by the government, political leaders or the intellectual elite. It should grow out of a vigorous democratic debate so that it represents the widest possible range of views, articulates the deepest aspirations of its citizens, and can be endorsed enthusiastically and owned by them all. An officially fabricated view of national identity has no emotional roots, lacks democratic legitimacy, and needs an unacceptable degree of moral and cultural engineering to overcome likely resistance.

National identity crisis

A well-organized political community generally goes about its business in a largely unselfconscious manner. It has a reasonably clear idea of what it is and what it stands for, and relies on this to conduct its collective affairs. When disputes occur from time to time, it generally knows how to debate and resolve them. A difficult situation arises when it undergoes massive economic and demographic changes, faces grave internal or external threats, is recovering from a traumatic period, or is paralysed by irreconcilable groups fighting bitterly over how it should be constituted. It then feels deeply disorientated, confused, directionless, and asks itself what kind of a society it is and wants to be. Different societies conduct the debate in different idioms, against different historical backgrounds and circumstances, and with different degrees of success. I shall take both the well-established and stable as well as the young, developing societies to illustrate the variety.

Britain began to undergo significant changes from the early 1960s onwards. As a result of the decolonization of most of the empire, its two centuries of imperial adventure came to an end, leading to a drastic shrinkage of its geographical expanse and political power. Thanks to the arrival of a large number of Afro-Caribbean and Asian immigrants from its erstwhile colonies, and their concentration in the major cities, British society began to become recognizably different and needed to find ways

of coping with its diversity. The British economy was in a state of
decline; its industrial productivity low, its technology outdated, the
quality of its industrial management poor, and its balance of payment
unfavourable. British political institutions were widely perceived to be
ineffective and commanded only limited popular support. The pressure
from influential quarters to join the European Community (EC) generated widespread fears about the loss of 'a thousand years of its history'.
The emergence of Scottish, and to a lesser extent Welsh, nationalism
aroused fears about Britain's territorial and political integrity. In short,
almost all the traditional sources of pride in terms of which the country
had constructed its collective identity, such as the empire, social cohesion, stable democratic institutions, industrial leadership of the world,
superiority to the rest of Europe, and political unity, were proving problematic. The cumulative impact of these and related changes was
considerable. Not surprisingly, they created a widespread sense of
disorientation, and provoked a debate on the causes of its decline and the
best ways of arresting it.

Enoch Powell was one of the first to address these questions with
great clarity. As he put it in 1963:[5]

> I suppose few nations have had, in a single generation, to confront the fact
> and the effects of such tremendous changes in their world situation as Britain
> has had to do in the last 30 years. In so short a space of time have a globe with
> one quarter of the land surface coloured red, our naval and air predominance,
> and our commercial, industrial and financial primacy become things of the
> past. History is littered with nations that have been destroyed for ever by the
> stress of lesser changes than these. But greatness does not consist in mere
> size, mere power. It lies in a realistic appraisal of the true stature of a nation,
> neither exaggerated, nor underestimated, and a faith in the unique possibili-
> ties for the future with which our history and our position have endowed us.

Powell argued that, since Britain had undergone massive changes in
such a short time, it should take a cool and critical look at itself, identify
its 'true nature', discover its 'innermost impulses' and 'collective
instincts', and build its future on that basis. For Powell, British identity
had four essential and interrelated components. First, it involved parliamentary sovereignty. The House of Commons was 'the personification
of the people of Britain; its independence is synonymous with their independence'. Second, Britain was an individualist society and had always
cherished the rights and liberties of the individual. This was more true of
Britain than of any other society, and its individualism, going right back

to the beginning of its history, was deeply embedded in the character of the British people. Third, the British national identity was grounded in and constantly nurtured by the ethnic and prepolitical unity of the British people. They were a cohesive people bound by the deep ties of kinship and loyalty to each other and to those who had migrated and settled abroad. Fourth, thanks to the country's geography and history, the British identity was distinctively singular and unattached. Britain was an island, not a part of the continent of Europe; a self-contained and detached entity with its centre of gravity located within itself. Its history reflected its geography and was uniquely global. For long periods of its history, Britain 'had stood with her face to the oceans, her back to Europe'. And even when it crossed the oceans to rule the world, like imperial Rome, it never left home and struck roots elsewhere.

Margaret Thatcher broadly shared Powell's analysis of Britain.[6] She was convinced that the country had declined steadily since the 1950s in all the major areas of life because it had lost its sense of national purpose, and that this was related to the systematic erosion of its identity. It needed to return to its roots and recapture the virtues and self-understanding that had once made it great. Like Powell, again, she was not clear about the causes of its decline, and blamed British self-forgetfulness, ignorance of history brought about by poor education, the liberal establishment, the permissive society, and the invasion of alien ideas from the rest of Europe.

With some important differences, Thatcher accepted Powell's view of British identity. She too stressed the centrality of parliamentary sovereignty, individualism and ethnic homogeneity. But, unlike Powell, she thought that Britain's ethnic minorities could not be repatriated or treated as second-class citizens, and that the best way was to assimilate them, both culturally and biologically, into the national 'stock'. She insisted that Britain was a part of Europe but not a European country. Like the rest of Europe, it was Christian; it had been shaped by the Roman Empire; its ancestors, such as the Celts, Saxons, Normans and Danes had come from Europe, and its language, literature, arts, architecture and music were heavily influenced by this. However, its history was quite different, and so were its values, institutions, character and outlook on life, so much so that it bore 'little resemblance to the rest of Europe'. Although long involved in continental politics, it was basically a global power, and should work with but avoid close institutional ties with its European partners.

Thatcher's view of British identity acted both as an anchor and a compass, giving her strong convictions, self-confidence, and a sense of direction. Since she knew that it was not in Britain's interest to leave the EC, she concentrated on so reshaping it that it became more hospitable to the preservation of the British and other national identities. At the national level she devoted all her efforts to restructuring British society and regenerating the British character. She used education as a major tool of cultural engineering and gave the state unprecedented educational powers. Her massive programme of privatization was designed not only to disburden the state of its economic functions and to demarcate clearly the boundaries of the state and the economy, but also to create the kind of 'vigorous' national character she desired. She made individual choice one of the central organizing principles of all areas of life, promoted the interests of consumers over producers, and dismantled or emasculated institutions suspected of nurturing corporatist ideas and aspirations.

Tony Blair and New Labour could not hope to dislodge the Conservative hegemony without offering the country a well-considered view of its identity.[7] New Labour had two choices: to offer a humane form of Thatcherism, or an alternative based on different values and views on Britain's place in the world. By and large, it opted for the former. Blair stressed British individualism but tempered it with some emphasis on social justice. In contrast to the New Right, he argued that Britain's political identity was plural and based on the equal partnership of England, Scotland and Wales and, subject to certain qualifications, Northern Ireland. Not parliamentary sovereignty but parliamentary democracy was central to British identity, and the latter was not only consistent with but also required devolution of powers to its constituent units. Blair also stressed Britain's long tradition of hospitality to immigrants, and its ability to integrate them. Although his view of Britain's history was free from the Thatcherite gloating over how it had 'civilized' the inferior races of Asia and Africa and 'saved' the rest of Europe from its internal barbarians, he shared her view that British colonialism was on the whole a good thing, and that the country should continue to give 'leadership' to the rest of Europe and the world. Blair appreciated that Britain remained a class-ridden society, and wanted it replaced not by the egalitarian society that many in his party advocated but by the American type of meritocratic society that Thatcher had also favoured. Like her, he too was keen to Americanize Britain in economic and social areas, but unlike her he was anxious that its political and cultural life should remain European. The idea of combining the best of Europe and

America was central to Blair's view of British identity, and was closely bound up with his view that its unique 'destiny' was to become a vital bridge between the two continents. Even his failure to get much in return for his support for the disastrous US-led war on Iraq did not alter his view.

Notwithstanding some notable contributions, the British debate on national identity remains disappointing. The complex origin of British individualism and its internal tensions remain unanalysed. There is little attempt to engage critically with its imperial history and to form a just view of what it did to its colonies and to Britain itself. There is no careful analysis of Britain's European heritage and relationship to the European Union, and the country remains uncertain or largely instrumental in its commitment to it. The dubious idea of becoming a bridge between it and the US, which is shared by no other European country, is not subjected to rigorous scrutiny, and continues to distort Britain's perception of its place in the world. Although it has largely accepted multicultural society as being integral to its identity and every public figure claims to take pride in it, its commitment to it remains precarious, and is often thwarted by a nationalist or assimilationist backlash. Gordon Brown has placed British identity, or what he calls 'Britishness', at the top of the public agenda, but largely limits it to 'British values' such as tolerance, fairness and enterprise, none of which is unique to the country. His proposal to restructure British political institutions and to call a national convention to draft a written constitution, as well as his remarks on British history, society and empire, suggest that the country might at last begin to give itself a coherent vision of its past and future.

Canada

Canada is another country where the question of national identity has dominated the public agenda since the early 1970s.[8] For a long time, Quebec was in no doubt that it was Catholic and French, and that the Catholic Church was the custodian of that identity. But because of the cumulative effect of urbanization, social atomization, secularization and the immigration of people of different races and religions, its social and political life underwent profound changes after the Second World War. This led to much anxious debate about what it once was and had since become, and whether and how it should define itself. The task of defining its national identity that had hitherto been discharged by the clergy was now taken over by the intellectuals, and the Quebec government replaced the Church as its guardian. In the new definition, Catholicism lost its earlier centrality to French language and culture. The nature and content of the French culture were nowhere clearly defined, but that did not prevent the emergence of the widely shared view that Quebec was 'essentially' French, that its cultural identity was under grave threat, and that the newly-formed alliance between its intellectuals and government had a vital role to play in defining, preserving and propagating it.

On the basis of the redefinition of its identity, Quebec's leaders argued that it was not just a province of Canada, or what was earlier called French Canada, but a distinct nation, and that, correspondingly, the rest of Canada did not consist of separate and distinct provinces but constituted a homogeneous English nation. Canada was a binational country, and the composition and functioning of its political institutions should reflect their equality. Quebec leaders also argued that it had a right to protect its identity, and hence to control immigration, to make French alone its official language, to require all immigrant children to go to French schools, and in general to do all that was necessary for that purpose. It asked the Canadian state to recognize it as a 'distinct society', regard its protection as one of its major national goals, and grant the latter rights not demanded or needed by the other provinces.

Quebec's demands, later taken over by the original nations of Canada, raised several questions about the nature and identity of the Canadian state. The first question related to the historical self-understanding of Canada. Was it an essentially Anglo-Saxon country containing several linguistic and cultural minorities, the French being one of them? Or a binational country founded by two distinct nations, and thus endowed from the very beginning with a dual identity? Or a trinational country made up of these two and the original nations? Or was it a multi-ethnic country composed of several distinct communities including the three major ones and several others that had later made it their home? In short, was the Canadian identity singular and homogeneous, two-in-one, three-in-one, or many-in-one? The answer to the question had profound constitutional and cultural implications.

The second question concerned the organizing principles of the Canadian state. Should it agree to the demands of the original nations and Quebec, and create not just an asymmetrical, though not necessarily unequal, federation but also a hybrid state based on both liberal individualism and a recognition of collective identities? Or should it refuse to compromise its much-cherished commitment to liberal individualism and reject all attempts to limit it in the name of Quebec's cultural self-preservation? Many Anglophones, including Pierre Trudeau, thought that if Canada opted for the former, it could no longer call itself a liberal society, and that this represented such a grave erosion of its identity that they could not live with it. Some others were prepared to compromise its liberal identity in the interest of national unity, but continued to feel deeply uneasy about it. A few, of whom Charles Taylor is the most eloquent spokesman, saw no reason why a liberal society could not accommodate collective rights and have a hybrid identity. While the recent official recognition of Quebec as a distinct nation ends one controversy, its implications remain unclear and could give rise to another.

The third question related to the nature of Canadian citizenship. Should Canada insist on equal and uniform citizenship and require all its citizens to belong to it in an identical manner? Or should it allow mediated and differentiated citizenship such that some could belong to particular national groups (say, Quebec), and through that to Canada, and thus become not Canadians *sans phrase* but Quebecquois-Canadians? This looks like, but is really quite different from, the more familiar hyphenated identities in the United States. The Polish-Americans and the Irish-Americans are all Americans, enjoying equal citizenship and relating to the American state in an identical manner. Their ethnicity does not adjectivize or qualify their citizenship, though this does not prevent them from organizing along ethnic lines to promote ethnic causes, and has only a limited cultural significance.[9] By contrast, the differential form of citizenship demanded by the French Canadians and the native peoples gives their ethnicity or nationhood a political significance, and ethnicizes and pluralizes the very structure of the Canadian state.

Quebec's demands were not the only factor precipitating a debate on Canadian identity. The other was the anxiety caused by the increasing cultural domination of the country by its powerful southern neighbour, the US, which led the Canadians to ask whether and how they differed from it. Many of them are convinced that they have a distinct national identity reflected in their cultural traditions, values, commitment to the welfare state, consensual ways of conducting their collective affairs, qualities of temperament and character, and positive attitude to the active role of government. They fear that this identity is being eroded, but few have clear ideas on how to safeguard it. Many of them think that, since Quebec marks out Canada from the US, accommodating it is in the interest of the larger Canadian identity, provided it does not undermine the country's unity.

Germany

In Germany too, the question of national identity has been a subject of much agonized debate, a debate initially provoked by the Nazi period and the Holocaust.[10] The trauma was too acute to allow Germans to raise disturbing questions very soon after the Second World War, and many of those who could have done so were politically too compromised or too diffident to address them. Most Germans sought to make a clean break with their recent past, and set about giving themselves a different political identity in the form of newly established democratic institutions. The study of history was replaced by social studies in many German schools, and systematic attempts were made to instil and nurture democratic culture. As the latter took roots and as a new generation of Germans with sufficient self-confidence and detachment grew up in the 1960s, they began to raise disturbing questions about the Nazi period and their parents' role in it.

They asked what the Nazi period told them about their society and why the German people had followed, in large numbers, a bunch of irresponsible demagogues. They also asked if the murder of six million Jews was 'singular' and historically unique, or whether it was substantially like other such 'genocides' as Stalin's liquidation of the Kulaks. If the former, it revealed the presence of dark and mysterious forces lurking in the German character. If the latter, it could be explained in terms of the usual political and personal factors, although that did not diminish its enormity. In either case, the question remained as to how the Germans could do such a thing. They were no more evil than human beings elsewhere, and the same nation that produced Adolf Hitler had also produced Kant, Herder and Goethe, not to mention a long line of great musicians, artists and writers. Was the Holocaust an aberration, then? Or was the German identity deeply divided and schizophrenic? Or were its outrageous propensities merely the obverse of its noble qualities? Whatever the explanation, the Nazi atrocities had at least some basis in German identity, raising disturbing questions about how the Germans were to come to terms with it and guard themselves against such a recurrence.[11]

Another question concerned the continuity of the German identity and the so-called 'historicization' of the Nazi period. Was German history continuous, or did it fall into three distinct phases – namely, pre-1933, 1933–45, and post-1945? If it was continuous, how was the second period to be integrated with its historical self-understanding? If it was discontinuous, how could the discontinuity be explained, and the Germans arrive at a coherent conception of their history? Jürgen Habermas stressed the continuity of German history. He located German identity in its way of life and argued that, since the latter had remained the same over time and persisted up to the present, there was no rupture in German identity. As he put it, 'our identity is permanently interwoven with it, from bodily gesture through the language to the rich interplay of intellectual customs'.[12] This meant that present-day Germans were connected with Auschwitz 'not through contingent circumstances but internally'. His critics argued that he was confusing cultural and political identities and that, while the former was continuous, the latter had suffered a radical rupture. In their view, the Nazi period was not a necessary expression of the German way of life, but an aberration.

Yet another question related to Germany's postwar democracy. The Germans had now given themselves a new national identity in the form of democratic institutions, and stressed their European roots as a way of guarding themselves against internal aberrations. This raised the crucial question of whether constitutional patriotism was all there was to national identity. Habermas thought it was not only sufficient but also the only form of identity possible in a modern plural and 'post-national' state. Others disagreed. In their view, a nation could not be held together by the largely formal constitutional patriotism alone, and needed deeper emotional and cultural bonds. They also thought that so long as the Germans lived within the framework of the nation state, a post-national identity was both utopian and dangerous. Even they acknowledged, however, that since interpretations of their past were bound to differ, an attempt to ground the new national identity in a unified understanding of the country's history threatened the postwar consensus. This left Germans with two painful choices. Either they should eschew all attempts to give the new identity a historical basis, or to give it one and risk provoking the hitherto subdued right-wing reading of German history. The first alternative entailed a deliberate historical amnesia and was emotionally and intellectually difficult, while the second was fraught with unacceptable political risks.

The postwar division of Germany too raised important questions about its identity. Were there now two German states, both equal and legitimate? Or was there only one Germany, divided illegitimately into two states? If the latter, did its oneness consist in its prewar territory, its ethnicity, or – as was commonly argued – its nationhood? The overwhelming majority of West Germans and a large section of East

Germans were in no doubt that the Germans were a single nation and that West Germany was the 'real' Germany and a true heir to the German past. Accordingly, West Germans decided not to give themselves a constitution, as that would imply an endorsement of the division, but instead a Basic Law (*Grundegesetz*), which was to remain effective until such time as the country was united. Not surprisingly, when the two halves were reunited, the Unification Treaty simply extended the Basic Law over East Germany and incorporated it into West Germany. Acutely aware of the role of collective memory in the maintenance of national identity, the Treaty sought to wipe out the memory of East Germany by avoiding every possible mention of it. As in postwar Germany, post-unification Germany sought a clean break with its recent past as the only way to give itself a secure identity. Since the unification was widely demanded, and the sacrifices it entailed were justified, in the name of the unity of the German nation, it seemed to some to be responsible for the subsequent rise of the neo-Nazi and other racist movements based on the slogan of 'Germany for the Germans' – precisely what most postwar leaders had been anxious to avoid.

Developing countries

Among the developing countries, India was one of the first to initiate a debate on national identity.[13] From the early decades of the nineteenth century onwards, its leaders had begun to ask why their country had fallen prey repeatedly to foreign invasions and rule. A large body of influential opinion thought that, after a brilliant start, the country had for centuries remained static, caste-ridden, fragmented, inward-looking and lacking in intellectual creativity and civic virtues. The only way to regenerate India was to make a clean break with its past by giving it a liberal, democratic and secular orientation. The modernists valued several aspects of its past, especially the classical, but thought that any attempt to resuscitate these fragments risked opening the door to Hindu revivalism and threatening the new identity. They also appreciated the need for a coherent conception of Indian history, but were again afraid that it would stir up controversy about the centuries of Muslim rule and open old wounds, of which the bloody partition of the country was a savage manifestation. After India became independent in 1947, Jawaharlal Nehru, its first and charismatic prime minister, threw all his weight behind the new national identity, or what he also called its 'national philosophy' or 'ideology'. As he won successive elections and claimed democratic legitimacy for it, he declared it the 'absolute' and 'unquestionable' foundation of the Indian state from which it would deviate at its peril.

In the 1980s, India threw up a new debate on national identity, which bears some resemblance to that in Germany. Some Hindu leaders argued that the Nehruvian view had failed the country because it was an alien implant and did not connect with its Hindu roots. They stressed the foundational and identity-determining role of the Hindus and pressed for a rather muddled alternative vision. As the modernists had feared, these attempts revived garbled collective memories of Muslim rule, stoked anti-Muslim prejudices and heightened Hindu self-consciousness, leading to the destruction of the Babri mosque in 1992 and the subsequent Muslim alienation. India continues to struggle to develop a just and balanced view of the kind of country it is and wishes to be, and of the contributions of the Hindu, Buddhist, Muslim, European and other civilizations that have shaped it.

The kind of debate on national identity that has taken place in India is to be found in all developing countries. At independence, Algeria declared itself a modern and secular country. A few years later, cries of 'depersonalization' and 'loss of national identity' were heard in many parts of the country, and demands were made to 'repersonalize' it by restoring the country's 'traditional Islamic identity'. As the movement gathered momentum and led to a fierce clash between the two groups, the Algerian republic faced its most severe crisis. Democratic elections in the early 1990s gave the Islamicists a majority, which the frightened secularists subverted with the help of the army.[14]

Like Algeria, Iran under the Shah opted for a secular national identity. But unlike Algeria, India and postwar Germany, the Shah sought to give himself and his modernist project a historical legitimacy by embedding it in his country's pre-Islamic past and downplaying the role of Islam. Refusing to see Islam as just one phase in Iran's long history, the marginalized mullahs began to assert its centrality to the country's identity. As the modernist project bit deep into the traditional institutions and threw up disaffected groups in rural and in particular urban areas, the fundamentalists under Ayatollah Khomeini won enough popular support to establish an Islamic republic. Among other things, they read its history from the 'Islamic point of view' and virtually wrote its non-Islamic roots and influences out of existence, propagating a unidimensional and homogeneous view of its identity. As the Islamic republic is running into problems, Iranian intellectuals are returning for inspiration to critical strands within their Islamic and pre-Islamic past. Other countries in Asia and Africa have faced, or are facing, similar battles.

They are now joined by the countries recently liberated from the communist rule. Their debates on national identity centre not only on appropriate paths of economic development and the possibility of establishing democratic institutions, but also on the centrality of religion, the place of indigenous or 'imposed' minorities in national life, and the best way to interpret and incorporate the years of communism in their self-understanding. In Poland, the Catholic Church, for long a guardian of Polish identity, especially during the communist rule, is increasingly being challenged because of its resistance to the consolidation of liberal democratic institutions in terms of which most Poles now define their identity. In some cases, such as Bosnia, the stark contrast between the country's self-conception and the outsiders' view of it has added a new poignancy to their search for national identity.[15] Most Bosnian Muslims see themselves as Muslim Europeans, as European as the rest and differing from them only in their religion, whereas most of their neighbours and others further afield define them as European Muslims – that is, Muslims like their counterparts in other parts of the world and different only in their geographical location. The latter view de-Europeanizes them, and presents them as an illegitimate and potentially dangerous presence in an 'essentially' Christian Europe.

Worried about its ability to meet contemporary challenges, Japan too is beginning to take a critical look at itself. In 2004, the government-appointed Commission on Japan's Goals in the Twenty-First Century proposed a fairly extensive overhaul of large parts of the country's identity. Since it now has a substantial number of permanently settled immigrants and needs more, the Commission recommended that it should abandon the idea of 'ethnic purity' and see itself as a multicultural society held together by civic nationalism. Traditionally, it has been inward-looking and a prisoner of *mura-ishiki* ('village mentality'). It now needs to become open and outward-looking, and to take a greater interest in other countries and cultures. The school curriculum should be revised appropriately, and English made a compulsory second language. Japan, the Commission argues, has a strong conformist tendency and loves an 'excessive degree of homogeneity and uniformity', summed up in the popular proverb, 'The nail that sticks up must be hammered down'. It should now aim to foster individuality, critical thinking, and 'individual empowerment' among its people. The Commission also suggests that

Japan should affirm the Asian dimension of its identity, see itself as both Asian and Western, and redefine its place in the world appropriately.

Some observations

I have so far sketched the various and sometimes confusing ways in which the concept of national identity entered the political discourses of different countries and the kinds of debate it provoked. In each case, there was a general sense of decline, disorientation or discontinuity, and a widespread desire to develop a coherent self-conception that could give the country a sense of direction and self-confidence, and around which its people could be united. This led to wide-ranging debates on the country's history, its strengths and weaknesses, its hopes for the future, the character of its people, and the causes of its decline. Different social groups advanced different views, and one that enjoyed wider support used its power to shape the country in its image. Debates on national identity were never politically innocent, and both reflected and sought to legitimize particular interests and systems of power. Since these debates had their origins in a sense of crisis, they shared several common features, such as the study of history, a celebration of its great events, some degree of self-criticism and a search for scapegoats. However, since the nature and causes of the crisis differed from country to country, the debates were conducted in different idioms and at different levels.

In Britain, the debate on national identity was triggered by several interrelated factors, of which the general feeling of *economic and political* decline was the most important. Given the country's imperial and industrial history, the debate also had an inescapable historical orientation, and was centred on the qualities of character that had once stood it in good stead and which many thought should be revived. In Germany, the debate on national identity had a largely *moral and political* origin. It was provoked by a profound sense of discontinuity and moral crisis caused by the Nazi experience and the anxiety about the stability of its postwar democratic institutions: its focus was on German political institutions and public culture. Unlike Britain and France, Germany was not unified until the late nineteenth century, and could not hope to revive or draw inspiration from an earlier historical period. While retaining links with its cultural past, the debate on national identity was therefore largely future-orientated.

The Indian situation was not much different. Since the country had been under foreign rule for centuries and had never before been united, it lacked a single and continuous past as a focus. Even the Hindu revivalists could only appeal to the great *cultural* achievements of classical India, and knew that these could not provide the *political* basis for its self-definition. The debate on national identity therefore centred on the *political and social* regeneration of India.

In Canada, the debate on national identity was provoked not by a sense of decline or discontinuity, but by disorientation and disunity generated by Quebec nationalism and to a lesser extent by the fear of American domination. The debate therefore took a predominantly *constitutional* form, and centred on redefining the structure of the Canadian state. In Iran, Algeria, Egypt, Pakistan and other Muslim countries, debates on national identity were initially political and cultural in nature, but later came to be dominated by the place of religion in national self-definition. Although the salience of religion is also to be found in India, Eastern Europe and elsewhere, it does not have the same urgency.

In different countries, debates on national identity involve different kinds of perplexity and agonizing choices. In those with a continuous and not too shameful a past, the present can be integrated with it, and the search for identity involves no discontinuity. In countries with a fragmented, discontinuous or disastrous past, the search for identity involves either a largely invented continuity or, more sensibly, a temporary break with the past and some kind of deliberately induced historical amnesia. Some of them can have either a future or a past but not both, at least for the present. Furthermore, since some societies cannot always turn to their past for inspiration and guidance, they either muddle through as best they can or seek inspiration from only the partially relevant historical experiences of other societies. Not surprisingly, they lurch from one extreme to another, experimenting promiscuously with different alternatives, and find it difficult to evolve coherent identities.

In developing societies, many of which are colonial constructs and have no continuous history or experience of a shared life, the question of identity can prove to be deeply divisive and intractable. National identity there needs to be created from fragments of the past, and views on it vary greatly. An even more difficult situation arises in societies with deeply divided national groups. Members of these groups share citizenship but not a common view of their history and a collective self-conception. In Israel there are strong Jewish and Arab identities, and at best only a thinly shared national identity. In Bosnia even a thin national identity is absent. Since such societies do not always have a hostile other, and indeed since each of its major groups is a hostile presence to the other, it is not easy to unite them around the kind of externally oriented overreaching notion of national identity that helped define Britain and other European countries in the nineteenth century.[16] Rather than become distracted by a debate on national identity, the best course of action for these societies is to unite their members around broadly agreed economic and political goals, and hold the country together long enough to allow them to develop enough experiences in common to foster over time a shared view of their identity.

5

Multicultural Society and the Convergence of Identities

Cultural diversity is an inescapable fact of modern life. Culture refers to a historically inherited system of meaning and significance in terms of which a group of people understand and structure their individual and collective lives. It defines the meaning or point of human activities, social relations and human life in general, and the significance or value to be attached to them. It is embodied in its beliefs and practices, which collectively constitute its fuzzy but recognizable identity. To say that almost every modern society is culturally diverse or multicultural is to say that its members subscribe to and live by different, though overlapping, systems of meaning and significance.[1]

Cultural diversity in modern society has several sources. Many societies include several ethnic, religious, cultural and other communities, with their more or less distinct bodies of beliefs and practices. Some of these communities were long denied self-expression in the name of nation-building or a hegemonic ideology, and are now keen to exercise their newly won freedoms. Modern men and women, being profoundly shaped by liberal individualism, take pride in making their own choices, and experiment with different ways of life. Globalization exposes society to different currents of thought, and its members either incorporate some of these in their ways of life, or panic and reactively revive traditional forms of life. The increasing reassertion of religion further reinforces diversity.

Immigration is another important source of diversity. It involves both skilled and unskilled labour recruited to meet the country's needs, and those involved bring their ways of life with them. Multinationals move their staff around from one country to another. People move freely within such regional units as the EU. Members of diasporas return to their lands of origin in large numbers, either in their old age (as in the case of India, China and Britain), or because these countries have now become more prosperous than when they left them (as in the case of Ireland, Spain and Portugal), or because they are now free of the political problems that had precipitated their original departure (as in the case of South Africa, Botswana, and some former communist countries), and they all bring with them the ideas and practices acquired abroad. Asylum seekers and refugees bring their ways of thinking and living. Since none of these and other sources of cultural diversity are likely to disappear in the foreseeable future, and since new forms of diversity appear as the old die out, it is a more or less permanent feature of modern life.

The indigenous peoples, the territorially concentrated minorities, the subnational groups, the religious communities and the immigrants represent different forms of diversity and require different reponses. Since I cannot discuss them all, I shall concentrate on immigrants, the archetypal strangers to whom the society does not feel the same degree of commitment as it does to its own minorities, and who highlight the dilemmas and tensions of a multicultural society more than indigenous minorities do. The strange fact that much of traditional political theory has either ignored the subject or treated it inadequately provides an additional reason to concentrate on it.

We need to avoid four commonly made mistakes in the discussion of immigration.[2] First, since immigration is only one source of cultural diversity, we should not think nostalgically that society was culturally homogeneous before immigration began and could be made so again by ending it. Second, since immigrants belong to different religious, ethnic and other groups, we should neither racialize them as if they were all non-white, nor homogenize them and ignore their different expectations, cultural resources, and ways of relating to the wider society. Third, the diversity introduced by immigrants is not necessarily deeper or more extensive than that already obtaining in most receiving societies. The latter include individuals and groups who take vastly different views on such subjects as homosexuality, same-sex marriages, cohabitation, relations between parents and children, family discipline, the capitalist economy, and respect for the law. In almost all these areas, immigrants often share the 'conservative' views of the majority, and the moral and cultural divide between them and the rest of society is narrower and shallower than that separating its own members. We should not therefore exoticize immigrants, and think that just because they look different, speak differently and come form unfamiliar countries, their moral and cultural lives are, or must also be, quite different. This is not to deny that immigrant ways of life often differ from those of the receiving society in important respects, but rather to say that these differences should not blind us to their commonalities, and that they are not necessarily more intractable than those to be found in society at large.

Fourth, contemporary immigration differs from those of earlier times in many important respects and should not be expected to follow the same pattern, an easily made mistake that generates false expectations and much avoidable tension. Earlier immigrants at the start of the twentieth century and during the interwar period often came as refugees fleeing persecution, and felt profoundly grateful to the receiving society for giving them a new home and in some cases saving them from a certain death. They also came with families, which helped. They were keen to assimilate, had virtually abandoned their homelands, and neither wished to nor could retain close ties with them because of poorly developed modes of transport and communication. The fact that many of them belonged to the Judeo-Christian tradition and could rely on local churches and synagogues to ease their transition also helped. By contrast, contemporary immigrants have often been recruited for their labour and skills, so their relationship to the receiving society is largely contractual and lacks an element of gratitude. Many of them belong to the former colonies, and arrive with mixed emotions. They are keen to retain their ties with their homelands, which modern technology facilitates. The current cultural and political climate is also more hospitable to their desire to maintain their identity than was the case earlier. Western societies, including such immigrant societies as the US, Canada, Australia and New Zealand thus face a historically novel situation, and need both to unlearn the lessons of the past and to learn some new ones.

Assimilation[3]

An influential body of opinion, far more widespread than is generally assumed, argues that a society cannot be cohesive and stable unless its immigrants assimilate into the prevailing culture and become like the rest. Every society needs a common system of meaning and values, and if some of its members were to hold very different beliefs and values, they would disagree deeply on important matters and not be able to sustain a shared life. Some assimilationists give the argument an onto-logical basis, and maintain that human beings feel at ease with those of their kind and find it extremely difficult, even impossible, to identify with those that they recognize as strangers. This is, in their view, a basic fact of human nature, an ineradicable human instinct, which a society may disregard at its peril. So far as immigrants are concerned, the choice before them is stark and simple. If they want to be accepted as full and equal citizens, they should assimilate into the national culture, exchange their inherited or imported identity for one derived from their new coun-try and undergo a kind of cultural rebirth. Conversely, if they hold on to their culture, retain close ties with their country of origin, and in these and other ways remain different, they should not complain if the rest of society refuses to identify with them and treats them as being unequal. Neither choice is cost-free, and immigrants must decide for themselves which one is better for them.[4]

The assimilationist approach is not devoid of merit. A society cannot be held together unless its members share some basic beliefs and values. If some of them saw no value in human life, fairness, and respect for authority, or did not see the point of reciprocity and keeping promises, no common life would be possible. Furthermore, as people live together they tend to develop common habits, interests, tastes and values, and grow to be similar to each other, often in a manner they do not recognize or even like. The assimilationist, however, wrongly asks for a greater degree and range of unity than is possible or necessary.

It is not true that human beings prefer and identify only with those of 'their own kind'. If that were so, inter-ethnic and inter-religious friend-ships, neighbourhoods and marriages as well as reasonably successful multi-ethnic and multicultural societies such as Canada, Australia and the US would be inexplicable. In fact, no two human beings are ever fully or substantially alike, not even spouses, and parents and children. They share some beliefs, values, tastes and attitudes but differ in others, and learn over time to live with and even delight in their differences. Members of a society are no different. They are similar in some respects and different in others, and which of these acquires salience is not dictated by human nature. The Jews in Germany were more or less fully assimilated and accepted by the rest of their countrymen, but the situa-tion changed drastically when the Nazis singled out their race and defined them as the enemies of the country. Those who were of the 'same kind' before 1930 were now demonized as being of a different kind. Here, as elsewhere, 'kind' is a social construct, and who belongs to what kind is a matter of personal, and more often political, decision.[5]

Assimilation is not as simple and smooth a process as the assimilationist imagines. The assimilating person is never quite sure when she has become assimilated fully and whether she is accepted. She is therefore anxious to prove to herself and others that she has assimilated, is generally loud and earnest to show that she is not a counterfeit, which makes her strangeness even more visible and comical. She is also constantly at the mercy of others, who alone are in a position to certify whether or not, and how much, she has assimilated, and remains permanently subordinate and heteronomous. As if this is not enough, she needs to keep pressuring other members of her group to assimilate, because if they do not that reflects badly on her and is embarrassing. Since some of them might not, she must join others in condemning them or at least disown and keep her distance from them, with all the moral and psychological corruption this involves.

There are also other problems with assimilation. Modern societies are characterized by deep disagreements on such matters as ideals of human excellence, the best way to lead the good life, the structure of the family, and legitimate forms of sexual self-expression. Since the society lacks a comprehensive moral consensus, assimilation of immigrants can in practice amount to little more than ensuring that they accept a few basic values and social norms, which does not satisfy the assimilationist. The kind of assimilation that the assimilationist wants is also impracticable, because most people derive their fundamental beliefs from their religion, and not even the most aggressive assimilationist wants to suppress religious freedom. Marriage is another factor reinforcing cultural identity, as many immigrants tend to marry among themselves, and some prefer spouses from their homeland. The determined assimilationist would have to deny them the right to 'import' spouses, and violate both their basic human freedom and equal citizenship, as this restriction is not extended to non-immigrants. Assimilation is inherently limitless, as it springs from intolerance of differences, and even the smallest of these can continue to arouse anxiety and hostility.

Integration

Since the assimilationist demand is unjust, unrealistic and illiberal, many societies have in recent years proposed integration as an alternative model. Prima facie, it appears to be a perfectly sensible goal, as immigrants should be encouraged to become an integral part of society, and should have the same rights, opportunities and obligations as the rest. But when probed deeper, the idea of integration is not as innocent as it seems. It involves a particular way of incorporating outsiders into the prevailing social structure, and is sometimes either indistinguishable or only marginally different from assimilation.[6]

Integrationists rightly insist that immigrants should commit themselves to their new society, respect its institutions and values, and show it basic loyalty. They are also right to insist that they should participate in the common life of society and build up bonds with its other members as an earnest indication of their willingness to become its full members. Integrationists do not, however, stop there. Like assimilationists, they too see integration as a one-way process: the onus to integrate is placed on the immigrants, and so is the blame for their failure to do so. This is a misleading account of the process of integration. A Muslim girl, for example, might be unwilling to swim in shorts, or undergo an internal medical examination by a male doctor; or a Sikh boy not want to go to school without his turban. Unless the wider society accommodates such demands, except when they are patently unreasonable or excessively costly, it makes it difficult for these people to integrate. Immigrants might move out of the communal ghetto and buy a house in a white middle-class suburb. But if the residents of that area move out, these efforts at integration amount to nothing. Or they might adopt the ways of life and thought of the wider society, but if they are dismissed as pushy, presumptuous, not knowing their place, integration not only brings no benefits but also consigns them to a cultural limbo, uprooted from their own community but without acquiring a reasonably secure foothold in the new one. Integration, frustrated as much by segregation as by rejection, is a two-way process, requiring both immigrants and the wider society to adjust to each other.

A society is articulated at several levels: political, economic, social, moral and cultural. Immigrants might integrate at some of these levels but not at others. They might, for example, integrate economically and politically and play their full part as productive workers and active citizens, but prefer to marry among themselves, retain a strong commitment to their country of origin, confine their close friendships and social ties to their own community, or limit their cultural interests to their own traditions.[7] Integrationists see such partial or limited integration as a sign of separateness, a refusal to integrate, and devise all kinds of policies to discourage this behaviour. This is broadly the case even with the idea of 'pluralist' integration advocated by some multiculturalists. It too remains uneasy with self-chosen separation in some areas of life, and allows diversity only in the manner and pace of integration.

Some integrationists do not share such an extreme view of integration. They appreciate that immigrants might wish to, and indeed have a right to, retain parts of their cultural identity, and that integration could and should be 'thin', limited mainly to society's 'common institutions'. While they are right, they face an obvious problem. Some members of society might consider this enough, whereas others might argue that society cannot be cohesive unless integration is extended also to the moral, social and cultural areas of life, and that allowing immigrants to integrate partially is to privilege them over other members of society.[8] Since there is no conclusive way to resolve the debate, the 'thin' view of integration appears to be ad hoc, arbitrary, even inconsistent.[9] Even if an agreement could be reached on which areas of life are essential to integration, the problem remains. From the integrationist's point of view, integration is a highly valued national goal and defines the quality of one's membership of a nation. If the former is partial and limited, then so is the latter. Partially integrated immigrants remain suspect, and are viewed by some as legitimate targets for unequal or discriminatory treatment. The demand for integration, like that for assimilation, is insatiable. One can always ask why immigrants want to hold themselves back, why they cannot be like the rest, why they want to maintain their culture if they are as sincerely committed to society as they claim to be. The totalist and intolerant logic of integration is readily exploited by those so inclined. And as for those of a tolerant and liberal persuasion, they are always at a disadvantage, both because the onus of justifying limited integration is placed on them, and because they are arguing within a framework whose basic thrust is inhospitable to their liberal disposition.[10]

Like assimilation, integration is vulnerable to subtle forms of racism. Since integration is the goal, one is led to ask what kinds of immigrants can be integrated with relative ease, are less likely to make inconvenient demands, and with whom the rest of society would find it easier to identify. The integrationist logic requires a society either to avoid 'difficult' immigrants or to subject them to a harsher regime of control. In Europe and elsewhere, black, Muslim and other immigrants are seen as a problem in a way that others are not, and far more is often demanded of them. No one cares whether the American or even the Japanese immigrants to

Europe marry only among themselves, lead socially and culturally self-contained lives, or retain close ties with their countries of origin, but great anxiety is expressed in relation to the inferiorized or 'less desirable' groups. Muslims are accused of inadequate loyalty if they fail to issue loud and unambiguous condemnations of Islamic terrorism, but no such demands are, or were, made of Irish immigrants in relation to IRA terrorism, or of American immigrants when their government violates international law. Sometimes there are good reasons for such a differential treatment, but not always, and even when there are, the role of racism is not entirely absent. We need to guard against the tendency to apply different standards of integration to different racial and ethnic groups, not only because it is unjust and racist, but also because it breeds resentment among the inferiorized groups and hinders their integration.[11]

A moral contract

Rather than ask how immigrants can be assimilated or integrated, we should ask how they can become equal citizens and be bound to the rest by the ties of common belonging. Common belonging refers to a broadly shared feeling among the citizens that they form part of the same community, belong together, share common interests, are bound to each other by a common system of rights and obligations, depend on each other for their well-being, and wish to live together in peace for the foreseeable future.[12] It gives emotional depth to their citizenship, fosters bonds of mutual identification, and enables them to cope with the inevitable tensions of sharing a common life. Fostering it is our general objective, and all else is derived from it. It obviously requires some form of integration in the sense that immigrants should accept the obligations of citizenship and not be excluded or marginalized by the wider society. It also requires some degree of assimilation in the sense that they should share certain basic beliefs and values. However, integration and assimilation are the means, not the end, and their nature, forms, degrees and limits should be decided by their ability to serve their overall objective in the context of the constantly changing relations between immigrants and the wider society. Common belonging is a two-way process. Immigrants cannot belong to a society unless it is prepared to welcome them, and conversely it cannot make them its own unless they wish to belong to it, with all that this entails. Common belonging requires a broad consensus on what is expected of each party, and can only be achieved if each discharges its part of the moral covenant.

Immigrants arrive of their own free will and wish to belong to their country of settlement. The latter represents an intricate and complex way of life built up through the struggles and sacrifices of its members over several generations. Since the identities, lives and personal histories of existing members are bound up closely with it, they rightly feel possessive and protective about their society. They want to be reassured that immigrants value their membership of it, and understand and respect their society's way of life. Even the ordinary clubs and associations insist on rules of membership, and rightly expect new members to join it in good faith, observe its norms, and do nothing to undermine it. This is even more so in the case of political communities, which have recognizable identities and mean a great deal to their members.[13] The immigrants' obligations derive not only from their explicit consent, as John Locke argued, but also from the basic respect they owe to those among whom they have chosen to settle and their way of life.

The society in which immigrants have come to settle is a deeply cherished home to its members and deserves to be treated with appropriate respect and sensitivity. It is also their own and their children's future home, and requires a moral and emotional commitment. This does not mean that immigrants should sever their ties with their country of origin, or may not enjoy dual nationality or even dual citizenship, no more than a marriage requires that spouses disown their parental ties. Such a demand is unfair, impossible to meet, and unnecessary. What can be demanded of immigrants is that they should see their country of settlement as their home, whatever other homes they might also happen to have. It should mean something to them, have an intrinsic value, and not just be a place to make money or to escape persecution, and immigrants should provide reasonable evidence of their commitment to it. Such a commitment shows respect for the prevailing way of life, establishes their good faith, qualifies them for full membership, and entitles them to make such demands on the rest of society as their process of settlement requires.

Immigrants express their commitment to society in several ways. They should value its integrity and well-being, respect its structure of authority and laws, and in general discharge their obligations as citizens. They should participate in its common life, discharge their share of collective responsibility, find gainful employment, should not misuse the available welfare provisions, and so on. Participation in common life does not mean that they may not live or marry among themselves, carve out communal cultural spaces of their own, or lead partially segregated lives. Marriages, cultural life, and so on are matters of individual choice and should not be subjected to legal coercion and social pressure. And since other citizens are at libery to live their own social and cultural lives as they please, including marrying abroad, denying that liberty to immigrants involves treating them unequally. As long as they participate in the collective life of the society and discharge their obligations as citizens, their personal and social lives are their own business.

Immigrants also need to acquire the cultural competence necessary to find their way around the society's way of life. This involves learning its language, understanding and observing its rules of civility and norms of behaviour, and acquiring reasonable familiarity with its traditions and history. As they respect its values and norms of behaviour, they are likely over time to internalize these and make them part of their social and even perhaps *personal* identity, especially if they see the point of them. And even when they do not see the point of them, they should generally observe such values and norms in their social relations, for broadly the same reasons that women visitors to Muslim countries cover their heads without necessarily approving of the practice. There is nothing insincere, hypocritical or self-alienating about this, because it merely shows respect for the society's way of life and facilitates good relations with its members.

Society's responses

Just as immigrants need to commit themselves to the receiving society, it too should make a reciprocal commitment to them. They are new to it, and liable to much misunderstanding and negative stereotyping. They need time to acquire the necessary cultural competence, and in the meantime they lack a clear and coherent voice. Being outsiders, they are often resented by certain sections of society and made to feel unwelcome. They are also likely to face discrimination in significant areas of life. They suffer from various kinds of disadvantages resulting from poverty, lack of language, trauma of transition, confusion and worry about how to adjust to the new society, anxieties about their children, and the likely mismatch between their expectations and the reality of their new life. The wider society needs to ease their transition, and help them feel and become its full and legitimate members. This requires action at several levels.

Discrimination against immigrants in all areas of life, especially those such as citizenship rights, employment, education and housing that affect their life chances and where bonds of common belonging are forged, should be declared unlawful and subjected to appropriate sanctions. Discrimination takes several forms. It can be blatant or subtle, direct or indirect, as when it is built into the procedures and rules of an organization, and might be practised by individuals or institutions. It can also be formal or informal, as when shop assistants overcharge immigrants, or fellow-passengers on public transport make abusive remarks and change seats. It is particularly hurtful when it is practised by the institutions of the state, such as the police, immigration officers, the courts and civil servants. The state is expected to treat its citizens equally, is the authoritative spokesperson for society, and its actions guide public opinion. When its institutions engage in discriminatory behaviour, they not only reduce their victims to second-class citizens, but also leave them with no redress. A discriminatory state imposes equal obligations but denies equal rights, and thus forfeits its legitimacy in the eyes of those it treats unequally.

While the law can tackle formal and institutional discrimination fairly effectively, its reach does not extend to informal and subtle discrimination. It cannot compel a passenger not to leave his/her seat or not to mumble abuse when an immigrant of a different colour sits next to her; or require a bank clerk not to keep him/her waiting an unduly long time. Although these actions taken individually are trivial and little more than sources of minor irritation, cumulatively they can create a regime of humiliation, wear down their victims, and build up powerful feelings of rage and hatred. There is no simple and foolproof way to deal with them. Heads of the organizations involved can be required to lay down standards of good behaviour, backed up by appropriate disciplinary procedures. Immigrant and other public-spirited civic organizations can expose such practices and use their consumer power to put them right. Since these practices spring from and derive their legitimacy from the general social ethos, church leaders, government ministers, public figures and the media have a vital role to play in reforming the society's moral culture. Ordinary citizens too facilitate integration by what they say and do, and it is their civic duty to play their part: in any society, the state is not and cannot be the only agent of social cohesion and harmony.

Immigrants suffer from several material, social, cultural, political and other disadvantages that impede their settlement, and tackling them calls for a comprehensive and coherent public policy. Their children, especially if they arrive as adolescents, might need remedial classes and some form of transitional bilingual education. Immigrants tend to live together partly because of discrimination and partly for reasons of physical security, emotional sustenance, ethnic clientele, locations of industries where many of them work, and ease of common cultural and religious practices. Such residential concentrations – or what are pejoratively called ghettoes – have their own economic and cultural logic, and should be accepted. They not only do not stand in the way of integration, but can even facilitate it, because personally and socially secure individuals are more likely to have the confidence to reach out to the wider society and experiment with its ways of life and thought.

Residential concentration is worrying when it is involuntary, confines immigrants to their own community, schools, economy, and so on, and rules out all but the minimum of contact with the rest of society. It then creates parallel societies with little in common apart from mutual indifference, incomprehension and even perhaps hatred. As the experience of many multicultural societies demonstrates, immigrants tend to move out of ethnically concentrated areas when they feel physically secure, acquire cultural self-confidence, improve their economic prospects, and feel sure that they will not face rejection. All this obviously depends quite heavily on government policy and the general social climate. If, for some reason, residential concentration persists, ways need to be found to encourage ethnic mixing in a manner that avoids conflict and promotes common interests. Housing estates could encourage ethnically mixed tenants; schools could draw their pupils from different ethnic groups; when this is not possible, ethnically concentrated schools could explore ways of involving their pupils in common curricular and extra-curricular projects with those of mixed schools, and so on.

Since the economy plays a vital role in the integration of immigrants, we need to devise well-targeted and group-sensitive policies to liberate them from the cumulative cycle of disadvantage. Removing discrimination in employment and promotion is obviously the most important, and requires an effective enforcement machinery with powers of investigation, determined action by heads of organizations, and a programme of positive action to identify and redress the disproportionate absence of relevant groups from different sectors of the economy. The run-down areas where immigrants are often concentrated need to be regenerated, and require a greater allocation of public resources and tax and other incentives to attract business. Helping immigrants to acquire valuable skills, improving the educational performance of their children, help with start-up capital, loans at lower rates of interest, and advice on how to start and build new businesses are valuable tools of public policy. Monitoring admissions into academically good schools and institutions of higher education is also necessary, as deliberate or unwitting discrimination by them blocks immigrants' upward mobility and hinders integration among the elite.

The situation is, of course, never quite as simple as this, and is sometimes made more complicated by the welfare state. Since need is often the only consideration in welfare provision, immigrants tend to be preferred over local people, and this can lead not only to hostility but also to injustice. As an example: since immigrants sometimes have larger families and often are poorer, they are given priority in the allocation of public housing over local people, whose needs are less acute but who might have been waiting much longer, given promises, have lived in the area for generations and have built up a strong social network. They feel bitter and treated unjustly, and sometimes rightly so. Although the answer lies in expanding housing provision, that takes time and comes up against the inevitable scarcity of resources. Since we cannot make need alone the basis of a claim, we should find just ways of weighing up different kinds of claims and fine-tuning the welfare state, such as assigning points to individuals. This is not easy, and whatever policy we follow leads to injustice to some groups and consequent discontent. The best way to deal with this is to explain honestly why the situation has arisen and, whenever possible, compensate those involved in other ways.

Sometimes group-sensitive policies are criticized on the grounds that they practise reverse discrimination, intensify ethnic consciousness, and militate against a common sense of belonging. Although this criticism has a point, the dangers it highlights are often exaggerated and can be guarded against. The kinds of policies I have suggested often represent a programme of positive action rather than positive discrimination, with its fixed targets and quotas. They are intended to remove obstacles to equal and fair competition and to tackle disadvantages, not to give arbitrary and unfair preference to immigrants. The policies apply not just to immigrants but to all who suffer from severe disadvantages. And if, in some cases, immigrants receive greater attention and help, this is only because their disadvantages are greater and have been compounded by discrimination.

The argument that ethnically orientated policies intensify ethnic consciousness and work against a shared sense of community is largely misconceived. A colour-blind approach makes sense when those making decisions are blind to colour, but when colour consciousness shapes their behaviour and is a source of discrimination, one needs to acknowledge its existence, identify its targets, remove their disadvantages, help them acquire equal competitive capacity, ease their integration into society, and create over time a genuinely colour-blind society that is so relaxed about ethnic differences that it takes no notice of them. Ethnically orientated policies perpetuate ethnic consciousness if they are open-ended, homogenize ethnic communities, prefer them unfairly over the rest, set up rigid quotas, and ignore wider social and economic inequalities. They have the opposite effect and become a means of integration when they are part of a general egalitarian policy, concentrate on clearly defined groups, and justify their differential treatment on grounds of fairness, special needs and social cohesion.

Like the lives of other members of society, a good deal of an immigrant's life is lived at the local level.[14] They regularly interact with their fellow citizens as neighbours, fellow workers, friends, shoppers, and spectators at sports events, and build up strong ties based on common interests and loyalties. Local attachments are free from the problems that arise at the national level, where foreign policy, national symbols and other issues become important. An immigrant can be proud to be a New Yorker without feeling troubled by and implicated in the US invasion of Iraq. Local ties are also easier to consolidate because, while fellow citizens might say 'You are not really Dutch', they are less likely to say 'You are not a Rotterdamer'. It is striking that the same young Turks who said they did not feel German replied in overwhelming numbers that they belonged to Frankfurt and could not imagine living elsewhere, and that the young Muslims who claimed not to feel British said that Bradford was their home and that they would not be happy elsewhere. People often generalize their local experiences and form an image of the country and their place in it; this is how a sense of nationhood is constructed. Other things being equal, the stronger the local ties and identity, the greater the sense of rootedness, and the weaker the impact of conflicts occurring at the national level.

It is therefore vital to build up inter-ethnic bonds at the local level through neighbourhood associations, sports clubs, trade unions, local branches of national political parties, charitable associations, chambers of commerce and inter-faith networks. These associations bring together different communities in the pursuit of common interests, and develop mutual understanding, and habits of co-operation and trust. Civic authorities too can do much to foster a strong sense of civic identity that can transcend ethnic differences and form the basis of the larger sense of national identity. They can do so by ensuring adequate representation for immigrants in their major institutions, involving them in common projects, sponsoring ethnic events, encouraging multi-ethnic cultural, literary and other festivals, and by designing public spaces so that they reflect and normalize diversity.

Educational institutions, especially schools, play a crucial role in creating a common sense of belonging. They should prepare their pupils for life in a multicultural society by sensitizing them to the reality of differences, and cultivating such vitally necessary multicultural skills and virtues as sympathetic imagination, tolerance, openness to other ways of life and thought, curiosity and mutual respect. They should promote intercultural literacy, foster better understanding between different cultural groups, and help them to acquire a shared pool of ideas and values. While they should obviously teach and assign a central role to the history, culture and traditions of the wider society, they also need to teach the history and culture of immigrants, explaining where they or their parents came from, why, and their experiences of migration and settlement.

Although multicultural education is directed primarily at the second and subsequent generations, it has a profound and often unnoticed effect on the first generation of immigrants. It avoids generational rupture with all its disastrous consequences, reassures parents that they will not lose their children to an 'alien' culture, and removes their suspicion of schools. Part of the reason why the first generation of immigrants sometimes resist participation in the common life of society and deliberately keep their distance from it is related to their understandable desire to provide an alternative cultural environment for their children, and to counter the assimilationist ethos of schools. When that anxiety is allayed by a programme of multicultural education, an important reason for their segregation is removed. This should also reduce the demand for separate ethnic and religious schools that might have their value but sometimes stand in the way of a common sense of belonging. And if for some reason such schools do exist, they should be required to teach a common national curriculum, promote intercultural understanding, and draw a proportion of their staff and pupils from other groups.

As I argued earlier, a common sense of belonging is easier when both the majority and minority communities feel at ease with themselves and with each other. If the minorities feel threatened, besieged, fearful of losing their culture, they turn inward, become defensive, and tend to avoid all but the minimum of contact with the rest of society. This is equally true of the majority. If it feels that it is no longer in charge of its future, and that its way of life is subjected to relentless erosion, it becomes defensive and intolerant, and either closes its doors to immigration – which is generally not possible – or falls prey to the unrealistic and self-defeating project of assimilation.

A sensible response to this has to be at several levels. The country's immigration and asylum policy should be fair, transparent, coherent, publicly debated and consensually grounded. The government needs to explain to its citizens why it has a moral and legal obligation to admit desperate refugees, and why it is in the country's interest to give them all the help they need to settle down. Similarly, it should explain why it needs immigrants, how many, to do what and with what benefits to the wider society, and to follow this up with independently audited periodic reports. It needs to distinguish between legitimate public anxieties about immigration and its racist rejection, and allay the former while combating the latter. If legitimate anxieties and fears remain unaddressed, and are not even allowed to be expressed in the name of political correctness, frustration builds up and takes aggressive forms. Those involved feel alienated from and turn against the political system that has no space for their views, and opt to support racist and right-wing political parties.

The distinction between legitimate fears on the one hand and blatant racism and xenophobia on the other is not easy to draw, especially as the latter often disguises itself in the former's respectable rhetoric. However not to draw it at all or to confuse the two is to create serious problems. If the public policy on immigration and asylum were to be transparent, based on the clearly stated economic needs and moral obligations of the country, and commanded the support of major political parties and leaders of public opinion, it should be relatively easy to identify racists and xenophobes. Since the battle against them is never conclusively won, statesmanship consists in isolating them skilfully and challenging their changing rhetoric and tactics.

Convergence of identities

As I argued in the previous chapter, a political community requires a broadly shared conception of its identity, and the latter should be inclusive and reflect its diversity. When the immigrants begin to settle, the prevailing definition of national identity needs to take them into account if they are to feel at home in and identify with the country. This is never a smooth process. Since national identity is ultimately about the ownership of the country, about who does and does not belong to it and whose interests and claims should be accorded priority, it becomes a site of contestation between those who think the country is theirs and those who want to share its ownership.[15] The resulting struggle is informal, unplanned and unorganized, conducted in multiple forums and in different idioms.

The history of the US provides a good example of this. For decades after its foundation, Americans were expected to be white, Protestant and of British descent. Other European immigrants, some of whom, such as the French and the Dutch, were associated with the founding of the country, were seen as insiders-outsiders, citizens enjoying a second-class status and expected over time to assimilate into the Anglo-Protestant culture and 'stock'. Subsequent European immigrants, indigenous peoples, black slaves, Asian immigrants, Jews and others faced even greater problems. Over time, and after a considerable struggle, American society became more open and had no tightly organized social or cultural structure into which its immigrants had to fit, as still remains the case in many European societies. The American identity too lost its narrow racial and cultural associations, and became available to all its citizens. An American can now be white, black or yellow, Protestant, Catholic or Hindu, native-born or a recent arrival, and does not have to speak with a standard accent. Black, Asian and newly naturalized immigrants have no hesitation in identifying themselves as Americans, and neither their fellow citizens nor outsiders are in the least puzzled by such claims. This uncoupling of national from ethnic, religious and other identities is a remarkable historical achievement, in no way unique to the US, but one of its greatest contributions to the theory and practice of multicultural societies.

National identity refers, among other things, to how the political community is represented in the imagination of its people. Since literature and the arts are the paradigmatic vehicles of representation, they play a vital role in constructing national identity and giving it a cultural and emotional depth. Not surprisingly, literature, especially the novel, and the visual arts have played an important part in the creation of the modern nation state. They have highlighted the commonalities between its distant and diverse members, challenged their inherited prejudices, rendered different places, groups, generations and historical times mutually intelligible, and woven them into a single temporal and spatial narrative. When immigrants arrive, their experiences too need to be rendered intelligible to the rest of society and incorporated in a suitably retold national story. A British example illustrates how this tends to happen.

Thanks to the work of its great literary and artistic figures, Britain often evokes images of serene Home Counties, manicured landscape, church bells, quiet Sundays, dreaming spires, emotional self-discipline, the art of understatement, and reserved gentlemen with their bowler hats and rolled-up umbrellas. As a result of the work of ethnic minority and other writers, artists, musicians, and so on, and some of the imaginative programmes transmitted on the television, Britain now also evokes the multicultural images of mosques and temples, elderly gentlemen walking with their children to Friday prayers in response to the call of the muezzin, Diwali celebrations in public squares, the noisy multi-ethnic streets of big cities, spicy food, saris and steel bands, as well as many hybrid images reflecting intercultural experimentation. British identity is increasingly being expressed in a plurality of images, and it is capacious and heterogeneous enough to allow its different communities and regions to find their representation in it. This makes it easier for them to take ownership of it and build common emotional bonds with each other.[16]

A similar process also occurs in relation to national symbols. In the mid-1980s, racist groups in Britain flaunted the national flag at their meetings and sought to make it an exclusive symbol of white Britain. Not surprisingly, the ethnic minorities found it difficult to relate to it, and some even felt threatened by it. Over time, many of them began to reclaim the flag by displaying it on ethnic and multi-ethnic occasions. This became particularly evident at the Sydney Olympics in 2000, and was reinforced at the Athens Olympics four years later, when the medal-winning black athletes did the lap of honour draped in the Union Jack. Their action had a double meaning, which was not lost on the British public. They were saying that they belonged to Britain and were proud to do so. They were also saying that Britain belonged to them as well, that they were its equal citizens, and that the flag and the national anthem symbolized them as much as the rest of their fellow citizens.

As immigrants come to be accepted as part of a country's national identity, the country looks at its past and constructs its historical narrative from a multicultural perspective. New facts are discovered, and the familiar ones seen in a new light. In Britain, for example, it is now widely accepted that black people have been here since Roman times, that after the abolition of slavery in 1833 they married local women and a sizeable section of the country's population is a product of this, that Muslims and Indians have been a significant presence for at least three centuries and there was a Muslim Peer as early as 1889, and so on. The racial and ethnic mix of the British people, the 'mongrel' character they have acquired over the centuries, and the diverse foreign influences that have shaped Britain's culture are all widely acknowledged without embarrassment and sometimes with pride.

As a political community begins to appreciate its multi-ethnic composition, it realizes that its current diversity is not recent or alien, but an ongoing feature of its history, and comes to feel at ease with it. For their part, immigrants appreciate that the country has known many like them in the past, and that they too will one day become a valued part of it. This makes it easier for them to relate to it and take ownership of its history. This gives rise to complementary transformations in their self-understanding. The receiving society recognizes that it now has new members, expands its self-definition or sense of identity to encompass them, and its citizens no longer think of themselves as a majority in opposition to an immigrant minority. For their part, immigrants realize that they are no longer immigrants but a part of society; not a minority, but equal citizens like the rest. Their cultural sense of identity is not abandoned – as the traditional American conception of immigration as 'rebirth' implies – but becomes a more or less valued component of their new identity that they share with the rest of their fellow citizens. Common belonging with immigrants is ultimately about the expansion and convergence of the identities of the two parties that are central to it, and is secure when both the language and the consciousness of majority and minority are transcended.

6

European Liberalism and the 'Muslim Question'

Unlike the US, with its sizeable Muslim population, it is widely held in many influential circles in the EU that its more than 15 million Muslims pose a serious cultural and political threat, and that this shows, among other things, that multicultural societies do not work.[1] Sometimes this view is stated explicitly; but more often it takes the form of an attack on multiculturalism for which Muslims are largely held responsible and which is a coded word for them. It cuts across the political and ideological divides and is shared, albeit in different degrees and for different reasons, by right wing nationalists, conservatives, liberals and socialists. In this chapter I critically examine the basis of this view, paying particular attention to how the Muslim identity has evolved over the years, and why liberals, the champions of minority rights, cultural diversity and civic as opposed to ethnic nationalism, feel threatened by it.

Emergence of Muslim identity

Although Muslim immigrants had begun to arrive in Europe to feed its labour-hungry industries from the 1950s onwards, they were culturally invisible until the 1970s and politically until the late 1980s.[2] Most of them came alone, intending to stay for a few years and then return home with enough savings to give them a better start in life. They had little command of the language of their country of settlement, were unused to the urban environment, and harboured a deep sense of inferiority, especially those coming from former colonies. They knew who they were, generally lived among their own people, did not see themselves as immigrants, and had little anxiety about maintaining their homeland-based identities. Since they faced racial discrimination, they united with other similarly placed groups to fight it, and acquired an additional, externally imposed and in a few cases freely accepted, racial identity of 'blacks'.

As Muslims abandoned their plans and even hopes of returning home, they were joined by their wives and began to raise families. They worried about how to bring up their children, to ensure intergenerational continuity, transmit their culture, religion and language, and counter the assimilationist pressure of the wider society. This increased their interest in the culture, institutions and practices of the society to which they had hitherto remained indifferent, and they began to form a view of their place in it. By and large, they defined their identity in religio-national terms. They were Pakistani, Indian, Algerian or Moroccan Muslims, not Muslims *simpliciter* but rooted in the cultures of their homelands. The society in which they lived could not be defined so easily because, although it was Christian, religion did not play an important role in it. They saw the culture as basically secular, and the question for them was how to maintain their religio-national identity in a secular environment.

Muslim immigrants set up welfare and cultural associations along religio-national lines. They built mosques, whose number increased dramatically in the 1970s, and began to demand that state schools make appropriate provisions for their children including *halal* meat, facilities for prayer, exemption of girls from sports, swimming and other activities that required them to wear shorts, and teaching children their history and culture. They could not expect their children to acquire and value their historical identity unless they set them appropriate examples and provided a suitable domestic environment. Accordingly, Muslim immigrants reorganized their personal lives and began to press for appropriate provisions in workplaces, hospitals and so on for themselves, and in particular for their women.

Since European states have traditionally seen themselves as nation states based on a homogeneous national culture, and since their earlier immigrants had made no such demands, the schools, workplaces and other public institutions often resisted Muslim pressure. This led to tension, court cases, public debates and protests. As a result, Muslims now became an unmistakable *cultural* presence and a source of public anxiety. Much agonized discussion took place throughout Europe on how to integrate them culturally. Different European countries worked out different models, France opting for assimilation, Britain for integration, the Netherlands for the 'pillarized' form of multiculturalism, and others for one or more of all three.[3]

From the late 1970s, and in particular the early 1980s onwards, the situation took a political turn. Although their pursuit of cultural demands and the resistance they encountered had already begun to politicize the first generation of Muslim immigrants, and thrown up political organizations, the second generation – which was now reaching adulthood – began to play a crucial role. Having grown up in a European society, young Muslims did not share their parents' inhibitions and diffidence, and well knew how to find their way around in the political system. More importantly, they increasingly began to define themselves in exclusively religious terms, not as Pakistani or Algerian Muslims, as their parents had done, but simply as Muslims. They did so for several reasons. Since they had limited contacts with their parental homeland, it meant little to them and was at best a minor element in their self-definition. In order to be politically effective, they needed to transcend ethnic and cultural divisions and build up nationwide organizations, which could only be based on their shared religion. Many of them, especially the girls, also chafed against parental constraints, and found it strategically useful to counter them by studying and suitably reinterpreting the Qur'ān. The fact that many young Muslims were embarrassed by some aspects of their parental culture reinforced the desire to return to the 'true principles' of Islam. Since the wider society too had begun to refer to them as Muslims, and associated negative ideas with the term, Muslim youth in the spirit of 'black is beautiful' asserted their Islamic identity with pride.

International events too played an important part in reinforcing the consciousness of Islamic identity. The basically non-violent Iranian revolution, in which almost all the violence came from the side of the Shah, and whose impact on Muslim consciousness was broadly comparable to that of the Russian Revolution of 1917 on the European left, gave Muslims the confidence that they could topple Western-supported regimes and offer an alternative to Western modernity. The Afghan resistance to Soviet occupation brought together Muslims of different nationalities, forged among them a common identity, and convinced Muslims the world over that they could defeat a determined superpower. Western dependence on oil exposed its vulnerability and awakened Muslims to their enormous potential economic power. The continuing Arab–Israeli conflict, the Israeli invasion of Lebanon in 1982, and the Muslim struggle against injustices and oppression in different parts of

the world gave them common global causes and sharpened the awareness of the *umma*, or the global Muslim community, a concept that
earlier had played only a marginal role in Muslim history. The historical
memory of the centuries-long Ottoman empire and the way it was
dismantled by European powers was increasingly revived, and used to
intensify the Muslim sense of humiliation and the desire to revive its
glory. By the mid-1980s, pride, power, the sense of victimhood, the
tantalizing dream of what over a billion of them, forming a majority in
fifty-five countries and a significant presence in just as many, including
the West, could achieve if they put their mind to it, and the deep anxiety
that all this could easily be lost through internal divisions and Western
manipulations, combined to form an increasingly global Islamic identity. European Muslims shared and asserted that identity, and felt part of
a worldwide community. The fact that they were courted and their religious institutions and activities generously funded by the oil-rich
Muslim countries, especially Saudi Arabia, reinforced this trend.

The growing importance of religion in Muslim self-definition and
others' perception of them made European Muslims intensely sensitive
to how their religion was represented in the West. Salman Rushdie's
Satanic Verses, published in 1989, was read against this background,
and widely seen as an anti-Islamic work written by a lapsed,
Westernized and Indian Muslim to impress and curry favour with a
predominantly Western audience. The protests it generated both
reflected and intensified Islamic identity. In France, there had been a
growing feeling that its Muslim population had remained only 'paper
French', French in their passports and nothing else, and needed to be
integrated. The Commission on Nationality, appointed in 1987,
produced a year later its two-volume report entitled *Being French Today
and Tomorrow*. The report insisted that Muslims should be 'absorbed'
into the cultural mainstream, and their religious and cultural differences
confined to the private realm. It was in this climate that *l'affair du
foulard* flared up. It acquired particular significance from the fact that
1989, the bicentenary of the French Revolution, witnessed aggressive
statements of the country's republican and secular identity. Muslim
youth, almost all male, in Britain, and Muslim girls in France led the
battle for Islam, quite often against the wishes of their parents, and
demanded that the state should recognize, respect and make public
space for it. By the late 1980s, Islam became a powerful *political* presence in Europe, its power deriving from its number, militancy, firm
sense of identity and global connections.

Bosnia was another important milestone in the development of Muslim self-consciousness. It had two unique features. It was in Europe's backyard and should have been of particular interest to it, and its Muslims were 'racially' no different from other Europeans. In spite of the geographical proximity, 'racial' similarity and the considerations of enlightened self-interest, European governments not only did nothing to protect the Muslims, but even prevented them from obtaining arms elsewhere. For many Muslims, this indicated European apathy, even antipathy, towards Muslims, and how little Europe cared for their lives. Some even conjured up the lurid nightmare that, if they lowered their guard, Europeans could perpetrate another Holocaust against them. In April 2005, twelve Danish cartoons, published in *Jyllands-Posten* (in which even the Prophet Mohammed was not spared) and the commentaries that accompanied them led Muslims to conclude that not only they as a community but their very religion was regarded as backward and unfit to be part of civilized Europe.

European anxiety

As the politically visible Muslims began to define their identity in religious terms from the late 1970s onwards, Europeans began to wonder how to integrate them and turn them into loyal citizens. A sizeable and influential section took the pessimistic view that this was virtually impossible, or at least exceedingly difficult. Such distinguished liberal leaders as Helmut Schmidt in Germany and Roy Jenkins in Britain even thought it a mistake to have admitted them in large numbers. Islam, they argued, was inherently undemocratic, which was why no Muslim country had so far thrown up a stable democracy, and almost all of them strenuously resisted internal and external pressures to introduce one. European Muslims could not be counted upon to respect democratic institutions, and at best offered a prudential and instrumental loyalty to them. Since Muslims privileged the *umma* over the nation state, they were far more interested in global Muslim causes than in their fellow citizens, and could not be trusted to be good citizens. Islam, in their view, was also profoundly illiberal and collectivist. It opposed freedom of expression, secularism, critical thought, personal autonomy and individual choice, and mocked such hard-won minority freedoms as the recognition of homosexuality, cohabitation, and gay and lesbian partnerships. Some liberals worried about an anti-secular alliance between

Muslims and Christians, and the likely dominance of religion in public life. Others thought that the fear of Islam would lead to the resurgence of conservative values. Cardinal Simonis of Utrecht confirmed these fears when he remarked: 'Political leaders ask whether the Muslims will accept our values. I ask what values are these? Gay marriage? Euthanasia? We are disarmed in the face of the Islamic danger: we must recover our identity.'

But even those Europeans who were sympathetic to Muslims thought them too demanding. When the request for *halal* meat was met, they asked for time off for prayer in workplaces. When the latter demand was met, they asked for the banning of blasphemous books. And when that request was met or seen off, they wanted recognition of polygyny. And after that, they pressed for interest-free loans, Islamic banks and insurance companies, and so on and on. In the ultimate analysis they wanted to live in Europe on their own terms. Their apparently innocent demand that the state should respect and accommodate their identity was part of the wider goal of replacing the 'heathen' and 'decadent' European with an Islamic civilization. For these and other reasons, it was argued, they were an enemy within, an unassimilable cultural and political presence, which had to be contained and neutralized. This involved judicious use of force, aggressive assimilation, promoting liberal interpretations of Islam, and denying them the right to bring culture-reinforcing spouses from their homelands. Many leading politicians, including liberals, also thought that admitting Turkey into the EC, as it then was, would gravely compound the problem and should be resisted at all cost.

The terrorist attacks in New York, Madrid, London and elsewhere had a traumatic effect on Europeans, as on others. Hitherto they had seen Muslims as a culturally threatening but manageable presence; they now developed a morbid fear of them. Furthermore, this fear became transformed into the fear of Islam as a religion in whose name the attacks were believed to have been perpetrated. All Muslims *qua* Muslims are now suspect, and those in Europe are assimilated to and seen as an undifferentiated part of the worldwide *umma*. They are expected and even asked to condemn terrorist attacks in any part of the world in the strongest terms, and those remaining silent or appearing lukewarm are assumed to be in sympathy with the attacks.

Thanks to the widespread distrust of Muslims and the belief that they do not wish to, and cannot, integrate, there is today an extensive moral panic.[4] This has led to a growing spirit of intolerance and a nationalist backlash in almost every European country. The veil that had been around for some time dominated public debate in Britain in 2006, and government ministers have refused to fund and have official dealings with the Muslim Council of Britain because of its allegedly inadequate condemnation of terrorism and weak control over Muslim youth. France has passed a law banning the *hijab* and even the Sikh's turban. In the liberal and culturally relaxed Netherlands, a Muslim leader who refused to shake hands with a woman minister for cultural reasons and volunteered to greet her in other ways was widely attacked in the media. In Greece, Spain and Germany there is a strong opposition to building 'too many' mosques, especially in prominent places, because they lead to 'Islamicization' of the country and alter its 'visage'. There is a demand in many European countries that dual nationality should be disallowed, and that all immigrants should unequivocally opt for the citizenship of their country of settlement. As a way of, among other things, integrating and fostering patriotism among its Maghrebian population, the French National Assembly passed a law on 23 February 2005 requiring all 'high school history courses and textbooks' to emphasize the 'positive dimension of the French colonial era'. Although this extraordinary law was declared unconstitutional by the Constitutional Court, it is striking that the National Assembly passed it, and that a large number of its conservative and even liberal members saw nothing wrong with it.[5]

In some European societies there are deliberate attempts to demonize and generate powerful feelings against Muslims. Take the following excerpt from an article by Daniel Pipes and Lars Hedegaard, entitled 'Something Rotten in Denmark'? that appeared in *National Post*, a Danish magazine, in the aftermath of the Danish cartoon affair. Although the article was widely criticized for its factual errors and alarmist tone, it had many supporters. The fact that it was published itself speaks volumes:[6]

> For years, Danes lauded multiculturalism and insisted they had no problem with the Muslim customs – until one day they found that they did. Some major issues: Living on the dole: Third-world immigrants – most of them Muslims – constitute 5 per cent of the population but consume upwards of 40 per cent of the welfare spending. Engaging in crime: Muslims are only 4 per cent of Denmark's 5.4 million people but make up a majority of the country's convicted rapists . . . Self-imposed isolation: Over time, as Muslim immigrants increase in numbers, they wish less to mix with the indigenous population. Importing unacceptable customs: Forced marriages . . . are one problem. Another is threats to kill Muslims who convert out of Islam . . . Fomenting anti-Semitism: Muslim violence threatens Denmark's

approximately 6,000 Jews, who increasingly depend on police protection . . .
Seeking Islamic law: Muslim leaders openly declare their goal of introducing Islamic law once Denmark's Muslim population grows large enough – a not-that-remote prospect. If present trends persist, one sociologist estimates, every third inhabitant of Denmark in 40 years will be Muslim.

The fear of Muslims has prompted deeply perplexed European leaders to ask what else to do to counter the 'Islamic threat'. In addition to pursuing even more vigorously the strategy they had evolved in the 1990s, many European countries are devising new tools, such as greater surveillance of Muslims, a better network of informers, stronger anti-terrorist laws, detaining people on suspicion, making 'glorification' of terrorism a criminal offence, monitoring mosques, banning imams from abroad, requiring imams to show competence in local languages, greater supervision of their training and sermons, requiring Muslim leaders to accept greater responsibility for the behaviour of their fellow-religionists, denying dual nationality, and imposing stringent conditions of citizenship. Although many Europeans realize that such measures severely restrict the civil liberties of not only the Muslims but all others, and violate some of their deeply cherished values, they see no other way to deal with the 'Muslim problem'.

A critique

A careful examination of European societies shows that while the anxiety informing the reaction outlined above has some basis, it is exaggerated. The terrorist attacks in Madrid and London, which between them took nearly 400 lives, were all mounted by Muslims. They involved about two dozen young people, a third of whom were neither Spanish nor British citizens, and not even immigrants. It is widely reported that several terrorist attacks have been foiled in France, Germany and Britain since 2004. If this is true, and there is no reason to doubt it, they would most certainly have led to considerable loss of life. In Britain, there are estimated to be 200 terrorist networks involving just under 2,000 identified individual terrorists under surveillance, all hatching plots at different stages of development. The two recent failed terrorist attacks in London and Glasgow were mounted by about a dozen Muslims, though none of them was a British citizen. Between 500 and 3,000 British Muslims are estimated to have passed through al-Qaeda training camps in Afghanistan. Several al-Qaeda cells were recently uncovered in

Germany, France, Britain and Italy, and there is no saying how many more still exist, what their targets are, and how much damage they can inflict. The military group al-Muhajirin in Britain pumps out the most rabid *jihadi* propaganda against the Jews, Hindus and the West in general, and says on its website that its aim is to act as a 'fifth column' preparing the way for a 'worldwide Islamic revolution'. Although most of this is recent, the incitement to violence goes back much further. It was threatened against Rushdie in 1989. And on the eve of the first Gulf War, Omar Bakri, leader of *Hizb al-Tahrir* (the Party of Liberation), had called on Muslims to assassinate Prime Minister John Major, saying that Bakri and many others 'will celebrate his death'.

While a small group of disaffected young Muslims, acting alone or in league with militant groups abroad, have shown active disloyalty to their country of settlement and should be condemned, the overwhelming majority of European Muslims have a good record as a law-abiding community. Since the 1960s, there have been four Muslim riots in Britain compared to eight race-related riots by Afro-Caribbeans. One of them concerned Rushdie's *Satanic Verses*, others police insensitivity and racist marches through Muslim areas. All were relatively minor and lasted barely a couple of days. France witnessed three riots during this period, almost all triggered by local grievances or police high-handedness. And even the week-long riots in 2006 were related to persistent discrimination, high unemployment and police insensitivity. They were limited to the young, did not challenge the authority of the state, and involved neither religious demands nor religious leaders. Britain has 300 Muslims in its armed forces, and the chief of staff, Sir Nicholas Walker, who recently praised their loyalty and commitment, asked for more Muslim recruits.

Even when subjected to blatant discrimination, such as not being allowed for years to build mosques in parts of Italy and Greece, or denied state funding for their schools on the same lines as Christian and Jewish schools in Britain, Muslims have either suffered quietly or protested peacefully, but rarely taken the law in their own hands. They have also taken considerable pride in their country of settlement. Muslims, both young and old, appreciate the rights and freedoms they enjoy in Europe, many of which are not available in most Muslim countries, and value the support of their fellow citizens in their struggle for equality and justice. In a British survey in 2004, 67 per cent of Muslims said they felt very or fairly patriotic, 11 per cent that they were mildly patriotic, and only 15 per cent, mainly under 40 years of age, claimed not to feel patriotic at all. In a BBC poll conducted just after the terrorist attacks in London, 78 per cent of Muslims and 73 per cent of the rest of the country said that immigrants should pledge their primary loyalty to Britain, and 91 per cent of Muslims and 93 per cent of the rest of the country said that immigrants should respect the authority of British institutions. The situation in the rest of Europe is broadly similar.[7]

As for the extraterritorial loyalty to the *umma*, it is neither unique to Muslims nor often amounts to much in practice. The Jews press the cause of Israel and their counterparts in other countries, as do Indians, Chinese, Pakistanis and others. What matters is whether the bulk of European Muslims are prepared to be disloyal to their country in order to promote the interests of the *umma*, and the answer to that is largely in the negative. Just over two dozen British Muslims fought with the Taliban, and they were condemned by most of their community. Although we do not have the exact figures for France, Italy, the Netherlands and elsewhere, the proportion of Muslims joining the Taliban there was even smaller. When terrorist attacks took place in Spain and Britain, the bulk of the Muslim community roundly condemned them, showed their solidarity with the victims, and undertook to put their communal house in order. After the recent unsuccessful terrorist attacks in London and Glasgow, they organized peaceful marches and placed page-long statements in national newspapers condemning them and declaring them incompatible with the principles of Islam. When two French journalists were taken hostage by the Islamic Army in Iraq to pressurize the French government to lift its recently imposed ban on the headscarf, French Muslims mobilized as never before, and insisted that the Islamic Army had no right to speak in their name, and that their primary loyalty was to their compatriots.

Like millions of their fellow citizens, a large number of European Muslims, though by no means all of them, were bitterly opposed to the second war on Iraq, but remained content to join peaceful protests against it. Had they been so minded, they could have been far noisier, tried to sabotage the war effort in countries belonging to the 'coalition of the willing', refused to pay their taxes, courted imprisonment, formed a human shield in Iraq, and used other familiar tactics. The fact that they did not do any of these things is significant. In Britain, when the Imam of Finsbury Park mosque, who preached hatred of the West and urged support for the terrorists, was arrested and his mosque raided, there was some outrage but also quiet satisfaction that some action had at last been taken against him and his associates.[8]

Muslims have also shown respect for democratic institutions. They have participated in local and national elections, stood as candidates in fairly large numbers, joined mainstream political parties, and accepted the decisions of the majority. When a Muslim parliament was set up in Britain in the 1990s by a pro-Iranian group to discuss issues of common interest and provide Muslims with a distinct political voice, it received little general support and became defunct, largely because of wide-spread Muslim hostility and factionalism. Calls for separate Muslim parties throughout Europe have gone unheeded, and Muslim candidates standing on Muslim platforms in local and national elections have almost always been defeated.

It is sometimes argued that the Muslim support for democratic institutions and loyalty to the state are largely a matter of political expediency and remain precarious. The argument makes a valid point, as reasons for supporting democratic institutions do matter, but it does not apply to a large majority of European Muslims. As the extensive debate among them shows, they are exploring the moral dimension of their relationship to their country of settlement, and beginning to articulate a theologico-moral theory of political obligation.

While a small minority dismisses democracy as a form of polytheism (*shirk billah*) that deifies people and sets up their sovereignty in rivalry to that of Allah, most Muslims take a different view. Democracy, they argue, does not deify people, but subjects their will to clearly stated constitutional constraints, including basic human rights. It shows respect for human dignity, protects fundamental human interests, ensures responsible use of power, guarantees freedom of religion and institutionalizes *shura* (consultation), all of which are not only consistent with but often enjoined by the Qur'ān. Although an enlightened monarchy might be able to achieve these objectives, it is heavily dependent on the character of the monarch and inherently risky. The Prophet was one such individual, but it is naïve to imagine that all societies can produce someone like him on a regular basis. For most European Muslims, democracy is therefore a better form of government than any other, and they have a moral obligation to support it. This does not mean that they approve of its current liberal form. Many of them would like it to be more respectful of religion and less secular in its orientation, but most of them agree that its basic institutional structure is worthy of their support.

Political participation is being given a similar theologico-moral basis. While a small minority such as the *Hizb al-Tahrir* dismisses it as *haram* (or sinful) because it involves working with secular political parties and accepting the authority of secular political institutions, most Muslims take a very different view. The *fatwa* by Taha Jabir al-Alwani, chairman of the North American Fiqh council, asks Muslims to participate in political life because it enables them to promote worthwhile causes, protects basic human rights, ensures responsible rule, and improves the quality of information about Islam and Muslim interests. For al-Alwani, political participation is not just a 'right' that can be surrendered, nor a 'permission' that may be ignored, but a 'duty' that must be discharged.

Loyalty to the state too is defended on Qur'ānic grounds. The Qur'ān places high value on the sanctity of contracts, and enjoins Muslims to show loyalty to the state in return for its physical protection and respect for basic freedoms. This argument was commonly made by British Muslims when a small number of them wanted to fight with the Taliban and against British troops. It was further clarified in the *Fatwa on British Muslims* issued by Shaykh Abdullah al-Judai, a member of the European Council for Fatwa and Research. The *fatwa* insisted that one of the Muslim's 'highest obligations' was to respect agreements and contracts, that they were contractually bound to their country of settlement, and that they 'cannot take up arms' against it even in order to defend Muslims elsewhere. This last point is disputed by some Muslims, largely members of a militant *shi'ite* group that lacks popular support.[9]

As far as the basic European values and practices are concerned, Muslims do not have much difficulty with many of these. Human dignity, equal human worth, equality of the races, civility, peaceful resolution of differences and reciprocity are all either enjoined by Islam or can be read into it. Although polygyny and female circumcision are practised by some groups of Muslims, they are disapproved of by others and are in decline. It is hardly surprising that the laws banning them provoked little Muslim protest in any European country. Two areas that have proved particularly contentious relate to the great values of gender equality and freedom of expression.

Gender equality, though resisted by some, is being accepted increasingly by the majority of European Muslims. Women vote in elections and stand for public office without facing much male opposition. Muslim girls stay on at school and do better than boys. A fairly large number of them pursue higher education, though the number is smaller than for boys, often because of parental discouragement. However, this is changing for the better. Muslim girls have been discouraged from pursuing certain occupations, but that too is changing. They enjoy less social freedom and are sometimes forced into arranged marriages, but they are rebelling against this, with some success. The struggle for gender equality is fought in many families. And while the rebellious young girls and women are subjected to intimidation and violence that has led to nearly a dozen, sometimes horrifying, cases of 'honour killing' and many more of abduction each year in Britain alone, Muslims are beginning to take collective action with the judicious help of the state. Young girls also invoke the authority of the Qur'ān in their struggle, arguing that sexist practices are conventional in origin and lack a religious basis. This requires them to study the Qur'ān well enough to interpret it. While *prima facie* such a diligent study of religion appears to be conservative, its intentions and outcome are often radical, as is evident in the growing popularity of 'Islamic feminism'.

Issues relating to free speech have provoked the greatest Muslim anger, and an equally fierce reaction against them. Muslims do not question the value of free speech, but rather its scope and limits. After all, they use it to criticize the West, highlight their grievances, press forward with their demands, challenge some of their own ugly practices, and are its beneficiaries. Many of them value it not only on instrumental but also moral grounds, and find theological support for it. The Qur'ān could not have been passed on and its message widely disseminated without free speech; the sticking point comes when free speech is in conflict with Muslim religious sensibilities.

The Rushdie affair, the first Europe-wide public expression of Muslim anger and a turning point in the European perception of Muslims, involved death threats against a creative writer for 'mocking' and 'lampooning' Islam and its founder, and that in a language most Muslims thought 'filthy' and 'scurrilous'.[10] As mentioned earlier, when a conservative Danish newspaper published cartoons about Islam and the Prophet Mohammed in 2005, many of them not particularly offensive, Muslims all over Europe and the rest of the world mounted vigorous and in several cases violent protests, leading to nearly a hundred deaths, though none were in Europe. Ayaan Hirsi Ali, a nauralized Somali Muslim then living in the Netherlands, was threatened with death and had to go into hiding because her documentary *Submission* showed words of the Qur'ān written on the back, stomach and legs of a partly dressed woman to highlight women's oppression in the name of Islam. While she remains unharmed and has now joined a rightwing American think tank, Theo Van Gogh, who directed the film and declined protection, was shot and carefully decapitated with a kind of butcher's knife. When challenged by a petrified bystander, Muhammed, his assassin, is reported to have said that his victim had 'asked for it' and that 'now you all know what you can expect'.[11] The Moroccan–Dutch painter, Rachid Ben Ali, received death threats because of the homosexual themes in his work and his satirical treatment of fundamentalist imams. Fearing reprisals, several critical scholars of the Qur'ān write under pseudonyms. 'Christoph Luxenberg', a pseudonymous author, argues that some key words in it are derived from Aramaic, the language group of most Middle Eastern Jews and Christians, and have meanings quite different from their conventional readings. He fears that even this might be too much for some Muslims.[12] Muslims do have a problem with a critical and historical study of the Qur'ān, and it is likely to take decades before they become used to it.

While small groups of Muslim militants have reacted violently against the works of 'Luxenberg', Ben Ali, and others like them, many either ignore or dismiss them with varying degrees of disapproval. The *Satanic Verses*, and to a lesser extent *Submission*, are in a separate category because of the kinds of issues they raise. Even here, there is no unanimity among Muslims. While a sizeable group considers violence justified in such cases, many disapprove of it. However, even they think, often wrongly, that these works stretch freedom of expression beyond acceptable limits. There is thus a deep difference of opinion between the liberal and Muslim views on this point, and it is likely to throw up acute conflicts from time to time. One should not, however, get it out of perspective. It is not a disagreement over the value of freedom of expression, but rather over a trade-off between it and offence to religious sensibilities. Nor is it a disagreement between Muslims and liberals, for the Muslim view is shared by many other religious groups and some liberals, and the liberal view enjoys some support among an albeit small number of Muslims. The editor of *Jyllands-Posten*, which published the controversial cartoons in 2006, had three years earlier rejected those about Jesus on the ground that they would offend Christians. In October 2005 a French court ordered a marketing company to remove posters featuring a tasteless depiction of the Last Supper. As long as Muslim protests are peaceful, non-intimidating and stay within the limits of the law, their dissenting voice need not arouse undue anxiety. Indeed, liberals should welcome it out of respect for the principle of freedom of expression, to show Muslims in public discussion why others feel disturbed by some of their views, and as a useful corrective to the excesses of its absolutist champions.

Accommodating religion

One of the major causes of European anxiety about Muslim immigrants is related to religion. Liberals in general, and European liberals in particular, have long been troubled by religion. For some, it rejects many of the central principles of liberalism, such as humanism, individualism, critical rationality, commitment to scientific inquiry, freedom of thought and belief in progress, and represents a reactionary and obscurantist form of thought. Others take a more discriminating view of it. They welcome it as a necessary corrective to human hubris and a valuable moral resource provided it is suitably rationalized and reformed, and does not seek to dominate political life. Whether their secularism is comprehensive or narrowly political, almost all liberals are convinced that political life should be organized along secular lines. The state, they argue, is equipped to deal with material and moral interests, not with the destiny of the human soul. Since it deals with matters that all citizens have in common, its affairs should be conducted in a secular language that they all understand and share, and in terms of public reasons they can critically assess. It is inherently coercive, and must stay clear of religious and other areas in which coercion has no place. It should treat all its citizens equally and respect their freedom of conscience, which it cannot do if it is tied to a particular religion.

In the liberal view, Muslims challenge this historical consensus and threaten to reopen long-settled controversies. They reject not only the comprehensive secularization of society but also its more limited political form, and introduce religion into political life at several levels. They make demands based on religion, such as a particular form of animal slaughter, taking time off for prayer during working hours, and exemption from certain laws and practices. They want the state to protect their religious beliefs and practices by restricting the freedom of expression and imposing an unfair burden on others. They reason about political matters in religious terms, debating whether the Qur'ān allows loyalty to the state, support for democratic institutions, political participation, equal rights for women, or participation in a particular war. In these and in other ways, Muslims introduce a theological form of political reasoning in which others cannot participate, but by the outcome of which they are deeply affected. This rules out any form of shared public discourse, the *sine qua non* of common citizenship. Liberals wonder how a secular political system can cope with this sudden intrusion of religion, especially one that rejects any form of private–public distinction on which all modern states are based. Their anxiety is further compounded by the fear that the Muslim example might encourage other religious groups, and lead over time to the disintegration of the liberal political order.

Although liberals are right to worry about the danger posed by militant Islam, their anxiety in the European context is exaggerated and arises largely from a misunderstanding of how European societies are actually constituted and conduct their affairs. No European society or political system is secular in the sense in which liberals use the term. Subject to the qualifications discussed in Chapter 8, its Christian heritage has shaped, and continues to shape, its vocabulary, self-understanding, institutions, ideals and practices. The ideas of human dignity, equal human worth and unity of humankind derive their moral energy from it, and reappear in liberalism in their secularized form. The views of human nature and history that inform much of European political thought and practice, many of its current laws and practices, and even such trivial things as treating Sundays, Christmas Day and New Year's Day as public holidays, are all further examples of the continuing influence of Christianity. The fact that their historical roots are often forgotten and religion survives as culture does not mean that their religious basis or overtones go unnoticed by non-Christians. Muslims, and for that matter devout Christians, do not introduce an alien element in an otherwise secular society. Rather, they state loudly in the same language what the rest of society says in a quiet whisper.

The theological style of reasoning about political matters that worries liberals is not unique to Muslims. Anti-abortionists, pacifists, some groups of environmentalists, champions of global justice, and opponents of Sunday trading reason from within the Christian, Judaic or some other religious tradition. And even some liberals only reproduce the basic Christian beliefs in a secular language, as becomes clear when they are pressed to articulate and defend them. Contrary to what liberals imagine, our public life does not, and cannot, rest on a homogeneous view of public reason, for the latter is not a neutral and sanitized species of reason but is, like all other forms of reason, embedded in (no doubt revisable) particular traditions or philosophical frameworks. Our public life is inherently plural and includes several different forms of reasoning, such as the secular, the religious, a mixture of the two, and the countless varieties of each of them. Liberals wonder how citizens can communicate across different moral and political languages; in fact they manage reasonably well.

Since many of these languages are precipitates of European history and form part of its common heritage, Europeans grow up acquiring considerable familiarity and even a measure of sympathy with some of them, and do not even notice their society's mixed discourse. Unbeknown to them, they themselves sometimes speak in several moral languages. And when they do not speak a language, they often understand it well enough to respond to its speakers. From time to time there are no doubt passages of incomprehension and breakdowns in communication, and then they seek to improve their knowledge of other languages, find a common language, turn to translators and interpreters, leave the matter unresolved, reach a tentative compromise, or do one of several other familiar things. What is troublesome about Muslim political reasoning is not its religious character but rather its unfamiliarity. And the answer to that lies in greater interaction, sympathetic dialogue, multicultural education, and Muslim representatives acquiring a reasonable competence in other languages, especially the secular.

Secularism is a complex concept. Since religion matters to the large majority of Europeans and an attack on it can easily provoke public disorder, no European political system excludes it from political life. At the same time, no European state allows it to colonize political life and threaten its citizens' liberties. The history of every modern European state is a story of how best to balance these requirements. All European states are secular in the sense that they do not impose a religion on their citizens or make citizenship rights dependent on subscription to that religion; are not generally guided by religious considerations in making laws and policies; and do not derive their legitimacy from religious sources. They do, however, allow religion its proper place in political life, including religion-based political parties and a religiously grounded political rhetoric. They also have institutional mechanisms for maintaining regular contact with major religious organizations, and many provide public funds to enable the religious organizations undertake secular activities.

Britain funds Anglican, Catholic and Jewish schools, and its government informally but regularly consults religious bodies on matters relating to them. In France, religious schools, most of them Catholic, receive a public subsidy, and in three out of its nineteen *départménts*, clerics are civil servants and appointed by the state. In Germany, the Jewish community, Catholic dioceses and regional Protestant churches enjoy the status of publicly recognized corporations, a uniquely German legal category. The state collects taxes (*Kirchensteuer*) from members of churches on their behalf and hands over the money to the churches after deducting the agreed administrative charge. Nearly 80 per cent of publicly funded nursery schools are run by churches on behalf of the state, and so are a number of hospitals and other welfare institutions. The Netherlands has its 'pillars', which include its major religious communities. And while the most secular France refuses to take any notice of group differences, it recognizes those based on religion and regularly consults the representatives of the officially recognized national organizations of Catholics, Protestants and Jews. Whether European states are right to do any of these things is an important question that does not concern us here. The fact is that they *do*, and we should begin by accepting it as a fact of political life.

Within this framework, Muslims pose no major problem. All that most of them ask for, and what European states should do, is to find ways of accommodating Muslims without radically altering the existing structure. This is broadly what is happening in practice, in some cases proactively, and in others after considerable resistance. France has set up a Council of Muslim Faith, a national representative body, with the right to speak on behalf of French Muslims, and this enjoys a consultative status. In the Netherlands, Muslims are part of 'pillarization' and are provided with state-funded religious schools and television channels. In Belgium, Islam has been a full member of the Council of Religions since 1974. Spain, which had been subject to Islam for centuries, tried for years to define its identity in opposition to it. In November 1992, it reached an accord with the Islamic Commission of Spain similar to that reached with other religious communities. The accord dealt with Muslim demands, such as the provision of *halal* meat, specific burial places, the right to take religious holidays, the recognition of religious rights in hospitals, prisons and the armed forces, tax relief, the authority to perform civil marriages, and religious education in public schools. Although parts of the accord remain unimplemented because of a lack of funds and political will, it represents a public acceptance of Muslims as an equal religious community alongside the others.

European societies have in these and other ways accommodated Muslims without compromising their secular character. Muslims are given regular access to power, their religious interests are taken into account, and their demands discussed and conceded, shelved or rejected. At the same time, the secular historical settlement remains firmly in place, and Muslims have not generally asked for (nor will or should be allowed) any changes to it. Indeed, since the existing arrangements treat them with respect and give them full and equal religious freedom, often far greater than they enjoy in sectarian Muslim societies, these arrangements rightly claim and generally receive their moral support. They also make it easier for Muslims to challenge the militant minority's mindless fulminations against the 'godless' land of 'infidels'. Liberal society has far greater intellectual and institutional resources and is far more flexible than its theorists imagine.

Defending liberal society

Many Europeans argue that Muslims are deeply uncomfortable with the basic ethos and constitutive principles of liberal society, and are unable or unwilling to give it their moral allegiance. Muslims, they contend, dismiss liberal society as materialistic, soul-less, permissive, individualistic, self-indulgent, given to the satisfaction of every passing desire, sexually obsessed, centred on rights rather than duties, committed to the cult of self-expression and self-fulfilment, and in general devoid of a spiritual basis and hence incompatible with a truly human life. Since Muslims explicitly or implicitly proclaim themselves to be the enemies of liberal society and want to overturn it by 'civilizing' the Europeans, they are considered a mortal threat to it.

While the European anxiety is not wholly misconceived, it homogenizes Muslims and treats them as an undifferentiated mass. Some are opposed to liberal society, some others are fully committed to it, most fall between the two. Furthermore radical criticisms of it are also advanced from different angles by conservatives, Christian and Jewish leaders, socialists and even liberals. If such critiques were to be considered subversive and unacceptable, all these groups and not just the Muslims would have to be declared enemies of liberal society. Liberal society values criticism and diversity of views, and relies on them to revitalize itself. It should therefore welcome Muslim criticisms, engage in a dialogue with them, and accept what it finds valuable in them. The only politically relevant question is twofold. First, are Muslims willing to adapt themselves to liberal society and live as good citizens? Second, which is more important, how can liberal society legitimize itself in their eyes and secure their moral allegiance?

As for the first question, we saw earlier that even the first-generation Muslims had no problem adjusting to liberal society and accepting its obligations. They did not organize their personal lives in the same way as most of their fellow citizens, but that did not stand in the way of their discharging their duties and responsibilities as citizens. As for the second and third generation Muslims, they grow up imbibing the ethos and values of liberal society and are at ease with it. They cherish their privacy and autonomy, and make their own choices and decisions in important areas of life. They reject parentally arranged marriages and insist on choosing their careers themselves. Even the young girls who wear the *hijab* or the *voile* and follow religious practices do so freely and not under pressure. Indeed it is this exercise of autonomy and the consequent expression of their self-chosen Islamic identity that distinguishes their religiosity from that of their parents.

In some areas young Muslims do wish to organize their social life differently from the rest of society, such as the structure of their family, the Islamic banking and way of doing business, and preference for a communal way of life. Unless these practices violate important moral values, they remain a matter of individual choice and should arouse no anxiety. Indeed they represent what J. S. Mill called 'experiments in living', add to the richness and vitality of society, and should be suitably accommodated by liberal society, as some of them are already doing.

The question of how to defend liberal values and secure Muslim allegiance is more complex. Liberals ask Muslims to give these their wholehearted moral allegiance. They do not want to say that 'this is how we do things here', because while that argument is valid in relation to local customs and traffic rules, it does not apply to moral values, where it smacks of moral coercion.[13] Liberals want to convince them that these values are correct, and think that this requires transculturally compelling reasons to be given. While such reasons are available in the case of some liberal values such as respect for human life, human dignity and equal human worth, they are not in the case of such others as individualism, personal autonomy, choice of spouses, and minimum restraints on freedom of expression. There are good reasons for the latter, but they are internal to the liberal tradition and not transcultural. While liberals find them convincing, even self-evident, they do not convince many Muslims. Other immigrant groups face similar difficulties, but many generally give in because they find supporting reasons within their tradition, or out of self-doubt, timidity and prudential considerations. Many Muslims do not give in, because they are as certain of their values and as determined to live by them as are the liberals, and worry deeply about the erosion of these values under the liberal impact.

The stage is now set for mutual hostility and suspicion. Each fears the other, not just politically but morally and culturally, and sincerely believes that it cannot survive without defeating the other. The fear is particularly acute among liberals and leads to a veritable panic. Unlike the religious Muslims who feel sure that God is on their side, liberals have no such certainty, and must protect their values and way of life themselves. Having long thought that history was on their side, they now find that it is acting capriciously and signalling the return of the 'dark ages' that they saw off successfully several centuries ago. Like most such panics, the liberal panic is partly fuelled by a lingering self-doubt. Despite much agonized reflection in recent years, the more self-critical liberals realize that they cannot make a transculturally compelling case for some of their cherished values. Compelling others to live by the latter therefore gives them an uneasy conscience, and since Muslims have precipitated it, they have become a moral irritant, an object of fear and resentment.

The liberal gets into this difficulty because s/he claims more for his/her way of life than is warranted. The liberal way of life is historically contingent and embedded in a particular culture or form of social self-understanding. It is not underwritten by history, mandated by human nature, or grounded in universal reason. Good internal reasons can, however, be given in support of it, such as those based on the society's history, experiences, moral traditions, cultural and religious heritage, circumstances and level of development. These reasons do not (and there is no reason why they should) convince all human beings and command their allegiance. It is enough if they are good reasons, publicly debated, and carry conviction with all or most members of the liberal society. The liberal society represents one good way to organize human life, and that is a strong enough moral basis to stand up for it and to use such compulsion as is unavoidable and prudent. It is not the best, the most rational, or the only universally valid form of a good society. If the liberal makes such a claim, as many Europeans liberals do, s/he not only cannot redeem it but ends up accusing Muslims of being irrational, morally obtuse and backward, which is not a way to win them over. The liberal should aim not to convince Muslims that the liberal way of life is the best but rather to get them to see that it is one good way to live, not to assert that this is the only acceptable way to be human, but rather that s/he and others understand their humanity in this way and have good reasons to commit themselves to it, which Muslims should respect. His/her aim should be *limited* in the sense of defending a particular society rather than prescribing a universal model, and *modest* in the sense of making a good case for it without claiming that no rational person can fail to be convinced by it. If some Muslims remain unpersuaded, they would at least see why others are persuaded, and why they should go along with them for moral or prudential reasons.

Once culture is explicitly recognized and brought into the political discourse as a source of claims, an additional form of reasoning is available to both liberals and Muslims. The latter could argue legitimately that when they offer good reasons for their cultural beliefs and practices, these should be respected and suitably accommodated. For their part, liberals could argue that Muslims should respect the prevailing cultural beliefs and practices when good reasons are given for them. Such an appeal to mutual cultural respect has several advantages. It reassures Muslims that their culture is valued by the wider society, and that they need not panic and turn inward or become intransigent, and it reassures the wider society that it remains in charge of its cultural life, that Muslims will not seek to undermine it by irresponsible demands, and that the differences between the two are to be resolved through a rational dialogue conducted in a spirit of mutual commitment to a common life.

An appeal to mutual cultural respect also often avoids and sometimes even resolves otherwise intractable disagreements and controversies. Since the cultural argument works both ways, it is perfectly valid for the two parties to say that one of them cannot be expected to respect the deeply held cultural beliefs and practices of the other unless the latter also does the same. It is often forgotten in the heat generated by the *l'affair du foulard* that over ninety five percent of Muslim girls in French schools avoided the *hijab* largely out of respect for the French culture and its reasons for placing a high value on *laicité*, not because it went against the French custom or some universal value.[14]

Difficult situations arise when both parties feel equally strongly about their cultural norms. A few French Muslim girls did insist on wearing the *hijab*, and so did Fereshta Luden, a Muslim teacher in Germany, to considerable public outrage.[15] Such clashes could be between two important cultural norms, between a human right and a cultural norm, and sometimes even between two human rights. There are good arguments on both sides. The French *laicité* and the German principle of religious neutrality should be modified to allow the *hijab* and other defensible Muslim beliefs and practices. But equally, these traditions are valuable historical achievements, embody important values, exceptions to them alienate the majority, which is not in the Muslim interest, and set a precedent whose unexpected long-term consequences can be unfortunate. In such situations of what John Rawls calls reasonable disagreement, it is wrong to claim that only one course of action is truly rational. Good reasons on both sides require and create a space for mutual accommodation and compromise. What form these should take depends on the context.

Islam and multicultural society

Like their counterparts elsewhere, European Muslims have some difficulty in coming to terms with multicultural societies, and this aggravates European anxiety. There is almost no religion whose followers do not think it the best one of all, and this sense of superiority is particularly strong among Muslims. The Qur'ān is believed to be unique in being the literal, unmediated, exhaustive and final revelation of the divine will. According to it, the Word of God was also revealed to Jews and Christians, whom it therefore respects and whose prophets it reveres. Since their revelations, however, are believed to have suffered corruption because of human mediation and the failure to live by them, Islam is supposed to 'confirm', 'continue' and 'complete' them. Although Islam is pluralist in relation to them while they are *not* in relation to it, its pluralism is articulated within an absolutist framework. As the Qur'ānic verses say, 'O mankind! The messenger has come to you in truth from Allah: believe in him, it is best for you.' And again, 'Whoever seeks a religion other than Islam, it will never be accepted of him.'[16] Although Jews and Christians, 'the people whom God has guided', are to be respected and left free to practise their religions, they remain legitimate targets for conversion to the 'most perfect' religion. As for other religions such as Hinduism, they are dismissed as polytheistic, idolatrous and unworthy of respect. The remarkable military successes of early and medieval Islam generated among its followers a triumphalist spirit, and seemed to them to confirm their belief in its absolute superiority. During the centuries of European colonization, this belief was and, in their current state remains, almost the sole basis of their collective pride, and has a powerful appeal for the overwhelming majority of them.

The belief in the absolute superiority of Islam is reflected in the constant invocation of its past glory by moderate and militant Muslims alike. It is also evident in many of its beliefs and practices. While Muslims have a duty to convert the followers of other religions, they are not themselves free to convert to another religion, this being apostasy, an act of treason, meriting punishment in both this world and the next. Most Muslims are anxious that others should learn about their religion, but few take much interest in the religions of others. They may marry non-Muslim women, but do not allow others to marry theirs, and expect those marrying within Islam to convert to it. This cannot be attributed to the current Muslim feeling of siege or fear of loss of identity. Even in the self-confident Ottoman empire, where Jews and Christians enjoyed considerable tolerance, they were treated as second-class citizens lacking the right to participate fully in its political life. While they were free to convert to Islam, they were strictly forbidden to convert Muslims to other faiths or to marry Muslim women.

Because of all this, the attitude of many European Muslims towards a multicultural society is one-sided. They understand it in the light of the millet model of the Ottoman empire, in which different communities followed their own customs and led more or less self-contained lives. They welcome a multicultural society because it gives them the freedom to live by and propagate their own religious beliefs and practices. But many of them also feel uncomfortable with it because it puts them on a par with, and exposes them and their children to the influence of, other religions and secular cultures. As Shabbir Akhtar, an influential British Muslim thinker during the Rushdie affair, put it, 'Our inherited (Islamic) understanding of religious freedom and the nature and role of religion in society is in the last analysis being fundamentally challenged by the new religious pluralism in Britain.'[17] In his view, and that of many others, religious and cultural pluralism presents Islam as a religion of Muslims in a way that Judaism is of Jews and Hinduism of Hindus, and implicitly rejects its claim to universality and absolute superiority.

Such an approach to multicultural society leads many Muslims to take an instrumental view of it, to welcome it because, and only to the extent that it gives them the space to maintain their identity. It also encourages a narrow and static view of multiculturalism, not a transformative and open-minded dialogue between people belonging to different cultures and religions but a compartmentalized cultural universe in which different groups live out their ghettoized existence. As a result, large groups of Muslims tend to withdraw or to keep a comfortable distance from the wider society, and deny themselves the opportunity to interact with others, understand their views and concerns, and take a critical view of themselves. This partly explains their current tendency to be unduly defensive about their religion and history, see slights where none might be intended, get minor criticisms out of perspective, fall prey or react disproportionately to misguided rightwing provocations, and in general to appear to want to live in Europe on their own terms.

European Muslims are no doubt changing, but they have a long way to go before they are able to participate enthusiastically in the creative tensions and controversies of a multicultural society, and make the contribution to which their great history and civilization entitle them. For the first time in their history, they are living in large numbers in societies where they are neither the rulers nor the subjects – their historical situation – but rather as fellow citizens enjoying equal rights with the rest in plural liberal democracies.[18] This requires them to rethink traditional views on their rights and obligations, their relationship to other religions and cultures, and their response to modernity. Some of their thinkers, such as Mohammed Arkoum and Tariq Ramadan, have just begun to do so, and their ideas are receiving sympathetic attention not only among Muslims in the West also in Muslim countries. If this trend continues, and Muslim intellectuals in Europe successfully develop a creative Euro-Islam, they could play a vital role in starting long overdue debates and offering valuable guidance to the global *umma*.

Muslim youth

I have argued that, while a Muslim presence in Europe does not constitute a political and cultural threat and can, if handled with wisdom on both sides, enrich European life, a small but deeply alienated group of young Muslims is a legitimate source of concern. In almost all European societies, young Muslims underachieve educationally and are among the poorest. Take Britain, for example. Over half its Muslims live in areas with the most deprived housing conditions, compared to 20 per cent of the total population, and their unemployment rate is twice the national average. Nearly 70 per cent of Muslim children live in poverty and receive state support, and some 36 per cent of them leave school without qualifications. These socio-economic disadvantages are compounded by the experiences of discrimination and marginalization. Young Muslims are also alienated from their parental culture, which they either do not understand or find conservative, backward, restrictive and not a source of pride. There is often limited emotional intimacy between parents and children, and very little meaningful conversation. Problems relating to drug abuse, mental health, personal relationships and sexuality are considered taboo and rarely discussed in families. Not surprisingly, many parents and elderly family members admit ignorance of what their younger members think, feel and do, as was confirmed in the case of some of those involved in the London terrorist attacks in July 2005.

Although they have grown up in Britain, many young Muslims lack roots in the country, and feel alienated from it as well. This is so for several interrelated reasons. Residential concentration in some parts of the country means that they lead parallel lives, go to predominantly Muslim schools, and have limited contact with their white counterparts. Unemployment denies them the opportunity to participate in one of the most important areas of life, and to get to know and become an integral part of British society. Those who succeed in breaking through the barrier sometimes find that the wider society fears and takes a demeaning view of them, and that its view of its national identity is too narrow and exclusive to find a respectable place for them.

Detached from their parental and British cultures, alienated young Muslims tend to form their own groups based on a shared subculture of defiance and victimhood. Some turn to drug trafficking, prostitution, gang warfare and petty crimes. It is striking that young Muslims form 9 per cent of the prison population, which is considerably higher than among their white counterpart. There is an increasing trend towards drug addiction among young Muslims, and a disturbingly large number of single mothers in London are Muslims. Many of those who avoid crime turn to Islam to give them a sense of dignity and identity, a particularly noticeable trend among college and university students.

Although, as we saw, religious consciousness is quite strong among most Muslims, it takes a different form among the alienated youth. Their parents' Islam is largely traditional, tied in with the culture of their homeland, and bound up with their ethnic and other identities. They revere the Qur'ān but their Islam is not centred narrowly on it or textual in character. They have no Arabic and rely on the traditionalist *ulema* drawn from their native homelands to interpret it for them. The Islam of young Muslims could not be more different. Many of them read Arabic, have direct access to the text, and interpret it themselves or rely on others like them. Their Islam is 'purged' of local culture and is textual in its orientation. It is not woven into and a taken-for-granted aspect of their lives as it is for their parents, but a self-consciously adopted badge of identity needing constantly to be asserted, an ideology providing them with a clear programme of action. Since it is a matter of conscious commitment, it is shadowed by a deep fear that the commitment might weaken or become diluted. They therefore become loud, rigid and uncompromising in their religiosity, both in order to guard themselves against the fear that they might slacken, and to ask others to pull them up if they should do so. It is hardly surprising that, compared to their parents, a much larger majority of those between the ages of 16 and 24 favour Islamic state schools over secular ones, want women to wear headscarves, prefer the *sharia* to British laws, and believe that a Muslim converting to another religion deserves death.[19]

Freed from the ethnic, national and other ties, and turning to religion as the sole basis of their identity, young Muslims are available for mobilization by militant groups with a global agenda. These groups idealize and flatter them by describing them as the 'true elite' charged with the responsibility of standing up for the honour of the *umma*. The pursuit of global causes gives them a sense of power, a purpose, a thrill, a sense of belonging, and a ready network of friends. The biased Western foreign policies, the invasion of Iraq, and the scandals of Abu Ghraib and Guantanamo Bay give their anger a moral edge and intensify their sense of victimhood.

There is also another important factor at work. Joining the ranks of Muslim fighters in different parts of the world and engaging in terrorist acts at home and abroad involve risking one's life, to which young Muslims, like others, are naturally averse. This is overcome by an increasingly popular interpretation of Islam among the young that thinks nothing of human life. Death in the cause of Allah is a mark of the elect, a calling, an expression of one's love for him. It also opens the door to paradise, where one is reunited with the loved ones who have died, and eventually with those one has left behind. While the latter are on earth, they would be well looked after by Allah as a reward for one's noble deed or by other members of one's group. Death is seen as nothing but a wink, marking the end of a brief and painful sojourn on earth and the beginning of a happy eternal life. Giving up one's life is thus made virtually cost-free and represents a perfectly rational choice, though of course the true believer sees it in much more grandiose terms.

An intriguing and highly complex combination of these and other factors throws some light on why some young Muslims are drawn or strongly sympathetic to terrorist activities. Unemployment, marginalization and poverty do not by themselves lead to terrorism, but they generate widespread resentment against or apathy to the wider society, and create a climate in which there is pervasive indifference to, or a weak and passive acquiescence in, terrorist activities. Even when some family members of some of the British terrorists had a vague idea of what their young people were thinking of doing, and did not like the idea, they either half-convinced themselves that the young people did not mean it, turned a blind eye or thought the matter too complex to worry about. The identity vacuum, created by the alienation from both parental and wider social cultures and filled by obsessive religious identity, is an important activating factor, and explains why young people and not others are drawn to terrorist activities. It links up the individuals involved with globalized Islam, and brings them within the sphere of militant groups. The reading of Islam propagated by these groups makes death not only virtually cost-free but also a special obligation on the intellectual elite, and has a particular appeal for the well-educated.

The British situation is reproduced in different forms and degrees across the rest of Europe.[20] Relative unemployment rates for young Muslims are broadly similar in France, Germany, the Netherlands and Spain, yet anti-discrimination legislation is relatively weaker. Few Muslims occupy high public offices or represent their country abroad, and symbolize their integration. As for educational underachievement, average income, child poverty, residential concentration, percentage of prison population and inter-ethnic friendships, some European societies are marginally better on some indices and worse on others. But all have a small but significant rootless, deeply alienated and sulking Muslim underclass defining its identity in exclusively religious terms. This group sees itself as Muslims *in* Europe, Muslims who happen to live in Europe without any commitment to it, not as Muslims *of* Europe – that is, those who see it as their home – let alone as *Europeanized* Muslims or those who share its culture and values. Islam is the sole basis of their personal and public identity and is freed from the moderating influence of other identities. Since this is precisely what the Hizb al-Tahrir, the Wahhabis, the Salafis and others advocate, these young people gravitate towards them.[21]

Reclaiming Muslim youth requires addressing some of the factors discussed earlier, and is the joint responsibility of both Muslim communities and the wider society. Senior politicians and public figures throughout Europe say that this involves 'winning their hearts and minds', but no one has a clear idea of how hearts and minds (which are not the same thing) function and what winning them means and involves. It cannot mean that the alienated youth should come to love their country of settlement as 'winning the hearts' implies, nor that they should endorse all its policies uncritically or take a liberal or 'moderate' view of their religion as 'winning the minds' implies. These things are not in the outsider's control, and not even necessary. Rather, we should aim at the more modest and realistic goal of ensuring that they become responsible citizens, discharge the basic obligations of citizenship including respect for the law, and over time develop a sense of common belonging with the rest.

Although such widely canvassed proposals as asking the parents to report on the activities of their children, an extensive network of informers, requiring universities to report on Muslim students, spying on what the imams say in their Friday sermons, and restricting the overseas visits of young Muslims cannot be ruled out under all circumstances, they are fraught with grave danger and often counter-productive. They not only alienate Muslim communities but also destroy the very trust and cohesion they need to carry any kind of moral authority with the young. Teaching citizenship in *madrassas* is of marginal value, because that is not where much of the *jihadi* ideology is picked up. And even if it sometimes is, formal classes on moral values can have only a limited impact. Requiring the imams to be trained in European societies too has only a limited value because the *jihadi* ideology is picked up not only from them but also from a variety of other sources, and there is no reason why the locally trained imams should be 'moderate'. In the days of globalization, ideas and passions flow through countless channels, and the solution cannot be entirely local.

Individuals develop a commitment to their society and form a view of their place in it on the basis of their experiences of how it perceives and treats them, and that should be our focus. European societies need to give young Muslims a stake in society, hope for a better future, and the opportunity to develop and enjoy multiple and mutually moderating identities. They should develop well thought out educational, economic and other strategies to tackle the roots of their disadvantage and alienation, and do so in consultation with young Muslims. Society should also treat these young people with respect, and so define its identity that all Muslims, including the young, feel themselves to be an integral and valued part of it. Thanks to the dominant ideology of the nation state, West European societies equate the national with cultural identity, and the latter with the Judeo-Christian heritage. It is therefore widely held that one cannot be both a Muslim and a full citizen of the country, at least not in equal measure. This is why white converts to Islam are often believed to have abandoned not only their religion but also their culture and national identity. Just as Europeans are beginning to deracialize national identity and to accept that a European can be white, brown or black, they also need to de-religionize it.

While guarding against murderous attacks by all necessary and legitimate means, societies should stay within the law, respect human rights and avoid appearing to single out Muslims. No government measures can work without the co-operation and support of the Muslim communities, and governments must do nothing to forfeit this. Foreign policy necessarily has domestic implications, and cannot be framed in isolation from them. This is particularly so in our interdependent world, where groups of citizens are part of a global network. While European societies cannot be held hostage to sectional pressures, though they sometimes are, both justice and the need for a national consensus require that their policies in relation to the Middle East and elsewhere should be much more even-handed than they have been so far.

Muslin communities, too, have an equally important role to play. They need to take a long and overdue critical look at themselves, and find ways of overcoming the pervasive sense of victimhood and the tendency to blame all their ills on the wider society. Much of the discussion in Muslim communities rightly highlights the wider society's racism and Islamophobia, but wrongly ignores what the communities themselves can do to regain their individual and collective agency and regenerate themselves. Muslim communities need to repair their disintegrating social fabric, build strong families and supporting networks, take greater interest in and responsibility for their youth, and reform those social and religious practices that stifle and alienate it. Their intellectual and religious leaders need to offer a way of reading Islam that connects with European modernity, and counters the perverted interpretations popularized by the al-Qaeda and its associates.

Global causes are important and worth pursuing, but they can also become a convenient escape from the vital task of revitalizing the community of which one is a part and where one can make a difference. Furthermore, it is not enough to keep blaming the West and especially the United States for the sorry state of the Muslim world. Many Muslim societies are willing accomplices to Western domination. Their complicity, oppressive regimes and iniquitous treatment of Muslim and non-Muslim minorities too need to be exposed and challenged in an even-handed manner. In the age of globalization, Muslim struggles for dignity and equality in Western Europe are inseparable from those in the global *umma*.

A closer co-operation between governments and Muslim communities raises difficult questions about the traditional private–public distinction, the nature, role and the legitimate sphere of action of governments, and challenges some of the current liberal views on the subject. Liberals generally insist that a government should not interfere with what goes on in religious gatherings and what the leaders preach there; that it has no business taking an active interest in how parents bring up their children and relate to them; that it is none of its concern where people go for their holidays; that it should stay clear of how people interpret their religious texts and the kind of debate they throw up, and so on. These and many other related restraints are being breached, and liberals need to ask if we are right to do so, when and why.

7

The Pathology of Religious Identity

I argued in Chapter 2 that human beings have plural identities and that these need to be balanced. Not all identities are equal in their scope, depth and importance: some cover large and important areas of human life and shape the way others are defined and regulated. The religious identity is one of them. For believers, their religion is the source of their world view and values, the ground of their being, their ultimate frame of reference, and governs all areas of their lives. Other identities, such as the national and the cultural can also acquire this degree of importance, but they do not generally have the same range and depth or deal with matters of equal concern.

The religious consciousness is articulated in terms of the two interrelated ideas of transcendence and faith. It rests on the assumption that the empirical world, the world as we know it through observation and experiment, is not self-sufficient and depends for its origin, meaning, ground or principles of conduct on a source lying outside it. Although religions differ greatly in the way they define the transcendental principle or being and relate it to the world, they all share this assumption, which the secular world view rejects.[1] Since the nature of the transcendental source and its relation to the world are not a matter of empirical evidence, religion involves faith.

By its very nature, every religion faces several challenges, of which two are of particular interest to us. First, although it involves faith it cannot be a matter of faith alone. It needs to establish a satisfactory relation between faith and reason, both because reason is an important human faculty, and because otherwise faith lacks a regulative principle, opens the door to all manner of absurd beliefs, and undermines the integrity of the religious faith itself. Second, every religion aims to guide the individual in the organization of his or her personal and collective life, and provides a set of moral and political principles. It needs to strike a balance between its worldly and transcendental concerns, and between the freedom of the individual and the power of the religious authority in achieving the desired form of personal and social life.

Not all religions get these two things right. And even when they do, their adherents might misinterpret them. Concerning the first, they might take the view that the divine will is exhaustively revealed in a particular scripture, that they have no right to sit in judgement on it, and that they have an absolute obligation to carry it out in its minutest detail. As for the second, they might use the religion to extract a moral and political programme and deploy its organized power to change their society in the light of it. In the first case, they suspend or marginalize reason and reduce religion to an uncritical faith. In the second, they turn it into the equivalent of a secular ideology, usually of the militant kind. In the political context, the former subordinates politics to religion, while the latter places shifting political considerations at the heart of religion and politicizes it. In their own different ways, religionization of politics and politicization of religion, which represent opposite ends of the religious spectrum, corrupt both religion and politics. I shall take each in turn and show how and why this is so.

Scriptural literalism

The scriptural literalist represents a classic case of someone for whom religious identity more or less transcends reason and is not amenable to rational investigation or criticism. As he understands it, human beings have to make a basic or fundamental choice concerning how to organize their lives. Since this choice is the basis of all others, it cannot itself be based on anything outside it, and involves an ultimate commitment. Rationalists commit themselves to reason and rely on it to navigate their lives. Religious people commit themselves to God and base their lives on His revealed Word. Both are a matter of faith or ultimate commitment, rest on non-rational foundations, and neither can justify their respective commitments in a non-circular way. For religious persons, the rationalist is therefore not entitled to accuse them of irrationality or 'blind' faith and claim superiority over them. In fact, the opposite is the case: while the rationalist makes the finite and fallible human reason the basis of his/her life, the religious person more sensibly relies on the infinitely superior and infallible divine reason.

While thus far the literalist argues like other religious people, he goes on to differ from them in the way he understands his religion. For him the divine reason is articulated in a particular scripture, an inerrant source of fundamental truths about human life and all the guidance human beings need to lead a good life. Limited human reasoning obviously cannot comprehend it in all its richness and complexity. Parts of it are bound to appear strange, elusive, irrational, even wrong to the believer, but he must not allow this to shake his faith in these. He should accept his limitations and hope that one day he might with divine help come to see the point of them. It is presumptuous of him, and shows a lack of basic trust in God, to sit in judgement on, let alone question, His revealed Word, and pick and choose what he likes and approves of. God is the only authority he accepts, and he may rightly disregard all others when their demands go against divine injunctions.[2]

Literalists confront us with an uncompromising stand. When asked to be reasonable, they rejoin that they do not understand what this means. If it means that they should entertain the possibility that they could be mistaken in their religious commitment and might one day revise their beliefs, they reply that they cannot see how the Word of God can ever be mistaken, and what new evidence or argument could conceivably cast doubt on the existence of God or on the fact that a particular scripture represents His self-revelation. If being reasonable means that they should not interpret their religion literally, they rejoin that they are being asked to commit the blasphemy of sitting in judgement on the revealed Word and deciding what in it is valid or true. If, finally, it means that they should not follow their religion too scrupulously or dogmatically, and should adjust to the limitations of the world, they repy that this amounts to abandoning religion. They are charged with the task of challenging and changing the corrupt world, and cannot submit to it meekly. Furthermore, just as one cannot be half-honest or half-sincere, one cannot be half-religious. One either takes one's religion seriously and follows its injunctions to the letter, or takes liberties with it and ceases to be faithful to its teachings. The former is likely to appear rigid and dogmatic to others, but that should not worry the faithful follower: the fault lies not with him/her but with those who expect their religion to give them an easy life.[3]

Although scriptural literalism has an air of internal consistency and exercises considerable influence over many religious people, it is deeply flawed. It argues wrongly that rationalism rests on faith, and that commitment to reason is no different from that to religion. Unlike the latter, rationalism is not a commitment to a substantive body of beliefs. It is procedural or methodological in nature, and implies no more than that one is committed to being guided by reason and evidence. Even as a procedural principle, it is not arbitrary or an act of faith. It is at bottom a commitment to disciplined thinking. Like any other human activity, thinking is governed by rules. If we are to think at all, which we cannot avoid doing, we should do so properly, not haphazardly and chaotically but in a disciplined and systematic manner, and that involves assessing evidence, making valid inferences, taking into account relevant factors, withholding judgement and keeping an open mind when evidence is inconclusive or reasons are evenly balanced, and accepting responsibility for one's decision.

Rational or disciplined thinking can also be defended on other grounds. It gives us a reliable knowledge of the world, and enables us to control and subject it to our needs. It ensures order, consistency and predictability in social relations without which human life is virtually unliveable. It dispels false fears, exposes impossible dreams and fantasies, regulates our choices and desires, facilitates self-determination, subordinates short-term goals to long-term objectives, and in these and other ways both expresses and promotes human freedom. It makes morality possible by countering the pull of emotions and prejudices, enabling us to appreciate the claims of, and do justice to, those outside our limited circle. It also ensures that our beliefs and actions are based on careful thought, that we take responsibility for them, and that the demands we make on others are legitimate and defensible.

Unlike the commitment to a faith, that to reason is in principle self-critical and self-limiting. It involves acknowledging that emotions, spontaneity, intuitions and gut feelings have a legitimate place in human life, that they may be valuable sources of knowledge and moral guidance, and deserve respect. It recognizes that faith might also be an appropriate response in certain situations, and makes room for it. It accepts its own fallibility, and is open to views that challenge it. It recognizes too that different areas of life involve different kinds of evidence, inferences and forms of reasoning, and should not be assimilated to a single model. It is, of course, true that some rationalists consider reason alone to be the 'essence' of human beings, or give it a supremely privileged place in human life, and marginalize and offer a highly distorted account of other human capacities. It is also true that some of them take the philosophical, the scientific or some other form of reasoning to be the only valid form, and either reduce all others to it or dismiss them as defective. The rationalists who take such a dogmatic view of reason and exempt it from critical self-reflection are not much different from those making an uncritical commitment to faith, and open to the same objections. There is, however, no good reason why the commitment to reason should take such a narrow and dogmatic form. Basically, it involves being guided by reason and evidence, and hence being sensitive to the role and contributions of other human faculties and the limits and diversity of reason. In so far as it is not, it is being inconsistent, even irrational.

The commitment to reason, then, is qualitatively different from that to the revealed Word, and is not a leap of faith. We can go further and argue that literalism itself necessarily involves and is parasitic on a commitment to reason. The literalist argues that he commits himself to God because human reason is limited. He needs to show how he knows this, and has to rely on reason to highlight its limits. He says that a particular scripture reveals God's will, and needs to show why he thinks so, especially when followers of other religions take a different view. Furthermore, there are several religions, and the literalist needs to show why he commits himself to one of them in particular. He might say that it is the best and superior to all others, but that calls for reasons. Or he might say that it is his religion in the sense that he was born and raised into it. It is surely open to him to leave it in favour of some other, and he needs to give reasons why he has not done so. He has grown up with numerous beliefs and practices, some of which he is bound to have abandoned or revised. He needs to give reasons why he makes religion an exception. Many believers also seek to convert others to their religion. They cannot do so without showing that their religion is better, and that means giving reasons. Seeking to convert others implies that religious commitments are revisable, and can and should be abandoned when good reasons are given, a view the literalist (inconsistently) denies in relation to himself.

The inescapable role of reason also extends to the reading of the scriptures. Scriptures of all religions, including the revealed ones, were composed over a period of time, written down not by their founders but their followers, and based on human decisions as to what did and did not belong in them. They are written in a particular language, with all its biases and limitations. No scripture can therefore claim to represent the 'pure' Word of God, and demand to be taken literally. Scriptures are inevitably dense, complex and articulated on several levels, each of which needs be carefully identified and read appropriately. Since profound truths about human life cannot always be stated in a propositional language, they are often communicated through parables, allegories or cryptic aphorisms, which need to be patiently decoded and explicated.

The moral principles lying at the heart of religion are necessarily abstract and general, and require interpretation and elucidation. The meaning of 'thou shalt not covet thy neighbour's wife' depends on who is one's neighbour, what 'to covet' means, whether a passing fantasy counts as much as a serious infatuation, and whether the prohibition is limited to the wife in the narrow sense of the term. 'Thou shalt not kill' is just as ambiguous. Does this include germs? This is physically impossible. Does it extend to animals, and commit one to strict vegetarianism? Even when the injunction is limited to humans, questions arise as to what killing means, whether it includes letting die, how important intentions are, and whether one might kill in self-defence, to save a child, in a just war, or to spread or defend the Word of God. One cannot follow religious injunctions without interpreting and understanding their meaning, and that involves identifying their underlying reasons. Human reason is thus at the very heart of religion, and human beings simply cannot live by faith or the sacred text alone.

Every religion involves not only a scripture but also a founder whose life and utterances are just as important, if not more so. The two need to be read together and their discrepancies resolved. The scripture, further, has wholeness and integrity, and is underpinned by a particular vision of human life and destiny. The heart of every scripture lies in its vision; much of the rest of it is meant to explicate and popularize it, and cannot enjoy the same hermeneutic status. No single sentence carries its meaning on the surface. It has to be related to the rest of the text and interpreted in the light of its central vision. Although the scriptures are meant to be valid forever, they were written in a particular language, composed at a particular time, and addressed to particular people whose fears, anxieties and aspirations they reflect. We need to know what the words meant at the time in elite and popular discourses, how the different parts were put together, in what contexts and by whom, and how and why different schools of interpretation grew up over time and built up a complex tradition of scriptural discourse. Since the scriptures contain different kinds of material, we need to separate its empirical and historical assertions from its moral and spiritual principles, show why the former could be wrong and discarded without damaging the latter, and appreciate that not everything in them is or can be inerrant. No interpretation of a religion can be regarded as being satisfactory unless it takes all of this into account. Even then, it is possible that it could be mistaken. After all, there is hardly a past interpretation of any religion, including those offered by its authorized representatives, that has not subsequently been revised and even rejected. No one may therefore claim infallibility or finality for his or her interpretation and suppress dissent.

Literalists violate these and other principles that are essential to interpreting a religion. They concentrate on the scriptures, and either ignore the founder or make no attempt to integrate the two. They pick out isolated sentences and do not locate them in the larger textual context. They read them literally and do not probe their deeper meaning. They degrade the scripture into a kind of dictionary or manual and violate its integrity. They abstract the text from its historical context, and read it as if it were a philosophical treatise written only yesterday. They treat every sentence, be it empirical, moral or theological, as if it had the same status and was equally sacred. They do not engage in a critical dialogue with other interpretations of the text and show why they are mistaken. By claiming infallibility for their own interpretation, they imply that they know God's mind as well as God does Himself, and thus are guilty of an egregious blasphemy.

Even if the literalist were to meet all, or even most, of the hermeneutic criteria of scriptural interpretation, s/he would not be out of trouble. The scripture enjoins a whole host of things, and a consistent literalist needs to follow them all. S/he does not – indeed cannot – and is invariably selective. A Christian literalist, for example, cannot both condemn abortion and endorse wars in which many innocent children get killed, or talk of God's boundless love for humankind and at the same time breathe hatred for a large part of it. Muslim and other literalists face similar difficulties. The literalist thus is doubly inconsistent, being selective when all selectivity is ruled out by his self-proclaimed attitude to the scriptures, and giving no reason why s/he selects particular parts over others.

Every religion articulates a vision of human life that no individual can fully realize in his or her life. No Christian, for example, can take the attitude of the carefree bird in the sky that worries not about tomorrow, or eliminate all possible traces of covetous thoughts about his/her neighbour's ox or ass or other belongings. Believers simply cannot function normally and lead balanced lives unless they take a relatively relaxed attitude to their religion, use their reason to identify its central values, and live by at least some of them within the limits of their capacity. They acknowledge and regret their inevitable failures, and cope with them in various ways, such as blaming human nature, asking God's forgiveness, doing charitable deeds, and praying for greater strength in future.

Literalists are no different. They might be more observant, but they too cut corners and make compromises. They might be scrupulous in following particular injunctions, but are invariably lax or negligent in relation to others. Their claim to be true to every scriptural utterance, or at least every moral injunction, is a lie repeatedly exposed by their practice. It is important to emphasize this, because they assert their superiority over their fellow believers, and blackmail them into feeling guilty by arguing that one is either fully religious or not at all, and that only they belong to the former category. Both assertions are false. No one can live by every injunction of his/her religion, and hence leading a religious life is necessarily a matter of degree. Furthermore, there is no standard or foolproof way of following one's religion, because its central principles can be interpreted and prioritized in different ways, and the literalist's is only one of them.

As the history of all religions shows, the literal approach to religion is often a reaction against the liberal. The latter leads to diversity of interpretations, pluralism, disagreements and lack of finality, which causes panic among believers and generates a strong but misguided pressure to return to the scriptures and read them literally. By its very nature, the scriptures do not carry their meaning on the surface. They need to be interpreted, and these interpretations necessarily vary. The literal approach cannot guarantee the certainty and finality that the believer seeks, and there is simply no alternative to living with and, whenever possible, finding a consensus between inescapable disagreements. Literalism is logically incoherent as well as morally unliveable, and undermines the religion it claims to uphold.

While challenging the literalist's approach to his religion, we might also challenge his interpretations of the particular scriptural statements that he cites in justification of his actions. We may show, as we generally can, that these statements do not mean what he says they do, that he takes them out of context, that they are interpolations, or that they are qualified or contradicted by others. The Qur'ān, for example, says that Jews and Christians are not to be 'taken as allies', but limits it to a particular historical context, and it also says that as People of the Book, they should be respected and trusted. It says, again, that Islam is the only true religion, but also that God has given different religions to different people. Both propositions are consistent when read in their context. The literalist, who concentrates on either alone and detaches it from its context, misunderstands their point and limits.

Literalists argue that they have an absolute and unconditional obligation to obey God, and that all their other obligations, including the political, are derivative and contingent. There is nothing wrong with this view, because it does not matter on what grounds individuals respect the civil authority as long as they acknowledge an obligation to do so. Their demand that they may disobey a law that goes against a religious injunction need not worry us either, for we can accommodate it by exempting them from it, as we do in the case of conscientious objectors. The difficulty arises when they refuse to recognize the legitimacy of the political authority, and pick and choose which laws to obey.

Take the case of Hassan Butt, a British Muslim activist. He sees himself as 'nothing but a Muslim', and insists on approaching all areas of life, including the political, 'Islamically'. As he says, 'My allegiance is to Allah, his *Sharia*, his way of life. Whatever he dictates as good is good, whatever as bad is bad.' When asked if he had an obligation to obey British laws, he replied in the negative. Voluntary immigrants were bound by the 'covenant of security' as the Qur'ān enjoins, but those born in Britain, such as himself, were not: 'They did not ask to be born here, neither did they ask to be protected by Britain.' 'Islamically', he therefore owed no allegiance to the British state, 'none whatsoever'.[4]

Butt and others like him are confused and inconsistent. He did not ask to be born a Muslim either, yet he takes his religion extremely seriously. He did not ask to be born of particular parents, and yet he generally acknowledges his obligations to them. It is inconsistent of him not to apply the same argument to his citizenship. Although he did not ask to be born in Britain, he had the freedom to leave it. The fact that he chose to stay implies that he has accepted the covenant of security and is bound by it. He has enjoyed not only British protection but also its welfare, educational and other provisions, entered into all manner of relations with his fellow citizens, and encouraged them to entertain certain expectations of him. Since the Qur'ān requires that he should do good to those who have done good to him, he owes the 'Islamic' duty of reciprocity to his fellow citizens, including the duty to respect the law.

While thus far we have argued with the literalist on his own ground and exposed his contradictions, we might now cast the argument much wider. The political community of which he is a citizen includes countless others as well, and they all demand the same rights as he does. Some of them share his religion, others belong to other religions or to none. And even those sharing his religion take different views of it. Just as he holds certain beliefs dear and wishes to live by them, so do they. And just as he does not want them to impose their religious beliefs on him, nor do they. He might say, as Hassan Butt and his counterparts in other religions do, that his religion is superior to all others and that he may claim rights others cannot. As we saw earlier he cannot establish this in a non-circular way, nor show why others are wrong to make a similar claim.

This means that they all need to agree on a form of association that respects their equal rights and is acceptable to them all. A liberal democracy meets this requirement. It is just because it treats all its members equally. It does not impose particular religious beliefs on them, and thus respects their integrity. And it is the only form of association capable of commanding general acceptance. Literalists therefore have a moral obligation to respect its institutions and laws. Even if they were to deny a moral obligation, we could show that they have a prudential obligation to do so. The state ensures a stable and secure environment in which they are able to practise their religion and lead a life of their choice. If they demanded to live on their own terms, they would put themselves in a state of war with the rest, with all that entails. Their enlightened self-interest, if nothing else, requires that they should discharge the basic obligations of citizenship.

The dialogue with literalists then can go a long way to undermine their views. It might not, however, succeed in winning them over and securing their compliance. They are obsessed by certain scriptural utterances and cannot let go of their determination to live by them. At this point, we reach the limits of dialogue and need to follow a different strategy. We should enter their world of thought and ask why they approach and read the scripture in this manner. No reading of it is entirely open-minded and purely cerebral. One brings to it certain assumptions, anxieties and fears, asks it certain questions, and expects the answers to fall within a particular range. This is one of the reasons why every religious text is read differently in different societies, and in the same society in different periods. A remark that in one age or society is ignored, given only passing attention, put in abeyance or left as an unresolved puzzle can easily become an obsession or acquire excessive importance in another.

Literalism tends to flourish in a climate of fear and anxiety. When individuals feel that outside groups or social processes are undermining their religion or breaking up their religious community, they panic and hold on desperately to their religion, especially its easily accessible central text. They have no interest in its subtle and nuanced reading. They want uncomplicated guidance, and latch on to isolated sentences that seem to them to sum up their predicament and address their concerns. We cannot loosen the hold of literalism without understanding and, when relevant, tackling the causes of the underlying fears and anxieties. Argumentative reason, which has done much to clear the ground, must now yield place to politics with its inescapable struggles, negotiations and compromises.

Fundamentalism[5]

Every society is subject to small and large changes, and generally has the resources to deal with them. A difficult situation arises when it faces what I shall call a moral crisis or a crisis of identity and integrity. This can happen for internal or external reasons. A society might undergo profound changes in economic, social and other areas of life, causing massive dislocation in the prevailing pattern of social relations, affecting the material interests of important groups, weakening the moral norms in terms of which its members structure their lives, and generating a widespread feeling of anomie and disorientation. A moral crisis may also occur when a society is subjected to foreign conquests or systematic external manipulation and domination. Its self-respect and pride are wounded, and it wonders how it should regenerate itself to stand up to outsiders and take charge of its destiny. In either case, particularly when the crisis is caused by a combination of both internal and external factors, there is a widespread yearning for a new moral order. Since religion is an important source of moral certainty and is a pervasive force in most societies, their members turn to it, especially if they have tried and failed with secular alternatives.

The moral crisis takes different forms in different societies. It is muted and has a limited impact in modern Western societies because they derive their world views and values from several sources, of which religion is only one, and because they have built up powerful economic, political, educational, cultural and other institutions that are capable of resisting and limiting the disturbing effects of the moral crisis. However, even here, the impact of a moral crisis should not be underestimated.

While Western societies are largely secular, they derive some of their moral values from Christianity and are nurtured and sustained by a deep religious undercurrent. In Britain, the Thatcher Government, faced with what it saw as a decline in moral standards, attacked the Churches for failing to define and enforce Christian values and for 'dabbling' in social and political issues that in its view fell outside the religious sphere. In the US, in which religion plays a far greater cultural and moral role than in Europe, it has often dominated the political agenda and regularly thrown up strident religious movements. The religiously inspired and highly influential neocons, Huntington's plea (1996, 2001) for a return to religion, and Evangelical pressure for the rebirth of America are all recent examples of this.

The situation is quite different in many non-Western societies. They are, or were until recently, the playthings of external powers, suffer from a deep sense of humiliation, and are desperate to turn the corner. Religion is the sole, or major, source of their world views and values, and they naturally turn to it for guidance and inspiration. Since their economic, political, cultural and other institutions are relatively undeveloped and often lack popular legitimacy and authority, they are unable to deflect, contain or even participate in the articulation and resolution of the moral crisis. The moral crisis is therefore not only unusually acute, but its resolution is also left almost entirely in the hands of religious leaders. If these societies happen to be subject to sustained modernizing influences, as they almost invariably are, they fear secularism and the likely loss of religion, their major hope for moral renewal. The moral crisis then becomes politically charged and causes a veritable panic.

Religious leaders respond to the moral crisis in several ways. Traditionalists blame it on the decline in the authority of traditions under the impact of modernization, scepticism and rationalism, and urge their revitalization. Revitalists urge a return to the original principles of religion or to a past golden age. Reformists seek to purge the religion of obscurantist beliefs and practices, and urge its reinterpretation and reform. There is another response which, for want of a better term, I shall call fundamentalism. Although the term is currently used so loosely that it has lost all meaning and coherence and one is tempted to reject it, there are good reasons to retain it and to give it a fairly precise meaning. It captures the twofold fact that the movement I am examining aims to reduce religion to its so-called fundamentals, and to use them to radically restructure and give a fundamentally new orientation to society. This was also broadly how the term was used in the early decades of the twentieth century in relation to Christianity. In spite of its Christian provenance, many leaders of the Islamic movements that exemplify this response seem to think that it broadly expresses what they have in mind, and have either adopted or indigenized it.[6] The term *banyadgarayan*, meaning fundamentalism, was first used by Ayatollah Khomeini's followers and has since become popular. The Arabic *al-usuliyyah al-Islamiyyah* has a similar thrust. The *Usulis* have no use for traditions and much of the past. They want to distil the basic or original principles of Islam and use them to restructure society.

These and other reasons are obviously not conclusive, and we may give this movement some other name. The basic point is that it has a distinct character, and that *whatever* name we give it should not be extended indiscriminately to others that might look like it but are logically quite different. Although fundamentalist movements have appeared, and continue to appear, in all societies, they are occurring in their stark and unchecked simplicity in some contemporary Muslim societies, and hence I shall draw most of my examples from them. My analysis, however, applies to these movements in whatever religions and societies they occur.

The fundamentalist argues that society has become degenerate because it has lost its moral moorings, that this is caused by the corrosive climate of secularism and scepticism brought about by globalization and rationalist influences, and that it can only be regenerated by reconstituting it on religious foundations. Secularism is the fundamentalist's greatest enemy and constant target of attack. In order to reconstitute society on a religious basis, he seeks to capture the state and, when this is not possible, to influence it by putting his sympathizers in power and mobilizing public opinion. For him the purpose of political power is not merely to maintain law and order or ensure justice, but to create and sustain a truly moral order.[7]

Even as the fundamentalist redefines the nature and role of the state, he also redefines the nature and role of religion, taking a stand on the allegedly unshakable foundation of the 'pure Word of God' as embodied in the sacred texts. He rejects the traditionalist view that the texts are inseparable from and should be read in the light of the tradition. For the fundamentalist, the latter is human, fallible, stands between man and God, is prone to corruption, and dilutes the divine message by making all manner of compromises. By contrast, the texts are inerrant, uncontaminated by human limitations, and the sole source of infallible guidance.

By detaching the text from the tradition and making it the basis of religious identity, the fundamentalist creates the vitally necessary conceptual space both to interpret the text and to undermine the authority of the traditional discourse built around it.

The fundamentalist approaches the sacred texts with two closely-related objectives in mind. First, he seeks to extract a moral and political programme around which the faithful can be mobilized; that is, he looks for the religious equivalent of a secular political ideology. Second, he aims to provide a neat, unambiguous, exclusive and easily intelligible definition of his religion. He seeks to distinguish it sharply from other religions and to provide a kind of checklist in terms of which the believers can define and distinguish themselves from others.[8]

The sacred text is incapable of serving either purpose. It is articulated at metaphysical, ontological, eschatological, moral, social and other levels, and politics is only a small part of it. It offers a highly complex way of seeing the world that cannot be reduced to a neat ideological programme and easily distinguished from others. Its moral principles are absolute and uncompromising, and cannot be accommodated to the shifting demands and interests of various social groups, in particular the petty bourgeoisie and the rural migrants to the cities who, for various reasons, bear the brunt of the moral crisis. Faced with these and other difficulties, the fundamentalist has only one alternative, to simplify the scripture by extracting its so-called fundamentals. Since he considers the scripture to be inerrant, he cannot and does not dismiss the rest as wrong; rather he considers it to be comparatively less fundamental. While the fundamentals are non-negotiable, the historical, factual and other material may be reinterpreted, revised and contextualized. This distinction enables the fundamentalist to be at once both rigid and flexible on his own terms.

Although he thinks otherwise, the fundamentalist's choice of the so-called fundamentals is influenced inescapably by the circumstances of his society, his diagnosis of the causes of its degeneration, the sources of threats to its identity and survival, and the limits imposed by what is likely to be acceptable to his followers. He cannot therefore avoid imposing his personal and political preferences on the sacred texts. This is not to say that he dishonestly reads his political project in the texts, though he might well also do that, but nor is it the case that the project is logically entailed by the texts, as he claims. His reading of the sacred text shapes, and is in turn shaped by, his political concerns. The two flow into each other so subtly and surreptitiously that he is often a victim of unconscious self-deception.

The fundamentalist needs to show how he decides which beliefs and practices are fundamental to his religion. He invokes the idea of 'dynamic interpretation' to justify his choice and convince the doubters. The 'essence' or 'true' meaning of the sacred text, he argues, is discovered not by constant meditation on it, as the traditionalists and others argue, but by means of a 'dynamic' reading of it. This involves two things. First, since the sacred texts are meant for all times, including his own, he argues that it must be read in the light of prevailing needs, problems and challenges. This historicizes the text while also insisting on its timelessness. Second, he argues that the text is meant to be realized in history and involves an active engagement with the world. The true meaning of the sacred text therefore unfolds and becomes evident only in the course of a struggle against evil, and is disclosed not to a contemplative scholar but to 'God's humble soldier'. For Khomeini, Maulana Maudoodi's theological commentaries on the Qur'ān had an air of unreality about them because they 'have not been written in the process of a revolutionary struggle'.[9] The struggle exposes the nature and mode of operation of evil, gives an insight into the kind of battle good has to fight, reveals the 'secret rhythm of the universe', and has a profound epistemological significance. Sayyid Qutb claimed to offer an 'activist exegesis' of the Qur'ān, and insisted that its true meaning became clear to people 'only if they are actively engaged in an actual Islamic movement'.[10] The similarity this bears to the Marxist idea of the unity of theory and praxis is too obvious to need elaboration.

The fundamentalist's activist epistemology and dynamic interpretation of the scripture give him a vital hermeneutic advantage over his rivals. The traditionalist legitimizes his interpretation of religion in terms of the tradition, the literalist in terms of a close and diligent reading of the text, and the liberal reformer appeals to his detailed knowledge of its historical context and the current state of scriptural scholarship. The fundamentalist does not compete with them on their own ground, but skilfully undermines their authority. His epistemology rules out an appeal to history, tradition and textual scholarship, and privileges the activist. The focus is not on how to validate an interpretation of the scripture, but rather on *who* is best qualified to offer it. In the fundamentalist view, such an individual should be both a person of deep faith and an activist trying to realize its truths in practice, for his activism is not only an earnest demonstration of his faith but also a source of his privileged epistemological insights. As Khomeini put it, a cleric who prefers fasting and prayerful reading to political struggle 'will never know' his religion.

Unlike the conservatives, the literalists and the traditionalists who endeavour to live by their religious beliefs as faithfully as they can, and either leave the corrupt world alone or strive to change it by the power of their example, the fundamentalist declares a war on it and seeks to reconstitute it on a wholly new foundation. He is, above all, a revolutionary, seeing religion as a revolutionary struggle and the believers as soldiers in God's army. For Maudoodi, Islam is a 'revolutionary ideology', very like Nazism, Fascism and communism and different from them 'only in its aims'. He understands *jihad* not as a spiritual but a 'revolutionary struggle', and urges Muslims to form an 'international revolutionary party'. Syed Qutb thinks of true Muslims as *talia* (the vanguard) fighting for a 'revolutionary theological programme'. For Khomeini, the faithful are *hezbollahis* – members of the Party of God. Ibrahim Yazdi, one of his three most influential supporters in exile, declared on the eve of his master's triumphant return to Tehran in 1979 that they were the 'Trotskyists of Islam'.[11] Ali Shariati, the principal ideologue of the Islamic revolution in Iran, was deeply influenced by Frantz Fanon, and insisted that Black Shi'ism, the religion of mourning that forms the mainstream of Shia history, had to be replaced by Red or revolutionary Shi'ism. Since fundamentalism competes with radical secular ideologies on their terrain, it cannot avoid taking over their vocabulary, methods of action and modes of organization.

Far from being a fossilized relic of the past and oblivious to the demands of the contemporary world, the fundamentalist is really a modernist seeking to define and structure his/her religion in modernist terms. The ideas that religion is God's 'project' for humankind, that it requires a revolutionary struggle, that the scriptures are an ideological text providing a social and political programme, that the right to interpret them is earned by acquiring appropriate religious and activist qualifications, that the faithful must be mobilized for action and form the party or army of God, and that religion can and should be rationalized and reduced to a simplified system of beliefs are all *modern* ideas. Even Islam, which rejects the separation of state and religion, has never previously been seen in quite this way. Fundamentalism does, no doubt, revolt against parts of modernity, but with modernist weapons, in a modernist spirit, and in the interests of a modernist view of religion. It is at bottom an illegitimate child of modernity, and inconceivable outside it.

Since fundamentalism is suffused with the spirit of modernity, it has little difficulty in coming to terms with the modern world. It accepts the modern state and the ideology of nationalism.[12] Although uneasy with the critical spirit of modern science, it is fascinated by and exploits to the full its technological and organizational resources. It has proved to be extremely skilful at manipulating religious rituals and the media, including television, which is incompatible with the Islamic embargo on visual representation, and which the conservative Saudis were able to domesticate only after much theological sophistry. As Khomeini put it: 'for Islam the requirements of government supersede every tenet, including even those of prayer, fasting and pilgrimage to Mecca'. Contrary to the general impression, fundamentalists have come to terms increasingly with modern science as well, so long as it is understood as a body of knowledge rather than an attitude of mind, a critical inquiry or a culture.[13] Khomeini rarely referred to miracles, and subtly marginalized the hidden twelfth imam believed to be in occultation for the past few centuries. Having insisted initially that universities should teach only the 'Islamic sciences', he later retreated on this point, saying that they should concentrate on 'secular knowledge', albeit in a spirit of 'Islamic independence'. Whatever its intentions, fundamentalism cannot reshape the secular world without imbibing its spirit and ethos.

Even as the fundamentalist's religion consists of little more than a few simple beliefs abstracted from a highly complex theological system, his moral programme rarely rises above conventional morality.[14] This is so largely because he defines the right moral order in terms of the traditional pattern of social relations, and reflects the anxieties and demands of such social groups as the petty bourgeoisie and urban migrants. He extols the patriarchal family and the virtues of self-discipline, hard work, thrift, obedience, clean living, humility, piety and so on, and condemns gambling, adultery, gender equality, premarital sex, homosexuality, sexual promiscuity, drunkenness, pornography, divorce, illegitimate children, abortion, sex education and parental permissiveness. Social justice, egalitarianism and rejection of the unrestrained capitalist pursuit of profit that are central to (or can at least be shown to be a powerful strand within) Islam are rarely paid much attention. Khomeini and others advocated them initially but dropped them later when they met with resistance.[15]

The fundamentalist needs to explain why his society and religion have long been in decline, and why the Word of God has proved to be ineffective. According to Khomeini, 'true Islam lasted for only a brief period after its inception' – in fact, barely a hundred years – and has since been followed by the age of apostasy and *jahiliyya*. Although the fundamentalist blames the corrupt religious establishment, he knows that is not enough, because he needs to explain why it became and remained corrupt, and why there was no elite or popular movement against it. For the most part he takes the easy option of blaming human sinfulness, by which he means the innate human propensity to prefer the world over religion, and thus to rebel against God. He takes a dark and pessimistic view of human nature and emphasizes the power of evil. Although he cannot deny that God will eventually and in the fullness of time ensure the triumph of good over evil, he is convinced that evil triumphs in the short and medium terms. God therefore needs human help. And since most humans are believed to have only a weak commitment to God, this help can only come form the religious elite. It is their job to serve God's cause by leading the fight against evil and protecting the majority against its natural propensity to sinfulness.[16]

The fundamentalist project of reconstituting society on a religious basis obviously involves considerable violence. At one level, it is no different from the violence to be found in all revolutionary struggles. It is a 'military necessity' and intended to defend the theo-political project against its enemies. As Khomeini calmly reassured the weak-hearted, 'The glorious Imam [the first Shi'ite imam] killed in one day four thousand of his enemies to protect the faith.' In two respects, however, the fundamentalist violence is quite different. It is 'holy': that is, not born out of hatred and vengeance but from a deep commitment to the cause of God. After all, as the fundamentalist constantly reminds his followers, even God resorts to the 'overwhelming terrors and fire of hell', not because He cannot find better ways of coping with human frailties, for nothing is beyond God, but because He considers them thoroughly well-deserved.

Second, in the fundamentalist view, all believers have a collective responsibility to safeguard their religious identity. Backsliding by any of them lowers the level of collective discipline, sets a bad example to others, and damages the spiritual well-being of all. Believers therefore have a dual obligation – to conform to the requirements of their religion and to be an example to others; and to make sure that others do so too. The stronger their religious credentials, the greater is their right and duty to keep an eye on others, report them to the appropriate authorities, and under certain circumstances to administer instant justice to them. Such violence is in the victims' own interest as it saves them from further sin and the consequent terrors of hell. As Khomeini put it, it 'does them service for their eventual punishment will be less'.

Fundamentalism, then, is a distinct phenomenon whose various components hang together well enough to give it a clear identity. It arises in a society with a deep and pervasive sense of disorientation and degeneration, and consists in using the institutions of the state to reconstitute it on a religious basis. It centres on the sacred text, abstracts it from the tradition, offers an activist reading of it, and extracts from it a politically relevant ideological programme. It is revolutionary in its aspirations, authoritarian in its structure, conventional in its personal and social morality, and elitist in its approach. It is militant, puritanical, aggressive and violent, and offers an extremely narrow and simplistic view of the identity of the religion concerned. Although it revolts against some aspects of the modern world, it is an essentially modern phenomenon, borrowing heavily from and competing with secular ideologies on *their* terrain and in *their* terms. It reconstitutes religion in the image of modernity, even as it copes with modernity within the limits of religion.[17] Its answers to the moral crisis, to which it owes its origin, are shallow, and subvert both the religion it claims to uphold and the society it seeks to save. Far from regenerating society, it traps it in a politically manipulated religious straitjacket and dries up all sources of creativity.

Specificity of fundamentalism

It is often argued, wrongly in my view, that fundamentalism is common to all religions. In an interdependent world, religions borrow each other's good and bad features. Since fundamentalism is often a source of considerable political energy, even the religions that are structurally inhospitable to and have no history of it sometimes tend to mimic it in order to mobilize their followers. The question, however, is whether it comes easily and naturally to every religious tradition, whether its occurrence provokes strong internal resistance or at least unease, and whether it succeeds in securing a mass following. It would seem that fundamentalism is largely limited to some forms of Islam and Protestant Christianity. This is not to say that other religions cannot be perverse, but rather that the kinds of perversity they throw up usually do not include fundamentalism.

As I have argued, fundamentalism seeks to regenerate an allegedly degenerate society by radically reconstituting it on a religious foundation by political means. As an ideological and political movement, it is only possible under certain conditions, of which the following are the most important. First, it implies that religion is capable of being separated from society and, since the latter is inescapably bound up with culture, from culture as well. For the Taliban as for Khomeini, Islam is the same everywhere, just as 'mathematics and chemistry' are. Such differences as exist are derived from local cultures and should be stamped out. Not surprisingly, the Taliban banned traditional and highly popular forms of music, arts, styles of dress, forms of worship and social practices as being un-Islamic. When a religion is deeply embedded in and cannot be abstracted from a social structure – as is the case with tribal religions, Hinduism and to some extent Judaism – it lacks the conceptual resources to transcend, evaluate and transform the society concerned.

Second, fundamentalism presupposes a sacred text. A religion with-out a text, such as a tribal religion, is nothing more than its traditions, and its adherents lack a means of judging or challenging them. They can, of course, mount an internal critique of them, but this cannot be radical and comprehensive. Third, fundamentalism requires that a religion should have a *single* sacred text or, if it has several, that there should be a clearly established hierarchy among them. If it has several texts of equal status, its adherents are at liberty to choose any one of them. They will not then share a common identity and cannot easily be defined, distinguished and mobilized on the basis of a shared body of beliefs.

Fourth, fundamentalism presupposes that a religion should grant the believer direct access to the sacred texts. If only its officially accredited representatives are permitted to read and interpret them, or if no new interpretation of them is allowed, it is not open to anyone to challenge the established authorities and practices by appealing directly to the authority of the texts. This is why Protestant Christianity is more vulner-able to fundamentalism than Roman Catholicism, and those Islamic schools that permit *ijtihad* (an interpretation of the Qur'ān) are more prone to it than those who have 'closed the door' to it. Finally, funda-mentalism uses the state to reconstitute society, and presupposes that a religion permits such a use of the state. If a religion is inherently anti-political or even apolitical, and so defines the religious identity that it cannot be enforced, or totally disapproves of the use of violence, then it cannot be chartered in the fundamentalist cause.[18]

The more of these preconditions a religion meets, the more likely it is to throw up fundamentalist movements in times of moral crisis. Not all religions are equally vulnerable to such movements. And when they do appear, they take different forms depending on the nature of the religion, the crisis it faces, and the society in which they occur. The case of the

Hindu religion, or Hinduism as it is popularly but mistakenly called, illustrates the point.

Hinduism satisfies few of the necessary conditions for fundamentalism. It has no single generally agreed sacred text, and leaves its followers free to choose any one of several. It has no doctrinal unity, and there is no belief to which all Hindus are required to subscribe. It is almost entirely concerned with social conduct, and leaves its members free to believe what they like as long as they conform to the prescribed norms of their caste. Like Judaism, but unlike Islam and Christianity, Hinduism is an ethnic or communal religion, which is why it has no established machinery for conversion and lacks the necessary critical distance from the social order in which it is embedded. It is socially conservative and hostile to the idea of using the state to reconstitute society. For these and other reasons, it lacks the necessary conceptual and institutional resources to produce and sustain a fundamentalist movement.

This has not prevented some Hindu groups from mimicking fundamentalism, but with only limited success: they have neither a clear programme of action nor a vision of what a Hindu India should look like. They cannot even agree on who is a Hindu, let alone a 'true' Hindu. Is s/he one who believes in castes? But castes do not go back very far into the past, have varied over time, and do not in their current form conform to their scriptural idealization. What is more, almost all Hindus are deeply embarrassed by the practice of untouchability, a product of the caste system. One might say that a Hindu is one who subscribes to certain beliefs. But which ones? They vary with castes, sects and regions, and in any case a Hindu is free to choose whichever of them appeals to him or her.

Dayananda Saraswati tried to 'semitize' Hinduism, but could neither give the *Vedas* the status of the Bible, let alone the Qur'ān, nor distil basic Hindu beliefs. Later, V. D. Savarkar tried to define *Hindutva* – the essence of a Hindu – but came up with nothing more than that a Hindu was one who looked upon India as his or her *pitrubhumi* (fatherland) and *punyabhumi* (a sacred or holy land).[19] Savarkar had to admit that, on his definition, even the Indian Christians, Buddhists, Jains, Sikhs and Parsis qualified as Hindus! The Bharatiya Janata Party (BJP), widely referred to as a Hindu fundamentalist party, has run up against a similar difficulty. After several unsuccessful attempts, it concluded that a Hindu was one who had Hindu *bhāvanā* (a Hindu disposition or goodwill towards the Hindus) and Hindu *mānasikatā* (a Hindu attitude of mind or way of looking at the world). The BJP was unable to give any meaning to these nebulous concepts, and has virtually abandoned all attempts to define a Hindu. It is further constrained by India's secular tradition, which the Supreme Court guards most jealously, and democracy, which requires the BJP to court Muslim votes. Not surprisingly, it has some non-Hindus in its ranks and campaigned successfully for a Muslim President of India when it was in power.

The nearest Hindus have come to producing a fundamentalist movement is the *Rashtriya Sevak Sangh* (RSS). It is militant, advocates 'just violence' and even an 'epic war' against non-Hindus (mainly Muslims), and seeks to restore traditional Hindu values. When examined closely, its religious and ideological content is meagre. It has no coherent definition of a Hindu, and no clear idea as to which of the conflicting Hindu values to stress. It wants to revive some Hindu cultural practices but has no interest in Hindu religious beliefs, does not want a theocratic state, and is vague about the public role of religion. Some of its well-known spokesmen are avowed atheists and think little of their own or any other religion. Basically, the RSS is not a religious but a political and cultural movement driven by a rabid hostility to Muslims, and to a lesser extent Christians. Some of its leaders would no doubt like it to become a fundamentalist movement of the kind found in other religions, but feel frustrated by the plurality and heterogeneity of Hinduism, not to mention the constraints imposed by India's vibrant democracy.

If we examine other religions, such as Buddhism, Jainism, Judaism, and even Sikhism, we might find that while they can all be dogmatic, militant and murderous, fundamentalism as I have defined it is alien to them, and not a useful concept in understanding their pathology. They might mimic it, but they cannot usually sustain it. All religions are tempted to fill a political vacuum, and in doing so suffer profound distortion. Fundamentalism represents a distinct kind of distortion of the religious identity. Rather than expect all religions to throw up a fundamentalist movement, we should ask why some do so but others either do not or contain it with relative ease.

8

Challenges of the Multicultural World

Attitudes to cultural diversity within and between societies are closely related. Those who welcome the former generally tend to feel sympathetic to, or at least at ease with, the latter. Conversely, those who believe that cultural diversity is a source of social instability feel deeply worried about the multicultural world and think it inherently conflictual. Their response to it is twofold. Some believe that since all societies should, or are likely over time to, converge on a single culture under the impact of modernization, globalization and the spread of democratic ideas, we should ensure that this is not obstructed and, whenever possible, promoted by appropriate pressure. Others consider such convergence unlikely or undesirable, and argue that our concern should be to manage the inevitable conflicts as well as we can, and be militarily ready to deal with those that get out of control. Both views have their strong advocates, and draw their inspiration from the writings of Samuel Huntington. I shall begin by examining Huntington's basic thesis critically, and go on to argue that a dialogue between civilizations, conducted with an open mind and in full knowledge of its limits, is the only sensible way to deal with the multicultural world.

Clash of civilizations

In the 1990s, Samuel Huntington advanced the influential view that the end of the Cold War had inaugurated a new era dominated by a clash of cultures.[1] At the local level, cultural conflicts took the form of ethnic or tribal conflicts, and globally, which was his main concern, that of a clash of civilizations. He argued that while his thesis did not explain all conflicts, it did explain most of them, and offered a better way of understanding the contemporary world than did rival theses.

Huntington's thesis is articulated in terms of the following five propositions.[2] First, the quest for cultural identity is a central human concern. It involves asking who we are, where we belong and feel most at home, what we stand for, and how we should organize our individual and collective lives. To know who we are is not only to know who we are *not* but 'often' also who and what we are *against*. Human beings identify with those who share their cultural identity, and feel threatened by those who do not. 'Faith and family, blood and belief' are the things that matter most to people, and for which they are willing to lay down their lives.

Huntington thinks that while the concern to retain and affirm one's cultural identity is an integral part of human nature and arises in all societies, it has acquired greater significance and urgency in recent times. He does not explain why this is so, and how its current form differs from the earlier ones. Sometimes he attributes it to globalization, especially its tendency to destabilize societies and bring together different cultures. On other occasions, he attributes it to the decline of political ideologies brought about by the dissolution of the Soviet Union. In either case, he is convinced that the 'velvet curtain of culture has replaced the iron curtain of ideology', and that cultures are the 'flashpoints' of our times.

Second, Huntington argues that no society can be based on a political creed or political institutions alone. It needs a shared cultural basis, which gives it a sense of purpose and direction, shapes its institutions and gives them legitimacy and vitality. 'East Asian culture' is the 'cause' of both the economic success of East Asian societies and their failure to build up stable democratic institutions. And the Islamic culture explains 'in large part' the failure of Muslim societies to establish democratic systems of government. A society that lacks a homogeneous culture or disavows it in favour of some other, or a mixture of the two, is self-divided and can never be stable. It has no enduring identity, centre, guiding principles, or sense of direction. A multicultural society, a society of many cultures, is a contradiction in terms, a veritable nightmare. This is why, Huntington argues, the Soviet Union, Yugoslavia, Bosnia and other multicultural societies fell apart.

Third, although there are countless cultures and cultural groups in the world, Huntington thinks they can be grouped into six and 'possibly' seven civilizations on the basis of their shared values and world views.

These are Western, Islamic, Sinic, Japanese, Hindu, Latin-American and 'possibly' African. A civilization is 'the broadest cultural entity', the 'highest cultural grouping of a people', wider than tribes, ethnic groups and national societies, but short of the species.[3] To deny their existence is to deny the basic realities of human existence.[4] This is why modern nation states increasingly define their identity and interests in civilizational terms, making civilizations rather than nation states the basic players in world politics. Peoples and countries with similar cultures are coming together. Peoples and countries with different cultures are coming apart.[5]

As Huntington defines it, a civilization has an objective and a subjective dimension. The former includes language, history, religion, customs, and social structure and institutions, of which religion is the 'most important' and a 'central defining characteristic'.[6] Sometimes Huntington argues that religion has always been central to civilization; on other occasions he thinks that this is only true of the modern world in which religion is 'a central, perhaps the central force that motivates and mobilises people'.[7] The subjective dimension of civilization consists in the 'subjective self-identification of a people' – that is, whether they see themselves as belonging to and feel at home in it.[8] Huntington does not think that the two dimensions of a civilization might conflict, and that people might feel alienated from 'their' civilization and be sympathetic to some other.

Fourth, Western civilization, Huntington's primary concern, is deeply shaped by its Greco-Roman and Judeo-Christian heritage, and has a distinct identity reflected in its commitment to individualism, individual rights, liberty, equality, tolerance and the spirit of critical inquiry. These values have long been a part of and are unique to it. As he puts it in one of his characteristic gnomic utterances, the 'West was the West long before it was modern'.[9] Its leaders have a duty to safeguard its remarkable achievements against both internal and external threats. The former come primarily from the multiculturalists who challenge and undermine its cultural identity, and the latter from other civilizations, especially that of Islam, which has a long record of hostility towards Christianity, and whose leaders 'never have a good word to say' for it. While all Western societies have a duty to safeguard their civilization, the US has a special responsibility because of its unrivalled economic and military power. The West, Huntington argues, simply cannot survive as a distinct civilization without American resolve and leadership.[10]

The US can play its great historical role only if remains true to itself. It is fundamentally an Anglo-Protestant country, 'founded in large part for religious reasons' and committed to certain 'absolute standards'.[11] Its national identity, shaped by the beliefs and practices of its original English settlers, has remained constant throughout its history, and been the basis of its unity and vitality. Although the country has subsequently welcomed millions of immigrants from all over the world, it is not a land of immigrants, as is commonly argued, because they became assimilated into and never challenged or compromised its original or foundational identity. Since the 1970s, however, many of them have become culturally assertive, pressing for the recognition of their cultural identities and seeking to make the country multicultural. America must resist this trend. 'A multicultural America is impossible because a non-western America is not an America'.[12] Since it is increasingly in danger of forgetting its roots and its historical mission, Huntington argues that its self-renewal consists in 'restoring' the influence of religion.[13]

Fifth and finally, Huntington argues that, since every civilization has a distinct identity, none, including the Western, can claim universal validity. 'Western belief in the universality of western culture suffers three problems: it is false, it is immoral and it is dangerous', and an intervention in the affairs of other civilizations 'is probably the single most dangerous source of instability and potential global conflict'. Rather than seeking to shape other societies in its own image, the West should accept the fact of global diversity, minimize inter-civilizational conflicts, establish peaceful relations with others, and evolve a minimally acceptable body of international rules and laws. At the same time, it should do everything in its power to ensure the survival of its own civilization and safeguard its interests. While it is China that will be the next great power, at present it is Islam that is generating most conflicts.[14] Muslims consider Western civilization to be materialistic, corrupt and immoral, but also highly seductive, and they hate and fear it the most. Convinced of their cultural superiority and obsessed by the inferiority of their power, they are the most implacable enemy of the West. The West should contain or subdue them at all costs, strengthen international institutions that 'reflect and legitimate Western interests and values', understand other civilizations so that it can work with them, and ensure that the North Atlantic Treaty Organization (NATO), the central instrument of its defence, excludes those lacking 'cultural affinity' with it.

A critique

Huntington's thesis captures some aspects of the contemporary world and contains valuable insights, which is why it has proved to be influential. As he rightly argues, economic and political interests alone do not determine human behaviour. Cultural identity and belonging matter to people, especially in our unstable and globalizing world, and shape their self-understanding and responses to others. Cultural and civilizational conflicts, further, cannot be reduced to and explained in economic terms alone. The hostility of several Islamic groups towards Western civilization, for example, springs primarily from moral and religious concerns and is not always a conflict of economic interests. As Huntington again rightly argues, the views and values of a civilization cannot be universalized uncritically. Rather than moralize international relations and render the existing conflicts even more intractable, it is better to accept genuine differences and to evolve a framework of rules within which conflicts can be managed and some kind of global order maintained.

In spite of these and other insights, Huntington's thesis is deeply flawed. Cultural identity matters to people, but so do other things such as decent existence, justice, self-respect and the respect of others. People also fight and die for them, not just for their faith and family. This has been the case throughout history, and our age is no different. It is therefore wrong to single out cultural identity as the sole or even a central human concern, either in general or in modern times alone. Furthermore, culture does not exist in a vacuum. It is linked to economic, political and other institutions, and both shapes and is shaped by them. Cultural reductionism is just as misguided as economic reductionism. Huntington abstracts culture from wider human interests and social institutions, and is led to reify and treat it as if it followed an independent internal logic of its own. Since culture is a site where major social and economic conflicts are played out, no cultural conflicts are exclusively cultural, even as few social conflicts are without a cultural dimension. We fail to understand the nature and causes of cultural conflict if we concentrate on culture alone.

Since the culture of a society is interwoven with its economic, political and other institutions, its beliefs and practices favour some individuals and groups over others, and perform the crucial ideological function of holding the society together by legitimizing it in their eyes. While its beneficiaries generally welcome and are prepared to die for it, others chafe against its treatment of them, resist it in all-too-familiar ways, view its decline with indifference, and might even prefer to die fighting against it. 'Who we are' and 'what we stand for' receive overlapping but different answers from different groups. The orthodox Brahmins and the 'untouchables' in India define Hindu identity in different ways. The Nazis and the German Jews defined the German identity, and the southern slave owners and black people in the US defined their American identity quite differently. A culture's identity is never homogeneous, settled, or free from contestation.

The concept of civilization, central to Huntington's thesis, is just as problematic as that of culture. His distinction between culture and civilization is unclear. Although he says different things on different occasions, he seems to think that they are basically the same and only differ in the fact that a civilization is wider than and includes several cultures. This raises the question of what they must all share in order to belong to a common civilization. Despite considerable equivocation, his general view seems to be that cultures sharing a common religion constitute a common civilization, which is why he defines and classifies them in the way he does. This is odd, for he talks of a 'possible' African civilization without showing what single religion is common to all Africans, and whether those who converted to Islam or Christianity belong to a different civilization. His difficulty is further compounded by the fact that he nowhere defines religion, and uses the term indiscriminately. He says, for example, that Confucianism, a strange term that turns the loose body of teachings of a sage into a closed system, lies at the heart of the Sinic civilization. Confucianism is not a religion in the conventional theocentric sense of the term, was not understood as such by Confucius, and is not perceived in this way by many Chinese today.

Even if Huntington were to give a coherent account of religion, his theory would remain deeply flawed. Christianity has certainly played a crucial role in the formation of Western civilization, but then so has Greco-Roman thought. Since at least the early decades of the nineteenth century, secular culture too has become an important strand within it. For these and other reasons it cannot be called Christian without serious qualification. Furthermore, the process of secularization has taken different forms in different Western societies, struck deeper roots in some more than in others, and has appropriated and rejected different aspects of their Christian heritage. Christianity plays a less important role in European societies than it does in the US, and even in the former its nature and role vary from country to country. If religion is the basis of civilization, Western societies are too diverse to be subsumed under a single civilization.

One could go further and question the very idea of sharing a common religion. India and Nepal have been profoundly influenced by 'Hinduism', another strange term that turns a loose and disparate body of beliefs and practices into a closed doctrinal system and does not correspond to the self-understanding of 'its' followers. In India, the Hindu religion has undergone profound changes under the impact of Buddhism, Islam, Christianity, secular modernity and the unique historical experiences of the country, with the result that it shares little in common with its Nepalese counterpart save a few general beliefs and symbols. Again, Indonesia, Iran and Egypt are all Muslim societies in the sense that most of their populations define themselves as Muslims. However, they are culturally quite different, have had very different histories, and Islam, which is only one of their formative influences, has come to terms with their pre-Islamic heritage in quite different ways. Not surprisingly, they define Islam differently and give it different kinds and degrees of importance in their social and cultural life. In so far as their cultures are shaped by Islam, they show similarities, but in so far as their Islam is shaped by their different cultures and history, they display marked differences. To claim that they all belong to a common Islamic civilization is to give a misleading account of them.

Huntington stresses similarities between various cultures, and groups them under a common civilization. There is no reason to stop here. Like cultures, civilizations too are both different and similar. They represent different visions of human life, and organize it differently. They also, however, address common problems of human existence, are subject to common natural and social constraints, and reflect universally shared human capacities and emotions. They have also interacted over the centuries and borrowed each other's beliefs and practices. Globalization brings them still closer and facilitates cultural exchanges. Since civilizations are not self-contained and irreducible wholes, they share much in common and are best seen as partners in a global conversation.

Since Huntington's view of civilization is confused, his classification of it remains arbitrary. Since the 1700s, Western civilization has influenced all others so deeply that it has become a powerful presence in their lives, and is no longer confined to the West. India has many of the elements that Huntington associates with Western civilization, such as political democracy, the tradition of critical inquiry, individual choice, and a long exposure to modernity, yet Huntington thinks that it cannot be considered a Western civilization. He talks of a Latin American civilization, but does not show what is unique about it, and disregards its large

Western heritage, including Christianity. At one level, Russia has long been a part of Western civilization and shares its religion, but Huntington thinks otherwise. No single civilization unites the whole of Africa, with its religious, cultural, racial and ethnic diversity, yet Huntington thinks that it 'possibly' shares one. Rather than identify the constitutive features of different civilizations and show that they are really different, he takes the easy but mistaken step of dividing the world into several geographical areas and turning them into so many civilizational units.

Huntington sees civilizations as being internally unified, coherent and easily distinguishable wholes, and that is not true of any of them. The Japanese civilization has Shinto, Confucian and Buddhist components, which govern different areas of life and do not form a coherent whole. Hindu civilization includes monist, monotheist, pantheist, polytheist, agnostic and atheist strands of thought, which have often been at odds with each other. Latin-American societies are a product of native Indian, European, American and other influences, which each of them has absorbed quite differently, and lack a homogeneous civilization. The traditional Sinic civilization is a product of Buddhist, Confucian, Taoist and other currents of thought that have often fought bitter intellectual battles and do not give it a coherent identity. Indeed, in China, it is not uncommon to be simultaneously a Buddhist, a Confucian and a Taoist, such that one can enjoy nature in the morning as a Taoist, work hard during the day as a Confucian, and reflect on the vicissitudes of life in the evening as a Buddhist.

Western civilization, Huntington's main concern, and to which he thinks his thesis most clearly applies, is just as eclectic and heterogeneous. He takes the conventional view that it is a product of the Judeo-Christian and Greco-Roman traditions, and ignores the profound historical influence of Arab, Islamic, Chinese, Indian and other currents of thought. More importantly, he naïvely assumes that the former two traditions fit in nicely and form a coherent whole. They are in fact not two but four traditions of thought, and are quite different in their world views and values. Greek rationalism, views on human life, political values and aesthetics have only limited parallels in Roman culture, which itself underwent great changes during its long history. Both, again, pull in very different directions to Judaism, with its novel ideas of fideism, monotheism, law, God's relation to man, man's to nature, and the best form of life. While Christianity grew out of Judaism and initially remained close to it, it had from the third century CE onwards begun to develop quite different ideas on human nature, divinity, eschatology, salvation and the good life, partly because of its obsessive concern to break with its source and partly because of its openness to Greek philosophy and Roman political institutions. To talk of the Judeo-Christian tradition is to imply that these are continuous and basically say the same thing, and thus to omit their crucial differences; a somewhat similar message is conveyed by lumping together Greek and Roman world views and values. As several keen students of Western civilization have pointed out, it has never been possible to integrate its heterogeneous heritage, and the constant tension between its contradictory trends offers important clues to its strengths and limitations.

Its subsequent development also reflects diverse and sometimes incompatible influences. Following the dubious conventional view, Huntington identifies the Renaissance, the Reformation and the Enlightenment as three major stages in its development, and assumes that they form part of a harmonious and quasi-teleological sequence, with each stage consolidating and building on the earlier one. This is simply not true. The Renaissance was largely a movement *outside* Christianity and turned to Europe's pre-Christian roots for inspiration. The Reformation was a movement *within* Christianity and turned to its origins to redefine it and mount a powerful attack on what it took to be the misguided theology and the corrupt religious practices of the Catholic Church. The Enlightenment was primarily a reaction *against* Christianity and sought to articulate a secular view of the world. Not surprisingly, these three intellectual movements had quite different concerns that often brought them into conflict. The classical humanism of the Renaissance did not cut off humankind from the universe and take a hubristic view of humans in a way that the anthropocentric humanism of the Enlightenment did, and was acutely sensitive to human frailities. In contrast to both, Reformation humanism was theologically grounded and represented an uneasy blend of rationalism and fideism, and took a dualistic view of human nature. The three movements naturally entailed quite different views on human dignity, society, ideals of human excellence, the place of religion in political life, and the nature and purposes of the state. These differences are evident in the very different ways in which contemporary political ideologies, including liberalism, have been and continue to be defined.

Western civilization then does not have a singular identity. It is made up of different and conflicting strands of thought, and includes robust rationalism and a deep – and at times naïve – religiosity, acute sensitivity to human limitations and a Messianic belief in the possibility of creating a heaven on earth, moral universalism as well as relativism, egalitarian and hierarchical impulses, and authoritarian as well as liberal tendencies. It also includes a belief in human equality and brotherhood as well as a hegemonic and patronizing attitude to the rest of the world, a commitment to the sacredness of human life but also a wanton and instrumental disregard of it, individualism as well as collectivism. Sometimes one tendency gains ascendancy over the other; often, however, they limit and regulate each other, and ensure that the civilizational pendulum does not swing too far in either direction.

Since Huntington places religion at the heart of civilization, he praises and blames it for the latter's virtues and deficiencies. He traces the current malaise of Muslim societies to Islam, attributing to it a historically unchanging essence and ignoring the various economic, political, social and international factors that have brought about the malaise and encouraged a particular way of reading Islam. And he goes equally wrong in understanding the major sources of Western civilization, arguing inconsistently that it is a product of Greco-Roman and Judeo-Christian influences, but also that most of its central values are derived from Christianity. As we saw earlier, the former is largely true, but it does not give Western civilization a singular identity. As for the latter, it is at best a half truth. Christianity has influenced the West deeply but in many cases only after it had been reinterpreted and reformed and new values had been read into it.

The ideas of social equality, tolerance, critical rationality and democracy are central to contemporary Western self-understanding, but none of them can be traced directly to Christianity. Christianity regards every human being as sacred and inviolable, and has an egalitarian potential, but this spiritual equality does not imply and did not for centuries translate into social and political equality. It excluded, persecuted and humiliated the Jews; early Fathers justified slavery; and the Catholic Church justified serfdom and did not condemn chattel slavery until the eighteenth century. Tolerance is not central to Christianity, as the history of early Christianity, the Crusades, the Spanish Inquisition and the religious wars of the sixteenth and seventeenth centuries show. Even theologically, Christianity has had considerable difficulty giving a coherent account of and finding a secure place for toleration in its moral and political theory. When Christian thinkers came to appreciate its value, they largely limited it to dissenting movements within Christianity and did not extend it to atheists or even to other religions, a matter they did not address adequately until the Second Vatican Council, and have not fully resolved even now.

Although freedom of conscience can be read into Christianity, it was rejected by the Catholic Church for centuries on the grounds that it was the custodian of individual conscience and that error and misguided conscience had no rights. Democracy is not Christian in its origin, for the belief in popular sovereignty sits uncomfortably with the ideas of revealed truth and Biblical inerrancy, and was long opposed by Catholics and Protestants alike on religious grounds. Freedom of inquiry is not Christian either. It is incompatible with its claim to represent the final truth and was not evident in its treatment of heretics, Galileo, Bruno and many others. Active and participatory citizenship too is not Christian in origin, and was often viewed as a moral distraction by Saints Augustine, Ambrose, Thomas Aquinas and many other eminent theologians. Since most of these ideas are largely modern, we may stand Huntington on his head and say that the West became West *only after* it became modern.

As I have argued, all civilizations are products of diverse influences and contain different and sometimes contradictory currents of thought. It is therefore hardly surprising that many strands of thought in one civilization have their counterparts in another. The Indian, Islamic and Sinic civilizations have rationalist, liberal, radical, religious and anti-modern strands of thought, just as the Western civilization has, and these are in constant tension. Islam's current fundamentalist tendency, for example, clashes not only with Western liberalism, but also with its own liberal tradition, and finds its echo in the Christian fundamentalism of the West. This means that civilizations do not clash, only their opposite strands or interpretations do. And the clash is as much within civilizations as between them. It is therefore deeply misleading to talk of an inherent clash between Islam and the West. The two civilizations have common roots and share far more than the ideologues of either appreciate.

Huntington's idea of a clash of civilizations is methodologically flawed because it reduces them to one of their many strands of thought. It is also biased ideologically, because he chooses the worst strand in other civilizations and the best in his own. For him, Islam is all about fundamentalism, and Western civilization is all about liberalism, and the two are radically different. Huntington complains that Muslims have nothing good to say about the West. This is true of the militants, but not of many others who have long admired and continue to copy much that is valuable in the West. And he ignores the fact that Christian fundamentalists and even others including himself do not have anything good to say about the Islamic civilization either. This methodological and ideological bias prevents him from appreciating the virtues of other civilizations and the limitations of his own. It is striking and a measure of his civilizational narcissism that he rarely looks at the all too obvious darker side of Western civilization and history, and asks how it might benefit from a creative and critical engagement with others.

The fact that civilizations might represent different, and even incompatible, world views and values does not of itself lead to a clash. They can live side by side in a spirit of indifference or mutual respect, as almost all of Huntington's civilizations save the Western and the Islamic have generally done for centuries. Civilizations clash when one of them is intolerant, messianic, missionary, unwilling to let others live in what it takes to be ignorance and darkness, or for economic and political reasons that are then articulated and justified in civilizational terms, or both. So far as the current conflict between Muslim and Western societies is concerned, it has complex roots. Some groups of Islamic militants are at war with the West because they either wish to restore the earlier era of Islamic supremacy or resent modernity, of which they take the West to be the source and champion. Their conflict is primarily, though not exclusively, civilizational and broadly supports Huntington's thesis. Millions of ordinary Muslims, and even some of their militants, however, are motivated differently. As we shall see later, they are driven by anger at the way Western powers, especially the US, have for decades interfered in their internal affairs, propped up and even installed corrupt regimes, played off one of them against another, encouraged wars between them and mounted ones of their own, subverted progressive movements, humiliated them, and in general used them to serve Western economic and geopolitical interests. Their conflict with the West is basically politico-economic in nature. Although their spokespersons sometimes articulate it in civilizational terms, there is no reason to be fooled by their rhetoric.

Like cultures and civilizations, societies also are plural, particularly the modern liberal society with its emphasis on individual choice, and openness to outside influences. The American culture, on which Huntington concentrates and to which he mistakenly attributes a homogeneous identity, is a good example of this. Its Constitution, the basis of its historical continuity, has provided a capacious framework within which cultural plurality has flourished. This plurality has in turn shaped its interpretation, so that while the Constitution has formally remained the same, its meaning and implications have changed substantially over the years. Huntington argues that America's foundational or core identity is Anglo-Protestant. This renders native Americans invisible, and ignores the ways in which their brutal treatment remains the dark underside of the country's history. It also ignores other groups of early settlers and the millions of immigrants who followed them. African slaves brought with them their native cultures, suitably reconstructed them in the light of their American experiences, and gave the wider culture a distinct orientation of which the current multiculturalism is just one expression. The Irish and later the Jews and others did the same. American capitalism too has generated powerful cultural forces, and added new elements to the country's constantly evolving national identity.

Thanks to the increasing pluralization of American society, it today includes such diverse groups as the uncompromising secularists and the naïve creationists; the moderate Christians perfectly at ease with their society, and the fire-breathing Evangelicals at war with it; the ecologically sensitive Green movements and the corporate capitalists bent on exploiting nature; the libertarians and the social conservatives; and the modernists, the native Americans and the Amish. These groups represent different world views and values, and share only a limited consensus on what their society stands for and should stand for. The Founding Fathers of the republic would find parts of the contemporary American culture incomprehensible, deeply disagreeable, or even perhaps a betrayal of some of their ideals and hopes for the country. The Anglo-Protestant heritage, which Huntington wants to hold on to at all cost, is still there, but as just one, albeit quite powerful, current of thought among several.[15]

Given America's cultural diversity, any attempt to homogenize it on the basis of a nostalgic return to the past is as misguided as the Islamic militants' wish to return to the days of Prophet Mohammad. It also undermines Huntington's view that America should be the custodian of Western civilization. The latter includes countries that are neither Anglo nor Protestant, and America cannot presume to speak for them if its identity is defined solely in Anglo-Protestant terms. Indeed, since Western civilization is internally diverse, the claim by any Western society to be its guardian or even a spokesperson is hubristic and illegitimate. The fact that America has enormous economic and military power is not only irrelevant but even perhaps counts against it. It violates some of the great Christian values, such as the disapproval of wealth and money-making activities, contempt for greed and consumerism, non-violence and universal brotherwood, and *limits* America's claim to speak for Western civilization. At best, it can speak not for Western civilization as a whole but only for those of its values it cherishes and lives by.

Huntington's plea for a culturally homogeneous society is also ill at ease with his multicultural view of the world. As he rightly argues, cultural diversity is a constitutive feature of the contemporary world. America, and for that matter any other Western or non-Western society can cope with it only if it is used to living with its own internal diversity. It does not then feel threatened by the diversity of views and values prevailing in the world at large, and is likely to develop the skills and sensitivity needed to manage its relations with the world. A society obsessed with cultural homogeneity is bound to feel disorientated in the presence of diversity, and would want either to isolate itself from the world or, if it has the power, to eliminate diversity by shaping the world in its own image. America has oscillated between both views because, among other things, many of its citizens, especially the conservatives, have not come to terms with and grasped the implications of their multicultural society. As I show in the following chapter, far from being the cause of its weakness, America's multicultural society is a great source of its strength and vitality.

The case for dialogue

As different cultural communities come together in our globalizing world, possibilities of both co-operation and conflict increase. If we are to build on the former and minimize the latter, we should create the conditions for a patient and sympathetic dialogue. The dialogue, which I define widely to mean not only talking and persuading but also negotiating and reaching a compromise, has a dual focus: to foster better understanding by helping each participant to see the world from the other's perspective; and to address sympathetically the deeper political, economic and other causes of conflict. I shall take as an example the conflict that lies at the heart of Huntington's thought and finds its expression in the terrorist attacks in New York and Washington in September 2001. They show the extent and depth of hostility that al-Qaeda, other related Muslim organizations, and large groups of Muslims the world over feel towards the US. We might respond to them in two different ways.

First, we might argue that their perpetrators are callous and inhuman monsters driven by a blind hatred of the West, and in particular the US. Since they are non-state agents, they are, strictly speaking, not *at war* with it, but they are certainly *in a state of war* with it. The US and the West in general have a duty to defend themselves and do everything in their power to put these agents out of action. There is no reasoning with them because they are not rational beings but rather nihilists driven by irrational hatred. The only language they understand is that of force. They claim in self-justification that they have grievances against the West, which their peaceful appeals have failed to redress. This is a specious argument. It turns every act of injustice into a licence for terrorism, which is a recipe for chaos. What is more, the terrorists' long list of injustices is largely suspect, as these so-called injustices are the results of their own badly-managed societies and cannot be blamed on the West. And even if the West was to bear responsibility for some of these, tackling or even discussing them now would be taken widely to legitimize terror.

Second, it might be argued that, while terrorist acts against the West deserve to be punished or pre-empted, their context and causes should also be looked at. They do not occur in a historical and moral vacuum, and in fact began to be mounted only since the 1970s. Their agents are human beings like the rest of us, a mixture of good and evil, and do not enjoy throwing away their lives, turning their wives into widows and children into orphans. They risk their lives in terrorist acts because they feel humiliated, manipulated, trampled on, treated unjustly, have exhausted all peaceful means, lost their patience and see no other way of redressing their grievances. Rather than concentrate only on their reprehensible deeds, Western societies should engage in a dialogue with them, understand their grievances, see if these are genuine, ask themselves whether they bear any responsibility for these, mend their ways when they think they do bear responsibility and, when they do not, persuade them why they are wrong to vent their anger upon the West. They may not wish to enter into a dialogue with the West, but there is no reason why it should not reach out to them. Although they will not meet face-to-face, they care deeply about what the West thinks of them, partly because they are worried about the likely impact of its views on their supporters, and partly because they are anxious to distinguish between themselves and ordinary criminals. This is why they issue statements stating their demands and justifying their actions. They are recruited from and cannot function effectively without the active or passive support of the majority of the disaffected groups. The West's goal should be to win over both these groups by addressing their concerns and drawing them into a dialogue.

For a time, the initial US response seemed to be of the second type. While condemning the attacks and vowing to bring their perpetrators to justice, US spokespersons seemed to appreciate the need to address the attacks' deeper causes. Increasingly, however, the US began to veer towards the first response and is now firmly committed to this. Several factors seem to have played a part in this change, such as the relative ease with which the Taliban government was removed, the Israeli government's intransigence, domestic electoral considerations, the temptation to settle old scores with Iran, Iraq, North Korea and other states, the excitement of flexing the military muscle, and the heightened sense of existence offered by the incredible upsurge in American patriotism and sense of national solidarity.

Whatever the explanation, hunting down and eliminating potential terrorists and deterring others has now become the sole objective of the US. Prisoners taken in Afghanistan are not only treated harshly but systematically humiliated, over a thousand foreign nationals have been arrested with little explanation, and normal legal processes have been suspended in favour of military tribunals with the power to punish suspects on the basis of evidence that is neither disclosed to them nor subject to their challenge. Every country that is suspected of supporting potential terrorists is declared a legitimate military and economic target and threatened with dire consequences. The world is divided into friends and foes. The latter – the 'axis of evil' – are put under intense pressure and subjected to all kinds of harassment and sanctions. The former are asked to endorse all American actions, and even muted criticisms are seen as acts of disloyalty. The US is the sole judge of who is or is not a potential terrorist, and the sole executioner of its verdict. It is convinced that its sole aim must be to create a 'psychology of fear' and 'command respect for its power'.

This response is deeply flawed. It dismisses our fellow human beings as inhuman monsters, and makes no attempt to understand them and their actions. Since it dehumanizes them, it so blunts our moral sensibility that killing anyone even remotely suspected of sympathy to radical causes is considered to be legitimate. Indeed, governments in the Middle East and many other parts of the world proudly proclaim the numbers of 'terrorists' they kill every day, and expect to be, and generally are, rewarded by the US government and applauded by much of the Western media. A 'war on terror' fought in this way increasingly takes on a terrorist character and brutalizes all involved. Anti-terrorist terrorism has different and in some respects better goals, but its ethos, methods and language are no different from those of its enemy.

Not surprisingly the US government's rhetoric and behaviour display a remarkable resemblance to those of the terrorists. The latter call the US an evil civilization; the US returns the compliment. The terrorists say they are fighting for 'eternal moral verities'; the US says it is fighting for values that are 'right and unchanging for all people everywhere'. The terrorists say that every state working in league with the United States is a legitimate target; the US says the same about them. Terrorists refuse to draw a distinction between civilians and combatants; the US claims to draw one but does not feel too worried if it is ignored in practice. Terrorists aim to create global fear by demonstrating that even the centres of American financial and military power are not beyond their reach; the US aims to do the same. Both claim divine blessings for their respective projects; both talk of a clash of civilizations, a long and bitter war, and a fight to the finish; both are driven by rage and hatred, and claim absolute superiority for their cause. In these and other ways, the US ultimately becomes the mirror image of its enemy and profoundly corrupts its way of life. It cuts legal and political corners, curtails the liberties of its citizens, gives the executive excessive discretionary powers, authorizes intelligence agencies to transgress international norms and even to terrorize sections of its own citizens, releases danger-ous passions, militarizes the psyche of its people, and encourages a dangerously simplistic and Manichean view of the world.

When people are embittered, brutalized and prepared to throw away their lives, nothing the US does can terrorize and deter them. Indeed, it only confirms their poor opinion of it and hardens their resolve. There is a limit to what the US can do to intimidate and terrorize potential terror-ists and, once these options are exhausted, the country is left without resources. But in contrast, terrorist methods are limitless. When hijack-ing planes or kidnapping soldiers becomes difficult, planting bombs takes its place. When that is stopped, suicide bombing becomes common, extending to women and before long to children. And if that becomes impossible, biological warfare and hitherto unimagined forms of terror will appear on the horizon. Terrorist groups are mobile and shift their bases from one country to another. The US gets dragged into wars on many fronts and makes enemies everywhere, precisely what the terrorists want and what the US needs to avoid.

It took fewer than twenty determined individuals to cause massive havoc in New York and Washington. It is inconceivable that millions of sulking and disaffected people from whose ranks they came cannot continue to produce similar numbers in future. Terrorists require not only finances, training and so on, but also a supportive or acquiescent body of people, a justifying ideology, and widely perceived grievances around which to mobilize support. Dismantling their networks is never enough; their grievances must also be redressed. Muslims, numbering 1.3 billion and forming a majority in fifty-five states, are likely to make up about a quarter of the world population by 2024. If the West is not most careful, the current state of hostility might easily encourage a new hot and cold war that would be vastly different from the Second World War and the subsequent Cold War, to both of which it is often compared. The number of states involved would be larger, and so too the number of people. The issues at stake would be neither narrowly political nor as clear cut as in the other two wars. The West's vital interests would be involved, which was not the case previously, the new terrorist methods and forms of organization have no historical precedent, and the criteria for deciding who could be said to have won or lost are nebulous.

Potential terrorists and their sponsors or supporters must obviously be deterred by all legitimate means, including through carefully gathered intelligence, financial pressure, domestic vigilance and, when necessary, the judicious use of force. At the same time, the West must also address the deeper roots of terrorism that drive ordinary men and women to build up enormous rage and hatred, making them so desperate that they throw away their lives and overcome the normal inhibitions against killing innocent people. Some might be nihilists, or in the grip of a fanatical religious or secular ideology, or content with nothing short of global domination. They must be isolated and fought. They are, however, in a tiny minority, at least at present, and largely feed on the prevailing sense of injustice. We must therefore assure the large majority that their injustices worry us as much as they worry them, that they can count on us to redress them, that they do not need to give up on dialogue, and that we are all partners in a common cause. International terrorism is not caused by poverty and global inequality. The poor and the oppressed know that their enemies are located within their own countries. And while Western prosperity attracts them, they do not resent or hate it, as is often argued. They obviously wish, as does any morally sensitive person, that the West would use its resources and influence to eliminate global poverty in its own long-term interest as well as for humanitarian reasons, but in general they do not go and bomb

Western cities. The West arouses their anger and hatred only when, in their view, it bears at least some responsibility for their predicament by such means as propping up corrupt and despotic regimes, thwarting their economic development, controlling their resources and inflicting injustice and humiliation on them.

This calls for a dialogue between Muslim societies and the West, especially the US. The point of the dialogue is to deepen mutual understanding, expand sympathy and imagination, exchange not only arguments but also sensibilities, to get both parties to take a critical look at themselves, build up mutual trust, and to arrive at a more just and balanced view of both the contentious issues and their wider context. It must be robust, frank and critical, telling the truth as each party sees it, but always in the knowledge that it cannot be allowed to fail, because the only alternative to it is the vicious cycle of hatred and violence. The dialogue is at various levels. It is obviously about substantive economic, political and other issues, the immediate causes of conflict. All such issues have historical roots. The dialogue therefore has a historical dimension, and involves exchange of memories and a better understanding of the past. Since human beings define their interests, identities and relations with others from within their culture, it also has a strong cultural component and calls for a deeper understanding of each side's world views and values. The parties to the dialogue do not enter into it with a blank mind. As a result of their past and present experiences, they form a certain view of each other which, though not always fully articulated, shapes the assumptions, attitudes and suspicions they bring to the dialogue and acts as a background against which they interpret each other's actions. Each side needs to articulate and understand this framework if it is to grasp the dynamics of the dialogue.

Muslim societies are not homogeneous, and nor is the West or the US. The conservative Saudi or Kuwaiti royal families and their hangers-on do not see the US in the same way as their subjects and their counterparts in other Muslim societies do. This is also the case in the US, in which the neo-con view is rejected by many on the liberal and radical left. In each of them, however, there is a broadly shared perspective that cuts across the political divide and from within which many ordinary men and women view the other side. Not all members of society share it in all its details, but most feel sympathetic to it in different degrees, giving it a considerable salience in the way they tend to understand and respond to the other's utterances and actions. In order to get to the heart of these two perspectives, I shall ignore their nuances and differences of detail and state them in their raw simplicity. Below are the broad sketches of what they think of and would want to say to each other in a frank dialogue, starting with the Muslim perspective:[16]

You, the United States of America, are driven by an overweening ambition to dominate the world. Since you enjoy military superiority over the rest of the world put together, a situation without parallel in human history, you are determined to use it to turn other societies into pliant instruments of your will. You have repeatedly used vulnerable states to serve your interests and left them in a mess when they outlived their value. Despite all your talk of human rights and democracy, whenever progressive forces emerged in many parts of the world, you subverted them. You toppled Mosaddeq in Iran, Lumumba in the Congo and Allende in Chile, trained and helped terrorists in Guatemala, Nicaragua, Angola and Argentina, connived at the mass murders instituted by Samuel Doe, Presidents Suharto of Indonesia and Pinochet of Chile, and invaded Grenada. You were so determined to avenge your defeat in Vietnam and destabilize the Soviet Union that you stoked powerful religious passions in Afghanistan, and armed and trained Mujahideen and Islamic terrorists in utter disregard of all moral considerations and without any thought for the long-term danger this posed to Afghanistan and Pakistan. To contain Iran, you armed Iraq and encouraged, or at least did nothing to stop, a most brutal war between the two. And when the latter thought it could count on your support and punish Kuwait for helping itself to Iraqi oil during its war with Iran, you sent mixed messages. When it foolishly invaded Kuwait, you hit hard, imposed impossible conditions on it, and continued with a regime of punitive sanctions that killed hundreds of thousands of innocent children. Not content with that, you lied, cheated, blackmailed other countries, launched a wholly unnecessary second war on Iraq without any preparation or even thought for its aftermath, and unleashed dark forces against which many with some knowledge of the area had repeatedly warned you. The horrendous results of your action – daily atrocities, the collapse of trust and normal relations between its various communities, the civil war, terror by militias, plunder of the country's resources by your multinationals and contractors – indeed, a virtual Hobbesian state of nature – shame and condemn you.

You are grossly biased in your response to the Israel–Palestine conflict, demanding impossible concessions from the Palestinians, constantly shifting your goalposts and endorsing every act of Israeli belligerence. You shed crocodile tears over Palestinian suffering, but do all in your power to perpetuate it in the hope that they would become so demoralized and fractious that they would stop fighting for their rights. You have no regard for the Israeli Arabs either. They form nearly a fifth of its population, but are ghettoized, suppressed, watched closely, denied jobs in key sectors of the economy, and are nowhere to be seen in Israeli public life – not as ministers, ambassadors, vice-chancellors, senior civil servants, or heads of public corporations. Compare this to your own African-Americans, who only constitute just over a tenth of your population but are increasingly occupying the highest positions of power. Israeli Arabs do have a vote and a small representation in the Knesset, but beyond that its much vaunted democracy that you constantly hold up as a shining example is a sham for them.

You are Israel's staunchest ally, but hardly its true friend. You should know that Israel is a small country, that the Arabs will one day become strong and prosperous, and that they would then seek to avenge the humiliations and injustices the Israeli governments continue to heap on them. They might acquire nuclear or other destructive weapons. And even if they do not, they have the power of numbers before which the Israeli arsenal is ultimately of no avail. Israel has no choice but to continue to depend on your contingent goodwill, militarize its way of life, and bear an enormous economic burden. If you were its true friend, you would in its own long-term interest tell it a few home truths. You would not, partly because of the pressure of the misguided Israeli lobby and partly because you want to tie that country to your apron strings, make it do your dirty work in that region, and use its quarrels with its neighbours to sell them arms, control their oil and other resources, and increase their dependence on you.

You are convinced that you represent 'the city on the hill', and that you have a God-given right to shape the rest of the world in your image. You are determined to turn the world into a consumerist paradise, inhabited by self-absorbed and self-satisfied people who like Coca-Cola and hamburgers, Hollywood movies, freedom to do as their fancy dictates, and are guided by no higher moral and spiritual goals. You do not understand that the good life can be lived in several different ways, and that yours leaves much to be desired. It has its obvious merits, such as material prosperity, efficiency, public sprit, enormous self-confidence and national unity, but it also has its deep pathology. It breeds aggression, self-centredness, a corporate stranglehold over the political process, a cynical manipulation of public opinion, a regime of lies and deceit, an absence of mutual concern, blindness to the limitations of the human will, a callous disregard and even a contempt for the poor. While other societies have much to learn from you, you too can learn much from them. Rather than respect their differences, you aggressively universalize your way of life, push for globalization, deregulation, the opening up of domestic markets, the dismantling of the public sector and structural adjustment programmes, so that your poorly regulated multinationals can have a free run of the whole world. When your direct pressure does not work, you use the International

Monetary Fund (IMF) and the World Bank to achieve this goal, as if these international agencies were nothing more than branches of your own Treasury.

While exhorting the rest of the world to respect international law and treaties, you flout them at will. You disregarded the verdict of the International Court of Justice when it condemned your invasion of Nicaragua. You refused to ratify the Kyoto Treaty on climate change, the International Criminal Court, and the ban on anti-personnel landmines and biological weapons, and for years you stayed out of the UNESCO and refused to pay your dues to the United Nations because it refused to dance to your tune. You unilaterally decided to break the Anti-Ballistic Missile Treaty with Russia, you walked out of the Durban Conference on racism when its agreed protocol did not go your way, and so humiliated and manoeuvred Russia that it is now embracing xenophobic nationalism. You are becoming a moral free-rider, benefiting from others' willingness to discharge their share of the collective burden but refusing to discharge yours when it damages your short term interest. Your enormous power has made you a world leader and you have the potential to be a great force for good. Instead, you are behaving like an arrogant bully who would only relate to the world on his/her own terms.

You display a powerful Manichean thrust. The world for you is made up of 'goodies' and 'baddies'. In your eyes, you and those who go along with you represent the former; and the rest are evil and must be defeated. You define your identity in terms of a real or imaginary hostile other, are look-ing constantly for enemies, and are at peace with yourself only when you are at war with others. For forty years, you fought the Cold War and caused much havoc. When that ended, you found a new enemy in the shape of Islamic fundamentalism. You have now found, or rather created, another in Islamic terrorism, and your war with it will, in your own words, keep you busy for a long time. It boosts your arms industry, helps your construction industry, hogs lucrative contracts in the countries you invade, and gives you the opportunity to settle old scores with some others. A cynic might think that you needed Osama bin Laden's blood-curdling rhetoric to give your collective life moral meaning and purpose. It is about time you asked yourself why your civilization has become so war-dependent and mili-tarist, and why you scare the rest of the world, including your friends.

We Muslims have remained backward, divided and confused, and that has spawned fundamentalism, and even terrorism. The blame for that lies fairly and squarely at the door of the colonial powers, and more recently at yours. You support despotic and feudal regimes in Muslim societies, and actively help them or at least acquiesce when they crush democratic move-ments. Can you think of occasions when you sincerely and actively supported the latter? Divided, ill-governed, humiliated and oppressed

Muslim masses turn to their religion to generate a sense of community, mobilize their moral resources, fight corruption, to forge unity with other Muslim societies, to regain a sense of pride, and to live out their vision of a good society. You feel frightened because Islam does not fit into your secular world view, rejects some of your rules of the game, and mobilizes Muslim masses around causes that threaten your interests. You increase your support for oppressive forces, and further alienate and embitter our masses. They are not by nature or habit anti-Western or anti-American, but are made so by your actions. They are drawn to militant Islamists because the latter play up anti-American sentiments and promise to stand up to you. Terrorism is the only form of power available to the weak, the only means of asserting their pride and drawing attention to their anger and injustice.

You are wrong to think that Muslim masses are 'jealous' of your way of life or 'resent' your prosperity and power. Since they have no wish to follow your way of life, they cannot be jealous of it. And they do not want your power and wealth either, because their goals and ideals are different. All they want is to get you off their backs so they can freely rebuild their way of life. Millions of Muslims strongly disapprove of the terrorist attacks on you, for these go against the basic principles of Islam, give it a bad name, endanger the lives of Muslims in the West, and invite reprisals. However, they understand the anger and frustration that inspired these deeds, appreciate the sacrifices and altruism of their perpetrators, and cannot honestly condemn them without qualification. They are keen to help you to put an end to such acts if only you would agree to mend your ways, and join them in exploring how best to create a just world order.

I have briefly sketched the framework within which a large majority of Muslims, and not only they, perceive the US. The following statement represents the way in which many in the US see Muslim societies:

You, Muslims, misleadingly claim that yours is a religion of peace. Islam is an absolutist religion claiming superiority over all others and driven by the hegemonic ambition to convert the world. It insists that the Qur'ān is the sole authentic and exhaustive revelation of God, and that Mohammed is the last of the prophets (*khatem al-nabiyyin*). It pours scorn on the so-called idolatrous religions, including Hinduism, which it has despised for centuries, and on such others as Confucianism, which in its view are not religions at all. It does, of course, show respect for Judaism and Christianity, but only as primitive first drafts of Islam. This is why Islam extends its proselytizing activities to their followers, never grants them full equality, and harasses them in counties where it is in power. It is true that Islam is currently engaged in a dialogue with these religions. However, one should not read too much into this. The initiative for the dialogue has come not from Islam but from them, it is confined to a few intellectuals, and is not allowed to challenge Islam's belief in its absolute superiority. Islam has welcomed it only in order to present itself as a religion of peace, neutralize these two powerful religions, and enjoy the freedom to carry on its proselytizing activities.

You are not content to assert the absolute superiority of your religion. You are also driven by a hegemonic political ambition. You constantly hark back to your 'glorious' period of military and political expansion, celebrate without embarrassment your *futuhat* or initial *jihadi* wars, your rule over large parts of Europe, Asia and Africa, and the Ottoman empire. You resent Europe for defeating and marginalizing you, wish for *inqilab al-mawazim* (historical reversal of circumstances), and now want to replace us as a global power. This is why you want to unite the *umma* (the global muslim community), and acquire sophisticated nuclear and other destructive weapons. You have imperialist designs, and your attack on misleadingly called Western imperialism is not born out of a sincere desire to get rid of all imperialism but is part of a larger strategy to replace it with your own.

You talk of your great civilization and its superiority to ours. Nothing can be further from the truth. All your great achievements belong to the distant past. For the past few centuries you have been intellectual parasites, depending on the West for all your scientific, medical and technological knowledge. No Muslim society today has much to be said for it. All are corrupt, autocratic, degenerate, materialist, violent, and oppressive of their minorities, women and dissident sects. You claim that this is because they are not truly Islamic and have bartered away the true principles of Islam for the consumerist idolatry of the secular West. This is nonsense. No two Muslims are agreed on what a truly Islamic society is like. For some, only the *umma* can be the legitimate unit of governance; others justify the existing nation states. For some, Islam requires communal ownership of property; others disagree. For some, it requires rule by the *mullah*; for others, it calls for a moderately secular state. Indeed, since the general and vague statements of the Qur'ān can be interpreted in different ways, the very idea of a truly Islamic society is absurd. Whenever such a society has come into existence, it has turned out to be much worse than others. The Taliban regime was endorsed by many a fundamentalist Muslim, including bin Laden. The regime was most oppressive and brutal, raping women whose chastity it claimed to be safeguarding, persecuting Shi'as, grossly abusing political power, plundering public property, harassing followers of other religions, and destroying rare Buddhist statues. The Saudis have run their country like a private fiefdom, and some of them travel abroad to indulge some of the vices their religion condemns and which they punish with death at home. Their piety is a sham, which they seek to redeem by giving huge sums for building grandiose mosques and spreading the *wahabi* ideas. They fool nobody. We shall use them when our interests so require, but we have no respect for them whatever. They waste billions of dollars on buying gadgets they do not even know how to use, and which are meant not for use against the infidels but against other Muslims – the very *umma* they so idealize. The Iranian revolution promised a new beginning, but it has now degenerated into a crude and unstable theocracy mortally afraid of its people and resorting to terror and bloodshed to keep itself in power.

You blame the West for your current predicament. You could not be more mistaken. Many non-Muslim societies have had no difficulty in developing themselves. There is no reason why you should have lagged so far behind. Many of you sit on vast natural resources, and could have used these to modernize yourselves as well as your poorer cousins in the *umma*. We did support some of your despotic rulers. But all states, including Muslim ones, pursue their interests, lean on pliant rulers ready to sell out their country to line their pockets, and it is wrong to expect the West to be altruistic. It was, and is, open to your leaders to organize your masses around a progressive agenda. You either did not do so or did it in a manner that failed to resonate with popular aspirations. It is utterly irresponsible of you to blame us for not fighting your battles for you and not giving you stable and responsible regimes on a platter. Your backwardness is *your* responsibility and you should stop venting your frustrations on the West. It is about time you thought and behaved as adults taking charge of your destiny, rather than as children passively praying for the West to sort out your problems for you.

Many of you approve of and even admire terrorism, and the greater the loss of innocent lives, the greater is your sense of triumph. The more sensible among you condemn it and blame its perpetrators for hijacking your religion. This is intellectual and political cowardice. You do not explain why your religion is hijacked in this way, why there is no resistance, why this has happened in some but not other Muslim countries, and why a powerful alternative view of Islam is not developed and canvassed by your leaders. The responsibility for the corruption and misuse of your religion lies wholly on the shoulders of your political, religious and intellectual leaders. They need to take a critical look at it, ask what tendencies within it are susceptible to fundamentalist and terrorist interpretations, and these need to be fought or reinterpreted. They must also explore how Islam can come to terms with modernity, including modern science, liberal and democratic values, the spirit of critical inquiry, and independent thought. These and other ideas are an inescapable part of the Western way of life; we in the West are proud of them and determined to defend them at all costs. Contrary to what your conservative leaders say about the vices of *gharbzadegi* (westoxification) and the dangers of *hulul mustawradah* (imported solutions), millions of Muslims, when given a choice, opt for many a Western value and practice, such as the freedom to challenge orthodoxy, choose a career, run their lives themselves, to protest against oppression and injustices, to enjoy the normal pleasures of life, read Western literature, and, yes, to watch Western movies, including pornographic ones. The Western way of life has its limitations, some serious, and we are willing to learn from you but only if you can offer worthwhile ideas. You cannot do so as long as you refuse to put your house in order and come to terms with modernity.

You talk of Israel. Its democracy is not perfect, but then no democracy is. It is surrounded by hostile neighbours, who have done everything they can to intensify its sense of insecurity. Many Palestinians are still not reconciled to its existence and talk of its obliteration. Given all this, its treatment of the Arab minority, though not exemplary, is generous and better than that of the Jewish minorities in Muslim countries. Israel does have its share of fanatics, but it also has a strong peace movement. Most of its people would like the Palestinians to have a state of their own, if only they were to accept its existence and agree to live as good neighbours. The Oslo Accord offered a chance, but their confused and divided leadership threw it away. Many Israelis are tired of living under constant threat and well know the dangers of militarization and the huge economic cost their small economy has to bear. It is in your interest as much as theirs to build on this by suitable gestures of goodwill.

I have sketched above the broad outlines of the widely shared frameworks within which many in these two societies perceive each other. The views I have attributed to them are based on the public and private utterances of their spokespersons, and are inevitably partisan, polemical, hurtful and sometimes deeply offensive. Some of the points made by each against the other are based on ignorance and wilful or honest misunderstanding, while others contain different degrees of truth. If the dialogue is to succeed, each needs to listen to the other, reflect seriously on its criticisms, and take a fresh look at itself. When that happens and the intellectual frameworks of both undergo appropriate changes, there is at least a partial convergence of horizons. Each now carries bits of the other within itself and is able to conduct a critical dialogue with itself, a necessary condition of a meaningful dialogue with the other.

Self-criticism and a better and sympathetic understanding of the other are crucial if the dialogue is to get off the ground. In their own different ways, mutual ignorance and self-righteousness lead to closed minds and rule out any kind of meaningful communication. Against the background of the willingness to reconsider one's views and accommodate the legitimate claims of the other, the dialogue at various levels becomes more manageable. It is about specific political issues and conflicts. Our aim here should be not to expect quick and permanent solutions, but rather to ensure that each side better understands the concerns and constraints of the other, recognizes their long-term common interests, is prepared to take calculated risks, goes the extra mile in search of reconciliation, strives to reach a mutually acceptable compromise, and in its absence keeps the conflict under control. The dialogue is also about the interpretation and legacy of history, and the hope here is not that they will forget the past and embrace each other as long-lost brothers, but rather that both sides can, through better mutual understanding, lift the burden of history, remove the venom from their collective memories, and face their common future with a fresh and charitable perspective. The dialogue at the cultural level is equally challenging. The hope is that Western and Muslim societies (as well as others) will learn to avoid the interrelated vices of narcissism and mutual demonization, develop mutual respect, and reach a level of trust where deep differences are acknowledged but not allowed to get out of control.

Dialogue, I have argued, requires a commitment to reason – that is, to solve conflicts of interest and values by discussion, compromise and mutual accommodation – and to justice – that is, the willingness to recognize and respect the legitimate claims of others and not to pursue one's interests at the expense of theirs. Although these two are not as rare as the 'realists' suggest, they are also not as common as the optimists believe. Rich and powerful countries are so used to getting their own way that they chafe against the constraints of negotiation and compromise. Corporate capitalist interests seek control over global markets, and use their states and the media to maintain their exploitative relations with weaker societies. Many public figures, religious leaders, media proprietors and ordinary men and women on both sides sometimes make such a heavy moral and emotional investment in conflict that they feel disorientated in the absence of a real or imaginary enemy. Indeed, some of them are like addicts who need their periodic supply of rage and violence to confirm their sense of self-worth, and even to feel alive. Since war and conflict make mediocre politicians look like world statesmen and often benefit them electorally, they opt for them in preference to the less glamorous dialogue. Authoritarian and feudal regimes in several Muslim societies have no tradition of public dialogue. Since freedom of speech and organization are not allowed, they cannot even provide dialogical partners. Their rulers are corrupt or in league with foreign interests, carry little moral authority, and do not speak for their people, and the latter are not allowed to speak for themselves. The fanatics and terrorists who claim to speak for them are often self-absorbed, have their own agenda and lack democratic legitimacy.

All this makes dialogue very difficult, but we cannot give up on it because the only alternatives are either a vicious cycle of massive violence or acquiescence in the current regime of injustice. Since reason cannot flourish, or even have a chance of being heard, in an unreasonable world, both Muslim and Western societies need to undergo radical structural changes if they are to create the conditions of a rational dialogue. These include such things as a greater equality and dispersal of economic and political power within and between societies, freeing political institutions from the pressure of corporate interests, and establishing democracy in Muslim and deepening it in Western societies. They also include greater transparency in the way governments make their decisions, the public-spirited and impartial media providing truthful information and a range of views, stringent limits on the government's power to declare war or initiate warlike activities, and multiple public spaces for democratic action.

These are difficult and distant goals, but they alone offer the promise of a humane and just world. As a step towards it, we need to create a mature, watchful and well-informed body of public opinion at both national and global levels; and to consolidate powerful national and global constituencies that are committed to just and peaceful resolutions of conflicts, and are as well-organized and informed as those working in the opposite direction. One effective way to do this is to nurture a vibrant national and global civil society through cross-national forums, where intellectuals, ordinary citizens, students, teachers, journalists, trade unionists, activists, religious leaders, parliamentarians and non-governmental organizations from different countries can meet on a regular basis to exchange views, and to build up extensive and powerful networks committed to better understanding and concerted action.

The pressure of rational argument and public opinion does not always work, and needs to be backed up by well-organized popular movements at both national and global levels. Their purpose is not to replace dialogue but rather to create conditions for it by breaking down resistance, altering the balance of interests and empowering the people. Such movements, though sometimes defeated, have on other occasions been fairly successful even in authoritarian societies such as those belonging the erstwhile Soviet bloc, Pakistan, Chile, the Philippines and elsewhere. In the US, they were able to compel the government to engage in a dialogue with the North Vietnamese government and bring the Vietnam war to an end in the 1970s. Although American public opinion was slow to assert itself in relation to the second war on Iraq because of the government's mendacity and the highly partisan media, it did eventually compel even its most intransigent government to take a critical look at itself and initiate at least a tentative dialogue with Iraq's neighbours and insurgents. Reason needs to be reinforced by the moral and political power of a determined and organized public will if people are not to lose their faith in it and turn to violence or terror as the only available alternative.

9

Globalization and Culture

In the previous chapter I argued that intercultural dialogue is necessary to promote better understanding and to consolidate our growing sense of common humanity. While globalization generally facilitates this by bringing various cultural communities together and creating large areas of overlap and convergence, in some cases it also threatens the cultural identity of societies and causes a sense of panic that militates against a dialogue. In this chapter, I take a closer look at both these processes. But before I do so, some general remarks on globalization are necessary to set the context and see how it also has an impact on other areas of life.

At one level, globalization is not a new phenomenon. For millennia, societies have invaded, interacted and traded with each other, and some even built large empires; groups of people, some in their thousands, have moved across continents in search of better conditions; and religious missionaries have carried their messages to the furthest corners of the world. As a result, there has been a considerable exchange of technology, modes of production, knowledge, beliefs and social practices. These interactions, however, were generally patchy, dependent on the vagaries of nature and political conditions, and often rather marginal in their internal impact. European powers, from the sixteenth century onwards, not only widened and accelerated but gave them a new depth, and shaped the lives of their colonies at several levels. They dominated their economies, introduced new currents of thought and the truncated versions of modern political institutions, and divided up most of the world into closely integrated political, economic and linguistic units.

Since the later decades of the twentieth century we have entered a new phase in human history. As a result of decolonization, the newly independent countries are breaking away from the imperial straitjacket and forming new economic and political relationships. Revolutionary changes in the means of transport, communications technology, the mass media, the internet, and the exponential growth in trade in goods and services are bringing far-flung societies together and locking them into a system of global interdependence. The capitalist societies of the West desperately need new markets, labour and sources of energy and raw materials, and the developing countries need the West's technology, capital and markets. Such international institutions as the International Monetary Fund (IMF), the World Bank, the General Agreement on Tariffs and Trade (GATT) and the World Trade Organization (WTO) institutionalize, channel and reinforce global interdependence, require countries to open themselves up to global forces on pain of sanctions, act as agencies of global economic governance, and represent, in an embryonic and semi-institutionalized form, world government at the economic level. The collaboration between world financial markets, the spectacular increase in foreign-currency trading, and the transnationalization of production, with its multiple but complementary manufacturing sites, have given an added impetus to global integration. To take just one of countless examples, it is striking that the imprudent banking practices in such a small economy as Thailand in 1997 led to the collapse of the Russian rouble, massive loans to stave off a crisis in Brazil, and the intervention by the New York Federal Reserve Bank to prevent the collapse of a hedge fund damaging the US economy.

Since globalization occurs in a world of great inequalities of wealth, power, knowledge and productive capacities, most economic activities are concentrated among the rich countries of Europe, North America and East Asia, and the integration of their economies is greater than that of the rest of the world. Ninety per cent of all multinationals are based in G7 countries, and only a few of them are genuinely transnational or global. But even in these countries, globalization has not led to a supra-national, borderless economy following its own laws of motion and subordinating national economies to a single system of division of labour. To that extent it is still at an early stage, and subject to the complex logics of national economies and politics.

Globalization is not limited to the economy, though that is where it is most evident and extensive; it covers other areas of life as well, such as the political, the cultural and the moral. All states today are members of the United Nations, an event without parallel in human history. And most are signatories to and bound by global protocols, conventions and agreements. In spite of all their differences, they speak the universally familiar language of national interest, sovereignty, development, rights, equality and choice. Ideas, intellectual movements, the arts, literature, television programmes, films and other cultural artefacts travel more-or-less freely across national boundaries and have a global reach. Thanks to speedy and relatively easy modes of travel, millions of people are constantly on the move, acting as carriers of new ideas and experiences, and helping to create, each in his or her small way, the global consciousness of interdependence. Social activists and non-governmental organizations link across national boundaries, campaign for common causes, and form an embryonic global civil society. Globalization is also internationalizing higher education, leading to massive movements of students, the international recruitment of higher education staff (so much so that several Chinese and East Asian universities have outsiders in senior positions), the standardized criteria of student admissions and examinations, and international campuses of Western universities.

Globalization has also penetrated moral life. Ease of travel has heightened an appreciation of the fact that, despite their differences, all societies are made up of human beings much like each other, who face common problems and share much in common. The global reach of the media brings us vivid images of events in other parts of the world, and involves us in their lives. We feel addressed by stories of human suffering in distant lands, and translate our concerns in programmes of humanitarian aid and acts of humanitarian intervention. The 'Live Aid' concert in 1985 was broadcast to half the world and yielded US$4 billion for twenty drought-stricken countries of Africa. The 'Live 8' concert in 2005 was even more successful. Common environmental problems, the desire to preserve the global commons and the earth's scarce resources, the need to tackle diseases that show no respect for national boundaries, and the dangers of global warming have alerted us to our common vulnerabilities and dangers, and heightened our sense of interdependence. An interesting example of this was provided recently when helicopters fumigated many US cities to eradicate the potentially lethal West Nile virus that had arrived in the blood of a traveller or even perhaps in the gut of a mosquito that flew into a jet plane.

In all areas of life, globalization has both desirable and undesirable consequences for both developed and developing societies. In the economic sphere, it increases competition and productivity, expands markets, raises the level of prosperity in rich countries, improves the quality of products in developing countries and brings them up to international standard, reduces prices, and expands the range of consumer choice. It releases entrepreneurial energies, facilitates outsourcing –

which is not a zero sum game but benefits all involved, at least in the medium and long term, creates new forms of economic activity, transfers capital and technology, and raises the level of technical skills in and gives global access to the products of developing societies. These and other economic consequences profoundly affect other areas of life as well, including the way individuals perceive both themselves and others. The West was once seen as a world of dazzling artefacts that the rest of the world could only hear about and envy from a distance. Today, its products are accessible to all and can be enjoyed at home. In the past, it was quite common for people in developing countries to ask their Western visitors or relations to send or bring with them coveted items not available in their country. Thanks to globalization, this tendency has declined, and in some cases has even been reversed, as these items are now cheaper in the developing countries where they are manufactured or sold at discounted prices. The old sense of being left out of modern civilization and the consequent feeling of marginalization and inferiority is beginning to weaken in many parts of the world.

Economic globalization also has undesirable consequences. It ties the national economies of both developed and the developing societies to the vagaries of international markets, and puts them at risk from external manipulations and currency speculators. It reduces the developing countries to being the producers of raw material; floods their markets with cheap imports; discourages or destroys domestic industries; patents and monopolizes their traditional products; increases unemployment, at least in the short and medium term; and increases inequalities between and within societies. It also tends to cream off talent, and leads to a net transfer of resources from poor to rich countries that is only partially balanced by the remittances sent to the country by the immigrants. All this often distorts the educational system of the developing countries, where elite institutions are geared towards producing qualified manpower for the West. Indeed, in some of them, the offspring of middle-class parents are groomed for jobs abroad and channelled accordingly from an early age.

At the political level, globalization increases international co-operation, opens up the possibility of greater collective control over the forces of the market, creates a global public opinion, and encourages respect for international law. It generates pressure for the universal acceptance of basic democratic values, fosters a climate conducive to human rights, and provides forums for an appeal and a redress against domestic tyrannies. By building international institutions in which all states are, in principle, able to participate as equals in shaping the global order, it creates a global public space and promotes the spirit of human solidarity. Globalization, however, also has its dark side. It reduces a society's control over its affairs and weakens the power and authority of its democratic institutions. As more and more areas of national life are either decided by international bureaucracies or subjected to the play of global forces, its elected representatives have less and less power and find a ready excuse for inaction, or worse. Globalization also creates a footloose cosmopolitan techno-managerial elite sharing more in common with one another than with their fellow citizens, for whose betterment they are unwilling to pay higher taxes and make sacrifices. This fractures the community, weakens its sense of common belonging, and leads to deep and often irresolvable differences regarding the goals of public policy. Since globalization weakens the state's capacity to plan and equitably distribute its resources, it renders the poor and disadvantaged groups political orphans. This diminishes its legitimacy in their eyes, and increases its propensity to use repressive violence to shore up its declining authority.

Globalization has had an impact on states in highly complex and at times contradictory ways. Territorial boundaries, national differences, national culture and the nationally organized economy on which modern states traditionally relied to maintain their unity and legitimacy have been weakened, making them porous, vulnerable and less self-confident. States have no unified nation to underpin them, nor can they hope to become one themselves, and need to rely on their own resources to ensure social cohesion. Their sphere of autonomous action is limited, which affects the quality of their democratic culture. At the same time, globalization has also had the opposite effect. People turn to the state to protect them against the ravages of global forces and foreign competition, to hold society together, and to provide a cohesive collective identity that can give them a sense of belonging in a world in flux. Globalization creates economic inequalities and uneven regional development, and states are expected to deal with the consequences, including the use of such repressive violence as is necessary to quell disorder. Globalization thus requires states that are both repressive and liberal, strong in the conduct of their internal affairs and weak in their resistance to external forces, able to represent and speak for their people yet disconnected from many important areas of their lives. Different states cope with these contradictory demands in different ways and with varying degrees of success.

Some of these welcome and unwelcome consequences of globalization are inherent in it; others arise from its current neoliberal form, and yet others from the vast inequality of wealth and power in which it is embedded. It is difficult to say what form globalization will take in the future. While it proceeds unabated across national boundaries, it is also encountering resistance at several levels. Since it disturbs the expectations built up over three centuries of nationally organized ways of living, and has been of uneven benefit to large sections of people in both developed and developing societies, there is a considerable pressure to arrest it by putting up protective walls and restricting immigration. Environmentalists argue that it wastes energy, and urge restricted travel and local production to meet local needs. There is also a movement towards regional rather than global integration, based on the complementarity of the economies involved and the need to resolve local conflicts by fostering common regional interests. These trends represent not so much a rejection of globalization as an attempt to limit its scope and depth in certain areas.

The cultural impact of globalization

As in other areas of life, globalization has important cultural consequences, of which the following five are particularly important. First, it leads to what I might call 'sectoral convergence'. As technology, institutions, ideas and practices travel across national boundaries, they tend to create broadly similar patterns of human behaviour and relationships in the relevant areas of life. Globalization accelerates urbanization and gives rise to cities with their familiar ethos of anonymity, residential clusters, impersonality, crime, drugs and congestion, and all having similar problems requiring broadly similar solutions. The universal acceptance of the state as the only valid form of constituting society brings with it territorial boundaries and disputes, the army, the police, the bureaucracy, the secret service, the flag, the national anthem, and the institutionalized inequality of political power. Hospitals, industries, universities, courts, airports, armies and bureaucracies too tend to develop similar organizational structures and cultures. Despite their differences in cleanliness, efficiency, general ethos and professional competence, to walk into a hospital, a court, a factory or a university in New York, Kuwait or Timbuktu is to encounter a broadly familiar institutional and organizational culture.

Several factors are responsible for bringing about sectoral convergences. Common technology, which requires a broadly similar response, is one of these. Educational, economic, political, judicial and other institutions pursue similar goals, and the ways of achieving these are limited in their range. Those involved in running these institutions undergo similar training and acquire common expertise and professional culture. Most citizens are generally familiar – from direct experience, films, the television or hearsay – with the good practices of other societies, and make appropriate demands on their own. Demands of the international community, expectations of fellow professionals in other parts of the world, cross-country comparisons, and a desire for international respectability also generate pressures for broad global conformity.

Convergences in different areas of life are not only inescapable but also have much to be said for them. They facilitate travel, communication, social contact, international co-operation, and the exchange of experiences and ideas. One would hardly wish to travel to another country, let alone establish close economic, cultural and other contacts with it, if one could not be reasonably confident that, despite all the local variations and eccentricities, its airports, hospitals, transport and bureaucracy would function in ways one might anticipate, understand and cope with. Sectoral convergences create pockets of familiarity, make the relevant areas of life in other societies intellectually and emotionally accessible, and provide the bases from which to reach out to and make sense of those that are unfamiliar and opaque. Thanks to globalization, hardly any society today is wholly inscrutable or closed to us.

Second, globalization has given rise to a broadly common elite culture not limited to the higher echelons of the technological, business and political elite who meet regularly at Davos. It extends to managerial, professional, academic and other groups as well. They are often educated at similar, and sometimes the same, prestigious Western institutions, and acquire a similar ethos and modes of thought. They come from similar social backgrounds, and grow up in a broadly similar cultural milieu. They are in regular contact with their counterparts in other countries, co-operate with them on common projects, forge friendships, and care about their counterparts' good opinion of them. They attend the same conferences, speak the same language, follow similar life-styles, stay at similar or the same hotels, dress alike, even sport similar clothing, shoes and ties, develop similar manners and tastes, holiday in similar places, and entertain similar ambitions for their children. They broadly occupy similar positions in their societies, share similar views and anxieties about their status, and tend to relate to their countries and fellow citizens in a similar manner. They are cosmopolitans in the sense of being at ease with different cultures, but they are also generally well versed in and even proud of their national cultures. The former makes it easy for them to relate to outsiders, while the latter establishes their individuality and makes them interesting and useful.

Third, globalization is leading to a relatively narrow common culture among ordinary men and women the world over. People everywhere speak the language of human rights, elections, free speech, minority rights, democracy, national sovereignty and popularly accountable government. At the economic level they are familiar with the language of the minimum wage, the right to work, the welfare state, enterprise, efficiency and balancing the national budget. At the moral and social level, the ideas of individual choice, control over one's life, romantic love, self-respect, identity, the right to one's own opinion, sexual orientation and equality are a universal currency. Had it not been for the impact of a global trend, homosexuality would not be a subject of public discussion let alone public admission in India, South Africa, North Africa and elsewhere. Healthy living is a common concern, and has led to interest in jogging, regular exercise, the avoidance of obesity, campaigns against smoking, drugs and Aids, yoga, alternative medicines and sensitivity to pollution. This is not to say that these ideas are cherished equally in all societies or by all groups within them, but rather that they are intellectually accessible to them in different degrees, and that, when some groups invoke them, others (including those opposed to these ideas) know what they mean and why they are considered to be important.[1]

The narrow global culture also extends to consumer-orientated areas of life.[2] Shopping malls, domestic gadgets, fast-food outlets and consumer goods produced by Nike, Adidas, Rolex, Chanel and Levi-Strauss are almost universal, and carry their culture with them. McDonald's, for example, is now not just a chain of fast-food outlets, but a cultural institution, embodying a particular attitude to food and the customer, and represents such qualities as efficiency, predictability, cleanliness, speedy consumption and the centrality of technology. As customers get used to these qualities, they make similar demands on local restaurants, which feel the pressure to 'McDonaldize' themselves. The chain Ruskoy Bistro in Russia is consciously modelled along the lines of McDonald's, and Beijing's most famous Quanjude Roast Duck Restaurant sent its management staff to McDonald's in the US for training, copied its ethos, and even introduced its own roast duck fast food.

Dress, the unmistakable marker of a society's traditional identity, now crosses national frontiers in a manner unimaginable in the past. More and more men the world over dress alike, traditional clothes being confined largely to rural areas, special occasions, the indigenous peoples and self-conscious nationalist regimes. Even women, the traditional transmitters of cultural identity, are beginning to dress alike. Uganda legislated against miniskirts, but in vain. The Iranian mullahs put women back into the chador, but that did not work, and where it is worn, jeans and trousers are sometimes worn under it. Such commonality is also to be found in commercial and even residential architecture, interior décor, hobbies and forms of sexual self-expression. In many of these cases, a Western influence appears to be the most dominant, but not always. Indian, Chinese, African and other societies have also influenced the West in such areas as dress, hairstyles, and ideas of male and female beauty.

Fourth, as a result of globalization, cultural boundaries have become porous, leading both to the multiculturalization of national cultural traditions and the emergence of new cultural forms that fit neatly into none of them.[3] Although cultural interaction is uneven and heavily dominated by the West, it is not an entirely one-way process. Other cultures too take advantage of globalization and have an impact on each other as well as on the West. Indian films are a strong presence in the Middle East, Central Asia, parts of Africa and now increasingly in the West. Turkish soap operas are popular in Central Asia, and Egyptian ones in the Arab world. Indian cuisine, forms of spirituality, yoga and music are popular in the West, and to a lesser extent in other parts of the world. This is equally true of Chinese cuisine, martial arts, dance forms, systems of medicine and herbal remedies, and of African and Latin American music, art and literature. Islam is the fastest growing religion in the world, and Buddhism too has made a considerable impact. Brazil's Rade Globo exports its '*telenovas*' to more than eighty countries around the world, and one of the biggest television hits in Russia is a Mexican soap opera called *Los Ricos Tambian Lloran* (*The Rich Also Cry*). Australian television programmes such as *Neighbours* are watched in scores of countries. Along with the Westernization of the rest of world, there are also trends, albeit weaker ones, towards its Indianization, Sinization or Africanization.

Thanks to the greater exposure to other cultures and the willingness to borrow ideas from them, there is a considerable cross-over and fusion of styles, images, cultural idioms and sensibilities. African percussion rhythms and Indian music are combined with Western pop music. Rap (itself a hybrid product of African and Latin-American influences) and hip-hop music have travelled out of the US inner-city ghettoes to distant parts of the world, where they shape and are in turn shaped by, the local musical traditions. Western designers plunder Indian, Chinese and African styles in search of a 'seasonal look'. Writers and artists experiment with the genres and imageries of different literary and artistic traditions. Indian, Chinese, Middle Eastern and other culinary traditions have incorporated Western ingredients, vegetables and styles of cooking, even as the latter have incorporated theirs. Jokes and styles of humour of one culture find their way into another, and are either retained as a welcome alien presence or bought into a creative interplay with their local counterparts. Children grow up reading stories of distant lands, learning something about their peoples, myths and legends, and confronting and combining them imaginatively with their own. Even the otherwise exclusive religions, including the most self-assured among them, sometimes borrow each other's ideas on spirituality, sacredness and the meaning of life and death, and suitably redefine their own.

While this process of cultural fusion, which is not limited to creative minds and goes on, consciously or unconsciously, in the lives of millions of ordinary men and women, is not new to our age, it has received a new depth and momentum under globalization. Every culture today carries elements of some others, and displays different degrees of multicultural orientation. This is not to say that we are heading towards a single musical, artistic or literary tradition, but rather that these traditions are becoming porous, display family resemblances, and are now part of a global cultural mélange. It is hardly surprising that few educated people in most parts of the world today are, or would admit to being, ignorant of at least some of the great literary, artistic and musical achievements of other societies. In this sense, a minimum level of global cultural literacy is beginning to emerge. Although intercultural interaction is still heavily one-sided, relatively fragile, and resisted in many parts of the world, it is well under way, has its own momentum, and is just as widespread as economic and technological globalization. And while it is limited largely to the middle classes, it is spreading to other sections of society, who sometimes embrace it even more enthusiastically in order to overcome their social inferiority, assert their modernity, or to liberate themselves from oppressive social norms. This multicultural literacy is likely to increase as it becomes integrated into the educational curriculum all over the world and becomes a norm for succeeding generations.

Thanks to all this, there is almost no culture that is wholly strange to us.[4] At least some areas of it, be it music, cuisine, literature, myths or beliefs, are likely to be familiar to us, not only because we have learnt about them in schools, or from films or television programmes, but also because of their influence on our own culture. Such familiarity provides a platform from which we prise open the obscure or unfamiliar areas of other cultures and make these accessible to us. This gives us the confidence to relax in their presence, delight in their otherness, and enjoy the adventure of exploring their complexity still further. A new form of cosmopolitanism is increasingly evident, which grasps human unity not only in terms of human similarities as the traditional forms of moral universalism did, but also through human diversity. For the first time in human history, it is possible to say that we not only inhabit a common earth but are beginning to share a common world. Human beings everywhere have access to a free-floating mass of universally common ideas and images, and often draw on them in different degrees to define their sense of who they are and what they wish to be. Although they construct their identities differently, some of the elements that go into these are often shared.

Finally, globalization is leading to the pluralization of every society. While human beings have always known that other people live and think differently, their knowledge had largely been vague, based on hearsay, and a hostage to traditional prejudices and elite manipulation. Today, they encounter other people via the television or during holidays, observe their customs and practices, and form their own views. When outsiders are settled among them, as they generally are, they also interact with them to varying degrees, acquire some knowledge of their food, music, dress, habits, customs, values and norms of behaviour, and grasp their humanity in all its pleasing and bewildering complexity. In the past, when travel and communication were poor, immigrants found it difficult to resist the pressure to assimilate. Today, they remain connected with their erstwhile homelands through films, television, internet and frequent travel, and even feel the pressure to retain their cultural identity, sometimes in a form that bears no relation to the changes that the culture might be undergoing in their countries of origin. Unlike earlier societies, in which cultural homogeneity was the norm and differences lay beyond their boundaries, human plurality and diversity is today a pervasive and tenacious fact of daily life. While there is increasing homogeneity between societies in some areas of life, there is within each of them a considerable degree of pluralization. Both are part of the same general process.

Almost all contemporary societies are culturally diverse, and likely to remain so for the foreseeable future. The depth and impact of their diversity, however, vary greatly, and different societies respond differently to them. Western societies are convinced of their cultural superiority and do not generally think much of the moral values and beliefs of the non-Western immigrants settled among them. While valuing the arts, literature, music and cuisine of the new arrivals, they are expected to acknowledge the superiority of, or at least to live by, Western values. If non-Western communities meet this expectation, there is no problem, but when they do not they are seen as a threat to the national culture. In almost all Western societies recently, an influential body of opinion has mounted an attack on moral and cultural diversity, and some have thrown up powerful right-wing movements. Since Western societies are culturally self-confident and the threat is relatively feeble, they have generally been able to avoid, or at least to contain, a moral panic.

The situation in non-Western societies is both similar and different. Most of them generally have no problem coping with the relatively superficial aspects of Western culture, such as popular music, food, films, television programmes and dress, but feel threatened by its moral and political values. The latter assert their superiority and mock local cultures. They also have the powerful backing of international institutions, to whom many non-Western societies have to turn for badly-needed funds, which are provided on condition that Western values and practices are adopted. The situation is further complicated by the fact that Westernization entrenches the hold of the Westernized local 'elites', creates great inequalities of power and status, and complicates the task of creating a shared way of life and common interests. Because of their long colonial history, many of these societies are culturally diffident and do not quite know how to come to terms with the Western impact. Western culture thus is not marginal to their lives in a way that non-Western culture is in the West, but a serious intellectual interlocutor, a rival source of moral authority, and hence a powerful destabilizing force.

Non-Western societies are culturally diverse in quite different ways from their Western counterparts. Traditional and Western cultures compete for the minds and hearts of the citizens and are in a state of tension. In their social lives, non-Western societies define themselves in traditional communal terms, in their political and economic lives in individualist terms, and in their personal lives display sympathies towards both. They have one sense of time when they go to the office or place of work or take their children to school, and another when visiting temples, attending social functions or meeting friends. Firms, government buildings and offices represent one way of structuring space; private homes, community centres and religious buildings a very different one. Caste or tribal membership matters a great deal in social life, but is strongly disapproved of in political, economic and other areas of life. Since space, time, social relations, moral values, ways of relating to oneself and others are all informed by competing systems of meaning and involve constant conceptual leaps, almost all non-Western societies display varying degrees of cultural disorientation and yearn nostalgically for the simplicity of a premodern past. Like their Western counterparts, they too find cultural diversity troubling, though for different reasons and with greater justification. Neither can escape it in the age of globalization, and both alike need to find ways of coping with it.

US hegemony and national culture

Although cultural globalization has enabled several countries to make varying degrees of impact at the global level, it is heavily dominated by the West, and in particular by the US.[5] US cultural industries have the obvious advantages of access to vast resources, scale of production, a large domestic market, control of the global media, an extensive network of distribution facilities, aggressive marketing, an early start in mass production and, of course, the political prestige and support of a hyperpower. While these advantages are considerable, they are not by themselves sufficient. They would not, for example, succeed in turning Indian films into global blockbusters, or give Chinese popular music global popularity. Conversely, they have not succeeded in pushing North American arts, theatre and literary works high up the scale of global popularity. The US domination of global culture is limited largely to such areas as films, soaps, television programmes and popular music.

Some of the important factors that have contributed to US domination are related to the nature of US society, and the character and content of its cultural products. Unlike Europe and many other parts of the world, the US has neither a feudal past nor a highly stratified class society. Since its culture is not bound up with a particular group and carries little historical baggage, it is relatively light, open, experimental, and willing to repackage elements drawn from others. Being a multicultural and multi-ethnic society whose citizens are drawn from almost every country, the US is virtually a microcosm of the world. Creators of its cultural products have diverse backgrounds and are willing to experiment with the ideas, themes and techniques of other cultures. They bring to their work a well-developed multicultural sensibility, which in turn is nurtured and rein-forced by the multicultural ethos of the wider society. Since immigrants and creative minds from different parts of the world continue to come to the US, American cultural industries are constantly in touch with chang-ing global tastes and cultural forms. With their domestic multicultural audience, they have the added advantage of being able to try out their products on it. If they win its approval, they can be reasonably confident that their products will have a good chance of appealing to much of the rest of the world.

Because of all this, US cultural products tend to cut across national boundaries and appeal to a wide variety of tastes. They do so in one of two ways, representing two different forms of universality. In some cases they deal with what is basic to all human beings, is culturally as neutral and bland as is humanly possible, and requires no more cultural sophistication and emotional depth than is universally available. In others, they are culturally eclectic in their appeal, multicultural in their orientation, and have enough in them to engage different cultural tastes to different degrees. Most US films fall into the first category, much of US television and popular music into the second. In either case, US cultural products, especially those meant for a mass market, have a built-in globalizability. And when they cannot be globalized in their original form, they have enough cultural elasticity to be suitably adapted to local circumstances. It is this inherent or adjustable globalizability that is exploited by the massive and well-researched US centres of cultural production. Globalizability of content is not enough to ensure globaliza-tion. Some other countries also produce globalizable cultural objects and activities, but their potential remains unrealized for lack of the kind of advantages enjoyed by US cultural industries. Since the nature of the product and the power of the producer are both important, the US prof-its as much from the size and power of its economy as its multicultural society.[6]

Globalization, particularly the US cultural dominance, is seen in many parts of the world as a threat to their national culture, and is some-times referred to in such lurid terms as cultural invasion, cultural onslaught and even cultural imperialism.[7] The truth is more complex. No national culture is a homogeneous and tightly knit whole. It is composed of different strands, privileges some and devalues other forms of life, and has different impacts on different groups. This means that, while foreign cultural products might appear to be threatening to one group, they might seem emancipatory to another. Western ideas of social, gender and racial equality threaten the beneficiaries of the dominant hierarchical and patriarchal culture in non-Western societies, but are often welcomed by women, minorities and other marginalized groups. The depictions of nudity, wearing of scanty clothing or sexuality in Western films and television programmes that offend middle-class sensibility deeply arouses no anxiety among the urban and rural poor, who have long been used to it because of their poverty, social customs or traditional life-style, and who even welcome it as a way of challenging middle-class snobbery and superiority.

But even so far as the middle classes are concerned, the situation is quite complex. Although loud in their complaints, they are also often the keenest consumers of such films and programmes. Their prudishness is generally a recent phenomenon. It is their way of distinguishing themselves from, and claiming superiority over, other social groups, or the result of a widespread attempt to define their national identity in non-Western terms during the anti-colonial struggle. In either case, it often lacks deep roots in their traditional culture. Indian middle-class puritanism, for example, goes back not much further than the nineteenth century, and sits uneasily with the long Hindu tradition of celebrating sexuality, evident alike in its erotic temple architecture, popular religious stories, sexual exploits of gods and goddesses, and an extensive erotic literature of which the famous *Kamasutra* is a relatively timid example. This is also the case with many Muslim societies, whose puritanism is relatively recent and at odds with the exuberant sensuality of much Iranian, Turkish and Arab literature, music and social practices.

The talk of cultural invasion wrongly assumes that the indigenous culture is passive and powerless before outside influences. Under normal circumstances it is able to engage in a critical dialogue with them and to decide what to reject or accept, and how to indigenize, neutralize or adapt to local needs what it is powerless to resist. McDonald's outlets in Russia serve a different menu from those in the West, and set aside special hours and places for families. In Japan, McDonald's does not serve down-market junk food but caters to middle-class tastes and provides a locally sensitive aesthetic décor. Since their houses are generally small, young students in Tokyo spend hours upstairs in Wendy's restaurant, doing their homework, chatting with friends and turning eating places into social centres and even extended homes. Again, a society might accept Western dress, food, practices or manners but deny them dignity and status by confining them to culturally marginal areas or socially insignificant occasions. India, China and Middle Eastern countries are full of McDonald's outlets and prestigious Western restaurants, but such food is not generally served on socially significant occasions such as those relating to births, marriages and deaths. Similar restraints are applied to Western dress and music. These strategies of cultural survival and self-reproduction sometimes break down or are abandoned voluntarily, not so much because of the pressure of global forces but because they make less sense in an increasingly industrialized and urbanized society, or because of the declining authority of the traditional culture.

The impact of things Western, especially US films and television programmes, should not be exaggerated either. When the Soviet Union was dissolved, Russians, long denied access to these, embraced them with great enthusiasm, but as their country settled down and began to face problems of national reconstruction, domestic films and television programmes, which explored these problems sensitively, began to enjoy far greater popularity than the Western imports. Similar things have begun to happen in India. The national television, long used to the monopoly of the domestic market, broadcast boring, unimaginative and technically poor programmes. However, it improved considerably under foreign competition, and began to produce films and serials that not only won over the alienated domestic market but also enjoyed overseas popularity.

Although Hollywood films and Western television programmes are popular all over the world, their appeal is not uniform and is generally limited to the middle classes and urban youth. *Dallas* was a failure in Brazil and Japan, and American television programmes have not been among the top ten in any of the major West European countries. Even in many developing countries, domestically produced programmes generally top the ratings during peak viewing hours, with Western, especially US, imports filling in less popular slots during the day. The latter largely include films, especially the easily exportable action films, soaps, sports and children's programmes but not those on current affairs or documentaries, shallow slapstick comedies but not those involving subtle word play, culturally specific references and nuanced dialogues. The Indian version of the British *Who Wants to Be a Millionaire* was a success, but not those of the *Weakest Link*, *Columbo* and *Charlie's Angels*. Indians generally preferred family soap operas, with their usually rich, overdressed and heavily made-up characters playing out the traditional themes of tension in the joint family.

Nigeria has the world's third-largest film industry, and many of its popular films revolve around the themes of witchcraft and demonic possession.[8] By and large, they end with the practitioners of witchcraft being punished, and the virtuous rewarded. People want actors they can relate to, who look, speak and behave like them. Theirs is also a very expressive culture, which shapes their judgement on what is and is not good acting. Actors are expected to get angry or cry easily, and the self-restraint and calmness in emotional or difficult situations that is common in Western films has only a limited appeal. As Femi Odugbemi, President of the Independent Television Producers' Association, put it, Nigerians are 'a story-telling people' who love embellishment and elaboration, and like their stories to have a clear, didactic message. Western films and television programmes are watched, sometimes even enjoyed, but often lack an emotional grip.

Even when foreign films and television programmes are widely viewed, they are not necessarily popular in the sense of viewers approving of or even enjoying them; they might watch them out of curiosity or because they have nothing else or better to view or do. And even when they are popular, they are not always influential in the sense of shaping the viewers' attitudes. US films are hugely popular in France, grossing in the 1990s nearly 60 per cent of the total cinema revenue compared to about a third in the 1980s, but there is no evidence that they have shaped the French attitude to the US significantly. Indeed, people might watch and even enjoy US imports, but feel, or be made to feel, ashamed or guilty at enjoying these programmes and blame the US for corrupting them. This seems to be the case in some Muslim countries, such as Saudi Arabia, where the television and cinemas show little but US imports without inducing much respect or love for their country of origin.

This is also true of such powerful news providers and communication channels as CNN, Reuters, and even the BBC. People watch them but do not entirely trust them, which is why Al Jazeera, widely respected for its accuracy, freedom from political manipulation and respect for Arab and Islamic values, was able to mount a powerful challenge to them. It is striking that, while domestic programmes are subjects of serious public and private discussions among viewers, Western imports are not. This is so because they do not relate to their viewers, deal with their day-to-day problems, articulate their cultural, economic and other anxieties, represent their views or those of people like them, and guide them on how to survive and flourish in their kind of environment. Since the viewers do not feel addressed by these programmes, they do not take them seriously enough to engage with them critically. It is therefore never enough for the Western imports to indigenize themselves or adapt to local tastes. They need to take up local issues, use native talent and themes, and handle their subject matter in a culturally intelligible manner. When they do so, they generally cease to be Western except in their sources of funding, and sometimes not even in that.[9]

The culture of a society is embodied in and transmitted through its religion, literature, language, songs, food, dress, music, newspapers, films, radio and television programmes, the arts, body language, manners, children's comics, moral practices and so on. It is striking that those worried about the integrity of the national culture do not generally mind foreign imports in such areas as music, dress (except in relation to women), newspapers, books, food, literature, the arts and radio programmes, largely because they think that these are either marginal to culture (food and dress, for example) or involve only the educated and presumably therefore a culturally reliable elite (literature, the arts and radio programmes, for example). They see religion as being central to their culture, and feel sure that this is the least open to foreign influences. They feel the same way about their language, except when a foreign tongue threatens to overwhelm and replace it, as in Quebec and to some extent in India. What seems to cause the most worry are films and television programmes.

Sometimes this is because of the pressure from commercial lobbies. In France, opposition to US films was led by, among others, the French Gaumont company, whose head insisted, without any sense of embarrassment, that the French film industry should be protected 'if France wants to be the home to new Prousts in the future'. Other reasons, especially in non-Western societies, are related to the fear that films and television programmes reach out to the illiterate masses, who are believed to be particularly vulnerable to their influence, a complaint heard even in the US when Hollywood started producing films on a mass scale. The first assumption is correct, because films, and especially television, are the main sources of popular entertainment in developing countries and command a huge audience. The second assumption is dubious. It underestimates the shrewdness and maturity of the masses, who are not easily taken in by what they see on the screen, and have a good idea of what is and is not relevant to them or their kind of society.[10]

Regulating cultural imports

In the light of our discussion, we should be wary of measures taken to protect a society's culture. They sometimes spring from false anxieties, or are engineered by vested interests and self-proclaimed guardians of the national culture. They are likely to be unduly restrictive, and prevent the flow of critical ideas and movements. They are also generally too crude to cope with the subtle ways in which cultures influence each other, and too paternalistic to trust the good sense of those they seek to protect. While we are right to be suspicious of them, we cannot rule them out altogether. It is widely acknowledged that free trade in material goods between vastly unequal societies is not a fair trade, and that even the latter needs to be accompanied by well-directed aid to build up the trading capacity of weak and developing societies. The same argument applies with equal, if not greater, force to cultural exchanges which, if left to the forces of the market, can easily undermine a society's way of life. This happens under three kinds of circumstances.

First, when foreign cultural products enjoy overwhelming advantages including direct and indirect subsidies at home, the importing countries are often unable to compete with them on equal terms, and their cultural industries might face wholesale destruction. Take the case of the US. Its film and television industries recover most of their costs from the domestic market, and export their products at extremely low prices which their domestic rivals cannot match. It is often cheaper to buy and distribute third-rate US films than to produce native ones. Domestic producers, who are generally keen to make a quick profit, have no incentive to make films of their own, leading to the closing down of national studios. Sometimes, rich and powerful US companies take over domestic cinemas to show their films, denying outlets to their domestic competitors. On its opening weekend, *Jurassic Park* took over nearly a quarter of France's screens in large towns and cities, and provoked a legitimate outcry. Indonesia had long protected its film industry, and produced some excellent films. The situation changed when the US demanded easier access for its film exports in return for guaranteed Indonesian textile imports. In 1992, 66 out of 81 cinema houses in its major cities showed only foreign, mainly US, films, and domestic gems such as *My Sky, My Home*, which won awards in France, Germany and even the US, could not secure a domestic outlet. Although films require a large financial outlay and are therefore particularly vulnerable to foreign domination, similar things tend to happen in other areas as well, such as popular music, television programmes, and political and life-style magazines.

Second, societies best cope with foreign cultures when they have some sense of control over their affairs, and are fairly stable and self-confident. When they are subjected to a rapid and relentless flow of foreign cultural products that they are powerless to control, they feel helpless and lose their normal capacity to take change in their stride, especially in the developing countries where cultural self-confidence is often low. The norms, values and social practices, which have long held them together and guided them through difficult times, are threatened, leading to a pervasive sense of disorientation and moral panic. Unless they are able to regulate foreign cultural imports, they either passively watch the disintegration of their society or turn to religion, the most tenacious medium of continuity with the past and generally the least affected by foreign influences, and opt for a highly conservative view of it. When the Shah of Iran opened up his country to massive Western cultural influences, he created a veritable panic. His ruthless attempts to suppress the inevitable protests only intensified the opposition, leading to a vicious cycle of violence which the mullahs exploited. Although cultures cannot be preserved like museum pieces, and should and generally do change with the times, they do so best when the process of change is not hurried, pressurized or manipulated from outside or by an unrepresentative national elite.

Unlike in the West, secularism in many developing societies, for example, has not grown organically out of an extensive public debate and widespread consensus. It was and largely remains a project initiated and imposed, as a deliberate policy or a panic reaction, by a combination of an intellectual and political elite acting either alone or under foreign pressure. Since it is seen as alien or undemocratic, it has often failed to strike roots and continues to provoke strong reactions and reversals. Even after over eighty years and constant nurturing, it remains fragile in Turkey and depends on the armed forces to sustain it. Cultural changes take roots and last when the bulk of national opinion is behind them, and that requires time, patience, an extensive national debate and absence of external manipulation.

Third, in an open competition, best ideas and practices do not always win in the short run, and even in the long run. Under globalization, there is a danger that a society might be flooded with cheap cultural imports that have little aesthetic value and derive their popularity solely from their exploitation of basic human instincts. Domestic producers imitate them as the quickest and cheapest way to make money. Since members of society are exposed to nothing better, their intellectual and emotional growth becomes stunted, and they remain unable to appreciate anything that is emotionally demanding, intellectually subtle, or morally ambiguous. Fostering good taste and cultural sophistication is a worthwhile public objective, and may under certain circumstances require appropriate restrictions. It is true that the government is neither the best judge of good taste nor can it be trusted to promote this, but that does not mean that nothing can or should be done.

One might ask why it should matter if a society's cultural industries disappear and its members view only foreign films and television programmes, listen only to foreign music, read only foreign magazines and literary works and, as can easily happen, if its creative writers write only with a foreign audience in mind. After all, cultures should have no boundaries, and all that matters is that people should be exposed to the best in the world irrespective of its national origins. Although this argument has merit, there are several good reasons why it is important for a society to develop its own cultural industries.

Legitimate national pride and self-respect, development of local talent, the economic interests of local cultural industries, employment of local people, and the revenue generated by the exports of cultural products are some of these. There are also far more important cultural reasons. Out of disinterested intellectual curiosity as well as in the interest of social stability and self-reproduction, every society seeks, and indeed needs, to develop a more or less coherent conception of the kind of society it is, how it came to be what it is, and what it wishes to become. This is particularly the case when it is undergoing profound changes, which is the case with all societies today. It then needs to make sense of its bewildering experiences, articulate a more or less coherent view of them, and integrate them into its self-understanding.

Although ordinary men and women in their own tentative and informal ways do this all the time, creative minds have a particularly important role. They share its experiences, participate in its moods and tensions, understand its needs and aspirations, give voice to neglected experiences, uncover the inner structures of the prevailing forms of consciousness, interpret different groups to each other, and build common bonds between them. In these and other ways they render their society intelligible to itself, provide a common framework of ideas and images, and help to create a shared sense of community. Foreign cultural producers cannot do this. Their contexts and experiential basis are different, and so too are their central concerns, assumptions and modes of thought. A society without a flourishing cultural realm remains a mass of opaque and undigested experiences, fragmented, confused, and devoid of a language in which to understand and evaluate itself.

Not only the society concerned but the rest of humankind suffers a loss when its cultural vitality disappears or seriously declines. Its unique experiences and insights into the human condition remain unexplored, and others are deprived of its contribution to the global conversation. A culturally homogeneous world or one dominated by a single world view and system of values lacks richness and variety, a critical interlocutor, an awareness of the importance of the capacities and sensibilities it neglects or marginalizes. While every society should welcome great human creations irrespective of their national and cultural origins, these are grounded in particular experiences, reflect particular views of the world, and do not capture the human condition in all its variety. They need to be supplemented and vitalized by locally derived insights which, while sometimes inferior in their technical sophistication, are often rich in their experiential content and experimental vitality.

While welcoming intercultural interaction, we need to avoid global cultural homogenization and undermining the society's ability to sustain a creative cultural life. When it is put under intolerable pressure, as happens in the situations I described earlier, it might be justified in imposing some restrictions on its cultural imports. Since such a policy is open to the dangers highlighted earlier, it needs to be guided by clearly defined objectives, proportionate, time-bound, constructive, flexible, democratically arrived at, and based on a general consensus. It should not be confused with censorship, because its aim is to regulate and not stop external influences; nor with protectionism, because its aim is not to protect the existing culture but to enable it to change freely and at its own pace; nor with cultural isolationism as its aim is not to insulate a society against the global currents of thought but to create a level playing field and to allow it to retain some measure of control over its cultural life.

The long-term aim of such a policy should be to build up local cultural industries to a level where they have the confidence and the capacity to interact as equals with those of other countries. While encouraging a competitive climate, the state might protect and subsidize those cultural industries that are too weak to compete, too vital to its way of life to be left to the vagaries of the market, or are essential to the development of refined tastes. It might give financial assistance, tax exemptions, fiscal incentives and low interest loans to artists' co-operatives, small publishing houses and film-producing units, provide export subsidies, give domestic cultural products preferential treatment, disallow foreign competition in certain areas, encourage foreign collaboration in some others, ban dumping, impose duty on cheap or trashy cultural products, and limit foreign ownership of local cultural industries.[11] Different cultural spheres have different needs and require different policies.

Much can also be done at the international level. Rich and culturally dominant countries can help developing societies by building up their cultural infrastructures, training their personnel, and devising schemes for co-production and co-distribution. They could limit voluntarily their cultural exports, and stop giving their cultural industries direct and indirect subsidies. They might also find ways of exposing the cultural products of the developing societies to the wider world by such means as film festivals, sponsored art exhibitions and book fairs. This is being done, but not often enough, and is largely limited to the elite. There is also a good case for setting up a global cultural fund to be used for encouraging domestic cultural industries and nurturing local talents in developing countries.

Although there is much to be said for a free flow of ideas across national boundaries, we should not turn it dogmatically into an absolute principle. It occurs in a highly unequal context, whose distorting effects can be considerable. As I argued above, there are also other equally important values at stake. When they conflict, as they sometimes do, we need to strike a judicious balance.

10

Principles of Global Ethics

As I argued earlier, our interests in the increasingly interdependent world are intertwined and we face common problems requiring collective action. This calls for a widely agreed body of universal principles to guide our choices and regulate our relations with other societies. In this chapter I turn to this complex question and explore the nature, basis and content of global ethics.[1]

The historical specificity of global ethics

Every society is organized in terms of a body of values and norms that govern the relations between its members, the kind of life they should lead, and the qualities of character they should cultivate. They are embedded in its customs, practices, rituals and so on, are nurtured by the countless ties and shared social identity that bind its members, and collectively constitute its ethical life. As long as a society is self-contained, this is generally enough. When it comes into close contact with others and encounters strangers on a regular basis, however, it faces the question of how to relate to them. Since such general norms as hospitality to strangers that it might have are not enough, it needs to rise to a higher level of reflection, recognize their commonalities as human beings, and ask how human beings *qua* human beings should relate to each other. Since the norms regulating its relations with outsiders are not embedded in and nurtured by the kinds of strong ties that obtain between its members, it also needs to explore their motivational basis and sanctions.

It is hardly surprising that systematic Western reflection on the content and basis of universal morality first began during the Roman Empire, which brought different societies together and encouraged an extensive movement of people and goods. The inquiry started by the Stoics has dominated Western moral and political philosophy, and generated a rich body of ideas. The Stoic idea of natural law, the Christian ethics of human brotherhood, the seventeenth-century idea of natural rights, its nineteenth-century liberal version with its universal civilizing mission, the Marxist vision of human solidarity, the UN Declaration of Human Rights, and subsequent international covenants are all important products of this inquiry. They offer different statements of universal principles, ground them differently, and articulate them in different languages. Each is a response to the challenges of its time, and represents a particular vision of a good life. In several significant respects our age is different and calls for a new inquiry into the principles of global ethics.

Because of globalization, all societies are being bound into a system of interdependence and their actions, directly or indirectly, affect others. The domestic policies of rich countries, such as the subsidies they give to their farmers and industries, the tariffs they impose on imports from developing countries, and their weak regulatory regimes, and the political protection they give to their multinationals, profoundly affect the vital interests and sometimes ruin the lives of millions in the rest of the world. Civil wars in distant countries affect the supply of raw materials and the prosperity and well-being of the rest of the world, including the rich West. And these wars lead to a flow of refugees, whom we cannot turn away as we would stray dogs or intruders. For the first time in history, humankind also faces common problems, such as climate change, drug and human trafficking, terrorist threats, pollution, infectious disease and environmental degradation, and needs to find ways of acting collectively.

As a result of the global reach of the media, human suffering in distant parts of the world comes to us in vivid images, gets under our skin, and calls for a response. We might choose to ignore it, but not without some sense of guilt, or at least unease. Feeble though they are, some concern for the suffering of unknown others and the expansion of sympathy are shaping our moral consciousness, and paving the way for a vague but unmistakable sense of a global moral community. It is this that explains the historically unique phenomenon of humanitarian aid, popular pressure on governments to help societies in distress, anti-globalization protesters driven by concern about its impact on poorer parts of the world, the great personal risk taken by aid workers, doctors, nurses, journalists and others working in unstable countries, and the global campaign to cancel the debts of the poorest countries. The growing sense of human unity is also reflected in and reinforced by an increasing interest in the great scientific, philosophical and artistic achievements of other civilizations, translations of their works, and preservation of a common architectural and ecological heritage.

The profound transformation of the world presents new moral challenges, and radically alters the context and content of the traditional discussion of universal morality. We are increasingly bound together not only by common interests but also by fellow feeling and a shared fate, and see humankind not just as a biological species or a collection of human beings but as a *moral* community. Human beings entertain certain expectations of one another, especially of those in the affluent and powerful West, because of their greater capacity to cause harm and to offer help both directly and through the international institutions they control. And as the latter respond sympathetically, the expectations acquire moral legitimacy, set new moral and political norms, and reinforce the growing awareness of a global community. As the 'we' that constitutes and defines a political community expands to encompass outsiders, humankind begins to acquire some of the features of a loosely knit *political* community. Although there is no global government, there is a growing regime of global governance exercised by international financial and political institutions, conventions and treaties.

Not only is the scope of moral consciousness widening to encompass the entire human race, its content is also undergoing a profound change. Much of the earlier discourse on universal morality took a relatively narrow and individual-centred view of duties to outsiders, such as not harming them and keeping promises. That view is no longer adequate in the modern context. Through the growing sentiment of human interdependence and solidarity, as well as for reasons of enlightened self-interest, it matters to us how human beings outside our own borders lead their lives. And since many of their problems and frustrations arise because of the sorry state of their economic and political life, the latter concerns us in a way that it never did before. Our moral consciousness thus acquires a collective dimension in two interrelated respects. We feel, or should feel, concerned about the quality of collective life in other countries, and our efforts should be directed not so much at helping individuals as at assisting struggling societies to cope with their problems. And since we can help them effectively not by individual actions but by acting through our governments, our moral response too takes on a collective or political character. While individuals do have duties to relieve the suffering of other individuals, as the earlier theories of universal morality argued, these duties in our historical context are also politically mediated and take the form of political communities helping each other directly or through international institutions. This inescapable political mediation of our moral duties has no historical parallel.

Some of the moral questions we face today, then, are new to our age, some of the older ones have taken new forms, and even those that are common need to be discussed in a very different historical context. It is this radical transformation in the traditional discourse on universal morality that the term 'global ethics' highlights, and which at least partly explains why it is to be preferred over the older term. Unlike the term 'universal', the term 'global' stresses the collective and integrated nature of our moral life, and captures the twofold fact that humankind is becoming increasingly interdependent, and faces common problems requiring collective solutions. Unlike the term 'moral', the term 'ethics' highlights the facts that our moral life is embedded in the countless strong ties and the shared human identity that increasingly bind us together, and that our focus is not so much on the intentions, motives and inner lives of individuals as on the structures of social relations. Global ethics is not a new name for the centuries-old discourse on universal morality, but rather its historically novel form in the unique context of our times.

A global ethics is intended to provide the universally valid principles that should guide our choices and actions in the context of an increasingly interdependent world.[2] It explores the universally valid constituents of a good life, why it should matter to us how others live, and what duties we have to them. It is addressed to individuals as well as those collectivities through which they act, such as political communities, international institutions and multinational corporations. It explores how global institutions should be designed and what goals they should pursue so that they promote human well-being and increase humankind's capacity to take charge of its collective destiny. Like all ethics, a global ethics is also concerned with the virtues and the qualities of character that human beings need to develop in order to cope successfully with the challenges of an interdependent world.

A global ethics needs to satisfy four conditions if it is to serve its purpose.[3] First, it should be substantive enough to guide our choices, but not so much as to institutionalize a narrow vision of the good life. Since human beings understand human life differently, and assign different meanings and significance to human activities and relations, moral and cultural diversity is an ineliminable fact of life. It also has much to be said for it, as different cultures represent different forms of human excellence, develop capacities that others marginalize or suppress, and enrich and provide each other with a valuable interlocutor. A global ethics should leave sufficient space for and respect the diversity of moral traditions.

This is sometimes taken to mean, mistakenly in my view, that universal moral principles should be culturally neutral. They might be closer to one view of the good life than to another, and there is no obvious reason why that should necessarily count against them. Indeed, some of them might even be derived from one culture or view of the good life, and that too should not count against them. Moral principles may come from anywhere, and all that matters is whether they can be defended adequately. Their origin in a particular culture makes it likely that they might embody a narrow vision of the good life. While this should put us on our guard and calls for close scrutiny, it does not entail their automatic rejection.

Second, a global ethics should be based on a global consensus. This is important for several interrelated reasons. Moral principles require uncoerced intellectual assent, and those whom they are meant to bind should see their point. The search for a consensus also shows respect for other points of view, and guards against our natural tendency to universalize our own. It has the further advantage that all involved see the principles as theirs, and take ownership of them. This ensures their compliance and builds up a climate of trust.

Third, since a global ethics is intended to guide our conduct, it should be grounded in our historical context, including our current self-understanding, needs, aspirations and circumstances. Its universality could therefore be limited to our times. This goes against the widely-held view that universal moral principles properly so called must be valid for all times. While some moral principles might meet such a stringent requirement, others might not. And even the former are invariably thin, and need to be interpreted against the background of, and adjusted to, our circumstances and self-understanding. The idea of human rights, for example, presupposes that human beings are able to abstract themselves from their social, national and ethnic background, that they see themselves as bearers of certain claims, and that these claims should be given institutional protection. Since many premodern societies do not meet these conditions, the idea of human rights would have made no sense to our Stone Age or even Greek ancestors. It cannot, however, be rejected on the grounds that its universality is limited to our times. The fact that moral principles are time-bound does not mean that they are also space-bound. Since contemporary societies are within our reach, we can bring moral principles to their attention and press these on them, which is not possible in relation to past societies.

Fourth, a global ethics should be concerned with principles, not institutions, practices and policies. The latter are ways of realizing them in practice, and that necessarily depends on the traditions, circumstances and history of a society. When a principle is equated with a particular institutional form or way of defining it, a commonly made mistake, it becomes a vehicle for universalizing the latter, and risks being rejected by those who are sympathetic to it but not to the institutional or cultural baggage loaded on to it. We might have good reasons for thinking that a particular institution best realizes, or a particular interpretation best captures, the thrust of the relevant principle, but we should not be dogmatic about it and pre-empt human ingenuity.

Basis of a global ethics

In the light of our discussion, we need a historically relevant, relatively narrow and consensually grounded global ethic. This raises the question of how to develop it. Many past and present answers fall into one of two categories. Some appeal to an allegedly infallible, or at least dependable, source such as human nature, God, or cross-cultural or cross-religious consensus, whereas others devise procedural tests, such as Kant's universalizability principle or Rawls' veil of ignorance. Although both approaches contain important insights, neither is adequate.

Human nature is obviously central to a global ethics, which is not meant for Martians but people like us, and needs to take fully into account what human beings are like, can or cannot do, their needs and desires, their conditions of growth, basic life experiences, distinctive capacities and so on. Although an appeal to human nature, or rather to the basic facts about human beings, is necessary, it is by itself not enough. Since human beings lead organized lives and their nature has been profoundly shaped by layers of social influences, we have no access to it in its raw form and cannot easily separate what is natural from what is social. Furthermore, human nature contains different desires and tendencies, and cannot tell us which ones to satisfy, to what degree, and how to resolve inescapable conflicts. We approve of some of these tendencies and disapprove of others, and the required criteria themselves cannot be derived from human nature. Although human nature is relatively stable, it is also historically and culturally mediated. As self-creating beings, humans develop new capacities, dispositions, ambitions and forms of self-understanding across different historical epochs. These are as much a part of them as is their 'natural' or biological nature, rightly being called their 'second nature'. The ideas of individuality, choice, self-authorship, equality, autonomy, and mastery of nature are historically specific and not inherent in human nature. If we ignored them, our view of human beings would be highly impoverished, and the resulting ethics historically irrelevant.

The appeal to God faces obvious difficulties. Belief in God, assuming that we can agree on what 'God' means, is not self-evident, and cannot be established to the satisfaction of those who reject or remain sceptical about it. It also creates the familiar puzzle as to whether a principle is right because God wills and commands it, or because we have independent reasons to accept it. If the latter, God is not the basis of its authority. If the former, then in theory God could have willed a different principle. We find this inconceivable, because God could never will what seems patently wrong to us, thus presupposing that we have at least some independent knowledge of what is right and wrong. God might still be invoked to sanction or supplement morality, but He is not its sole source. God also speaks differently in different religions, and we have no means of deciding which of them represents His true will.

The appeal to cross-religious or cross-cultural consensus is useful as a starting point, but has its limits.[4] All religions share certain attitudes and sensibilities, such as a sense of transcendence, an acute awareness of human fallibility and finitude, and some conception of the sacred and the holy. However, they do not have many moral principles in common, and some of those that they do, such as a low view of women, hostility to outsiders, and intolerance of dissent and heresy, are morally unacceptable. Many religions do not value human equality and assign differential worth to different categories of human beings. Although all religions value freedom, at least in the choice of religion, some deny their adherents the freedom to reject it, and are so convinced of their truth that they resort to all manner of moral and spiritual coercion, including threats of other-worldly punishment, to convert outsiders. Although all religions value human life, they do not place much value on the lives of outsiders, heathens, apostates and idolaters. They cherish human dignity, but again limit it in various ways, and some even make it dependent on acceptance of the 'true faith' or belief in God. Some religions value the service of one's fellow-humans, whereas others either do not or consider it inferior to a life devoted to the solitary contemplation of God. Some value the environment and show respect for nature, while others do not. We can reinterpret religions and find in them different degrees of support for some, or even all, of these values, but that only shows that the values are derived from other sources and have been read back into or 'discovered' in religions. The appeal to a cross-cultural consensus runs into similar difficulties. Different cultures do not hold many values in common, and some of those they do are morally unacceptable. And in the case of the former, they are values not, or at least not merely, because different cultures say so, but rather because we see their point on independent grounds.

The second common way to arrive at a global ethics is to invoke various kinds of procedural devices. Broadly speaking, Kant's universalizability principle maintains that, if a maxim of conduct can be consistently universalized, it has a claim to universal acceptance.[5] Although Kant's principle has the great advantage of guarding against the influence of prejudices and self-interest, its difficulties are well known. Like all procedural tests, it does not stand on its own. It assumes that all human beings have equal dignity and that their claims deserve equal consideration. Unlike some of his followers, Kant realized this, and justified equality on the grounds that human beings were ends in themselves by virtue of their unique capacity for self-determination or acting in accordance with self-given laws. Although this is an important basis for equality, it does not explain whether and why we should extend equality to those, such as children and people with learning disabilities, whose capacity for autonomy is inadequately developed. Nor does it explain how such noumenal equality translates at the phenomenal level, and whether it entails equal access to the material and other conditions that are needed to develop that capacity.

The maxim that we should not render assistance to those in need can be universalized, but Kant resists it. He argues that 'a will which resolved this would conflict with itself' because occasions are bound to arise when every human being needs the love and sympathy of others. This is not a moral but a prudential argument. It also ignores the fact that some individuals might prefer to forgo others' sympathy and love in order to avoid the reciprocal obligation to help them in turn. Since individuals differ in their temperaments and preferences, one person might be able to will a maxim consistently, whereas another might not. Kant's principle cannot therefore deliver on its promise to offer an objective universal maxim. Furthermore, it implies that which maxim can be consistently willed and universalized cannot be decided independently of the empirical facts about human beings and their circumstances, which Kant's dualist metaphysics rules out.

Even if we abstracted Kant's universalizability principle from its metaphysical framework, difficulties would remain. It is better equipped to tell us what actions should be disallowed rather than which ones should be required. It is possible to universalize the maxim that one should always tell the truth, but also that one should tell a lie when it saves human lives or has beneficial consequences. Since the universalizability test is met by both, it does not tell us which maxim to adopt. Kant opts for the former, but this is no more than a personal preference. Furthermore, the test is centred on individuals, and does not help us to decide which maxims should guide the actions of states, multinational corporations and international institutions, which also have obligations. Since it is embedded in the individualist view of moral life, it is also culturally too specific to provide the basis for a cross-culturally valid global ethics.

John Rawls' view in his *A Theory of Justice* that universal principles are best arrived at by exploring what individuals would agree upon behind the veil of ignorance fares no better.[6] Although it ensures impartiality and filters out morally irrelevant considerations, it is open to several objections. He so oversimplifies the process of moral deliberation that it bears little relevance to human life as we know it. Individuals behind the veil of ignorance are almost identical, thinking in the same way and being guided by the same considerations as others. Furthermore, they all reason privately on the basis of their own interests, and do not engage in a transformative rational discussion that might force them to be clear about what they want and to change their views. Rawls even suggests that we might imagine a courier collecting their proposals, and informing them when they have come to an agreement. By removing religion, culture, nationality and so on, which profoundly shape people's views and values, Rawls makes moral deliberation and agreement infinitely easier than it is in reality.

There is also the question of the language in which individuals deliberate and communicate behind the veil of ignorance, as it is not difficult to think of several that lack the conceptual resources to express some of Rawls' central ideas, at least in a form that is crucial to the whole exercise. Furthermore, individuals behind the veil of ignorance can be conceptualized in several different ways, and Rawls does not explain why he abstracts greed, envy, desire for status, the impulse to gamble, and differences in the capacity to reason, but not self-interest and self-respect, and why he thinks that abstracting only the former set of human qualities provides the ideal conditions for a fair choice among free and equal persons. It is also difficult to see why the principles arrived at behind the veil of ignorance should bind individuals once they know the full facts about themselves and their circumstances, or acquire a historically specific 'second' nature. They might then wish to replace the chosen principles with others more suited to their circumstances and self-understanding, or disagree deeply about what they should be. Rawls claims to transcend history and legislate for 'eternity', an inherently implausible claim for any philosopher to make.

Rawls' original position is territorially bounded, and individuals within it deliberate about what principles of justice should apply within their political community. He does not explain why he thinks that the territorial boundary is not just a contingent historical fact but rather an irreducible and self-contained unit of moral deliberation. This is not to say that his view is indefensible, but rather that he does not provide good reasons for it and pushes it further than is warranted. One consequence of this is that fellow citizens acquire undue moral significance, and outsiders count for very little. Even when Rawls later addresses the question of global justice, he is unable to overcome the limitations of his statist framework, and ultimately gives an untenably minimalist and arbitrary account of duties to outsiders.

A global ethics, then, cannot be derived from some infallible source or foolproof procedural test. Rational deliberation is the only way to arrive at it. This involves examining different moral principles, weighing up the reasons for and against them, and settling on those that on balance seem more convincing and command a broad cross-cultural consensus. Moral deliberation is comparative in nature. We decide in favour of some principles rather than others not because arguments for them are irrefutable, for such certainty is rare in human affairs, but because they are stronger and more convincing than those for their alternatives. It is not, therefore, enough for the critic to say that our arguments are inconclusive, as that is a necessary feature of all moral reasoning; he or she needs to show that a much better or an equally good case can be made for the opposite principle. If s/he cannot, our decision stands. For example, while we can offer powerful arguments for both gender and race equality, these are rarely conclusive and incontrovertible. However, if we can show, as indeed we can, that those for sexism and racism are flimsy, self-serving, circular or ill-founded, we would have said enough to show that equality is a rationally defensible value to be preferred over inequality. Moral values have no foundations in the sense of an indisputable and objective basis, but they do have grounds in the form of well-considered reasons.

Reasons relevant to deliberation on a global ethics are of several kinds, of which three are particularly important. Some are empirical and appeal to the well-established and cross-culturally instantiated facts about human beings, such as that they are mortal, prone to disease, decay and pain, have certain basic desires, needs and capacities, flourish or wither away under certain conditions, suffer at the loss of loved ones, and have limited knowledge of themselves. These facts circumscribe the scope of moral principles as well as provide part of their content. They tell us what human beings can or cannot do, and set limits as to what can morally be expected of them. They also tell us what humans generally tend to do, and what a moral system should accommodate unless there are good reasons not to. Human beings, for example, generally wish to preserve themselves, have certain natural desires, and care more for those they love than for total strangers. A moral system that ignored or declared a war on these tendencies would be widely resisted and risks being discredited. It should acknowledge their reality, and find ways of regulating and guiding them.

Some other morally relevant reasons are rather complex in nature. For convenience, and because they have been the central preoccupation of moral philosophers, I shall call them philosophical reasons. They presuppose a particular way of understanding human beings, a more or less coherent conception of what it is to be human. We arrive at it by locating human beings in the world around them, identifying and critically reflecting on their distinctive capacities, and determining their meaning and significance. The resulting general conception of human beings provides a framework within which we discuss how they should be treated, and determine the relevance and weight of our reasons.

It is a fundamental fact of human life, and hence the inescapable basis of all moral deliberation, that human beings share the earth with other animals. At one level, they are like them, but at another, they are quite different by virtue of possessing certain distinctive capacities. This raises the question of whether they should be viewed as animals and treated on a par with them, or given an ontologically privileged status. Again, while human beings are all members of a common species and thus similar, they also differ greatly among themselves, sometimes as much as or even more than they differ from the animals. This raises the question of how to understand and assess their commonalities and differences, and whether they should be entitled to equal consideration, or whether some of them might be used in the service of others. These and other similar questions have an empirical basis, but they are not empirical questions. They have profound moral consequences, but they are not moral questions either. They are interpretive and hermeneutic questions – that is, questions about the nature of humanity, man's place in the world, the contribution humankind makes to it, and how best to interpret and understand human existence. All moral inquiry presupposes and is embedded in a philosophical inquiry of this kind, often called philosophical anthropology or simply philosophy of man.

Third, some morally relevant reasons are experiential or prudential in nature, and constitute what some earlier writers called practical wisdom. They are reflective distillations of the past and present experiences of different societies and the lessons that can be drawn from them. They tell us what is or is not practicable, what is likely to have which long-term consequences, how different social institutions and practices are related and so on. We can, for example, show by appropriate historical and contemporary examples that identification of state and religion corrupts both and undermines human dignity and freedom; that absolute power corrupts not only in the mundane sense of creating vested interests but also in the deeper sense of breeding self-righteousness and intolerance of disagreement; that the self-evident moral truths of one age turn out to be falsehoods in another, and that we should be wary of all such claims; and that institutionalized criticism is the best way to guard against the all too common illusion of infallibility. We can also show that inequalities beyond a certain point corrupt all involved, that degrading groups of human beings exacts a heavy emotional and moral price from its alleged beneficiaries as well as its victims, and that human freedom is best protected by setting up appropriate institutions and practices rather than by trusting the wisdom and good sense of the powerful. We might also appeal to a cross-cultural consensus to show why different societies in their own different ways felt it necessary to develop certain common practices, and why the latter deserve to be taken seriously. The consensus does not by itself settle the matter, as it could be mistaken or based on social conditions that no longer obtain. Its basic role is to assist reflection, highlight factors we might have ignored, and provide an additional reason when others are evenly balanced.

Deliberation on a global ethics is, then, a highly complex activity. It involves assessing, relating and weighing up reasons for and against different principles and values. It has an empirical component in the form of established facts about human beings, a philosophical component in the sense of a coherent framework for understanding human beings, and a practical component or knowledge of the broad consequences of and the connections between different social practices. These three components are closely related. We assess the significance of the established facts about human beings in the light of our general conception of them. And we critically assess the latter and choose between different conceptions on the basis of, among other things, these facts and the lessons of historical and contemporary experience. When individuals disagree about the principles of a global ethic, their disagreements can often, though not always, be traced to one of these three. Disagreements at each level require different modes of resolution. The empirical differences are generally easy to resolve, whereas the philosophical ones are often the most intractable.

Equal worth

Human beings are endowed with several capacities that mark them out from the rest of the natural world.[7] These include the capacity to think, reason, reflect, use language, imagine things unseen, dream of a better life, enter into moral relations with one another, pursue ideals and so on. Although these capacities are related, they are different in nature, and cannot all be reduced to any one of them. Reason is often taken to be the basis of them all, but it does not by itself explain why human beings are able to construct myths, compose music, pursue large causes or fall in love, unless we define reason in such narrow, formal and abstract terms that it loses all specificity. Human beings are not only rational and moral but also artistic, sensual, sexual, vulnerable, practical and needy beings, and the interplay of these and other dimensions constitutes and structures their humanity or human identity.

Through these capacities, humans introduce a wholly novel and uniquely human form of existence. They are able to rise above the automatic and inexorable processes of nature, understand and control them, carve out spaces of freedom, and act as self-determining and responsible agents. They build rich inner worlds of distinctly human emotions, enter into webs of fulfilling relationships with each other, and give depth and meaning to their lives. They also create a public world of aesthetic, literary, scientific, religious and other achievements, and introduce the great values of truth, goodness and beauty. This is not to advance the hubristic anthropocentric view that the universe derives its value from human beings, but rather that it is the richer for human contributions to it.

As beings capable of creating meaning and values and leading lives based on them, humans deserve to be valued themselves and have intrinsic value or worth. Worth is not a natural fact, like eyes and ears, but rather a status we ascribe to or confer upon them. It is a moral judgement and is, like all judgements, based on what we take to be good reasons for valuing freedom, beauty, truth, goodness, and a rich and meaningful life. Human beings have worth because they are capable of doing worthy things, and their worth is intrinsic because it is based on capacities and achievements that are not contingent but constitutive of their humanity. This is not 'speciesism' (surely a mouthful for which there must be a better expression), because we value human beings not because of who they are but because of their capacities and what they are capable of achieving and doing. It is, of course, possible that human capacities and achievements are all trivial in the eyes of God, and that the high value we place on them reveals a deep anthropocentric bias. We cannot, however, leap out of ourselves and judge ourselves from some superhuman point of view. Even the latter is ultimately constructed on the basis of what we think and value. The properties we ascribe to God and the standards by which we think He judges us are shaped and limited by our own categories of thought and values.

In so far as we judge ourselves by the standards we ourselves have set up, some bias does enter our judgement. But it is inescapable at this most basic level, and we reduce it by conferring value on other species that display some of these capacities, such as the higher animals and, if they ever arrive, visitors from other planets. The more human capacities an animal exhibits, the higher is, or should be, its status in our eyes, and the better is, or should be, our treatment of it. Even such higher animals as chimpanzees and gorillas, however, are qualitatively different from humans. They lack the capacity to create the great values on the basis of which we endow human beings with worth, and do not enjoy the same moral status as human beings. Not even the most ardent animal rights activist maintains that rats may not be killed to save crops or to stop disease, that if a starving lion was found attacking a child, we should not intervene, or that animal interests should take precedence over the human in situations of scarcity. Animals do, of course, have feelings, can be objects of affection, have needs, and even perhaps interests in an extended sense of the term. We should not therefore use them as we please, subject them to torture or painful experiments, or kill them for fun, but they are not our moral equals.[8] A man who bequeathed his property to his dog rather than to his young child or disabled wife would rightly be open to criticism.

Human beings not only have or, what comes to the same thing, should be accorded intrinsic value or worth, but have it in equal measure. This is sometimes denied on the grounds that, since reason is the *differentia specifica* of human beings, those endowed with it to a greater degree are better than other human beings and have greater worth. This view goes back to Plato and Aristotle, who not only privileged reason but divided it into theoretical and practical reason and considered the former to be higher than the latter. It also informed much of the Christian justification of slavery, was shared by many an eminent liberal, and underpinned European colonialism. There is no good reason to privilege reason, let alone theoretical reason, over other human capacities. We do so either because we believe it to be the basis of all other human capacities, or consider it to be the highest. Neither is convincing. Reason certainly informs and is presupposed by other human capacities, but they are neither derived from nor reducible to it. Those with greater reason are not necessarily more imaginative, capable of greater will-power, or more courageous, compassionate, caring or creative. Indeed, given the complex logic of human capacities, the more one of them, including reason, is developed, the less likely it is that others will be developed in equal measure. Human capacities do not form a harmonious whole, and the conditions for the fullest development of one sometimes militate against the development of others.

As for the second assumption, that reason is the highest human capacity, it is difficult to see how it can be substantiated. If reason is the highest capacity because it says so, the argument is circular. And as for the others, they indicate no such thing. Furthermore, it is not clear what standard is used to grade human capacities such that reason comes out at the top. It could be one of three, namely that it is the basis of all others, that it generates knowledge, and that human life is impossible without its guidance and regulative influence. As we saw, the first is suspect. As for the second, imagination and so on also play a vital role in arriving at knowledge, and in any case there is no reason why knowledge should be considered the highest value and given greater importance than love, courage and compassion. As for the third, while reason plays a crucial role in organizing life, will-power, the capacity for empathy, and love also do so.

Human beings have a range of capacities, and a reductionist account of them is inherently flawed. Different human capacities operate differently and play different roles in human life. One cannot take the place of another, and they do not always entail each other either. Since human capacities cannot be reduced to one of them and graded on a single scale, superiority in one capacity does not signify overall superiority or superiority *qua* human beings. Indeed, the very idea of grading human beings and establishing a hierarchy among them is logically incoherent.

This establishes a negative case for equality; that is, that there is no basis to assign differential or unequal worth to human beings. We can go further and make a positive case for it. Human beings have common needs that are as compelling in the case of one of them as that of another, and they are subject to common vulnerabilities and misfortunes that are as much a part of one man's life as that of another, and just as distressing to them. They need common conditions to flourish, and in their absence decay and wither away. They all seek meaning and fulfilment in their lives, and feel frustrated and disorientated when their lives offer neither. Although these commonalities do not by themselves entail equal treatment, they create a strong presumption in favour of it, and place the onus of justification on those seeking to depart from it. It is a matter of intellectual and moral consistency that those with similar needs should be treated similarly unless there are compelling reasons to do otherwise.

Yet another reason for equality relates to the fact that it leads to a richer and more relaxed society than does inequality. Human beings depend on each other for their sense of self-worth and all-round development. When they are treated as inferior or of no worth, they tend to internalize these images, take a poor view of themselves, aim low, fail to develop their talents, and build up resentment against those subjecting them to such treatment. By contrast, equality builds up their self-respect and gives them the confidence and energy to realize their potential. It also increases their respect for others, both because the latter treat them with respect, and because they appreciate that just as they value their own self-respect, so do others. Unlike inequality, which stifles the potential and stunts the growth of those treated as inferiors, equality releases their energies, unshackles their talents, and enables them to make their unique contributions to society. It also encourages different forms of self-expression, generates an ethos of achievement-based rather than status-based recognition, and creates a varied and vibrant society that benefits all. Inequality breaks up society into self-contained groups. Those at the top share no common interest with those at the bottom, not even social cohesion and better public services, because of their ability to buy their way out of the shared life. By contrast, equality creates common interests and experiences, and fosters the spirit of common belonging and common citizenship that lies at the heart of a viable political community.

Because of their unique capacities, human beings are capable of self-determination, pursuing self-chosen goals, leading fulfilling lives, accepting responsibility for their actions, entering into relationships of reciprocity with each other, and forming part of a moral community. In other words, they are moral persons or agents. Since they all share the capacity for personhood, they are equal *qua* persons. It is true that some are better able to organize their lives, make greater use of their opportunities, and even to be involved in more worthwhile activities. This makes them better persons but not more of a person than others, worthy of greater admiration but not of greater claims that go with personhood. Personhood presupposes an intellectual and moral threshold as defined by those basic capacities that are needed to function as self-determining and responsible individuals, and all who meet it deserve to be treated equally. There is also the acute practical difficulty of determining the degree of personhood of different individuals and adjusting our treatment of them accordingly. The most sensible and fair way is to treat equally all those who meet the threshold. We apply the idea of a threshold in many areas of life, and use it to determine formal equality. Once an academic organization or a legally constituted community, for example, meets certain minimum criteria or crosses a threshold and qualifies as a university or a state, it has the same rights as any other, although the others might be much larger, richer, older or better run.

Some categories of human beings, such as those who are insane or have severe learning difficulties do not cross the threshold of personhood, thus raising the question of whether they have less worth – or even perhaps none. Since they are not full persons, they do not qualify for equality as persons, which is why they are rightly denied some of the rights of persons, such as the rights to make their own choices, run their lives independently, and to vote. Although they are not full persons, they are human beings and should be accorded equal worth. Few, if any, human beings are wholly devoid of basic human capacities, and they are insane or disabled in a way that only humans can be. Conferring worth on such individuals also tests, affirms and reinforces our general commitment to human worth because, if we are able to value and stretch our compassion to include them, we are even more likely to value our more fortunate fellow humans. Furthermore, insanity and mental disability are not easy to define. Once we deny worth to such people and treat them as subhuman or a burden on society's resources, we risk undermining our historically developed moral inhibitions and denying worth to other classes of human beings such as the elderly, those who are physically disabled, and criminals. We well know from historical experience how dangerous it is to travel along this slippery road. It is in our collective interest to grant equal worth to all human beings and foster the right kind of moral sensibility.

I have argued that there is a powerful case for assigning equal worth to human beings, and that it is stronger than that for its opposites. The principle of equal human worth has several important implications. First, it implies that the individual's humanity does not end with his or her social status, and is the basis for equal claims on others. Under slavery, slaves are nothing more than this. Their status as slaves negates their humanity and condemns them to permanent inequality. In a hierarchical society, those on the lower rungs are considered to be inferior not just in their social status but *qua* human beings, and carry their inferiority in all areas of their life. They may not remain seated in the presence of their superiors, or dress like them, disagree with them, speak with a certain accent, go against their wishes, and are in general expected to demonstrate their subordinate status in small and large ways. The principle of equal human worth implies that all are entitled to equal respect, and that their subordinate status in a particular area remains limited to that area and does not affect their humanity.

Since the sense of an individual's worth in his/her own eyes is bound up with what others think of him/her and how they treat him/her, the principle of equal human worth requires a broad equality of social status, power and life chances. This does not mean that we may not admire some people more, because that depends on their individual capacities and achievements; nor that all should enjoy equal wealth and income, because that depends on their contribution to social well-being, and because the incentive of unequal reward is often necessary to spur people to greater efforts; nor that all are equally qualified to hold all offices, as that depends on their capacities and inclinations. Rather, it requires that such inequalities as are necessary or inescapable should satisfy certain conditions. They should not extend to basic civil, political and economic rights, and treat some as less than full human beings.

They should not be interlocking such that inequality in one area leads to that in others, or so entrenched and self-perpetuating that they close off worthwhile careers for, and deny equal life chances to, large sections of people. They should not be so wide and so deep as to allow some to opt out of the common life and lead a fortified and parallel life of their own, nor so comprehensive as to channel all ambitions and talents in one particular direction and discourage other legitimate modes of self-fulfil-ment and ways of life. Above all, they should not lead to such a wide disparity of power and status between or within societies as to breed arrogance and superciliousness among some and inferiority and help-lessness among others, and split society or humankind into two different species of human beings.

Second, the principle of equal human worth implies respect for the right of self-determination for all those who cross the threshold of personhood. They are capable of making choices, running their lives, and accepting responsibility for the consequences of their actions. They may make mistakes and even make a mess of their lives, but they should be free to learn from these errors. Others may point out their mistakes and offer advice, but should not take over their lives as if the individuals were children or incapable of independent agency. Such paternalism undermines their worth in their own and others' eyes, stunts their growth, opens the door to all manner of oppression, and represents what Kant called the 'greatest conceivable despotism'.

Third, the principle of equal human worth requires that all human beings should be able to lead lives that affirm and nurture their sense of worth. They flourish under certain material and social conditions, and have equal claims to them. Their fundamental interests include physical secu-rity, the satisfaction of their basic needs, good health, opportunities for growth, access to the cultural resources of their community, basic rights and liberties, and so on. They also include the development of those capac-ities without which they cannot function effectively and lead balanced and fulfilling lives, and those dispositions and drives such as the will to succeed, the determination to take hold of their lives, and the sense of pride and self-confidence without which they cannot make full use of their capacities. The organization and conduct of their collective life should also affirm and sustain their equal worth. This requires that they should be in charge of their collective destiny, their views should be sought, heard and respected in all major institutions of society, they should be able to partic-ipate in the conduct of public affairs, and should in general have the sense that they have the power to make a difference to their shared life.

Since human beings cannot affirm and realize their equal worth in the absence of these and related conditions, the latter constitute great human goods, and their opposites great human evils. Poverty, terror, institutionalized humiliation, degrading working conditions, subjection to the arbitrary will of others, a lack of basic rights, and being the playthings of their rulers and the impersonal forces of the market generate a sense of worthlessness and destroy the very substance of their humanity. The consciousness of equal human worth does not arise and cannot be sustained in a social vacuum. It needs to be embodied in social, economic, political and other institutions, and become a matter of daily experience.

Finally, the principle of equal human worth implies that we have the same worth as others, and that the grounds on which we should respect others require us to respect ourselves as well. As Kant argues, just as we may not treat others as if they were worthless, we also should not treat ourselves, or allow others to treat us, as if we were worthless. Degrading, demeaning or humiliating oneself is in principle little different from degrading or humiliating others, for both alike detract from our status as human beings. We acquire worth by virtue of being human or members of the universal human community. As its representative, we may not behave in a manner that denies our worth, either in our own case or that of others. This is why it makes sense to say that when one human being is degraded and his/her humanity is mocked, all human beings *qua* human beings are degraded. This happens in many other areas of life as well. When a son humiliates, mocks, abuses or blackmails his father, the latter may rightly say that he will not be treated in this way, not because he is personally disturbed about it but because no son should ever treat his father in this way. He is concerned not about his personal feelings but about a principle, a value, a norm, the dignity of the status of father, of which he sees himself in this case as a custodian. Even if he is prepared to put up with his treatment because he is too dependent on his son or too frightened, others may rightly uphold the principle and criticize or think badly of the son.

The principle of equal human worth generates duties to others.[9] It is common to distinguish between negative and positive duties – the duty not to harm and the duty to render positive assistance, and to make the latter optional or supererogatory. Although the distinction is *prima facie* plausible, it is ultimately unsatisfactory. Some duties fall under neither category; for example, the duty to acknowledge the equal worth of all human beings, to treat them with respect, or to tell the truth. Some others fall under either, depending on how they are interpreted; for example, the duty to highlight injustices or to support their victims in their struggle. Some other duties straddle or have elements of both. The duty to pull a drunkard out of a pond is positive because it involves active help; it is also negative because by not helping one would have caused his death. The cause of his death is not only his drunken state that caused the fall into the pond in the first place, but also others' inaction that failed to prevent its consequences.

Even when the two duties can be clearly distinguished, it is not clear why, as a rule, the negative duty should be considered binding or obligatory and the positive optional or supererogatory, and more stringent than the latter. Two reasons are generally given for this view. First, the principle of equal human worth requires that since others' interests have equal claims with ours, we should not harm them. The positive duty is grounded in the principle of benevolence which, although commendable, goes beyond that of equal worth and is not morally as compelling. Second, duties must be realistic and within the reach of all. If they were to be inflated, even those that are minimally necessary would be ignored. We cannot expect human beings to ignore their own self-interest, and should only require that they do not harm the interests of others. While these arguments make important points, they cannot carry the moral weight that is placed on them.

The first argument is flawed because it narrows arbitrarily the scope of the principle of equal human worth. We cannot be said to respect the equal worth of other human beings if we are indifferent to the quality of their lives. If they lead poor, empty and miserable lives, their humanity is degraded and their worth in their own and others' eyes is undermined. They address us and, if it is within our power to do something about them, we have a duty to do so. The principle of equal human worth entails both negative and positive duties, and it is our resources and other obligations that determine the scope of the latter. Benevolence within the limits of one's capacity is not optional but a duty, which is why a person who fails to attempt to save a drowning child, or report a crime or a fire, is considered blameworthy. In many societies, law explicitly imposes these 'good samaritan' duties on pain of sanctions. Although there is a distinction to be drawn between justice and benevolence, it is culturally conditioned, constantly stretched, and does not correspond to that between negative and positive duties.

The second argument makes the valid point that duties should not be unduly multiplied, but misunderstands what negative duty entails. The latter is not necessarily less demanding than positive duty. It requires that one may not pursue one's interests in a manner that harms others, but one can harm them in several direct and indirect ways. Driving a car or flying to a distant holiday may contribute to global warming, and thus damage others' vital interests. Buying the shares or even the products of a company that pays poor wages or imposes harsh conditions of work harms its employees. Doing one's negative duty thus requires a most careful consideration of the short and long term consequences of one's actions, which is never easy, and it imposes far greater limits on one's choices than is generally appreciated. It is also sometimes more difficult to discharge than positive duty. We do not always know whether and how our action or inaction damages others' interests, whereas we often know how we can alleviate their suffering and improve their ability to lead worthwhile lives. Indeed, it is precisely because we sometimes inadvertently harm others' interests and thus fail to discharge our negative duty that we owe them the duty of assistance to compensate for it.

Principles

I have so far been concerned to show how we might go about developing a historically relevant global ethics. Since outlining a fully articulated ethics falls outside the scope of this book, assuming that such a presumptuous exercise is even possible, I shall end by highlighting some of its central principles as they follow from our discussion in the earlier chapters and in this one. They are not the only ones, but they are some of the most important.

The first is the principle of equal worth. I argued earlier why all human beings have, or rather should be assigned, equal worth and what this entails. It implies that they make equal claims to the promotion of their fundamental interests, and imposes duties on others. We may not pursue our interests in a manner that damages those of others. And when others are unable to lead worthy lives, we have a positive duty to help them within the limits of our capacity and other obligations. These duties are unaffected by territorial boundaries because they bind us as human beings and not as members of this or that community.

Although rights are important, much of the current discussion of global ethics goes wrong in placing an excessive emphasis on them. All rights, including the so-called negative ones, involve both negative and positive duties. They can only be realized under certain conditions, such as a stable society, a well-functioning state, and availability of material resources. When these are absent, rights remain empty claims unless those in a position to help are placed under a duty of assistance. Universal declarations of rights are sometimes perceived as being instruments of Western domination and arouse hostility because, among other things, they entitle the West to demand that all societies should organize themselves in certain ways, but impose no negative or positive duties on it to help them to do so. A global ethics needs to be as specific in indicating who has what duties to whom, as it is in listing rights.[10]

The second important constituent of a global ethics is the principle of human solidarity. As I argued earlier, human interests are closely inter-twined in our interdependent world, and it is becoming increasingly difficult for the members of any society to lead secure and decent lives unless others do so too. We also face common problems and cannot tackle them on our own. Forces of globalization acquire a momentum of their own and reduce human beings to becoming their playthings unless the latter act collectively and use the forces to promote human well-being. Our actions have profound consequences for future generations, who have as much worth as we have, and we may not act in a manner that damages their vital interests. We inhabit a fragile planet with finite resources, and if some overuse them, everyone pays the price. All this means that the world is our collective responsibility, humankind as a whole should be our moral point of reference, and we need to think and act together in the spirit of human solidarity.

The third important constituent of a global ethics is the principle of respect for difference or plurality. As I argued earlier, different commu-nities develop different forms of life, cultivate different human capaci-ties and emotions, and cherish different values and ideals. Since human capacities and ideals cannot all be combined harmoniously, every way of life is necessarily partial. In attaining its characteristic form of excel-lence, it misses out or marginalizes many a valuable human capacity, emotion and value. Different communities, capturing different dimen-sions of human existence and exploring it from different angles, comple-ment each other, and each can learn from a critical and creative engagement with others.

Although human beings cannot escape their finitude and view them-selves from a transcendental or Archimedean standpoint, they have available to them mini-Archimedean standpoints in the shape of other cultural perspectives. An intercultural dialogue enables each cultural community to look at its beliefs and practices from the standpoints of others, appreciate their contingency and specificity, see their strengths and limitations, and in these and other ways assists their rational evaluation. Rationality or critical self-reflection is not an isolated individual achievement. It presupposes that we are able to rise above our beliefs and practices, and appreciate both that they could be different and do not represent the absolute truth. This in turn requires that there should be available to us other systems of beliefs and practices to act as our critical interlocutor. The plurality of cultures both highlights and offers at least a partial release from human finitude, and is the necessary condition of human freedom and rationality. It also gives us access to the insights and achievements of other cultures, widens our range of choices, and promotes human well-being.

When one appreciates the ontological and epistemological importance of plurality and difference, one sees other cultures, religions and so on, not as threats or rivals but rather as conversational partners, indeed as the very condition of one's growth. One does not merely tolerate or even respect them from a distance, but values and cherishes them, and wishes them well. When they flourish and develop their characteristic forms of excellence, one benefits just as their members do. The diversity of perspectives and their sympathetic and critical interaction is a universal human good, which we have a collective interest in promoting. This does not mean that all forms of diversity should be valued. The principles of global ethics tell us which ones are unacceptable. Nor does it mean that we should preserve or freeze existing forms of diversity. Cultural and other differences cannot be preserved like museum pieces, and the kind of dialogue I am talking about has a transformative effect on each of them. Rather, valuing diversity means that we should create conditions in which human beings, individually and collectively, are free and able to experiment with different ideals, values and forms of life, develop newer forms of diversity, and enrich others with their unique contributions.[11]

Taken together, these three principles point to a world in which human beings are equally valued; lead free and fulfilling lives; deal with their common problems and nurture their shared world in the spirit of human solidarity; and cherish and profit from their individual and collective differences. Whatever else we aim at, and there is much else, they represent the minimum that should guide our individual and in particular collective choices, and shape the structure and goals of global institutions.

11

Moralities of Partiality and Impartiality

In the previous chapter I argued that *qua* human beings, all human beings are morally equal and make equal claims on each other. They are also, however, bound to some of their fellow humans by special ties arising out of mutual commitments, promises, participation in common practices and membership of organizations, and make claims on each other that others do not.[1] These ties vary greatly in their intensity and depth. Some are shallow and formal, such as those to fellow members of clubs and to colleagues. At the other extreme they are deep, lifelong, and involve mutual identification and deep emotional engagement, such as those to one's parents, children, spouse and close friends. Many others, such as those to one's fellow citizens and neighbours, fall between the two extremes.

All special ties or bonds involve giving preference to those involved, and hence some degree of partiality. The deeper and more intense the bonds, the greater is the claim of those involved, and the greater is the role of partiality. This is why the world of close personal relations constitutes the realm of partiality par excellence. Since special relations involve partiality, they pose a challenge to the principle of impartiality. The question arises with particular intensity in relation to close personal ties. I shall therefore concentrate on these, and explore a way of resolving the conflict between the two moralities that could then be extended with appropriate modifications to other kinds of special relations.

Special relationships

The world of close personal relations, which for brevity I shall call 'identity relations' because of the mutual identification they involve, has

228

several unique features. Those involved matter to each other intrinsically, because of who they are, and not for some ulterior purpose they might serve. Each is, and knows that he or she is, special, unique, precious, irreplaceable in the eyes of the other, and may make claims that others cannot. When they need each other's help, it is not just the urgency of the need but the special character of the relationship that gives their claim its particular moral and emotional weight.

Second, the claims involved in these relationships are wide-ranging and extend far beyond those characteristic of other relations. One not only helps others when they need it, but also thinks and worries about them, feels for them, raises their spirits when they are feeling low, seeks ways of getting them out of difficult situations, pays them surprise visits, and is generous with one's time with them. One's spouse, parents or friends may legitimately complain if one is remiss in these respects, and even conclude that the relationship is no longer what it should be. One may share one's material resources with anyone in need but not one's thoughts, feelings or a sense of anxious concern, which are generally the prerogative of those to whom one is bound by special ties.

Third, one meets the claims of those involved not because one has a duty to do so, nor because this is how a moral being should behave, but as an expression of one's commitment to them – that is, for reasons internal to the relationship. To tell one's parents, children or close friends, or even to convey the impression, that one helped them out in difficult situations out of a sense of duty or because their claims had passed the test of impartiality would rightly be taken to mean that one either does not understand the nature of the relationship or has unilaterally decided to redefine and change its character.

Fourth, identity relations involve bonding, mutual exploration and increasingly deeper understanding, and invariably these take time to grow. In the course of their development, those involved help each other out in need, make small and large sacrifices, come to count on each other, and build up certain expectations. As a result, the principles of gratitude, fair play and reciprocity come into play, and their demands form an integral part of the relationship. Identity relations are thus subject to two related but distinguishable bases of moral claims – those grounded in mutual commitment, and those arising out of the acts of kindness over a period of time. Although the latter are expressions of the former, they have a certain independence, which is why they remain binding even when the relationship itself has ended and no mutual commitment is involved. When one divorces one's wife or breaks with a friend, one is free of the claims based on love and commitment, but cannot ignore all they had done during the life of the relationship. Affection or love can be contingent or short-lived, but its moral legacy in the shape of acquired obligations can last a lifetime.

Identity relations cannot come into existence and last unless those involved are mutually committed and special in each other's eyes. Partiality is inherent in them, both as their psychological basis and as an integral part of their internal morality. William Godwin asked what 'magic' there was in the pronoun 'my'. Unless the pronoun is used in a purely descriptive or referential sense, it signifies different degrees of identification or oneness. To call someone 'my friend' or 'my wife' is to say that are an extended me and part of my identity, that I am deeply committed to them, that they give meaning to my life, even that they *are* my life. There is thus as much magic in the pronoun 'my' as in giving depth and breadth to 'I', and that is quite a lot. If we take away the first person singular and all that forms part of it, human life loses its individuality, and with it much of its meaning and depth.

Partiality and impartiality[2]

Human life would be infinitely poorer and even perhaps unimaginable without close personal relations, and they entail a morality of partiality. Earlier I argued that all human beings have equal worth and that morality involves an impartial weighing up of the claims of all those who are or could be affected by one's actions. The two moralities clearly point in different directions. One privileges those to whom one is bound by special ties, while the other assigns their claims no special status. The tension between the two goes to the very heart of moral life and has been a subject of considerable discussion for over two millennia. Of the various attempts to resolve it, four have been most influential. Since these are well-known, a brief sketch of their basic theses should suffice.

First, one might argue that the morality of impartiality represents the only true morality. Morally relevant reasons are impersonal, objective and universal, and do not take into account personal ties and contingent social relations. As moral agents, human beings should transcend the latter and relate to each other in terms of their common humanity. Since they have equal worth, greater needs make greater claims, irrespective of one's relationship to those involved. The fact that someone is my mother or wife has a considerable emotional but no moral significance, and her claims carry no greater weight than those of others.[3]

This view is open to several objections. It draws an untenably sharp distinction between our humanity and the various special relationships into which we enter. Our humanity is what Hegel called a concrete universal, and is expressed and articulated, though of course not exhausted, in them. They are contingent in the sense that they could have involved different individuals or taken different forms, but not in the sense that they are marginal or incidental to human life. They add richness and depth to life, and form an integral part of it. Their claims are just as important as those derived from our common humanity.

Identity relations have a unique character that delimits the scope of impartiality. One falls in love with this woman and not that one, likes this man and builds up a close friendship with him rather than some other, and each entails certain commitments. By contrast, the principle of impartiality, interpreted strictly, requires that these relationships should be based on a careful consideration of the others' needs. One should not fall in love with the woman who is appealing, but rather one who is desperately lonely and needs one's love, or is given to a life of crime and could be weaned away from it if made an object of one's love. And one should cultivate a close friendship not with someone whose company one enjoys, but rather with a loner who finds it difficult to make friends and needs one's friendship more than the former does. Such an approach is the surest way to destroy the relationship, assuming that it is within our power to decide who to like and to love. Those involved are bound to find one's love and friendship patronizing, even insincere, and lacking in the spark, the deep emotional engagement, that lies at the heart of and gives meaning to these relationships. Identity relations generally begin independently of moral considerations, and the principle of impartiality comes in later to regulate their morality.

If the principle of impartiality were to be the sole basis of morality, one would either need to avoid identity relations, or so define and structure them that they do not make moral claims. Both of these were advocated by some Stoics, the first systematic theorists of this view in the West, and neither has much to be said for it. The Stoic sage is a citizen of the world, without family and friends, morally and emotionally committed to no one, and hence equally open and available to all. While isolated individuals might prefer and be able to lead such a life, it has no relevance to the overwhelming majority of humankind, whom some of the Stoics therefore arrogantly dismissed as being incapable of moral life.

Even so far as the sages are concerned, they have several involuntarily incurred ties and obligations that they may not disregard. They live within a particular community, benefit from its stability, prosperity, protection and cultural resources. Unless they wish to live as moral parasites or free-riders, they have obligations to it that they do not have to other societies. They also have parents, colleagues, co-workers and others, who too have claims on them, and whom they cannot treat as if they were total strangers. In short, even the sages are morally encumbered and subject to special claims.

The other alternative, in which one has special relations to one's family, friends and country but makes it clear to them that they have no special claims, fares no better. These relations cannot be formed and sustained unless one commits oneself to those involved and acknowledges the force of their special ties. No one would want to make an emotional investment in a relationship and suffer its inevitable ups and downs if one were to be treated no differently from a total stranger. Furthermore, special relations grow over time and involve countless acts of kindness, love and help, which one has a duty to reciprocate out of gratitude, fair play and reciprocity, and thus on the grounds of impartiality itself. The impartialist cannot consistently cherish special relations and ignore their psychological dynamics and internal morality.

Second, one might take the opposite view that only the morality of partiality represents the true morality. All moral claims arise from concrete relationships which build bonds between those involved and generate expectations. In human life, we do not encounter 'men' or 'women' but people who are involved with us in certain relationships. Common humanity is an abstraction, a largely empty logical category. It is not a moral relationship and cannot by itself generate moral claims. In this view, the morality of impartiality is doubly flawed. It goes against the basic tendencies of human nature and is psychologically unrealistic. It also subverts the very basis of special relationships and renders human life virtually unliveable.

While the partialist view, whose echoes are to be found in some followers of Epicurus, Edmund Burke and many a conservative and romantic writer, rightly stresses the importance and morality of special relations, it goes wrong in taking a narrow and ultimately incoherent view of them.[4] I argued earlier why human beings should be assigned equal worth, and why their fundamental interests make equal claims on us. If someone were starving or drowning, one would be morally culpable if one did nothing because one had no special ties with that person.

Their claims are addressed to us as human beings, and cannot be ignored or dismissed by a linguistic or conceptual fiat that places them outside morality. The fundamental interests of others also impose limits on the partiality inherent in special relations. A poor mother is right to do all she can to get her sick child back to health, but she may not rob her neighbour or kill a stranger to get the money she needs to pay her medical bills. Friends have strong claims on each other, but they may not engage in a criminal conspiracy or pervert the course of justice when one of them is in trouble. The internal morality of special relations is embedded in and regulated by the wider morality arising out of the principle of equal human worth.

The third way to resolve the tension between the two moralities is a variation on the second. It gives primacy to the morality of partiality, and introduces that of impartiality to limit its excesses. According to it, our lives are embedded in deep special relationships and governed by the claims and expectations inherent in these. Since other human beings also have claims on us, we have a negative duty not to harm their interests. Subject to the constraints this imposes on us, we are free to organize and follow the demands of our special relationships as we wish.

Although this view offers a promising way of integrating the two moralities and reflects what many people think, it is open to criticism. Like the second view considered above, it too is heavily biased, though to a lesser extent, towards the morality of partiality and provides only a severely restricted space for that of impartiality. I showed earlier why this is mistaken. Furthermore, this view interprets the principle of impartiality in extremely narrow terms, and emphasizes the duty not to harm others, but not that of positive assistance to those in need. As I argued earlier, the rigid distinction between negative and positive duties is untenable, and the principles of equal worth, which is the basis of negative duties, also entails the positive.

The fourth response is the obverse of the third, and finds support among ethical universalists.[5] It defines morality in impartialist terms and sees the morality of partiality as a means to it. According to this response, morality requires us to weigh up the equal claims of relevant human beings and meet those that are more urgent or promote the well-being of most. This runs into the obvious practical problem that, when all are supposed to care for the well-being of all, no one feels a strong sense of personal responsibility, and the claims of those in need are neglected. No child, for example, would receive adequate attention if its well-being were not made the primary responsibility of its parents. The general duty to promote human well-being is therefore best discharged by 'parcelling it out' among different individuals, depending on such things as their special ties, intimate knowledge, continuity of relationship, and the ability to promote the interests of those involved. Special relationships represent such a 'division of labour', and are a realistic 'administrative device for discharging our general duties more efficiently'.

Although this view is right to reject a radical opposition between the moralities of partiality and impartiality, and to appreciate that the former sometimes realizes the latter, it is unconvincing. The language of 'division of labour', 'parcelling out duties' and 'administrative device' makes sense within an organization where someone is in overall charge, has clear goals, and knows how best to distribute the necessary tasks. Moral life is not at all like that, and is much misunderstood when conceptualized in this language, even in its attenuated and metaphorical sense. Furthermore, while we have our respective spheres of action, our duties are not limited to them. We also have general negative and positive duties to others that fall outside our allotted spheres. The language of division of labour consigns them to a moral limbo, and not only does not give a coherent account of them but implies that they are less important, or even unimportant.

Even so far as one's special relationships are concerned, this view gives a highly misleading quasi-managerial account of them. It requires one to approach one's parents, children or spouse not as a son, a parent or a husband or wife but as a representative of society or humankind, as the occupant of a moral office. In so doing, it ignores the singularity and uniqueness of the relationship and turns it into something totally different. One cares for one's parents and children, not because someone needs to care for them and one is better placed than anyone else, or because one has a general duty to promote human well-being, of which this is an instantiation, but because one is committed to them and respects the claims of the relationship. This is why they would rightly feel insulted if told that one cared for them not because they meant much to one and were part of one's life, but because they fell within one's socially prescribed sphere of responsibility.

Resolving the tension

The moralities of partiality and impartiality, then, are both legitimate forms of morality, and neither can be dismissed as not morality at all or its inferior form.[6] Although they overlap, they rest on different bases, one on special ties and mutual commitment, the other on our common humanity and the principle of equal worth. Since they have different bases, neither can be reduced to the other. Both are central to moral life, and the claims of neither can be ignored save by those who have no special relationships, as in the case of hermits and monks, and perhaps not even by them, because of residual ties to the society in which they live. When they come into conflict, there is no neutral principle to resolve it. An appeal to consequences, often seen as such a principle, is committed to the morality of impartiality and is not neutral. It takes into account the number of people affected by one's action, or the quantity of pleasure, well-being or whatever else is used to evaluate the consequences, and ignores the agent's relation to those involved and the moral weight of their claims. In situations of conflict, one needs to assess the nature of the special relationship, the relative weight of the claims and needs of those involved as against those of others, one's circumstances, and so on. Sometimes the demands of impartiality are a priority; on other occasions, those of partiality. Such a weighing-up is a highly complex activity involving sensitivity to the context and the identity and fundamental commitments of the moral agent. It cannot be settled by some meta-ethical formula, and morally serious persons may rightly reach different conclusions.[7]

Although the conflict between the two moralities cannot be eliminated, like that between the morality of a good man and a good citizen (Aristotle) or the Christian and political morality (Machiavelli), and whatever one does is likely to leave some degree of moral unease, it can be reduced by restructuring our special relationships and those with human beings in general.

Special relations involve partiality and cannot be sustained without it. We are also, however, subject to the claims of other human beings and bound to them by both negative and positive duties. The question therefore is one of striking a balance, and determining what degree and kind of partiality should be allowed to enable special relations to be sustained and the basic demands of the principle of impartiality to be met. The fact that special relations require partiality does not mean that they should be open-ended. They admit degrees of partiality, and its limits can be set by the principle of impartiality. Such an approach cherishes and assigns partiality a valued place in human life, but locates it within a wider moral framework that delimits its scope and content.

An example will illustrate this point. It is perfectly understandable and morally right that a father should wish to give his children the best education he can afford and a good start in adult life. This affirms his commitment to them, and it is what they have come to expect of him as part of their relationship. However, since he has negative and positive duties to others, he is morally not at liberty to commit his entire wealth to them, or to use it to indulge all their whims and gratify their unreasonable demands. Nor is he morally at liberty to allow himself to be so taken over by them that he has no time, energy, affection or concern for others. He owes part of his time, energy, attention and wealth to others, and his family and friends have claims to the rest. They may resent these constraints, and that may damage the quality of his relationships with them. However, that would not be the case if they saw the point of these constraints, accepted them as the basis of their relationship, and defined their mutual claims and expectations accordingly. In these matters, the wider moral culture and social ethos play a vital part. If such views became the dominant norm, all entering into special relationships would frame their demands appropriately, and even enjoy them the better once they had lost their narrowness and exclusivity. All social relations, including the most intimate, rest on certain expectations, which define the nature and limits of partiality. And these expectations are not inherent in these relations but socially determined.

Some such way of reconciling the two moralities is central to many great religions, and premodern and some modern societies.[8] They insist that others have a claim on one's resources, and require their members to set aside a percentage of their wealth or income for the welfare of the needy. This is not charity or even benevolence, because what one gives to others belongs to them as of right or rather is owed to them as a matter of duty, and one simply has no claim to it. What remains, however, is exclusively one's own, to be used as one pleases and for which one is not accountable to others. One might choose to give away part of it to others, and then it is an act of charity or benevolence, or spend it on oneself and one's friends and family.

Many religions and societies also require their members to commit part of not only their material resources but also themselves to their fellow human beings. They expect members to devote their time, energy, thoughts, concerns and service to others, and make this an integral part of their way of life by devising appropriate norms, rituals, practices, pilgrimages and moral sanctions. Others are not outside the bounds of special ties and brought in later; rather, they are present from the very beginning and shape the ethos and ethics of the special relations. In principle, redistributive taxation and the welfare state have a similar moral basis. They assume that those with greater needs have a strong claim on those with the resources to help them. Since we do not always appreciate this, or since the use of the resources needs to be co-ordinated collectively, the task is allocated to the state.

This way of defining the morality of identity relations also holds true of less intense special relations, be they based on membership of a common organization or participation in a common practice. In each case, the greater claims of those involved in special relations are recognized, but these are balanced against those of outsiders, and defined and delimited accordingly. I shall discuss this in Chapter 12 in relation to the political community.

Just as we should redefine the scope and content of the morality of special relations, we should redefine the nature and morality of our relations to human beings in general. Since much of our moral theory has a strong rationalist thrust, it dissociates morality from emotions and defines it in terms of general rules and principles. As a result, other human beings remain distant, strangers, mean little to us, and confront us as peremptory sources of claims derived from certain shared properties. A chasm separates 'us' from 'them', and morality appears austere and coercive.

A richer and more coherent way to relate to other human beings is to see them not in their generalized otherness or abstract similarity but rather their concrete particularity, as beings like us, who are just as keen as we are to lead fulfilling lives, care for their families and close relations just as much as we do, and grieve at their losses and delight in their successes. We then put ourselves in their place, grasp their pain and struggles imaginatively, feel with and for them, see ourselves in them and them in ourselves, identify with them, and care for them as an expression of our human identity. We know what it is like to be in their situation, to be humiliated, to see children suffer for lack of medical attention, to be far from home and among strangers, to live in total insecurity, to achieve a lifelong ambition. Our relations with them are then not impersonal but emotionally charged and based on a vivid sense of how they feel and lead their lives.

They then appear to us not just as sources of claims but also as objects of moral concern, no longer distant strangers but beings with whom we empathize and who matter to us not only morally but also emotionally. We take their claims into account not just because the principle of equal human worth requires this, but also because we visualize how their lives would be affected if we did not, and the consequent sense of concern for and solidarity with them. When such identification with other human beings is fully developed, it takes the form of love for them and a passionate desire to see them flourish. In its less developed and more common form, it is a sentiment of humanity, good will towards all human beings, or simply fellow feeling. We should find ways of fostering such feelings and sentiments, and use them to give the principle of impartiality its moral and emotional energy. As I argued earlier, this is beginning to happen in our globalizing world, albeit in a fragile and haphazard form. We need to build on this and consolidate the sentiment of humanity by giving it suitable institutional forms.

As we develop the sentiment of humanity or fellow feeling and affirm our human identity, our relations with fellow human beings acquire some of the features of our special relationships, such as a sense of concern, emotional engagement and some degree of mutual identification. This is not to say that millions of men and women can or should ever become as close as, or matter to us as much as, our family and friends. That is psychologically unrealistic and even perhaps undesirable, as it might threaten the integrity of the special relationships that depend for their vitality on their exclusivity. Rather, our relations with human beings in general now no longer differ from our special relations qualitatively but largely in their degree and intensity of attachment. They do not represent two separate worlds of 'we' and 'others', one warm and based on identification, the other cold, based on abstract morality and lying beyond it. Rather, they constitute a single moral world with overlapping and mutually limiting concentric circles within which we move with equal ease. In the view that I am advocating, partiality and impartiality are no longer disjoined and seen as rival moralities. The former is structured in the light of and incorporates impartiality. And the latter is not impersonal and imperious but a form of generalized or reiterative partiality, seeing the lives of other human beings in the image of our own and acknowledging their equal worth.

12

Citizenship in the Global Age

In Chapter 11 I argued that the moralities of both partiality and impartiality make legitimate claims, and suggested ways of reconciling them in the context of close personal relationships. I now want to extend the analysis to political communities, and explore how we might reconcile our obligations to our fellow citizens with those to outsiders.

Exclusivist paradigm

Since the emergence of the modern state in the seventeenth century, a statist or exclusivist view of it has dominated political theory and practice.[1] This view involves the following interrelated beliefs. First, the world is divided into political communities or states, and each is a legally, politically and even morally self-contained entity. Every human being is a citizen of an identifiable state, and the two belong together. Its citizens are the state's exclusive responsibility, just as it is theirs. Second, every state is sovereign in the sense that it has a right to run its internal and, with some qualification, its external affairs as it pleases without being accountable to other states or external agencies. Sovereignty is inherent in it, something it possesses by virtue of what it is and to which it has a natural right, in broadly the same way that human beings are supposed to enjoy certain natural rights by the very fact of being human. Although things do not work quite like this in practice, every state aspires to sovereignty and believes that its independence is compromised and it is less of a state when for some reason it is unable to follow its own will. Third, the state derives its legitimacy from its citizens, and its sole duty is to promote their collective interests. It has a right to do all that is necessary for that purpose, and conversely it has no right to do anything that damages, sacrifices or compromises them. Finally, the citizen has a moral obligation to obey the state, and this takes precedence over all others, including such universal obligations as human beings might have to one another.

The exclusivist or statist view is deeply flawed. This was perceived with remarkable prescience by Hugo Grotius, Francisco de Vitoria, Francisco Suárez and other seventeenth-century writers, who were committed to the idea of human unity and worried that the newly-emerging states risked undermining this by setting themselves up as morally self-contained units standing between individuals and humankind in general. To say that humankind is divided into states is only partially true. The humanity of the citizen is not exhausted in the state, territorial boundaries do not negate the moral bonds that obtain between human beings, and every state remains embedded in a wider human community. Humankind *is* divided into states, but it also transcends and imposes moral limits on them. Although citizens are the primary responsibility of their state, they are not its exclusive responsibility. As I argued earlier, outsiders too have a legitimate interest in their well-being, and every state is morally accountable to these others for its treatment of them. The fact that its actions affect human beings outside its boundaries in our increasingly interdependent world reinforces its accountability and imposes further moral constraints upon it.

The sovereignty of the state, as traditionally defined, is a deeply problematic notion. It is morally incoherent because, for reasons discussed earlier, no state is morally at liberty to conduct its internal and external affairs as it pleases. It is also legally and politically incoherent, because sovereignty is not inherent in the state or a matter of its natural right. A group of people might unilaterally declare themselves to be a state, but it would not have the status and the rights of one unless other states accept it and are prepared to deal with it as a state. It can enjoy immunity to external interference, and its citizens can trade or even travel abroad, only when other states acknowledge it as one of them and accept the ensuing obligations.

This is evident in the practice of international recognition. New states function as independent agents on the world stage, enjoy membership of international organizations and enter into international agreements and treaties once they are 'recognized' by other states. While recognition is generally based on the state's ability to exercise effective control over its territory, the latter does not of itself generate the rights and immunities of statehood. Just as interpersonal recognition acknowledges and gives social reality to individuals, international recognition does not merely register an already existing state; it also partially constitutes it as, and confers upon it, the rights of a state. The state's sovereignty is thus derived not only from the will of its citizens but also from the consent of other states and, through them, of humankind as a whole. Sometimes a state might be recognized by some other states but not all, as in the case of communist China in 1950, or more recently during the break-up of the Yugoslav federation, either for arbitrary political reasons or because of the uncertainty about whether or not the state concerned meets the conditions of recognition. The new state has the status and rights of a state in relation to those who recognize it, but not to others.

Sovereignty, further, is not an end in itself but rather a means, a power that a state needs in order for its citizens to lead lives of their choice. In its traditional form it is becoming increasingly impractical in the modern world. All states today are enmeshed in a system of interdependence and cannot alone ensure their own security, plan their economy or maintain prosperity, let alone deal with such common problems as pollution, global warming, drug or human trafficking and the spread of contagious diseases. Each of them is faced with a choice. Either the state insists on going its own way and avoids alliances and organizations that restrict its capacity for action, or it co-operates with others and accepts limits on its freedom of action. In the first case, it retains its sovereignty but remains helplessly subject to external forces and the consequences of others' uncoordinated actions. In the second, its freedom is limited but its power to influence events and attain its basic objectives is increased. On any rational calculation, the latter represents the best course of action. Power is not a zero-sum game, because sharing it with others can not only generate more power than existed before, but it is sometimes the only way of preserving it. When sovereignty is shared with others and exercised co-operatively, the states involved are not subordinated to some higher authority; rather, they are partners in a larger unit and collectively decide the limits of their freedom.[2]

In the exclusivist view, the state's sole duty is to promote the interests of its citizens. This, again, is a half truth. Human beings have duties not to harm others' fundamental interests and, within the limits of their capacity, to help them to enjoy those basic goods without which no worthwhile life is possible. The state is a medium through which they discharge these duties and express their moral nature. While its citizens have the first claim on a state, others also have a claim on it, and it needs to balance the two. It may not therefore define and pursue its interests in a manner that damages the interests of others, and should share its resources with those in need. National self-interest is one thing, but national selfishness is another matter. The former recognizes the legitimate interests of others and defines itself accordingly, while the latter takes no notice of them and subordinates them to a narrow and aggressive pursuit of its own interests.

The profound limitations of the exclusivist view of the state become particularly evident in relation to humanitarian intervention, and deserve careful examination.[3] Such intervention is a relatively recent and increasingly common phenomenon that has emerged in some cases as a mask for reordering the world to suit dominant interests, and in others as a way of affirming human solidarity in times of crisis. In either case, it reflects the reality of global interdependence, and our uncertain response to it reflects our failure to develop an adequate political theory that is relevant to that reality.

When a state engages in acts of genocide, grossly maltreats its citizens or collapses under the impact of civil war, the rest of the world rightly feels a duty to intervene. Such humanitarian intervention is, however, caught up in a paradox. According to the exclusivist view, the state behaving outrageously is the business of its own citizens, not of outsiders, but humanitarian intervention takes the opposite view. The exclusivist view implies that the state should only use its taxpayers' money to promote their interests, and ask its soldiers only to fight and give their lives in nationally necessary wars; humanitarian intervention implies that the state may do both in the interest of outsiders. The exclusivist view requires that states should respect each other's sovereignty and scrupulously refrain from mutual interference; humanitarian intervention implies that this may be overridden under certain circumstances. The exclusivist manner of thinking implies that national interest alone should guide a state's relations with other states; humanitarian intervention requires it to act in a more or less disinterested manner in certain situations.

In the statist view, a state engaged in humanitarian intervention acts in excess of its authority, pursues objectives it has neither a right nor a duty to pursue, and violates the terms on which it is deemed to be constituted. If its citizens refused to pay taxes or its soldiers declined to fight abroad on the grounds that neither its constitution nor the tacit self-understanding that underpins every political community gives it the authority to impose these burdens, it would have difficulty in providing a satisfactory defence. Samuel Huntington expresses this view well when he says that it is 'morally unjustifiable and politically indefensible that members of the [US] armed forces should be killed to prevent Somalis from killing one another'. Robert Jackson makes a similar point when he observes, 'I do not see how democratic governments could sacrifice their own people if such sacrifice was necessary to protect human rights in foreign countries but nothing else was at stake', especially their vital national interests.[4]

Humanitarian intervention cannot, then, easily be reconciled with the exclusivist view of the state.[5] Since many governments rightly feel drawn towards it, they defend it in one of two unsuccessful ways. First, they argue that it is in the national interest, this being the only, or at least the most widely accepted, way of justifying the sacrifices of money and lives within the exclusivist approach. Although this is true in some cases, it is often quite specious in many others, and leads to much dishonest rhetoric. What is worse, it encourages the tendency to put things right retrospectively by setting up pliant regimes and hogging lucrative contracts for reconstruction in the states in which one has intervened.

Second, government leaders argue that public opinion demands humanitarian intervention. This is intended to legitimize the state's use of power for purposes disallowed by the exclusivist paradigm, and to overcome the resulting authority deficit. Such a strategy runs into difficulties. The authority the government claims to acquire in this way is uninstitutionalized, and does not have the same weight as its constitutionally derived authority to pursue the interests of its own citizens. Furthermore, since public opinion, which is now given a constitutional status, is invariably subject to media and government manipulation and is often deeply divided, the authority it is supposed to confer is inherently suspect and precarious. In a constitutional democracy, the constitution is the sole source of authority, and public opinion can only encourage the government to do what it has a duty to do but which it is for some reason reluctant to do. To use public opinion to derive rights and duties not sanctioned by the state's constitution is to perpetrate a fraud on the latter.

Even when the state undertakes popularly supported humanitarian intervention, it remains subject to the distorting constraints of the exclusivist paradigm. Its actions occur outside its territorial boundary, but the constituency to which it is accountable, and which it must constantly placate, is domestic. The disjunction between the two leads to perverse choices. In order to ensure that its citizens continue to authorize and support its actions, the government feels compelled to demand only the minimum possible sacrifices from them. The lives of its soldiers must be protected at all cost, and sacrificed only when unavoidable. If, say, twenty soldiers or civilians of the intervened country have to be killed in order to save the life of a single soldier of the intervening country, or if a large cultivated or inhabited area in the former has to be destroyed or vacated in order to give its army a strategic advantage, it is considered fully justified. The intervening country is also led to grossly oversimplify the situation, to present the intervened country as being pathetically devoid of regenerative resources, and to argue that its troops are constantly 'beating the baddies' and bringing hope to an otherwise hopeless country.

The moral reasoning behind this view is tragically simple. Since humanitarian intervention falls outside the state's normal duties as they are defined in the exclusivist view, it needs to be legitimized in terms of a popular demand that could easily go the other way if too many 'body bags' begin to arrive. The country that is being helped is expected to be profoundly grateful that another country is making human and financial sacrifices beyond the call of duty, and to appreciate that its saviour cannot be too pernickety in its choice of military tactics and targets or its treatment of prisoners and even civilians. Within the statist paradigm, humanitarian intervention necessarily appears as a gratuitous act of generosity, born out of a mixture of contempt and pity for the intervened country, and fuelled by a sense of resentment at the sacrifices one is morally blackmailed into making. These and related factors remove many of the usual moral constraints on the use of force, as we have recently seen in relation to the outrageous behaviour of some of the US and even British troops in Iraq, and to a lesser extent in Afghanistan.

Globally orientated citizenship

The exclusivist view of the state, then, is deeply flawed, and needs to be replaced by an inclusive or globally orientated view of it. The latter recognizes states as valuable communities that need to enjoy independence, but locates them within a society of states and the wider human community.

Human beings seek and need the freedom to organize and run their affairs without external interference for several interrelated reasons. Their independence expresses and realizes their collective will to constitute themselves as a separate community. It enables them to lead the lives of their choice, and to set up a form of government with which they can identify and enjoy ease of access and communication. They are self-determining individuals who have the intellectual and moral resources to govern themselves and to form their own ideas of the good life. They might make mistakes, but that is not unique to them, and they can be trusted to learn from them. They are affected directly by the consequences of their actions, and are more likely to pursue their common good than any outside agency might on their behalf. It is only by running their affairs themselves that individuals can cultivate their capacity for self-government, build up ties of common interest and sympathy, develop mutual trust, come to see their institutions and community as their own, and identify with and feel responsible for these in varying degrees.

States operate at two levels. First, they exist among other states and constitute a society of states. As collective entities representing their members' will to live as independent communities, they encounter each other as equals irrespective of their size, population, and political and economic power. They enjoy equal rights and obligations, equal representation in international institutions, and participate as equals in framing the conventions, agreements, treaties and laws by which they are bound. The society of states is not a Hobbesian state of nature but rather an association of independent and equal states, 'recognising themselves as mutually recognising each other' and accepting the corresponding constraints, as Hegel put it.[6] It is governed by rules and structured by institutions that ensure a measure of stability and civility in their relations, and which they have a common obligation to respect. It is striking that since the 1960s we have begun to bring increasing numbers of state activities under international law, and subject them to nearly three dozen conventions, covenants and treaties.

Second, as associations of human beings, states are embedded in and form part of a wider human community. They are moral units but are not morally self-contained. Humankind too is a moral community, and its members have certain negative and positive duties to each other. This means a number of things. Human beings are citizens of particular communities but also members of the global human community. No state may therefore stand in the way of normal interactions of human beings and such lawful relations as they choose to establish among themselves. Human beings have a legitimate moral interest in how others live, and may express their concern directly or through the medium of their state. Citizens of a state are not its exclusive responsibility, and it is accountable to the rest of humankind for its treatment of them. They have a duty to ensure that their state, which speaks in their name, does not define and pursue their interests in a manner that damages those of others and renders them such help as they need and it can give to lead worthy lives.

The two levels at which states operate have different but complementary logics. The first takes states as its basic units; the second gives pre-eminence to human beings and the universal community they form. The first takes cognizance of individuals as citizens of particular states; the second sees states through the prism of individuals. The first level is orientated primarily towards the stability of the international order, and the second towards human well-being. As members of the society of states, human relations are governed by the rules and practices states have agreed upon; and as members of the human community, by formally stated and unstated negative and positive duties.

Neither view is by itself adequate. The society of states leads to an exclusivist view of them with all its limitations, as discussed earlier. Stressing the human community alone violates the autonomy of states as it implies that other states and international institutions may disregard state boundaries and deal directly with the state's citizens. We need to see the world as both a community of human beings and a society of states, and harmonize their perspectives as well we can. Although the Charter of the United Nations rightly refers to both, it is heavily biased towards the latter.

Citizens, then, are members of both particular political communities and the wider human community, and have duties to their fellow citizens as well as to outsiders. The statist view denies the latter, and I have shown why this is mistaken. The cosmopolitan or ethical universalist view denies the special claims of the former, and is equally mistaken. It argues that, since political communities are contingent in the sense that their boundaries are arbitrary and membership is an accident of birth, one's fellow citizens have no stronger claims than human beings elsewhere. The territorial boundary of a political community is certainly contingent in the sense that it is often a product of international or civil wars, conquests or decisions by colonial rulers, and might have been different. However, over time, it becomes integrated into the lives of its citizens. They have generally lived there for generations, and their personal and collective memories are bound up with the territory. The territory is also the basis of their common life, the site of their history, and a witness to their struggles, triumphs and tragedies. Their religion, literature, rituals, social practices and cultural life in general are developed against its background and carry a distinct local flavour. In these and other ways the territory acquires a moral and political significance. It ceases to be a brute geographical fact and becomes their home, a place they shape in their image and by which they in turn are shaped, and which is inseparable from their personal and national identities.

The argument that birth in a particular community is an accident of no moral significance is doubly mistaken. Accidents are not devoid of moral significance. The fact that one is born a human being or with a particular body is an accident, but that does not detract from the fact that one's humanity is the basis of one's worth and claims on others, or that one's body is an integral part of one's identity. Furthermore, to call birth an accident is to utter a half truth. Birth is often intended and planned by one's parents and expresses their desire to widen their world by introducing a new member to it. And birth alone would not have culminated in a fully grown adult if the parents and the institutions of the wider society had not welcomed and nurtured the infant. Birth is not just a physical occurrence but a social and cultural event, involving special ties with, and hence appropriate moral claims on and obligations to, the wider community. This is one of the reasons why, in most societies, one inherits the citizenship of one's parents or acquires it by virtue of being born in a certain territory.

Members of a political community are bound to each other by countless ties. They have a common interest in maintaining a stable community, a system of basic rights and liberties, and a general climate of civility and mutual trust. They are required to pay taxes for the benefits of others, to die for their country, to defer their own needs in favour of the more urgent ones of others, and to bear their share of the burden of maintaining a common life. They benefit in various ways from their membership of the community, and acquire mutual obligations based on fairness and gratitude. Since they grow up within and are shaped by it, they are also generally attached to it, identify with it in varying degrees, and define their identity in terms of it. They see it as their community, feel responsible for it, take an active interest in its affairs, and feel proud or ashamed when it does or does not live up to their moral expectations of it. Through all this, relations between citizens are a form of special relations. Although they lack the immediacy, intimacy, intensity and depth of close personal relations, they too involve special bonds, commitments and different degrees of identification. Citizens therefore have duties to each other that they do not have to outsiders.

But while we are bound to our fellow citizens by special ties, we do also have duties to outsiders. These arise from the principle of equal human worth discussed earlier. In modern times, they are reinforced by two additional factors. Because of colonialism, many Western states are partly responsible for conditions of life in other parts of the world. They designed and ran their economy to suit their own interests, drew their territorial boundaries without regard to historical and ethnic considerations, imposed pliant political structures and leaders, transplanted large masses of people across continents, manipulated or created ethnic, religious and other divisions, and in some cases bought and sold people as slaves. Although the colonial rule is now over, it ended in many cases barely three decades ago, a relatively short time in the history of nations. Even after it ended, the economic and political lives of these societies continued to be manipulated by Western powers, either directly or through international institutions, multinational corporations and unfair trade arrangements. This is not at all to deny that these countries themselves bear much of the responsibility for disappointing performance, but rather that the Western powers are not wholly innocent either, and have a duty to help remedy the consequences of their past and present actions.

The second factor reinforcing our duties to outsiders is related to the moral and political compulsions of global interdependence that I discussed earlier. Our actions affect distant others, and we are responsible for their consequences. We face common problems, and cannot tackle these without seeking the willing co-operation of others and taking into account their interests. In a globalizing age, groups and societies judge themselves comparatively, and those feeling neglected or unjustly treated become breeding grounds for deep discontent and cause havoc in distant lands. The enlightened self-interest of each country provides an additional reason to be concerned about others.

Our citizenship, then, has both a national and a global dimension. For convenience, I shall call it globally oriented citizenship. It is wider and deeper than the traditional view of citizenship, which limits to a particular political community. It is also different from global or cosmopolitan citizenship. The latter implies that one is a citizen of the world, has no special ties to a particular community, no political home, and is in a state of what Martha Nussbaum calls 'voluntary exile', a condition she welcomes, but which is difficult to live in and for which there is little to be said.[7] When one grows up in a particular community one understands it better than any other, is bound to it by various ties, identifies with it in various degrees, takes an active interest in its affairs, feels responsible for it, and cannot treat it as if it were like any other. If one continues to live in the community and enjoys the benefits of its citizenship, one also acquires certain obligations to it, which one does not have to others. Furthermore, one is unlikely to carry weight with one's fellow citizens if they think one is not committed to them, and that they enjoy no special claims on one's loyalty. Apart from being perceived as a moral free rider, a voluntary exile deprives herself of the moral authority needed to persuade her fellow citizens to support her universalist goals.

In contrast to a global citizen who is in exile everywhere, a globally-orientated citizen has a home of his own, from which he reaches out to others with equally valued homes of their own. He appreciates the reality and value of political communities and is an internationalist rather than a cosmopolitan.[8] Internationalism reconciles the moral impulses lying at the heart of loyalty to one's community and to humankind in general, while avoiding their pathologies. The former stresses one's commitment to one's community but runs the risk of degenerating into an isolationist or expansionist form of self-centred nationalism. Cosmopolitanism rightly highlights our universal duties, but is too abstract to generate the emotional and moral energy needed to live up to its demands, and can easily become an excuse for doing nothing to improve the community one knows and can influence. When nationalism and cosmopolitanism are seen as the only alternatives, the pathology of one gives pseudo-legitimacy to the other. Internationalism mediates between the two and offers a better alternative.

With all their limitations, political communities in one form or another have long been an integral part of our lives, and we have a considerable knowledge of how to run and regulate them. They inspire their citizens to look beyond narrow self-interest, and to identify with millions of relative strangers whom they will never meet, and some of whose views and life-styles they might abhor. They also evoke loyalty and attachment, and can mobilize great moral energy. For these and other reasons they represent a valuable political resource. We should make full use of them, expand their moral boundaries to include outsiders, and mobilize the legitimate collective pride of their citizens to pursue wider human interests. This is a better way to proceed than to rely on a tenuous and free-floating cosmopolitan consciousness that is at best limited to only a few. A global human identity cannot be created by dismantling or bypassing national identities, because it then remains

abstract, distant and lacks a basis in lived reality. Rather, we should redefine, reinterpret and use them as its necessary stepping stones. A secure
national identity is built on strong civic and regional identities, a lesson
states have learnt after causing much bloodshed and social havoc in the
misguided belief that they were its enemies. The global human identity
is no different.

Our duties to humankind are best discharged through the mediating
agency of the state, and we become better globally orientated citizens by
activating our national citizenship. It is a common experience that those
who identify with their community and feel a sense of responsibility for
its actions are often the most likely to feel ashamed when it behaves
badly. Apathetic citizens, who have no interest in the conduct of their
government, are neither good national nor good global citizens.
Globally orientated citizenship calls for a democratic deepening of
national citizenship, and is not its rival but a necessary complement.

Globally orientated citizenship involves commitments both to one's
country and to humankind in general, each conditioning and regulating
the other. It requires one to ensure that one's country's policies do not
damage and, within the limits of its resources, promote the interests of
humankind at large. When a government props up dictatorships in other
countries, supplies them with dangerous weapons, corrupts, manipulates
and destabilizes vulnerable regimes or imposes unfavourable trade
agreements on them, the citizens have a duty to challenge this by organizing pressure and protests. The interests of other countries can also be
harmed in several less visible ways. Take the increasingly common practice of recruiting highly skilled manpower from poor countries. It creams
off their talents, and creates acute shortages of doctors, nurses, middle-
level managers, IT specialists, engineers and others, whom they badly
need and have spent a large proportion of their limited resources training.
The net transfer of resources to rich countries from poor ones is estimated to run into several billion dollars, far more than the remittances by
the skilled individuals to their homelands. The just response to this could
be twofold: self-imposed limits on the extent of such recruitments from
poor countries, and compensating them for the loss. The latter could take
the form of financial contributions or, better still, establishing educational institutions there and giving their students commensurate numbers
of scholarships to study in the West. There are many such cases of
uneven, and in part exploitative, relationships between rich and poor
countries, which a globally orientated citizen needs to address.

Globally orientated citizenship also involves an active interest in and a sense of concern for our fellow human beings in other parts of the world. Even as one values one's community, others value theirs. And even as one desires certain basic conditions of the good life, so do they. One wishes them well, takes pleasure in their success, and feels addressed by their problems when for some reason they are unable to lead decent lives. When their government maltreats them, practises genocide or ethnic cleansing, one feels a responsibility for them and mobilizes international opinion.

Globally orientated citizens should also strive for a world order based on the principles of global ethics discussed earlier. They should seek to design global financial and other institutions in such a way that they regulate global forces in the service of emancipatory purposes, promote universal human well-being and enhance humankind's capacity to control its destiny. These institutions provide a system of global governance without a global government, and their composition, objectives and modes of operation should reflect these moral concerns. As they do so, they begin to command universal respect, symbolize and nurture human solidarity, and become objects of global loyalty. They provide the vital global forums where decisions are taken from a global or humanity's point of view, and raise collective consciousness to the level required by the reality of global interdependence.

The IMF and the World Bank do not meet these conditions. They are rightly seen as Western instruments of global domination, and need to be radically reconstituted or replaced by others more representative in their constitution, democratic in their operations, and committed to the pursuit of universal human well-being. By contrast, the UN is fairly representative and transparent, and provides a neutral global space for deliberation. However, it reflects the world of the 1940s – over sixty years ago – not the one in which we live. It is dominated by the Security Council, in particular its five permanent members with their power to veto decisions that go against their interests. Its members see the UN as just another stage on which to pursue their narrow national interests rather than as a global body where they need to deliberate and decide from the wider humanity's point of view. National interest obviously cannot and should not be ignored, but it must be balanced against that of outsiders. Above all, the UN reflects and institutionalizes the society of states but not the universal human community. We need to find ways of giving the latter institutional articulation through other, complementary forms of representation within or preferably outside the already over-crowded UN. The widely canvassed global parliament representing people rather than governments has its attractions, but also serious limitations. Electing its members on a global scale is costly and an administrative nightmare. It is also unlikely to work in authoritarian regimes, which do not even allow domestic elections. More importantly, it is not clear how a global parliament should be related to the General Assembly, and what its role is. There is much disagreement about what representative institutions can best express an effective non-governmental global voice. However, we do need to evolve such institutions, and it is not beyond human ingenuity to come up with ideas. The suitably reconstituted World Social Forum is one of these, and no doubt practical struggles by the oppressed and marginalized groups the world over will produce others.

Humanitarian intervention

I argued above that political communities exist to create conditions for the good life. None of them is perfect. Gender, religious and other forms of discrimination, pockets of acute poverty, ordinary violations of human rights, racism, abuse of political power, corrupt politicians, pursuit of partisan and sectional interests, and the widespread crime and insecurity these create disfigure almost all societies. They are best tackled by the determined efforts of their citizens, and we rightly assume that the latter have the necessary intellectual and moral resources to do so.

A very different situation arises when a state proves itself unable to secure its basic objectives, and forfeits its claim to others' non-interference. This happens in two situations. First, the state might almost have collapsed, or there might be no effective civil authority, and then its subjects are placed in a quasi-state of nature. Since there is no state, the question of respecting 'its' autonomy simply does not arise. Sometimes, while the state itself might not have collapsed, it might be caught up in a protracted civil war which no group has any hope of winning, and which undermines its long-term stability and viability. Such a community is too deeply fractured to provide the internal unity needed for an autonomous life. Second, the state might be well-established but engage in acts of genocide, the expulsion of its minorities on a massive scale, or ethnic cleansing. These are not ordinary violations of human rights which it can be expected to put right in due course under internal or external pressure, and which its citizens can be expected to live with, but a declaration of war against large sections of them. Confronted by the might of the state and its regime of terror, they are powerless against it and need external help.

The two situations require different responses. The second is generally easier to deal with: it has an identifiable authority, a mechanism of collective action and a vested interest in self-preservation, and is therefore amenable to external pressure. The international community has several forms of action available to it. It might impose 'smart' sanctions, which should be well-targeted and hit those in power while causing minimal damage to ordinary citizens and the country's long-term viability. It might expel the state from all or major international bodies, deny it access to international travel, postal, telephone, banking and other facilities, and withdraw its recognition as a state for a specified period. It might make it clear that leaders of the country concerned will not escape investigation and punishment after their retirement or overthrow. In extreme cases, and subject to certain conditions to be discussed later, military intervention might be necessary as a last recourse.

Societies with failed or deeply fractured states are the most difficult to handle. They have multiple actors, none of them carrying much authority except that derived from their fickle militias. These societies are not easily targeted, and actions designed to hit the leaders' interests invariably affect ordinary citizens. The leaders have no moral commitment to their society, and do not care if their indiscriminate violence damages its long-term viability, and their hate-filled propaganda destroys such bonds as might exist among its members. Different ethnic and religious groups in these societies have no history of working together, nor shared collective memories, and distrust each other too deeply to form durable alliances.

Creating stable states in such societies is an exceedingly difficult and protracted task requiring great patience, forbearance and wisdom. Outsiders can play only a limited and largely facilitating role. They can identify the economic interests that drive different groups, and explore ways of reconciling them. They can encourage and press for power-sharing by throwing their weight behind appropriate federal structures, decentralization, fair regional and ethnic allocations of resources, and a constitutionally guaranteed system of individual and group rights. Outsiders could refuse to recognize arrangements that marginalize or exclude minority groups, and to deal with such states unless matters are put right. They can also discourage obsession with the nation state, in which the dominant group claims ownership of the nation and declares other groups to be anti-national and subversive.

The state is not the only agency through which the international community asserts itself. Much can be done at the level of civil society. International and local NGOs can do much to foster trust between different groups by developing shared projects and promoting better understanding. They can also be encouraged to try peaceful methods of conflict resolution, and begin to deal with conflicts before they threaten to get out of control. Even in societies that are fractured and scarred by civil wars, ordinary men and women sometimes play a significant, but largely unnoticed, role. In Croatia, peace teams with Serb and Croat members successfully prevented several reprisals against Serbs, with a real risk to their own lives. In Kenya, large-scale fighting between clans was stopped by Wajir Women for Peace, who appealed to and involved tribal leaders. Similar interventions were made successfully by women in Northern Ireland.

We have become so used to violence that that we have not devoted sufficient attention and resources to internationally organized non-violent methods of mediating and resolving conflicts. Rather than sending troops every time we feel the need to intervene, we might think of UN-supported or independently operating and non-violently trained men and women, drawn from the region or belonging to the same religion, interposing themselves between warring groups, either alone or in collaboration with local groups, and mobilizing popular pressure.[9] Since these people are unarmed, not allied to governments and are seen as well-meaning, they are unlikely to become targets of attack in the way that armed troops are. This idea might prove to be too optimistic, but it has had some success in the past and is worth considering, especially as armed intervention leads to a great (sometimes too great) loss of lives and property, and becomes more and more difficult to mount in view of its cost and the number of failing or failed states, currently estimated at nearly sixty.[10]

In both failed and repressive states, national and world religious leaders often wield considerable authority, and should be required to take responsibility. They should lead non-violent protests, reconcile warring groups, condemn and excommunicate those suspected of outrageous deeds, and even deny them funeral rites, as some religions do to convicted murderers and suicides. It is a sad commentary on certain religious organizations, and a sign of their deep corruption, that, for example, the Serbian Church leaders blessed their followers' brutalities; some Buddhist monks openly endorsed Pol Pot's mass murders; and even the Vatican's role in Rwanda left much to be desired. Such organizations and their leaders should be named and shamed, and called to account by the pressure of international religious and secular public opinion.

Situations are bound to arise when these and other actions might be impossible or ineffective. Military action may then become necessary if it satisfies four conditions. First, it should be lawful. It is self-contradictory to intervene in order to create conditions conducive to the rule of law if the intervention itself is in violation of international law. At present, international law on intervention is vague, confused, open to conflicting interpretations, and constantly stretched to accommodate pre-emptive, preventive and other dubious types of war. It should be formulated clearly, and should lay down strict conditions under which outsiders may intervene in the internal affairs of a state. Even then disputes are bound to arise in particular cases. These should be referred to the International Court of Justice, whose judgement should be final. We do this in domestic jurisdiction, where internal state actions are subject to judicial scrutiny. There is no reason why external state actions should be treated differently.

Second, since military action is heavy-handed, involves considerable human and financial cost, leaves a legacy of destruction and hatred, and is likely to provoke resentment against the groups on whose behalf it is undertaken, it should be based on the most careful calculation and planning. We should assess the comparative cost in human lives, its chances of success, the expectations it is likely to arouse in the country concerned, the attitudes of its major groups, and the precedent it is likely to set. We should also remember that viable polities are often developed in the course of struggle, that a premature or ill-conceived intervention is often counter-productive, and that the deep-seated political problems of a country cannot be solved in a hurry or by military means alone. Sometimes the warring parties need to be left alone to try their strength until they reach an impasse, at which time they might be more ready to accept, and even welcome, external intervention. In some parts of the world, there is a tendency to do nothing, and societies hope that outsiders will sort out their internal problems for them. External intervention should not perpetuate such a colonial mentality, which corrupts both the parties involved. The future of a state is shaped by the manner of its birth, and those that owe their existence to external agencies tend to remain dependent on them for a long time. While outsiders have a duty to help struggling states, they should not undermine the states' sense of agency.

Third, military intervention should be limited in its objectives. It should not become an occasion to dictate the composition of government, prop up groups too weak to survive the departure of outsiders, distort the normal play of political forces, or become an excuse to occupy the country. It cannot end all factional struggles either, as that takes time and is not within the power of outsiders. They are also part of the process of state-building and best resolved by those involved. The sole purpose of armed intervention should be to stop the cycle of violence, get help to civilians trapped in war zones, ensure a measure of stability, and hold the ring until the parties involved create a viable government. It should accept the ground reality, work with those who can deliver peace and stability, involve and give neighbours a stake, and not be distracted by the desire to hunt down and punish obnoxious leaders. Such a task is best undertaken after a measure of order is restored, and should be left to the people of the country, who alone have the legal authority to do so and can use it to achieve the necessary reconciliation between rival groups.

Fourth, military intervention should ideally be authorized by a body widely accepted as the voice of the international community. At one level, the duty of assistance falls on all states, and any state in a position to offer help should be able to do so. If there is a widespread feeling, based on reliable evidence, that the situation is desperate and that the rest of the world is for some reason unable or unwilling to act, individual states may need to intervene. This is why India and Tanzania were right to intervene in East Pakistan and Amin's Uganda respectively, and why any state or coalition of states would have had the right to intervene in the dark days leading up to the genocide in Rwanda. Although unilateral actions might be necessary in exceptional circumstances, they have their obvious dangers. States are likely to be guided by their own interests, and to use the intervention to settle old scores, favour particular groups or set up convenient regimes. Military intervention should be based on clearly stated principles to ensure consistency and avoid double standards, and that cannot be achieved by leaving it to unilateral decisions. The country in difficulty is likely to have greater confidence in the intervention and is more likely to co-operate if the intervention enjoys international legitimacy. Unless there is a widely acknowledged grave crisis and the rest of the world is for some reason unable to act, all interventions should require international authorization.

When the Security Council is paralysed by a veto or put under undue pressure by one or more of its members, as was the case with the second war on Iraq, the matter should be referred to the General Assembly under the broadly interpreted 'uniting for peace' procedure, as done by the US in 1950 during the Korean War. Greater use could be made of this provision than has been the case so far, and it could be redrafted and made mandatory in certain cases. The UN could act more effectively and more speedily if it had a rapid reaction force of its own, made up of units seconded by the members states for a specific period or, where possible, voluntary soldiers joining it as individuals rather than as representatives of their countries. The UN could set up a Standing Commission to offer independent advice on the states sliding towards collapse, likely situations of conflict, and how best to handle them. Since the UN is increasingly being given the responsibility for too many functions, some of these might be hived off to newly-created global institutions or to regional bodies.

As several recent experiences show, humanitarian intervention runs the risk of being turned into a profitable business. The infrastructure of the invaded country gets badly damaged or is deliberately destroyed in military action, and needs to be rebuilt. Its natural resources need to be developed, its armed forces have to be retrained and equipped with new weaponry, its schools and hospitals reconstructed, its ministers and officials protected by an elaborate security system, and so on. Since all this yields millions of dollars in income from inflated contracts, the intervening countries and their business enterprises are keen to get their share of it. Indeed, some multinationals are known to lobby for humanitarian intervention for this very reason, supported by similarly motivated local groups who even create or contribute to the crisis in the hope of reaping their share of its attractive harvest. The presence of the UN in a country means quick money for various groups. It creates jobs, rents houses, hires interpreters and consultants, and gives out contracts and subcontracts that sometimes go to those with close ties to the warring parties.

We need to find ways of freeing humanitarian intervention from such sordid considerations, and the enormous wastage of money that accompanies it. It helps to channel aid for reconstruction through recognized international and national NGOs, and to involve local residents in their work. It would also help if the decisions concerning the reconstruction of the country were not to be made by the intervening countries but by a neutral international body set up by the UN and operating under strict guidelines. It should invite international tenders, and its decisions should be monitored and subjected to a rigorous public scrutiny.

I have argued that we should see states as both autonomous and a part of the wider human community, bounded but open, self-determining yet accountable to the rest of the world, having obligations to their own citizens but also to others outside their boundaries. When seen from the perspective of such a non-exclusivist view of the state, humanitarian intervention appears in an altogether different light.[11] It is a logical extension of the duty of mutual help that states, as representatives of their citizens, owe to each other. It is not a way of sorting out undisciplined natives, pacifying one's troubled conscience or giving a veneer of respectability to the normally cynical conduct of international relations. Rather, it is an act of helping one's fellow human beings who, as all humans tend to do, have temporarily lost their self-restraint, cannot free themselves from bitter and often garbled historical memories, have fallen prey to malevolent manipulators masquerading as their leaders, become victims of divisions created by external powers, run up against problems too large for their moral and political resources, or been overwhelmed by atavistic passions. They need help, sympathetic understanding, wise and disinterested pressure, words of advice, caution and rebuke, a touch of force – all administered with the respect owed to fellow human beings, and with a view to repairing or restructuring the fractured framework of civility in a manner best suited to their traditions and history. When so conceived, humanitarian intervention is freed from the corrupting moral and psychological climate associated with the current practice of it, and becomes instead a way of expressing and nurturing human solidarity.[12]

Subject to certain stringent conditions, intervention, then, is just or at least justified in the failed and egregiously repressive states. One might ask if it may be undertaken to establish democratic institutions, and whether the case I have made for it requires us to give an affirmative answer. It is to this highly contentious question that I turn in the final chapter.

13

Promoting Democracy

The question whether democratic societies should promote democracy in non-democratic societies has dominated the public agenda in recent years.[1] Although it is asked in relation to the West, it could easily be asked in other contexts. In response to public opinion, India assisted the democratic movement in Nepal and put considerable pressure on the Nepalese king to agree to a constitutional monarchy. Some Indians have wondered if they should do the same in relation to Burma, Bangladesh and even perhaps Pakistan. The South African government is urged to use economic and diplomatic pressure to promote democracy in neighbouring countries, including Zimbabwe. There is no reason why other countries such as Malaysia and Brazil might not ask the same question in relation to their region. At present, however, only the West, in particular the US, has the necessary power and reach, and therefore I shall concentrate on it.

Those who think the West should promote democracy generally advance a mixture of moral and prudential reasons. Democracy respects such important values as human dignity, rights and equality and all who can promote it have a duty to do so. Since democratic societies do not generally go to war with each other, the universal spread of democracy is also considered to be the best way to ensure international peace and stability. Democracy is believed to have the additional advantage of discouraging domestic, and in particular international, terrorism. Since it allows the expression and redress of discontent, disaffected groups do not need to resort to terrorism against their own government or the outsiders deemed to be responsible for their predicament.

The critics find much of this reasoning specious, self-serving and dangerous, and think that the idea of promoting democracy is basically an imperialist project intended to shape the rest of the world to suit

259

Western interests. In their view, there is no good reason why democracies should not go to war with each other. That they have not done so is a historically contingent fact which could easily be otherwise if there were to be fundamental conflicts of interest between them, or if one of them for some reason felt deeply threatened by another. While free press and public accountability might guard against war-mongering, there is nothing to stop determined governments from manipulating and mobilizing popular passions against outsiders. Democracy does not rule out terrorism either, as the examples of India, Britain, Germany, Italy and Japan since the 1970s show. A country might engage in ethnic cleansing, repress its minorities or deny them effective redress, and thereby create a climate conducive to terrorism. If the government is in league with foreign powers and compromises vital national interests, its citizens might see no alternative to international terrorism to bring appropriate pressure to bear on it. As for the moral argument, the critics think it is particularly dangerous: all countries pursue their narrow interests, and are likely to use the promotion of democracy as a convenient moral excuse. Furthermore, democracy involves not just a set of institutions but also a particular kind of moral and political culture, which takes years to develop and in whose absence these institutions cannot flourish or even last. Societies need to achieve stability and build up an effective state before they can aspire to democracy. Over-zealous attempts to push them towards it not only fail to establish it but ultimately might make them unstable, as the case of Iraq so eloquently and tragically demonstrates.[2]

Since the debate on the desirability or otherwise of promoting democracy is conducted against the background of recent experiences in Afghanistan and Iraq, and the Bush Government's self-serving use of it, it lacks a broad historical and moral perspective. While not losing sight of the lessons of these experiences, it is therefore necessary to step back from current events and address the question in general theoretical terms.

The idea of promoting democracy in non-democratic societies raises four important questions. First, since democracy has taken different forms in different historical epochs and societies, what is it that we wish to promote in its name? Second, since we can legitimately promote and press on others what is good for them or in their interests, is democracy a universally desirable good? Third, if it is, do we have a duty to promote it, and what is its basis? Since there is much to be said for leaving each society free to organize its collective affairs, what is the best trade-off between the goods of democracy and self-determination? Fourth, and finally, if we conclude that, on balance, we have a duty to promote democracy, what is the best way to do so? I shall take each of these in turn.

What is democracy?

Historically speaking, democracy has been understood in several different ways.[3] The communitarian democracy of classical Athens is quite different from modern liberal democracy, and both again differ from the bottom up radical democracy advocated by Marxists and others. Constitutional democracy, in which people's powers are constitutionally limited, is different from the populist democracy that recognizes no limits on the popular will. Liberal democracy itself should not be homogenized. It could be representative *government*, in which elected representatives are free from institutionalized popular control and at liberty to take decisions as they think best, or representative *democracy*, in which people rule themselves through their representatives and expect them to carry out the people's clearly articulated will; and each of these two, again, can be organized differently. Since democracy can take different forms, we should resist the all too common temptation to equate it with a single form, promote the latter in its name, and foreclose choice. Different forms of democracy represent so many different ways of interpreting, institutionally articulating and balancing the central principles of democracy. Promoting democracy involves promoting these principles, not their particular interpretations or institutional structures.

At its most basic, democracy refers to a particular theory of political authority or legitimacy; that is, who should exercise political power, how and for what purposes. This is the context in which the idea of democracy first emerged in the West, and this is how it has subsequently been understood. Democracy stands for the view that citizens collectively are the source of political authority, and that they alone have the right to speak in their collective name and take binding decisions. They should govern themselves by means of general laws and aim to pursue their common interest. In a democracy, the will of the people is the sole source of legitimacy, and their interest or good is the sole basis of justification of laws and policies. People may govern themselves directly or through their representatives. Although elections are the most reliable and commonest way of choosing representatives, there can be other ways, so long as they ensure a free, fair and generally acceptable way to make a choice.

Citizens – that is, those enjoying full membership of the political community – collectively constitute the people or demos. Membership criteria might vary from community to community. They could be ethnic, cultural, religious, economic or based on some other consideration, and in each case the demos is defined and delimited appropriately. At the centre of democracy is the idea that these criteria should not be unjust, arbitrary or based on contingent circumstances. They should only require that claimants to citizenship should have some commitment to their society, and be able and willing to obey its laws and participate in the conduct of its affairs. Since all sane adults born within the community, or who have lived in it for a prescribed period of time, meet this requirement, a democratic society should grant citizenship to them all without discrimination. The history of democracy is a story of struggle against the various kinds of arbitrary limits on citizenship until a universal franchise is secured.

If people are to govern themselves directly or through their representatives, they need freedom of speech, including the freedom to express and exchange views, and to criticize the government. This freedom is not absolute and may be limited by law if this is justified on grounds of the democratically defined public interest. People also need independent sources of truthful information, and hence a free and impartial press that is independent of both the government and private interests. They need freedom of association, so they can exchange views, organize in pursuit of their interests, bring pressure on the government, and set up political parties. They cannot form, express and press their views unless they enjoy a basic sense of independence and self-worth, which they cannot do if they are at the mercy of and subject to the arbitrary will of their government or their fellow citizens. People therefore need certain basic rights, inviolable personal space, and the rule of law with all that it entails.

People as the ultimate source of political authority, popularly chosen and accountable government, universal suffrage, legal and political equality, freedom of speech, protest and organization, respect for basic human rights and the rule of law are some of the important constitutive features of democracy. No form of government that denies these can be called democratic. For convenience, I shall call them principles of democratic governance.

So long as they respect these principles, democratic societies may organize their conduct of collective affairs as they please, depending on their traditions, circumstances and self-understanding. Although liberalism and democracy are distinct bodies of thought, and a society can be one but not the other, they have become so identified in our minds that we frequently confuse what are in fact liberal values with democratic ones. This encourages intellectual disingenuousness, as when we push liberal values in the name of promoting democracy, and provokes avoidable opposition from many in non-western societies, who are sympathetic to democracy but not to liberalism. Basically, liberal democracy is a form of government in which liberalism is the dominant partner, and defines and sets limits to democracy. It is individualist in its ethos; rationalist in its orientation – in the sense of resolving disagreements by rational discussion and public reason; values choice; recognizes only the individual as its basic legal, moral and political unit; sees society largely as a voluntary association; rejects paternalism; and cherishes such rights as those to own property, the unlimited accumulation of wealth, and fairly extensive freedom of expression. It presupposes, and is an appropriate response to, societies that have a strong individualist ethos, are not deeply divided along ethnic or religious lines, and whose members do not all agree on and feel strongly about a substantive vision of the good life.

Societies such as classical Athens are quite different. They share a common vision of the good life, and their members are, and see themselves as, embedded in structures of thick social relations. They might therefore restrict the right to own property or freedom of speech when these threaten to undermine their way of life in a way that would be unacceptable in a liberal democracy. After listening to Socrates' self-defence, a large majority of Athenians concluded at the end of a public debate that his uninhibited intellectual inquiry was morally and culturally subversive, and gave him the choice of leaving, staying silent, or accepting the punishment of death. Their decision was democratic, though not liberal. Again, contemporary Quebec, determined to preserve its language and culture, requires Allophone (those who are not Anglophones or Francophones) parents to send their children to French-speaking schools. This is illiberal, at least from some views of liberalism, but it is arrived at democratically and serves widely shared collective goals. There is no reason why all democracies should be organized along liberal lines, so long as they satisfy the basic principles of democratic governance.

Multi-ethnic societies, especially those in which ethnic groups are territorially concentrated and have a history of mutual indifference or hostility, do not have a single demos, and need to devise ways of ensuring peace and stability long enough to allow their several communities to develop into a single people. They may grant rights to individuals as well as to groups, allow the latter varying degrees of autonomy provided that they respect their members' right of exit, recognize officially their diverse identities, introduce asymmetrical federation, and so on. This is the case in many contemporary democracies, including India and Canada. Although it leads to a highly complex democracy, it would be wrong to say that they are not democracies simply because they do not conform to the standard version of liberal democracy.

In some Muslim countries, attempts are being made to develop what are being called Islamic democracies.[4] These are committed to Islam and its vision of the good life, but they also value democracy and explore alternatives to individualist and largely secular liberal democracy. Since democracy locates political authority in the people, it has a secular thrust, but it would be wrong to say that it is conceptually incompatible with religion, or that a religion-based democracy is inherently impossible. Islam insists that sovereignty is ultimately derived from God. This can be reconciled with democracy by arguing that people are its inheritors on earth. Islam views the Qur'ān as the source of authoritative norms and injunctions, and expects it to play the part that a written constitution does in a democracy. This too should create no problems if their meaning and entailments are openly debated, and only those interpretations that command widespread popular consensus are made the basis of public policy. The role of the mullahs might be problematical, but this too can be dealt with by denying them an official or a privileged place, or by a suitable separation of powers that leaves the ultimate authority with the people.

Other difficulties are more acute. Are people free to modify, disregard or go against Qur'ānic injunctions? Can they opt for a secular state? Can they establish gender equality? Can they treat non-Muslims equally with Muslims? Can they allow apostasy? Can they elect a non-Muslim head of state? In each case, democracy requires that they should, but Islam seems to take the opposite view. In some areas, tensions can be resolved or reduced, but not in others. An Islamic democracy can ensure gender equality and even allow apostasy by reinterpreting the Qur'ān, as some Muslim countries have done. However, it cannot so easily allow a non-Muslim head of state, a secular government, or laws that go against the explicit injunctions of the Qur'ān. An

Islamic democracy thus can go a long way, but not all the way, to being a democracy even in the minimal sense in which I have defined the term. Like liberal democracy, Islamic democracy can take different forms and combine its two halves in different ways, ranging from one where Islam is the dominant partner to one where it does no more than give a certain ethos to a basically democratic public culture. It is clearly not a liberal democracy, but it does not pretend to be this, and might even have compensating advantages such as a strong sense of community, solidarity and providing a meaningful life.

At the heart of an Islamic or any other religion-based (or even hyphenated) democracy, there is a constant tension between the requirements of religion and democracy. However, this is not unique. Liberal democracy also contains a tension between the principles of liberalism and democracy: the former stressing individual autonomy and personal liberty and with a bias towards capitalism; and the latter stressing community and equality and with a thrust towards socialism or social democracy, so much so that for over a century liberals and democrats wondered if they could ever become partners.[5] The tension remains, but almost all liberal democracies have found ways not only of containing but also of benefiting from it. The Islamic democracy too could in principle develop along similar lines. There are, of course, important differences between the two. Despite their tensions in other areas, both democracy and liberalism have a secular and rationalist orientation, value public reason and autonomous civil society, and meet on common ground. This is not the case with Islam, or religion in general, and democracy. However, one should not exaggerate the differences, for no Western liberal democracy is wholly secular in its design, free from a Christian ethos, or immune to the powerful influence of religious groups. An Islamic democracy could benefit from a dialectic between its two halves, with Islam giving democracy moral and spiritual depth and egalitarian principles of social organization, and democracy subjecting Islam to the test of public reason and giving it a semi-secular ethos. Things might not work out quite like this in practice, but there is no reason to be dogmatic and foreclose new experiments.

Universal validity

The principles of democratic governance are universally valid and deserve to form part of any well-conceived system of governance. This is so on three related grounds, namely moral, political and prudential. Since these are well-known, a brief discussion should suffice.

Democracy institutionalizes and nurtures human dignity and a sense of self-worth. Its citizens are not the playthings of, or live on the sufferance and in fear of, others, but rather are independent agents enjoying self-respect, a measure of inviolability, and the power to shape their individual and collective lives. They have a say in the conduct of their affairs, are free to protest and join with others in redressing their grievances, matter equally, and feel empowered. Whatever their differences and inequalities in other areas of life, there is one where they meet as equals. Their legal and political equality also generates an appropriate momentum in other areas, and leads to demands for their democratization.

Politically, democracy creates conditions in which people are expected to form their own views on individuals and issues, defend these views before others, look at themselves from the standpoint of others, and transcend their narrow perspectives and interests. In so doing, they develop their powers of judgement, self-reflection and self-criticism, and expand their sympathies. Democracy also gives them a sense of ownership of their community, helps them to recognize its institutions as their common achievements, and generates an emotional commitment to them that nurtures and reinforces respect for the law and a sense of justice that every well-established community requires. They act justly and take an active interest in the affairs of the community, not only because they should, but because they want to as an expression of their commitment to and identification with it.

The principles of democratic governance can also be defended on prudential grounds. All power corrupts, not only in the material sense that those who have it want to hold on to it at all costs and use it to promote their interests, but also in the deeper sense of generating the illusion that they know what is good for others, and the concomitant vices of self-righteousness and moral arrogance. Democracy checks power by making it conditional and subjecting its exercise to critical scrutiny. Human beings, further, tend to look at the world in particular ways, and have their inescapable blind spots. The only way to overcome this is to create a public space where they critically engage with one another and arrive at a wider and more balanced view of the subject in question. With all its limitations, democracy is the best way to guard against partiality, corruptibility, intellectual and moral myopia, and the other familiar human frailties.

It is, of course, true that people can make mistakes, easily be mobilized around misguided causes, fall prey to peddlers of suicidal fantasies and utopias, and misjudge their long-term interests. This is, however, just as true, if not more so, of authoritarian rulers and despots as well as of allegedly infallible religious leaders. Furthermore, it is precisely because human beings are fallible and corruptible that they need to guard against their frailties by establishing appropriate institutions. Free speech, opposition parties, and the freedom to organize and protest ensure that information flows freely and is constantly checked, and that judgements and actions of those in, or seeking, power are carefully scrutinized. Non-democratic forms of government lack such self-regulating mechanisms, and are not only more prone to abuses but also have no protection against them. Democracy is not the best form of governance imaginable, but it is better than all others available at the present time. We should constantly seek ways of deepening and widening democracy to meet new challenges, and ensure that it does not become frozen in a set of historically inherited institutions and practices that might once have served society well but no longer do so.

It is sometimes argued that democratic principles are Western in their origins, historically and culturally specific, and should not be universalized.[6] This argument is deeply flawed. The principles are not all Western in origin, as many of them are also to be found in different forms in other parts of the world, including the Buddhist republics in classical India and the ancient city-states of Phoenicia, especially Tyre. Even in the West, they first appeared in classical Athens. Depending on how we define East and West, classical Athens could be considered to be either. Even if the principles were 'Western', however, nothing would follow, for their validity or otherwise is unconnected to their origin. After all, the modern state, nationalism and private property are even more unequivocally Western in origin, yet they are adopted enthusiastically by those rejecting democracy as being Western. The charge that the principles of democratic governance are culturally specific makes sense when democracy is equated with a particular form of it, usually the liberal. This is one of the reasons why I insisted at the beginning that we should detach democracy from its various forms as much as possible, and define it in terms of its basic or minimum constitutive principles.

Although democracy is a political good, so are others, such as political stability and economic development. It is sometimes suggested, that since they conflict, at least in the short run, we need a trade-off, and even that the latter two, being more central to human life, trump democracy. Although the argument makes sense in some contexts as I argue later, and should not be dismissed out of hand, it is unconvincing in its stark form. Let us take the alleged conflict between democracy and development. Democracy, it is argued, is wasteful, short-sighted, accustomed to thinking in terms of electoral cycles, in thrall to the dominant class that controls the media or contributes to party funds and sets the parameters of state action, and is biased towards the middle classes with their greater ability to manipulate the political system. All this is true, but the conclusion that development is better achieved under other forms of government does not follow. These defects are not inherent in democracy but in the way it is practised, and can be corrected by making it more effective. When well-organized, it mobilizes the enthusiasm and moral energies of its citizens and gives them a stake in their development. Furthermore, non-democratic forms of government not only include many of these defects but have additional ones of their own, such as using public resources for private gain, wasting them on grandiose projects and weaponry, mortgaging vital natural resources to the multinationals for a share in the spoils, favouring a small coterie of loyalists, locating industries in unviable but favoured regions, and so on. Unlike democracies, they have no institutional mechanism for exposing and correcting these defects, and bankrupt the country in a way that is generally unlikely in a democracy. Responsible and public-spirited authoritarian regimes can certainly run the country better, but that is equally true of democracies.

China is often taken as a counter-example, but the situation there is more complex. It has for long been hugely wasteful of its human talents and lives (especially but not only during the Cultural Revolution), and has devoted vast resources to armaments that could have been better spent on alleviating the poverty of its people. Although it does not have a democratic regime, there is some democracy within the Communist Party that ensures debates between different points of view and moderates the excesses of authoritarianism. Furthermore, China is increasingly beginning to realize that this is not enough, and that it needs democratic freedoms to expose rampant corruption, hold public officials to account, give voice to marginalized groups, and to highlight the inequity of local allocations of resources.

Compared to China, India's developmental record has long been extremely disappointing, but this has had more to do with the policies of successive governments than its democratic institutions. This became clear when it began to move away from its state-centred and heavily bureaucratic micromanagement of the economy, released entrepreneurial energy and promptly chalked up an 8 per cent growth rate. There is also the further question of why economic development is desirable. It matters because it creates the conditions for a good life for all or most of its citizens, and these include a sense of dignity, basic freedoms, and empowerment. If these are absent, economic development loses much of its point.[7]

A duty to promote democracy

We have a duty to promote the principles of democratic governance for three related reasons. First, as I argued earlier, the principle of equal human worth enjoins a duty to promote human well-being within the limits of our capacity, and these principles form part of it. Second, while democracies can be highly nationalistic, go to war with one another and intervene aggressively in each others' affairs in a manner that falls only just short of outright war, they generally have self-correcting mechanisms. They encourage a plurality of views, hold the government to account, punish it for gross misjudgement, cannot for long suppress dissent, and learn from their mistakes. President George W. Bush went to war in Iraq, but the processes of US democracy eventually caught up with him. Israel went to war with Lebanon in 2006, but the subsequent public inquiry showed how ill-advised it was and severely criticized its prime minister. The eight year long Iran–Iraq war in the 1980s that killed millions, many as a result of egregiously irresponsible military and political decisions, would be rare in democracies. Although the spread of democracy does not stop wars, it tends to make them less impulsive and less brutal, and contributes towards a stable and law-governed world. It also facilitates the kind of intercultural dialogue I talked about earlier, builds vital bridges across societies, generates a pressure for a peaceful resolution of conflicts, and fosters a mature and well-informed public opinion.[8]

Third, as we saw earlier, in our increasingly interdependent world, people's interests are interlocked. Gross misgovernment, oppression, ethnic, sectarian or religious cleansing, and failed states in other parts of the world affect the material and moral interests of all. They produce waves of asylum seekers and refugees who cannot be turned away as if they were stray dogs. Their suffering addresses us as moral beings, and our failure to respond to it diminishes us in our eyes. They also affect our material interests, such as the supply of energy and so on, make us target of their frustrations, and render the world unstable. The moral duty to promote conditions for a good life elsewhere is thus reinforced by the considerations of our own humanity and enlightened self-interest.

It is sometimes argued that every society has a right to decide its own form of government, and that others should respect its autonomy. While there is much to be said for this, the right to self-determination, as I argued earlier, is not absolute, and may be curtailed or overridden when it leads to a systematic and egregious violation of human freedom and lives. Furthermore, this right belongs to members of the community, not to its self-appointed and oppressive rulers, who may not therefore claim its protection. When citizens are subjected to a regime of terror they become political orphans. Rejected by their state, they look to the wider human community for help, and it has a duty to respond to them. Even as we are rightly worried about acute poverty and global injustices in poorer parts of the world, we should be equally concerned about the political conditions under which they live.

Ways of promoting democracy

While the duty to promote democracy is relatively unproblematic, the most difficult question is how best to discharge it. The use of force is not the answer. Democracy must be the free choice of the people, and it is self-contradictory to impose it by force. Force can certainly remove an oppressive ruler but it can neither establish a democracy nor even create some of the basic conditions for it. Advocates of force talk of people's natural 'yearning' or 'hunger for freedom', and naïvely assume that once the oppressive ruler is removed, democratic institutions and practices will spring up spontaneously. People might welcome the end of oppressive rule, and might even vote in the elections in large numbers, but constructing and running democratic institutions is an altogether different matter. It requires new habits of thought, new practices, mutual trust, self-restraint and different expectations of government, and all this takes years to cultivate.

No oppressive ruler can rule for long without building up an intricate system of oppression whose roots stretch deep into almost all areas of life, and co-opting a large number of collaborators, each a miniature version of him. Removing him does not end the system. Erstwhile collaborators present themselves as democrats, use their powerful contacts and resources to get elected, and entrench themselves. In the absence of an alternative system that has not yet had the chance to emerge, the old system with its intricate network is reproduced. Through the misguided use of force, the new democracy is undermined even before it has had a chance to establish itself.

When democracy is imposed externally, it is associated with aggression and an assault on national pride, and arouses widespread hostility. All kinds of otherwise divided groups, some made up of erstwhile collaborators, unite under the banner of nationalism and do their best to sabotage it. The external powers and 'their democracy' now become the new enemy, and memories of the repressive ruler recede into the collective unconscious. Driven by contradictory sentiments, ordinary men and women do not take ownership of the new institutions, which are meant to be in their best interests but in whose creation they had no role, and prefer to remain passive bystanders or worse.

The basic question, furthermore, is not how to introduce democracy but rather how to sustain it. Elections are easy to organize, and they can even be free and fair, though it is difficult to see how they can reflect well-considered popular choices when held in a climate of fear and chaos. Once elected, a government might refuse to hold elections in the future, suppress and harass the opposition, or decline to relinquish office when defeated. At least two to three elections are needed before democratic institutions and practices are consolidated, and one can be sure that the society is well on its way to democracy. External force might ensure that the first elections take place, but little beyond that, and could even frustrate further democratic developments.

Sometimes the examples of postwar Japan and Germany are cited as evidence that democracy can be imposed externally, but the situation in both countries was far more complex than such a simplistic account suggests. Both countries were defeated in wars they had themselves started. Foreign powers did not invade their countries to impose democracy; rather, they were already there and stayed on to design the new constitutions. Both countries were anxious to put an end to militarism, and welcomed democratic institutions. In both countries, the Allied powers stayed for several years, worked with and enjoyed the broad support of local leaders, and planned the new institutions co-operatively. Germany had a long liberal tradition and had lived under the Weimar Republic before it was overthrown. The new Japanese Constitution, passed in 1946 and adopted in May 1947, was widely discussed in the country. The emperor willingly agreed to become a constitutional monarch and went round the country indicating his new status. An impressive official delegation of seventy political and trade union leaders, industrialists and intellectuals visited Europe and the US to find out how democracy worked, in the same way that their predecessors had gone there several decades earlier to learn their technological know-how. Germany had the benefits of the Marshall Plan and the newly-emerging European common market. In neither country was democracy imposed by force. Force was used only to end the militaristic system, and what followed was the free choice of the people themselves, albeit under the pressure and guidance of external powers.

The European Union provides the best and hitherto the only example in history of how to introduce democracy by democratic means in societies that have never really known it.[9] It provided the accession countries with powerful incentives in the form of investment, access to a large market, monetary stability, aid and subsidies, international respectability, and the opportunity to shape the EU's decisions and acquire global influence. They saw the economic prosperity that membership had brought in Spain, Portugal and Ireland, and wanted something similar for themselves. Not surprisingly, large majorities in these countries were excited by the prospect of joining the EU and were willing to comply with its requirements, including the adoption of democratic institutions.

This was made easier by the fact that they were not asked to conform to a rigid model of democracy. They had to satisfy certain basic principles, subject to which they were free to make their own choices. The accession countries' representatives negotiated hard with those of the EU and agreed on what they needed to do in different areas. A clear plan was worked out, benchmarks were specified, and considerable time was allowed to make the changes. Financial assistance was given to cover the costs involved; seminars, workshops and training programmes were organized for administrative officials, politicians, journalists, judges and others; experts were seconded; and any difficulties the countries encountered were examined sympathetically and dealt with.

The EU model of promoting democracy contains many important lessons. It rightly relies on a mixture of self-interest, national self-respect, and moral and political pressure to persuade its future members to embrace democracy. It wisely lays down a mutually agreed 'road map', bears the cost of transition, offers technical assistance and advice, and closely monitors the pace and direction of progress. These are the sorts of things we need to do to promote democracy. The EU, however, is a relatively small club, with large resources to dispense. Its potential members are all neighbours and share a broadly common history and social structure. The democracy it demands is largely liberal in its orientation, which is unlikely to work in the case of Muslim and other societies that have their own ideas on the kind of democracy they want. The EU has also opted for a socially orientated capitalist model, and some countries might have different views on this. Its approach to the promotion of democracy therefore needs to be modified when applied at the global level.

While democracy can be promoted externally – though not, of course, imposed or even exported – the important question is whether outsiders can be trusted to do so in a systematic and relatively disinterested manner, and here the critics are right. Given its economic, political and military power and global contacts, the responsibility to promote democratic governance falls on the West. Although the West talks a great deal about it, its priorities are quite different, such as a misguided 'war on terror', making the world safe for capitalism, creating and protecting markets for its multinationals, a guaranteed energy supply at a relatively cheap price, and the preservation of its political, military and cultural hegemony. Its interest in promoting democracy is therefore episodic, self-serving, intermittent, half-hearted, selective, and often designed to embarrass inconvenient regimes (China and Russia, for example) or to provide a moral 'fig-leaf' to its imperialist adventures (Iraq, for example).

If the West is seriously interested in promoting democracy, and I have argued that it should be, it needs to do the following. First, it should realize that, in our interdependent world, the spread of stable democracy is as much in its own long-term interest as that of the country concerned.[10] It should therefore resist the temptation, which in the past it often has not, to destabilize politically inconvenient regimes, manipulate weak and fragile governments, play off rival groups against each other, arm them, and encourage and even instigate wars within and between states. Democracy requires strong and stable states enjoying legitimacy and popular support, able to act autonomously against outsiders and mediate effectively between warring internal groups. Weak states, or those perceived to be in thrall to or propped up by foreign powers or interests, do not meet this requirement, and cannot cope with the enormous pressures that an infant and diffident democracy generates.

The most useful role the West can play is to offer such help as the oppressed people need in their struggle against their rulers. This may involve economic and other sanctions and, in *extreme* cases, judicious and carefully calibrated intervention. As I argued earlier, oppressive rulers are not easy to remove without bloodshed. They also create an elaborate apparatus to consolidate their rule, and their removal can create a political vacuum and instability bordering on a Hobbesian state of nature in which warlords and militias thrive. Armed intervention to remove them must remain the last resort. It cannot, however, be ruled out altogether, as some argue. It was justified against Idi Amin in Uganda, Pol Pot in Cambodia, the Taliban in Afghanistan, and would have been justified against Hitler if undertaken at the right time. In these cases, the rulers either outraged 'the conscience of mankind' and simply could not be tolerated, or had been sponsoring terrorist networks, or had not developed a well-organized apparatus of rule and could be toppled with ease, or an organized opposition was available to provide an alternative. When these conditions are absent, armed intervention is counter-productive, as was the case in Iraq, would have been in Zaire under Mobutu, and would be in the case of Burma and Zimbabwe.

What situation falls under which category requires judgement based on reliable intelligence and a most careful analysis of the social and political situation of the country concerned. Since the intelligence is often patchy, and those willing to intervene cannot always be trusted to be disinterested, we need to be extremely cautious and endorse armed intervention only in exceptional cases, and when authorized by the UN and supported by the bulk of global opinion, including major civil society organizations that have some reliable knowledge of the country. When armed intervention occurs, its purpose should be to restore the country to its citizens, to remove obstacles to the development of democracy rather than actively to press for it. The outsider's role should be to advise, suggest ideas, urge reconciliation between different groups, reassure those who fear reprisals, and offer help to build up its democratic institutions, promote its economic development, and train its administrative and military personnel.[11] It should not seek to impose a particular form of democracy, set up a pliant regime, get caught up in internal conflicts, or try to run the country and become an occupying power.

Second, the West should recognize that one size does not fit all. Although democratic institutions have their own dynamics, they are only as good as those running them, and have a chance of success only if they are not too out of step with the prevailing system of social relations and power structure. The West should not therefore expect all societies to proceed along prescribed lines, or insist that democratic institutions and practices should be introduced in one sweep in their fully developed forms. Its first priority should be to encourage a stable, effective and popularly accountable government, and that might involve accommodating rival groups even at the cost of compromising some of the other principles of democratic governance. It should insist that certain basic rights (but not the full panoply of human rights) should be constitutionally guaranteed, good governance ensured, and civil society given the freedom to flourish, but should not press for more. Even so far as elections are concerned, the West needs to proceed cautiously. They can be deeply divisive, costly, polarize the community, raise issues that are best kept out, bring conflicts into the open, ratchet up political rhetoric and arouse deep fears, and waste scarce national resources on electoral bribes. If this danger is real, as it sometimes is, they should be delayed or replaced by other reliable and fair ways of eliciting the popular will and holding the government accountable, such as indirect elections or a council of tribal elders.

Third, while democracy is valuable for intrinsic reasons, it risks losing its legitimacy and popular support if it fails to ensure economic development. The West, especially the US, insists on a neo-liberal model that was at the heart of the Structural Adjustment Programme stridently supported by the Washington Consensus.[12] No Western society ever followed it during the course of its economic development, and it has proved to be a failure almost every time it has been tried. The discipline of the market is obviously important, and there is little to be said for an inefficient and bloated public sector, opportunistic subsidies to weak industries, and electoral bribes in the shape of writing off loans and unproductive investments. However, the market cannot be left alone. The neo-liberal model creates great inequalities that undermine social cohesion, leaves the state with few resources to contain discontent, denies it a significant presence in the lives of its people, and gives it limited power to deal with the consequences of an inevitably uneven development. Not surprisingly, it often requires authoritarian regimes to implement and deal with the consequences of its unfair and contentious policies. The weak and vulnerable groups, and infant industries, look to the state for help, which it is unable to offer when required to function within the straitjacket of the market. The logics of democracy and market conflict and, if the two are not balanced, popular support for both can easily evaporate.

Economic development calls for free and fair trade. Poorer countries need access to Western markets and a level playing field, neither of which they currently have because of high tariffs and the direct and indirect subsidies on which the West relies to maintain its competitive advantage. The protracted negotiations at Doha, as well as earlier ones, show how reluctant the West is to welcome competition, let alone respond generously to the needs of the poor. The latter also need index linking the prices of primary products to those of Western manufactured goods, and well-directed foreign aid to build their infrastructure and provide basic services to their people, and here again the Western record is disappointingly poor. It is true that aid is sometimes wasted or misdirected, but there are ways of guarding against that, such as targeting it for particular projects or purposes, ensuring independent monitoring, and involving responsible local and international NGOs. The promotion of democacy is inseparable from the pursuit of global justice.

Fourth, in many developing countries, democracy is resisted or does not survive the first elections for a variety of reasons. One of the most important is related to the ease with which those in power are able to plunder national resources, and the constant temptation that this provides to the military. Rulers sell, license or lease these resources to the multinationals of their choice and collect the kickback. They borrow vast sums of money from international institutions and bankers in the name of the country, pocket or waste most of it, and leave behind huge debts that impose crushing burdens on fledgling democracies. In Nigeria, military rulers plundered oil resources and left a national debt of US$30 billion, just under 80 per cent of its gross national product (GNP). In Angola and Mozambique, the debt–GNP ratio was four times as high; and Zaire, a vast mineral-rich country, was bled to death by Mobutu and his henchmen. The answer obviously lies in these countries themselves. They need to organize strong institutional checks, fight corruption, expose gross misuse of national resources, demand that these be used to meet the basic needs of their people, and in general mount a democratic struggle.

While outsiders cannot do their job for them and should not aggressively seek to shape the outcome of the struggle, they can make it easier. International law could require that the property of those found to have plundered national resources cannot be lawfully inherited and remains liable to expropriation. There could be internationally agreed restrictions on both the borrowing privileges of unrepresentative rulers, and their right to dispose of national resources. The strange and apparently perverse practice of secret Swiss bank accounts needs to be ended, and there should be effective mechanisms to track down the flow of funds. We also need tighter laws than at present to stop multinationals and foreign governments from using direct and indirect bribes to gain their ends, and to check the illicit trade in precious metals that is often the source of much internal struggle and bloodshed.

Finally, the West needs to approach the promotion of democracy in a spirit of humility. The widely popular language of 'exporting' it implies that the West has perfected the product and has nothing to learn from others, which is why it is better to talk of 'promoting' it. Although Western societies had an early start and have made considerable progress in the direction of democracy, they leave much to be desired. The first election of President George W. Bush, the unembarrassed champion of the promotion of democracy, remains under a cloud. African-Americans in some southern states of the US, who are unlikely to want to vote for him, faced avoidable difficulties in registering and casting their votes. Most of the US media were heavily biased in the lead-up to the second war on Iraq, as several independent investigations have shown, and misled the country. The British democracy had no institutional resources to stop its determined prime minister from bouncing his Cabinet, Parliament and country into a most unpopular and disastrous war on Iraq, or even to expose the lies and half truths told to justify it and punish any of the individuals involved. Large masses of people in all Western societies feel powerless, manipulated and deeply alienated from the political system. The press is free from government control, but not of corporate interests, for whom it is a way of making money and promoting a political and economic agenda rather than the public responsibility to provide impartial and truthful information and analysis.[13]

Democracy, then, needs to be promoted not only outside the West but also within it. Indeed, many non-Western societies have developed fascinating ways of deepening it and empowering people, from which it can learn. Examples include participatory budgeting in Brazil, which gives citizens a say in determining local priorities and deciding how a proportion of the tax revenue should be spent; the people's courts that rely on conciliation to resolve disputes and the fairly extensive public interest litigation in India; and the cultural and linguistic empowerment of minorities in South Africa. Promoting democracy would have a greater chance of success if the West saw it not as an export but rather as a co-operative global project to be pursued in the spirit of partnership.

To conclude, the principles of democratic governance constitute some of the important features of a good society, and represent a universal good. They presuppose certain economic and political conditions. These take time and can only be created by progressive struggles within each society. Its task, however, is made easier if others stop attempting to manipulate it in the pursuit of their narrow self-interest, facilitate its economic development, and generously render such advice, encouragement and help as it needs in a spirit of human solidarity. The promotion of democracy can be a paternalist, and even an imperialist project, when defined and pursued in the hegemonic form currently favoured by some dominant groups in the West. But it can also be the opposite, and an expression of our shared humanity and the duties arising out of it, if it is understood along the lines I have suggested. A blend of political realism and moral idealism dictates that while exposing and vigorously challenging the former, we should continue to press for the latter.

Notes

Chapter 1

1. For globalization, see Benyon and Dunkerley (2000), Scholte (2000) and Berger and Huntington (2002).
2. The term 'identity', in the sense in which I use it, became very popular after the Second World War. It had become so inflated by the 1970s that many, such as Robert Coles and W. J. M. Mackenzie, were complaining that it was 'driven out of its wits by overuse' and had become the 'purest of cliches'. Cited in Brubaker and Cooper (2000, p.3). Even in the late 1960s, some had thought that 'the terminological situation had gotten completely out of hand' (ibid. p. 37). Its usage has been much refined in recent years and has regained currency.
3. See Hegel (1961 and 1995). For a fuller discussion, see Parekh (1982, chs 4 and 5).
4. See Parekh (1981 and 2000b).
5. There is a common but mistaken tendency to define philosophy in a certain way and apply it mechanically to whatever happens to be the subject of inquiry. As Aristotle said, the mode of philosophizing should be appropriate to its subject matter, or else it distorts the latter. The difference between his theoretical philosophy (*Metaphysics*) and practical philosophy (*Ethics* and *Politics*) is well known. What is less widely appreciated is the structural difference between the latter two – that is, the ways Aristotle discusses moral and political life.

   Political philosophy is done differently in different civilizations, and benefits from a comparative perspective; see Dallmayr (1989 and 1999).

Chapter 2

1. For a good history of the various senses of the term, see Gleason (1983). See also Brubaker and Cooper (2000). Even Erik Erikson, a leading theorist of identity, uses the term in different senses. Sometimes he takes it to mean a sense of sameness or unity of personality, while on other occasions he takes it to refer to authenticity. A sense of identity is attained when one feels most deeply and intensely active and alive, and 'a voice inside speaks and says "This is the real me"'. At yet other places he equates it with

279

'aggravated self-consciousness'. See Erikson (1968, pp. 15, 50, 246, 300). See also Friedman (1999, pp. 226, 318–19). For a valuable discussion of the origin and development of the contemporary discourse on identity, see Elio Zarentsky's article in Craig Calhoun (1994).

2. Amélie Rorty (1976, p. 2) puts this well: 'What sorts of characteristics identify a person as essentially the person she is, such that if those characteristics changed, she would be a significantly different person, though she might still be differentiated and reidentified as the same?' See also Taylor (1989, p. 27), who offers a richer and substantive account of personal identity, on which I draw: 'My identity is defined by the commitments and identifications which provide the frame or horizon within which I can try to determine from case to case what is good, or valuable, or what ought to be done, or what I endorse or oppose. In other words, it is the horizon within which I am capable of taking a stand.'

3. Giddens (1991, pp. 52ff) shows how modernity is closely tied up with the development of a reflexive construction of the self.

4. Giddens (1991) provides a valuable insight into how what he calls self-identity or a sense of self emerges in modernity. Erikson explains well what this achievement consists of: 'I must register a certain impatience with the faddish equation. . . of the term identity with the question "who am I"? Nobody asks this question except in a morbid state or a creative self-confrontation. The pertinent question would be "what do I want to make of myself and what do I have to work with?"' (Erikson, 1968, p. 314).

5. Aristotle's account of choice highlights this factor. 'What is chosen is something in our power which is desired after deliberation. Choice, therefore, must be a deliberate desire of something in our power' (*Nicomachean Ethics*, III, 3. 113 a9). For Aristotle, every choice involves deliberation, and is in that sense reasoned. But the deliberation might be inadequate or shallow, and hence a reasoned choice might not be rational.

6. Maslow (1971, pp. 295ff). He thinks that certain 'choices' are a matter of 'inner necessity' or 'compulsion', and are best expressed as 'I have to' or 'I must', rather than 'I want to'.

7. Hayden (2001).

8. See his preface to the Hebrew Translation of his *Totem and Taboo*, cited in Fay (1993, pp. 211–12). See also Freud's address to the Society of B'nai B'rith in Vienna in 1926, cited in Erikson (1968, p. 20). He also talks of the 'safe privacy of a common mental construction', a commonality known only to those who share it.

9. For a valuable discussion, see Appiah (2005).

10. For a perceptive discussion, see Sen (2006, ch.1); see also Creppell (2003). As should be clear from the previous discussion, I take a different view from Sen's on the role of choice in human life.

11. Einstein once remarked, 'When I came to Germany fifteen years ago, I discovered for the first time that I was a Jew. I owe this discovery more to Gentiles than Jews' (quoted in Berlin, 1980, p. 147). Although no one seems to know who said the following, it makes a similar point: 'I was satisfied with being black until I discovered I was nonwhite.'

12. Cited in Gutmann (2003, p. 137).
13. A man seeking amputation of his healthy leg told a BBC interviewer that his leg 'is a wrongness; it is not a part of who I am'. This is somewhat similar to transsexuals feeling trapped in the wrong bodies. See Carl Elliott, 'Is Ugliness a Disease?', *Guardian*, 26 August 2003, pp. 10–11.
14. Williams (1995).
15. 'In order to have a sense of who we are, we have to have a notion of how we have become, and of where we are going' (Taylor, 1989, p. 47).

Chapter 3

1. For a helpful account of the politics of identity, see the editor's chapter in Calhoun (1994). For good discussions, see Kourani (1988), Appiah (2005), Young (1990), Phillips (1995) and Kastoryano (2002).
2. For an excellent discussion of the ways in which the demands of identity are moderated by, accommodated in and used to deepen democracy, see Gutmann (2003). Since all identity groups do not understand her democratic principles the way Gutmann does, she underestimates the difficulties involved in reasoning with them.
3. The term 'politics of difference' is used by some to mean the same as 'politics of identity'. For others, mainly the post-structuralists, it refers to a politics that is concerned to decentre established identities by uncovering the differences they conceal. As I argue, they sometimes coincide and on other occasions diverge.
4. For a valuable discussion of the ways in which demands of identity are scrutinized in public debates, see Gutmann (2003). For a valuable empirical discussion, see Mitra (1999).
5. Discussions of recognition wrongly assume that it is a modern phenomenon. Many premodern Western and non-Western societies granted it as a matter of fact, although their reasons for doing so were rarely theorized. Indian and Islamic societies were in this respect more articulate.
6. Barry (2001a, 2001b) are the best polemical examples of this.
7. Identity politics is not always the politics of the left or of opposition. It could be right-wing, as in the case of racists or religious orthodoxy. It is equally characteristic of established or dominant groups. Since their identity is institutionalized and hegemonic, they do not need to assert it openly.
8. There are other forms of politics than those of recognition or redistribution, but I ignore them in this chapter.
9. Wolff (1988) and Hinton (2002).
10. Miller (1995, 2005), Rawls (1999) and Goodhart (2006).
11. For a valuable discussion of these issues, see Fraser (1995a and 1995b). For an insightful critique of the narrowly defined distributivist view of justice, see Young (1990). Young goes wrong in tying justice too closely to the loosely defined concept of oppression, thus depriving it of a focus.
12. Cited in Haley (1966). See also Du Bois (1989) and Ellison (1952).

13. Peter Tatchell, a well-known and controversial gay rights activist in Britain in the 1980s and 1990s, puts the point well:

> We can create our own homo-affirming community and safe queer space where we do not have to justify ourselves or plead with hetero-sexuals for acceptance. We can give each other the support that straight society denies us. Developing the lesbian and gay community as a focus of counter-culture and counter-power helps undermine the grip that homophobia has on our lives. A well organised, powerful queer community is more difficult for straights to ignore. From a position of strength, we can better challenge hetero-supremacism. (*The Observer*, 19 June 1994)

For Einstein Jews were able to withstand the humiliation and hatred of the gentiles because of a strong community. See Berlin (1980, pp. 147–9).
14. I owe this point to Amartya Sen.
15. Tully (2000, p. 471).

Chapter 4

1. Cited by T.K. Oomen in May *et al.* (2004, p. 138). In Israel, the orthodox Jews, numbering about a tenth of its population, say the same about their country. Judaism is several thousand years old and God's gift. By contrast Israel is barely sixty years old and a human creation; for the ultra-orthodox Jews it is even considered illegitimate. Their national or political identity means little to them compared to their religio-ethnic identity.
2. Although national identity has some features in common with individual identity, it differs in important respects. It has the advantages of recorded history, public debate and institutional articulation, and the disadvantages of involving large numbers, a long past, dominant interests and ideological manipulation.
3. The excessive preoccupation with difference vitiates the discussions of both personal and national identity. It is strikingly absent in many conservative writers; see, for example, the discussion of national identity in Oakeshott (1962, chs 5 and 7). The obsession with being different is largely a legacy of certain forms of liberalism and, of course, Romanticism. It is to be found in J. S. Mill's *On Liberty*, ch. 3, where individuality is sometimes equated with being different. For references to the celebration of difference as the basis of identity in Herder, Schleiermacher and others, see Kedourie (1960, ch. 4).
4. *Newsweek*, April 1992. For a very different view, see Hill, C. (1989, p. 203): 'We have a great deal to be ashamed of in our history. We promoted and profited by the slave trade; we plundered India and Africa . . . we forced the opium trade on China, attempted to suppress the American, French and Russian revolutions, and were guilty of centuries of oppression

of the Irish people. I do not want a school history which boasts about our victories over lesser breeds – Spaniards, Frenchmen, Germans, Russians, Argentinians – nor over helpless colonial peoples.'

5.   See Lewis (1979, pp. 86–7), Cowling (1978), Casey (1982, pp. 23ff), Crowther (1983) and Thatcher (1988).

6.   See Skidelsky (1989). The *Sunday Telegraph* ran a series of fifteen articles on the state of Britain. These were later collected in Hutber (1978).

7.   See Parekh (2000a). For valuable discussions of the subject, see Kumar (2003) and Bryant (2006).

8.   For a good summary and discussion of the Canadian debate, see Cairns (1991), Kaplan (1991), Tully (1992) and Taylor (1993). Philip Resnik (2005) offers a passionate statement of why he thinks the country is basically European in its values and views.

9.   Walzer (1992, p. 46) puts this well:

> it is not the case that Irish-Americans, say, are culturally Irish and politically American . . . Rather they are culturally Irish-American and politically Irish-American. Their culture has been significantly influenced by American culture; their politics is still, both in style and substance, significantly ethnic . . . It remains true, however, that what all the groups have in common is most importantly their citizenship and what most differentiates them . . . is their culture.

Since liberalism is currently more severely tested and contested in Canada than in almost any other Western country, and since most Canadian writers on it are also politically engaged, the recent Canadian contribution to the development of liberalism displays unusual richness and depth. Indeed, thanks to Charles Taylor, Will Kymlicka and Joe Carens, a distinctly Canadian form of liberalism has now come of age.

10.   The most useful place to follow the German debate is the famous Historikerstreit debate, now helpfully collected in Knowlton and Cates (1993); see also Heimannsberg and Schmidt (1993). For obvious reasons, trust between generations and the transmission of experience and views from one generation to another, without both of which a society cannot preserve its continuity, were effectively shattered in Germany. This created a disturbing void at the very heart of the young Germans' sense of personal and national identity.

11.   The fear of the past was so deep that many West Germans hotly debated what to call their divided country. An influential group preferred 'Federation of German Länder'. Theodor Heus, the first federal president, thought this implied an 'evasive action before one's own identity' (*ein Ausweichen vor sich selbst*) and persuasively advocated the name of 'Federal Republic of Germany'; see Hucku (1987, p. 69).

12.   Knowlton and Cates, op. cit., p. 165.

13.   For a fuller discussion, see Parekh (1991, pp. 35–48 and 2006a). The appeal to a 'new national philosophy' is to be found in the rhetoric of almost all newly independent countries.

14. Karpat (1982).
15. The debate on national identity also extends to history and archaeology. The Slovenes insist that they are Europeans, not Balkans, and should *therefore* avoid certain habits and practices. Many Hindus insist that they are Aryans and indigenous to India, and hence own the country. Many Pakistanis trace their history not to India but to central Asia and Persia, from where many Muslim invaders came to India. In all these cases, the basic concern is to define the identity in a way that legitimizes certain goals and gives the identity a historical depth.
16. For an excellent discussion of Britain, see Colley (1992). Her frequent use of the term 'Britishness' gives her analysis a wrong orientation and is best avoided. Being British or French is a way of relating to one's fellow citizens, not a set of some uniformly shared qualities as the term 'Britishness' (like redness) implies. Unlike Colley, many writers on the subject make the common mistake of equating national identity with national character. Although the two overlap, they are conceptually distinct and belong to different traditions of discourse. National identity refers to the kind of political *community* we are, national character to the kind of *people* we are. The former refers to citizens collectively, to what they share as an organized community; the latter to them distributively, to the qualities they are supposed to share as individuals. National identity therefore has an institutional focus, a historical orientation in the sense of some account of how the community came to be what it is, and is political in nature and a matter of collective self-definition. Unlike national identity, national character, which is largely given, refers to psychological dispositions, qualities of temperament, and so on. While the concept of national character is problematic in a culturally diverse society, that of national identity is not. Immigrants can be expected to share national identity but not national character. Ethnic nationalism equates the two; civic nationalism keeps them separate.

Chapter 5

1. The term 'multicultural society' is generally used to refer to societies characterized by diversity, irrespective of how that diversity is derived and whether or not it is exclusively cultural in nature. This is how I use it.
2. These assumptions are commonly made in European societies, which do not see themselves as based on immigration. In those societies such as Norway and Denmark where most of the immigrants are refugees or asylum seekers and are expected to show gratitude, the expectations are greater than in those countries where immigrants were recruited for their labour and skills.
3. This is a standard nationalist and conservative view of social unity. Although often dismissed, it has subtly influenced the thought of even its liberal and socialist critics. It has also long been, and continues to be, a powerful force in the US; see Glazer (1993, pp. 122–36).

4. Margaret Thatcher used this argument repeatedly.
5. In the 1930s, Jews constituted just over 1 per cent of the German popula-
    tion, and were fully assimilated: 12,000 of them died defending Germany
    in the First World War, and 100,000 of them served in the army; 30 per
    cent of the Jewish soldiers were awarded the Iron Cross for bravery.
    Nearly half of Jewish marriages were with Christian partners. More than
    a third of Berlin's doctors and lawyers were Jewish. To highlight their
    German identity, many described themselves as Germans of the Mosaic
    persuasion. Some of them even objected to the influx of East European
    Jews, described by Walter Ratheneu, the Jewish foreign minister, as the
    'Asiatic hordes camping on the Brandenburg sands'.
6. For a good discussion, see Kymlicka and Opalski (2001). See also
    Vertovec (1999). Myron Weiner's article in the same volume uses 'inte-
    gration' interchangeably with assimilation and absorption.
7. In France, 'too much' religious practice indicates insufficient integration,
    and the demand is not only for the privatization of religion but also for
    decreased religiosity. Those who reduce the number of times they pray
    are deemed to be better integrated. A distinction is drawn between prac-
    tising Muslims (*pratiquant*) and believing Muslims (*croyant*); the latter
    indicates fanaticism and is a threat to integration. France sometimes uses
    these criteria to grant citizenship. A third of applicants are rejected each
    year because they fail on questions relating to dress, religiosity, language,
    etc. One lawyer from Morocco was asked how many times he ate cous-
    cous, what newspapers he read, of what nationality most of his friends
    were, and so on; see Bowen, (2007, pp. 195, 196).
8. Even in Canada, which takes a broad and plural view of integration, diver-
    sity and separateness are associated by an influential body of opinion with
    disunity and fragmentation. For a further discussion of some of the theo-
    ries of integration, see my 'Three Theories of Immigration' in Spencer
    (1994).
9. See Kymlicka and Opalski (2001, p. 48). The integrationist would reject
    what he calls 'thin' integration as not really being integration. It is not
    clear why Kymlicka thinks that integration can be limited to common
    institutions, which he then defines broadly to include educational, acade-
    mic, welfare, economic and political institutions (p. 35). Sometimes he
    talks of 'cultural integration' without spelling out what this entails.
10. This is particularly evident in the French and German discourses on inte-
    gration. In recent years it has also become quite prominent in the British
    discourse. MORI reported in 2001 that two-fifths of respondents felt that if
    immigrants are to integrate, they 'should not maintain their culture and
    lifestyle'. Four years earlier, British Election Study showed that 71 per cent
    of white respondents believed that immigrants should 'adopt and blend into
    society'; see Saggar (2003). The Runnymede *Report on the Future of Multi-
    Ethnic Britain* produced by the Commission I chaired argued that equal
    treatment involves respecting and accommodating differences, and that
    there was nothing wrong with looser integration and immigrant separate-
    ness in certain areas. Not only the conservative but even the liberal and

socialist media felt deeply troubled by this and attacked the Report. Such a totalist view of integration has persuaded me that the language of integration, which I had myself used in the past, is best avoided.

11. Banton (1999) acknowledges that the term 'integration' with its connotation of wholeness and unity is 'very far from ideal'. In another article he calls it a 'treacherous concept'. As he rightly observes, immigrants might be integrated at the local but not the national level, or vice versa, making it difficult to decide whether they can then be said to be integrated. Banton, however, continues to use the term 'because there is no alternative expression which is not open to even greater objections' (2001).

12. For an excellent discussion, see Mason (2000, ch. 5). While he sometimes equates common belonging with integration (p. 151), the general thrust of his argument is to separate the two. A multicultural society needs to bear in mind what Confucius said about the wise man: 'The exemplary person seeks harmony rather than agreement; the small person does the opposite' (*Analects* 13:23; 1:12; 2:14; 15:22).

13. It is striking that while immigration has long been a part of European history, hardly any political theorist has systematically theorized it. Most of them assume that citizens are all native-born.

14. Much discussion of social unity and national identity ignores this vital fact, and hence pays little attention to what can be done at the local level.

15. For a further discussion, see Parekh (2006b, pp. 230ff).

16. For a fuller discussion, see Parekh (2007c). I am here indebted to Mason (2000).

Chapter 6

1. Articles and editorials in major national and local newspapers and magazines as well as parliamentary debates in European countries provide countless examples of this. This view is also reflected in serious works of political and social theory. For an insightful study of European Muslims, see Klausen (2005).

2. It is striking that Islam in Europe became an important area of research from the 1980s onwards. The European Science Foundation sponsored a collaborative Europewide project in the mid-1980s. Sweden convened a conference appropriately called 'The New Islamic Presence in Europe' in 1986. It is against this background that the Rushdie affair in Britain and the headscarf affair in France burst on the scene in the same year. Both involved young people, sometimes acting in opposition to their parents. Europe had now discovered and begun to fear its Muslims.

In the US, a distinctly Americanized version of Islam is beginning to emerge based on a clear separation between religious and secular matters, the individual's right to interpret the Qur'ān, giving the lay governing boards of mosques final authority over the Imam, etc. Some commentators even call it Presbyterian or Baptist Islam. See Haddad and Smith (2002, pp. 128ff). See also Esposito and Burgat (2003).

3. In Britain, multiculturalism has been welcomed by liberals and even conservatives since the 1970s. During the Thatcherite period, it was viewed with disfavour by conservatives, but liberals remained its strong champions, and even the Conservative Government did little to arrest its progress. Although the Rushdie affair dampened liberal enthusiasm for it, they continued to support it. In recent years, especially after the events of 11 September 2001 (9/11), more of them are turning against it, arguing that it ghettoizes communities, gives them a licence to continue dubious practices, and militates against common values and national cohesion. Most of the examples they give refer to Muslims. A similar trend is evident in the Netherlands, where multiculturalism was much valued for years and is now being blamed for Muslim 'separatism'. France, Germany, Belgium and Spain were never very keen on multiculturalism, and now think that they were right to take this position.

    Much confusion in the discussion of multiculturalism arises because the term is used in two opposite senses. For some, it means treating each cultural community as a world unto itself and involves cultural relativism. For others, including myself, it means that no culture is perfect and that it benefits from a critical dialogue with others, and involves rejection of cultural relativism. Once the definitional differences are cleared up, there is often no serious disagreement between those who reject and those who favour multiculturalism. For most valuable discussions, see Phillips (2007) and Modood (2007). Many who accept a multicultural society reject multiculturalism because they think it turns what they consider a regrettable but inescapable fact into a value.

4. In the Netherlands, Immigration Minister Rita Verdonk announced that immigrants would in future be compelled to pass an examination in Dutch language and culture and attend 350 hours of classes before becoming permanent residents; see *Time*, 28 February 2005, p. 37. In Belgium, Filip Dewinter, the leader of the Far Right Vlaams Belang Party, which won nearly a quarter of the national vote in the regional elections in June 2004, wants to prevent Muslim immigrants from marrying in their home countries and bringing their spouses into Belgium; see *Time*, op. cit., p. 38. In Britain, some members of the Labour Government and many of its liberal supporters endorse this idea.

5. For a variety of reasons, Muslims in the US do not arouse this kind of cultural anxiety. Many of them are economically better off, and are not residentially concentrated. Historical memories of Islam are also different. The geographical distance from Muslim countries is greater, and the percentage of Muslims is smaller. Since the census does not gather information on religion, their number is estimated to be between three and six million – that is, less than 2 per cent of the population. At most, only 10 per cent of new immigrants are Muslim. Since they are drawn from many different countries, they do not form organized communities. About a third of American Muslims are African-American converts, and hence Islam is not seen as a wholly foreign religion. The US sees itself as a country of immigrants held together by Constitution rather than as a nation

state based on a shared culture, and is less nervous about cultural and other differences. Its political structure both permits a greater range of ethnic diversity and prescribes clear limits to it, channelling immigrant demands in certain directions. US society and culture are not as tightly structured as they are in Europe, leaving greater space for and being less judgemental about diversity. Since the US is much more religious than Europe and allows the public expression of religion, Muslims feel more comfortable with it.

It is striking that Muslim immigrants arouse anxiety in ways that other religious and ethnic minorities do not. This is related to their number, the kinds of demands they make, their forms and degrees of self-assertion, and, of course, the contemporary international situation. Historically speaking, the anxiety provoked by Muslims bears a resemblance to that associated in earlier times in some countries with Jews and Catholics.

Contrary to popular misconception, Islam has undergone more drastic changes than almost any other religion. Turkey under Kemal Atatürk underwent extensive secularization, including changes in dress, script and so on that has no European parallel. Libya under President Gadaffi broke the hold of the *ulema,* insisted on an officially sponsored radical interpretation of Islam, and even encouraged Muslims to date their calendar from the Prophet's death rather than the *hijra.* Nasser proclaimed a socialist interpretation of Islam and nationalized Al-Azhar University in 1961. Almost all of these and other changes occurred during periods of crisis, were largely initiated by determined governments, and did not grow organically from a sustained process of cultural criticism and change. This may partly explain why they remained precarious.

6. Cited in Pieterse (2007, p. 192).
7. See ICM Survey for the BBC, Radio 4, 24 December 2002. Rather surprisingly, the proportion of those claiming to be patriotic was higher among men then women (71 per cent as opposed to 59 per cent). Predictably, it was higher among those at the top of the occupational hierarchy than those at the lower end (73 per cent as opposed to 60 per cent) and in the older generation rather than the younger (90 per cent as opposed to 60 per cent).

    Such polls can be highly misleading and should be read carefully. Words like 'patriotic' and even 'primary' loyalty mean different things to different people, including the pollster and his/her subjects. Many people love their country but would not call themselves patriotic because of the exclusivity, uncritical loyalty and intensity of passion associated with this. Our vocabulary in this respect is too poor and limited to express the range of emotions one feels towards one's country and its people, and these two are not the same.
8. Most of his audience consisted of young Muslim men whose parents took a different view of him. The Islam of the first generation of immigrants is heavily folkish, oral, tied up with local culture, and traditional. That of their children and grandchildren, however, is textual, learned in mosques

and schools, lacks historical continuity, is shaped by intellectuals rather than mullahs, and is often strident.

9. The *Muslim Manifesto* published by Kalim Siddiqui's London-based Muslim Institute in 1990 took a different view. While agreeing that Muslims have a duty of loyalty to the state in which they have settled, it argued that such loyalty was overridden if in conflict with the *umma*. The Institute was openly committed to Ayatollah Khomeini, and reflects a minority view.

10. For a background to the Rushdie affair, see Parekh (1990).

11. The assassin of Theo Van Gogh had been featured a few years earlier in a Dutch magazine, with his picture on its cover, as an example of successful Muslim integration into Dutch society. He later joined an international gang of Muslim terrorists.

12. See Paul Cliteur's 'Cast Your Discomfort Aside', *The Times Education Supplement*, 18 February 2005.

13. Although Brian Barry talks a great deal about culture, he does not offer a systematic analysis of it. He often equates it with customs and thinks that it rests on the authority of tradition. He does not realize that culture could involve reasons that are internal to it.

14. The French case is complicated by the fact that, since Christian pupils are allowed to wear the crucifix, Muslims girls complained of discrimination. France could ban the crucifix or at least the cross as well, but dare not do so for fear of provoking public disorder and falling foul of human rights. It therefore argued that, unlike the crucifix, the *hijab* was ostentatious and had a proselytizing dimension, and thus subverted the principle of *laicité* in a way that the crucifix did not. Although this argument is not as specious as its critics suggest, it cannot bear the weight the French government puts on it.

Wearing a *hijab* can symbolize many different things. It can be an act of subjection to parental or communal pressure and a sign of inequality. It can also signify the process of personal spiritual development or turning inwards, and be a statement of self-chosen identity. As some French girls put it, it made them more restrained and inward-looking, and less extrovert, and that is what they wanted. It can also be a way of conveying to the boys without having to say it that they are not interested in certain kinds of activities or relationships. Since the *hijab* is open to conflicting interpretations, the school authorities and the government face a difficult decision. The French government took it to signify subordination, a denial of gender equality and pressure on other girls to do the same. This enabled it to show that the ban did not contravene Article 9 of the European Convention on Human Rights, which protects the 'freedom to manifest one's religion and beliefs'. Switzerland and Turkey have taken a similar legal route.

In this connection, a story, probably apocryphal, is relevant. There was a discussion at a tribal meeting in Kabul about ending the practice of women walking several steps behind their men. Young radicals insisted the women should not only walk alongside but ahead of men. This will show the world that the country has begun to change and bring more

American dollars. To their surprise, the greatest support came from the conservative elders, for two reasons. Since all roads were mined, men would not only be spared an early death, but be free to marry again! The same view, but different meanings and contradictory reasons!

15. In Germany, the teacher is a public servant representing the neutral and impartial state, and expected to be above political, religious and other markers of identification. This is why s/he is required not to go on strike, to wear neutral dress, and so on. When Fereshta Ludin decided to wear a headscarf in the school, she was told not to. She took the matter to the Federal Constitutional Court on the ground that she had a human right to practise her religion. Although the Court shared the general unease about her action, it had no alternative in law but to rule in her favour. There have been other such cases where exemptions from established practices were granted to accommodate the right to religion.

    Several writers complained that human rights were being used to change their culture and that Germans were losing control over it. While some of them did not wish to change any established custom, others wanted to draw a line at practices they regarded as central to their way of life. This involves striking a delicate balance between respecting human rights and upholding valuable cultural traditions. It is not obvious that human rights should automatically trump traditions. Courts may feel legally constrained to take that view, and then their decisions alienate a large majority and become contentious, as happened in Germany. Such matters are therefore best settled politically. Johanne Kandel, a keen advocate of Christian–Muslim dialogue, expressed this view well when he asked Muslim organizations if they were right to use human rights to 'push through their interpretation of Islam by means of the German Courts' and maintain practices that might be deeply offensive to the majority of Germans; see his article in *Islam und Gessellschaft*, Nr. 2, Berlin: Friedrich-Ebert Stiftung, no date.

    Every liberal society contains structural tension. It is committed both to human rights and to particular cultural traditions. When interpreted in a certain manner or pressed beyond a certain point, human rights might undermine the latter. Conversely, if the cultural traditions were to set the limits of human rights, these would emasculate them. Much good sense is required on the part of both the majority and the minority to maintain their balance.

16. Other verses such as 2: 136, 5: 48, 6: 83–96 and 29: 46 display a pluralist spirit.

17. Akhtar (1989, p. 102); see also his 'Is Freedom Holy to Liberals?' in Parekh (1990).

18. Europe is not *dar al-Islam* (an abode of Islam), but nor is it *dar al-harb* (the land of unbelief or war) because its large Muslim population is born here, enjoys all the rights, and has begun to shape the ethos of the wider society. It requires Islamic scholars to develop a new category with its own appropriate claims and obligations. Zaki Badawi, a distinguished Egyptian–British theologian, invented the third category of *dar al-sulh*

(the land of contract). It is helpful, but goes wrong in seeing Muslim citizenship as nothing more than contractual in nature.

Some Muslims mistakenly see their presence in Europe as comparable to the Prophet's *hijra* to Madina, and draw misleading conclusions from it. As Ismail al-Faruqe puts it, 'This is our Madina. We have arrived, we are here' (quoted in Fuller, 2003, p. 185). The Prophet founded a new community with its own rules and structure of authority; Muslim immigrants are not like that. The Prophet migrated to avoid persecution; Muslims are voluntary migrants. For a creative interpretation of Islam that takes this into account, see Ramadan (2004).

19. Populous Poll, cited in a Policy Exchange Report, entitled *Living Apart Together*, 30 January 2007 (www.policyexchange.org.uk).
20. In France, riots began in the high-rise, decaying and overcrowded housing estates of Sous-Bois and Montfermail, where up to half the youth are unemployed and have nothing to do except watch television and peddle drugs. They are subject to frequent harassment and humiliation by the police. Almost a whole generation is lost in this way. It is worth noting that US ghettoes present quite a different picture from their European counterparts. They have more poverty and violence, but display a greater community spirit. Religion is generally joyful and uplifting, unlike many European ghettoes, where it is aggressive and sour. Women play a greater role in holding families together in the US ghettoes.
21. See Olivier Roy, 'Britain, Home-grown Terror', *Le Monde Diplomatique*, 5 August 2005, p.1, where he talks of 'born again' Muslims and the 'revolt of a generation adrift between its culture of origin and westernisation'; see also Modood (2005).

Chapter 7

1. Although the term 'atheism' is widely used, it is not without its difficulties. It is intended to deny the existence of God, but much depends on what one means by God. God is often understood in the sense popularized by monotheistic religions, and taken to refer to a singular and omnipotent being or principle. This is what an atheist is supposed to deny. However, one can believe in a limited God, or God as a ground rather than a creator, or not in one but in many gods, or even in each individual having a personal deity guiding his/her destiny. An atheist would need to deny this as well. S/he is thus basically committed to the view that the world as we know it by empirical or scientific observation is self-sufficient and can and should be understood in its own terms. This is what is meant by a secular view of the world, raising the question of why we need the term 'atheism'. A secular person calls himself an atheist because some people believe in some kind of God and he wants to reject such a view. Atheism thus is a derivative category in a way that secularity is not.

Strictly speaking, a secular person does not so much deny the existence of God as remains indifferent to the whole debate. S/he sees no reason why the idea of God, and hence His existence or non-existence, should be taken seriously. Atheism could mean indifference to the question about the existence of God (as in 'amoral' or 'asocial'), or denial of the existence of God. A secular person is primarily an atheist in the first sense, and derivatively in the second. Secularity and atheism involve different kinds of debate. The latter seeks to refute arguments for the existence of God, and enters into a philosophical–theological debate. A secular person asks why s/he should enter the debate at all, what aspects of the world or human experience requires us to invoke the idea of God, and whether it really explains them.

2. The style of reasoning is the same among the literalists of all religions. The ultra-orthodox and even orthodox Jews, who say that God promised the land of Judea and Samara to the Jews, and that Israel has an absolute duty to reclaim them, are no different from their counterparts in other religions, and can be refuted along the lines discussed later in the chapter.

    It is estimated that there are 90 million evangelical Christians in the US, and that 59 per cent of Americans believe that St. John's prophecies foretold in the Book of Revelations will be fulfilled, probably during their lifetime! John Sutherland, 'God Save America', *Guardian*, 4 May 2004.

3. See the interview with Hassan Butt, a Muslim activist (2005). His views are echoed by many Muslim literalists, evangelical Christians, and their counterparts in other religions. For him, there can be no 'moderate Muslim'. 'If someone believes that it [the Qur'ān] is the incontestable word of Allah, how can he take a moderate view? He must fight if it is the will of Allah' (ibid. p. 32). Hassan has since changed his views, and is now an extremist target.

4. Ibid., p. 33.

5. For a fascinating study of fundamentalism, see the three volumes of Marty and Appleby (1991–3). Even here, fundamentalism is treated as a universal phenomenon occurring in all religions. See also Caplan (1987). Even in this otherwise excellent collection, the term fundamentalism is used by the contributors to cover all religions and all kinds of conservative movements.

6. The term fundamentalism appears to have been derived from a series of booklets entitled *The Fundamentals* published in America between 1910 and 1915. In them, the term 'fundamentals' referred to the 'central' doctrines of Christianity. I thank David McLellan for continuing to educate me on the nature of religious consciousness.

7. For Islamic fundamentalism, see Algar (1985), Choueiri (1990), Piscatori (1984), Mortimer (1982), Hiro (1988).

8. See Choueiri (1990, pp. 9–10, 129–31 and 150ff).

9. Khomeini used the derogatory word *akhund*, meaning hidebound and confused clergymen, to describe them; see Piscatori (1984, p. 170). As Karen Armstrong puts it, 'What he [Khomenei] did with Shi'ite Islam was as revolutionary as it would be for the Pope to abolish the mass'; see Lännström (2003, p. 17).

10. For Qutb and others like him, knowledge of the ultimate reality is the best guide to action, and action is the best way to acquire that knowledge. See

Binder (1988, p. 198), who rightly draws attention to how close this view is to Marx.

11. Quoted in Kedourie (1990). See also Ali Shariati's distinction between black or traditional Shi'ism, which he strongly disapproves of, and revolutionary or red Shi'ism, which he strongly commends, in *Red Shi'ism*, Tehran: Shariate Foundation and Hamdani Publishers, 1979.

12. Roy (1986, p. 6). Islamic fundamentalism emerges from the 'modern institutions of society' such as colleges, science faculties and the urban environment, and not from 'the clergy and traditional circles'.

13. Fundamentalists reconcile religion and science in ingenious ways. Science is limited to the phenomenal world, where its value is great. The knowledge it provides is tentative, hypothetical and open to revision. One may therefore use it but cannot make it the basis of life. The laws of nature are believed to be designed by and owe their effectiveness to God. Atoms of hydrogen and oxygen do not by themselves produce water, but because God wills it to be so. For a good discussion, see Al-Azm (1993).

14. For a good discussion of how little Islamic fundamentalism reflects the spirit and thrust of Islam, see Nasr (1985).

15. Fundamentalism has a particular appeal for two groups of people. First the petty bourgeoisie – that is, such groups as the middle and lower middle classes, the shopkeepers, traders, merchants, artisans, peasantry and clerical workers. They enjoy some power and status in society, but these are now under threat. They are economically and politically unorganized, and when their interests are threatened, religion is often their only, or at least the most effective, means of mobilization. They build up their limited savings by means of hard work, thrift and an austere lifestyle, and feel threatened by a moral climate of self-indulgence. They rely on the willing co-operation, support and resources of their immediate and extended families, and depend heavily on conventional morality to sustain their relations with each other. More than almost any other section of society, the petty bourgeoisie therefore cherish conventional morality, define their self-respect and moral integrity in terms of it, and expect their religion to emphasize and enforce it. When that morality collapses or is under serious threat, the very foundations of their personal and social world are shaken.

Another group making similar demands consists of first-generation and sometimes even second-generation migrants to the city. The traditional values, forms of interdependence and self-understanding on which they generally rely in the villages do not make much sense in their new environment. As a result, their lives lack rootedness, coherence and moral anchorage, and their sense of identity and continuity is subjected to intolerable pressure. They are also disturbed by the life-styles of their urban fellow religionists, and the liberties taken with religious beliefs and values. They find that these life-styles intrude into their own families, and undermine the traditional pattern of intra-familial and inter-familial relationships. Although their moral requirements and demands are not the same as those of the petty bourgeoisie, they share enough in common to join them in demanding a firm reassertion of their religious identity. Both lack continuity and coherence in their lives, and have been wrenched or are in the process of being wrenched from the social world as they have hitherto known it. Such increasingly abstract individuals require and demand an equally abstract and simplified definition of their religion. Fundamentalism is a response to this demand.

16. Choueiri (1990, pp. 120ff).
17. Caplan observes that 'rationalism is a crucial characteristic of fundamentalism' (1987, p. 13).
18. Marty and Appleby (1991–3). Daniel Gold's analysis here shows that what he calls Hindu fundamentalism has little in common with its Islamic and Protestant counterparts, raising the question of why it should be so called. Donald Swearer, in his essay in Marty and Appleby, is unable to go beyond showing that Buddhists can be militant, yet he talks of Buddhist fundamentalism.
19. Misra (2004).

Chapter 8

1. See Huntington (1996, 2001). In talking of a clash of civilizations, he at least acknowledges that non-Western civilizations, including Islam, merit that description. For many others, the clash is between civilization (Western) and barbarism.
2. Huntington (1996, pp. 310, 312; see also pp. 40f, 309, 318).
3. Ibid., p. 43.
4. Ibid., p. 20.
5. Ibid., p. 53.
6. Ibid., pp. 42 and 47.
7. Ibid., p. 43.
8. Ibid., pp. 40f.
9. Ibid., p. 69. It is worth noting that the tendency to disjoin West and non-West and to write an autonomous history of the former is a modern phenomenon. Until the end of the eighteenth century, most books on the history of philosophy, for example, included, even began with, the Persians, Indians, Chinese and Egyptians. Voltaire called Confucious the first philosopher. By the beginning of the nineteenth century, this was replaced by a singular narrative beginning with the Greeks and taking no notice of non-Western traditions of thought. This trend is strikingly evident in Dietrich Tiedmann's eleven-volume history of philosophy that began in 1798. Two related factors were largely responsible for this change, namely European domination of the world and the definition of philosophy as an argumentative inquiry in preference to the earlier view of it as *Weltweisheit* (world wisdom). The view that philosophical ideas should be traceable to identifiable individuals also played a part.
10. Huntington (1996, pp. 305ff).

11. Huntington (2001, pp. 19, 15); Huntington (1996, pp. 305–6).
12. Huntington (2001, p. 19). This is why he thinks that 'Americans view atheists more unfavourably than most other countries, including socialists and homosexuals', p. 85. For him, US civic identity is inseparable from, and indeed rooted in, its ethnic and religious identity. Since its cosmopolitan elite fails to appreciate this fundamental fact, it cannot connect with the spirit of the American people. See Huntington (2004a).
13. See also Huntington (2004b), where he argues that the presence of an increasing number of Hispanics is challenging the Western identity of the US.
14. 'The underlying problem for the West is not Islamic fundamentalism. It is Islam' (Huntington 1996, pp. 217 and 312).
15. The US tradition is 'an amalgam of many traditions', none of which can be called 'the American tradition'. It is a product of the traditions of native Americans, Anglo-Saxons, slaves, early Dutch settlers, French Huguenots, Scottish-Irish, Irish Catholics, Jews and so on. See Lerner (1957, p. 22).
16. I draw here on Parekh (2002). For a different angle on the subject, see Parekh (2004b).

Chapter 9

1. See Giddens (1990).
2. For a fuller discussion, see Pieterse (2007, pp.89ff). Walking along the beach in Mumbai some years ago, I saw a young Indian, who seemed to be a recent migrant from his village, nibbling at his girlfriend's ear lobe. The confused girl, who knew only the printed instructions of sex, had little idea of the power of CNN over her male companion!
3. See Pieterse, in Featherstone *et al.* (1996). There is a cross-over of ideas of beauty and, thanks to intermarriages, there is even talk of a global face. *Newsweek*, 4 November 2003 referred to the emerging 'global standard' of beauty and hailed Saira Mohan's face as the 'perfect face', an example of a 'global face of beauty'. She has sharp cheekbones inherited from her Indian father, and a white complexion and round eyes derived from the French–Irish–Canadian ancestry on her mother's side. She could easily pass as Italian, Spanish or British, and even as an Indian if she wore a sari. Whatever one thinks of a global face based on national stereotypes, ideas of beauty are clearly crossing borders. In Asia, the round face used to be favoured; now the oblong face preferred in the West seems to be becoming more popular. Lean figures among men, and especially among women, are also more popular than before. Conversely, Eastern hairstyles and eyes seem to be gaining popularity in the West. See Thomas Fuller's 'Globalization Brings New Cultural Traits to India', *International Herald Tribune*, 14 September 2000.
4. See Cvekovich and Kellner (1997). The article by Axtmann is particularly relevant.

5. For a sensitive account of the way that US films and television programmes dominate the world, see Barber (1995). Visual and musical entertainment is the US's third-largest export after aerospace and pharmaceuticals. See also Cowen (2002), which takes a much rosier view of globalization than is warranted by his own evidence.

6. Explaining US's strengths, Joffe, a German journalist, observes: 'America has the world's most open culture, and therefore the world is most open to it'. Dominique Moise, a French critic of America, expresses a similar view. The message of the American cinema has a universal appeal because it is 'based on the openness of America and the continuing success of its multicultural society'. Cited in Nye (2002, p. 71). Although written from the US point of view, this a wise and thoughtful analysis of the implications of globalization.

7. See Goddard (1993) and Tournabouni (1995). This view underestimates the reverse process, in which the rest of the world shapes US ways of life and thought. As Kishore Mahbubani puts it, 'The West will increasingly absorb good minds from other cultures. And as it does so, the West will undergo a major transformation: it will become within itself a microcosm of the new interdependent world with many thriving cultures and ideas'; cited in Nye (2002, p. 80).

8. Jeevan Vasagar (2006) 'Welcome to Nollywood', *Guardian*, 18 March 2006.

9. Barber (1995, pp 90ff). Barber's book is one of the best on this subject.

10. For a balanced evaluation of the cultural impact of globalization, see Tomlinson (1999), Pieterse (2003) and Barber (1995).

11. Canada has often used cultural subsidies as a crucial element of its cultural policy. In the late 1990s, Canada, France and others opposed the Multilateral Agreement on Investments that had been negotiated through the OECD, largely to defend cultural diversity. As Antonio Muoz Molina, a Spanish writer put it, 'In Europe, unlike the United States, there is a consensus that culture is a public good, much like education and health, that cannot be left to the strict laws of the market' (*El Pais*, 17 April 2004).

Chapter 10

1. Global ethics has been a subject of criticism from three different directions. First, relativists deny its possibility. Second, some argue that, while it is possible, it is unnecessary, for each society should be free to lead the life of its choice. Chinese leaders have taken this line consistently for half a century. Third, some, mainly those from developing countries, argue that global ethics is possible but dangerous, as it can be and indeed often is used to justify imperialist projects.

   None of these criticisms is convincing. Relativism is incoherent, and stands refuted by the several universal declarations of rights that have been prepared and accepted by the representatives of vastly different national and cultural communities. See Parekh (1999). The second criticism is incoherent, because the universal principle that each society should be free to decide how it wishes to live is itself universal in nature. It also entails the untenable view that egregious misdeeds in other societies, including genocides, make no moral claims on the rest of humanity. The third criticism makes an important point, but is basically directed not at moral universalism per se but at its particular form and use. I thank Joseph Raz for a most helpful discussion on the subject.

2. By global ethics, I mean a systemic study of ethical principles. *A* global ethic or ethics is the result of such a study, and refers to a particular body of substantive ethical principles.

3. For a fuller discussion, see Parekh (2006b, pp. 117ff). For a valuable discussion that takes a somewhat different view, see Gorringe (2006).

4. See the Declaration Toward a Global Ethic by the Parliament of the World's Religions, September, 1993 (Küng and Kuschel, 1993). Its introduction asserts that 'a common set of core values is found in the teachings of religions and that these form the basis of a global ethic'. The list is a mixed bag and includes common aspirations rather than shared values.

5. See Kant (1953, pp. 90, 98). For a critique of Kant's universalizability principle, see Jones (1999, ch. 8). For an attempt to save it by reinterpreting it radically, see O'Neill (1986, ch. 7, esp. pp. 130ff).

6. John Rawls (1971). Rawls is too much in the shadow of Utilitarianism to transcend its basic approach. He sets up his system in opposition to it, but keeps claiming that his principles of justice have beneficial consequences. What if they do not? There is also the further question of how to evaluate consequences.

    Dworkin highlights other important weaknesses: 'The device of the original position . . . cannot plausibly be taken as the starting point for political philosophy. It requires a deeper theory beneath it, a theory that explains why the original position has the features that it does and why the fact that people would choose particular principles in that position, if they would, certifies those principles as principles of justice' (Dworkin, 1981, p. 345). See also Beitz (1979) for a critique of Rawls' state-centred approach.

7. I draw here on a fuller discussion in Parekh (2006b).

8. This is one of several reasons why we should talk of our duties or responsibilities towards animals rather than animal rights. See Midgley (1986, ch. 5) and Clark (1977, pp. 43ff). For a different but ultimately unpersuasive view, see Regan (1983). Unlike the term 'human', the term 'animal' covers such a wide spectrum that one wonders if it is a coherent subject for moral analysis, let alone a bearer of rights.

9. For a valuable discussion, see Scheffler (2002) and Honderich (2006). The distinction between negative and positive duties is often taken to correspond to that between justice and benevolence, or between what should or should not be enforced by law. Beyond a certain point, this latter distinction is problematical. What are considered to be benevolent acts in one society are a moral duty, even a 'perfect' duty, in another. Even in the

same society, they are seen differently at different periods and by different groups.

10.   For a critique of an excessive preoccupation with rights, including human rights, see Parekh (2006c). Starting with the UN Declaration, most that followed it concentrated on rights. Although duties beyond a certain point are not easy to specify, the basic ones such as not to cause harm to others and to assist those in desperate need can be. A universal declaration of human duties, analogous to that of human rights, would cover such things as countries committing a certain percentage of their GNP to foreign aid, requiring them to observe certain norms in relation to each other, banning the sale of arms under certain circumstances, banning landmines and the use of cluster bombs, imposing certain duties on multinationals operating in poor countries, environmental protection and so on. Fragments of such a declaration currently exist in the form of international treaties and UN resolutions. A clearly articulated and universally agreed declaration would consolidate global ethical norms and act as a benchmark against which to judge countries.

11.   This implies non-relativist pluralism. I explore this in Parekh (2006b and 2007a).

Chapter 11

1.   MacIntyre (1984, p. 18) distinguishes sharply between a 'morality of liberal impersonality' and a 'morality of patriotism'. He argues, wrongly in my view, that patriotism is the highest political virtue and is 'systematically incompatible' with the standpoint of impartial morality. Patriotism is not necessarily a virtue; much depends on how it is defined and whether the *patre* is worthy of one's loyalty. Even when it is a virtue, it is not and cannot be the highest, because the *patre* is itself judged by certain general principles. It can and should be made compatible with impartial morality if it is not to degenerate into national selfishness and worse. For a critical discussion, see Forst (1994).

2.   For useful discussions, see Barry (1995), Nagel (1991) and Nussbaum (1996).

3.   'People should not show personal affection and love to others on the basis of arbitrary physical characteristics alone, but rather on the basis of traits of personality and character related to acting on moral principles' (Richards, 1991, p. 94).

4.   Oakeshott (1962, ch. 3).

5.   For a good statement, see Goodin (1985 and 1987).

6.   W. H. Walsh, in Berki and Parekh (1972).

7.   See Gewirth (1988).

8.   Rousseau has something like this in mind (1979, p. 441). In his book *Emile*, Emile tells his prospective wife: 'Sophie, you are the arbiter of my fate. You know it well. But do not hope to make me forget the rights of humanity. They are more sacred to me than yours. I will never give them

up for you'. At this point, Sophie 'puts an arm around his neck and gives him a kiss'. Here, as elsewhere, Rousseau carries his point too far and renders it untenable. 'Rights of humanity' are not 'more sacred', and do not automatically trump those of Sophie. What is needed is a balance between the two.

Chapter 12

1. For good critical discussions of the exclusivist view, see Nardin (1983) and Brown (1992).
2. For the uncoupling of autonomy and sovereignty, see Walker and Mendlouitz (1990).
3. For valuable discussions of humanitarian intervention, see Wheeler (2000), Walzer (1977 and 1998) and Pieterse (1998). The US-led intervention in Somalia in 1992 was the first UN authorized example of it. I thank Nick Wheeler for many long discussions on this subject.
4. See Smith (1989, p. 63); and Jackson, in Lyons and Mastanduno (1995, p. 76). Simon Jenkins thinks it 'difficult . . . to justify asking your own troops . . . to commit their lives to the defence of – what?', in 'Foreign Policy and Human Rights'. Foreign Affairs Committee of the House of Commons, Minutes of Evidence, 25 November 1977, p. 4.
5. I rely here on parts of Parekh (1997). I thank Joseph Nye, Jr for his helpful comments when he was a discussant at a lecture I gave at the Boston University's Institute of Philosophy in 2005.
6. Hegel (1995, §330–2). For Hegel recognition is both a right and a gift.
7. Nussbaum (1996). In a recent poll, 73 per cent of Americans saw themselves as citizens of both the US and the world, and 44 per cent felt strongly about it. See Nye (2002, p.138).
8. I am not happy with the term 'internationalism', but cannot think of a better alternative. It is state-centred, and relates to the society of states, not the universal human community. The term 'cosmopolitan' stresses the latter but ignores the states.
9. The NATO bombing of Serbia cost US$4 billion, and an additional US$20 billion to rebuild what it had destroyed, not to mention the lives lost, and yet it left the problem of Kosovo unsolved. It was neither authorized nor condemned by the UN.
10. 'The Failed States Index', *Foreign Policy*, vol. 149, 2005, pp. 56f. In all, these states include around two billion people, a third of the world's population. The figure of sixty states is higher than it should be because it also includes 'weak' or soft states.
11. This is well articulated in the Report of the *International Commission on Intervention and State sovereignty*. It rightly moves away from some of the assumptions of the current debate when it talks of the 'responsibility to protect', and redefines sovereignty.
12. For an excellent analysis of the complexity of global issues and ways of responding to them, see Griffiths and Potter (2007).

Chapter 13

1. The US invaded Cuba in the nineteenth century to 'liberate' it from Spanish 'despotism'. It offered a similar defence for its colonization of the Phillipines. While European powers justified their imperialism in liberal terms, the US has generally preferred the language of democracy. President George W. Bush is convinced that 'global expansion of democracy is the ultimate force in rolling back terrorism and tyranny' (*Financial Times*, 11 November 2003).
2. The argument here is that our primary concern should be with stability rather than democracy or even good governance.
3. For excellent accounts of the history and changing forms of democracy, see Dunn (2005) and Held (1996).
4. For a valuable discussion, see Bayat (2007). See also Esposito (1996) and Sachedina (2006).
5. See Parekh (1993).
6. This argument has generally come from almost every part of the world apart from Latin America. See Schaffer (1988).
7. See the article by Dasgupta and Maskin in Shapiro and Hacker-Cordón (1999). The fact that India is one of the very few developing societies to have sustained democracy for almost sixty years is best explained in terms of the quality of its early leadership, the democratic structure of the Indian National Congress before and after independence, a century-old programme of social reform before independence, absence of a revolutionary threat to the regime, India's regional and social diversity, the messy compromise reflected in its Constitution, the long tradition of dissent and public debate, and the country's plural culture.

    In all Western societies, democracy was introduced in at least three stages over at least a hundred years – first the removal of the property qualification, then gender, then age, and, in some cases, race. Independent India introduced universal suffrage at one go – an event without precedent – with all its opportunities and problems. When we seek to promote democracy in non-democratic societies, we do the same, and it is never without its problems. Since the West has no historical experience of this, it fails to understand how difficult these problems can be. Those regarded as socially, economically or generationally inferior are suddenly one's equals and, what is worse, one is expected to woo them to get their votes.
8. Since democracies can be bounced into wars by determined governments, we need to find more effective ways of guarding against this. We could require that no war should be initiated without the authorization of a two-third majority in both Houses of Parliament or Congress. If a war is really justified, the bulk of the community should be convinced of it, and one obvious test of this is that the overwhelming majority of the elected representatives are in favour of it. A bare majority shows that almost half of them are unconvinced by the reasons given for it, and a war involving a massive loss of lives and property, and increasing the vulnerability of the country to terrorist attacks, cannot be undertaken on such a basis.

Since a war can be sold on the basis of dubious or conveniently misinterpreted intelligence reports, as in the case of the second war on Iraq, we might also require that they should be checked, vetted and certified by a small body of independent and senior statesmen experienced in such matters, and pledged to confidentiality. I have canvassed both of these ideas in the British House of Lords, found support among quite a number of my colleagues, and resistance among many more: they think a majority is all that one can hope, and ask, for, and that intelligence should remain limited to the government.

9. Youngs (2004).
10. See the articles by Richard Falk and Samir Amin in Sheth and Nandy (1996).
11. For the importance of sensitivity to local interests in fostering democracy, see Chandler (2006).
12. See Dario Salinas Figueredo, 'Democratic Accountability in Latin America: Limits and Possibilities in the context of Neoliberal Domination', *Critical Sociology*, vol. 32, issue 1.
13. In a democracy, the media are vital sources of information and opinions for citizens, and affect the quality of democracy. They also exercise considerable political power, and shape government policies. We are therefore right to insist that they cannot be just business; rather, they are privately owned public institutions, and subject to public regulation. We may therefore not allow anyone to own more than a quarter of the national media, encourage new media through a media development agency, require them to publish corrections promptly, and to set aside a certain space for different points of view. We may also expect journalists to declare their business and other interests and not write on subjects involving conflict of interest, the kind of requirement we impose on elected representatives and other public figures.

There is also something to be said for cross-party Parliamentary committees holding public hearings, where editors of major media might be asked to explain their coverage of public events. An independent and publicly funded body could also periodically audit media coverage of important events and public figures, and grade them on a scale of accuracy and objectivity. Whatever we do, our main concern should be to maximize freedom of the media and minimize its biases and manipulations.

Bibliography

Akhtar, S. (1989) *Be Careful with Muhammed! The Salman Rushdie Affair* (London: Bellow Publishing).

Al-Azm, S. J. (1993) 'Islamic Fundamentalism Reconsidered', *South Asia Bulletin*, vol. XIII, nos. 1 and 2.

Algar, H. (1985) *Iman Khomeini: Islam and Revolution* (London: Routledge).

Appiah, K. A. (1997) 'Cosmopolitan Patriots', *Critical Inquiry*, vol. 23, no. 3.

—— (2005) *The Ethics of Identity* (Princeton, NJ: Princeton University Press).

Baggini, J. and Stangroom, J. (eds) (2007) *What More Philosophers Think* (London: Continuum).

Banton, M. (1999) 'National Integration and Ethnic Violence in Western Europe', *Journal of Ethnic and Migration Studies*, vol. 25, no. 1.

—— (2001) 'National Integration in France and Britain', *Journal of Ethnic and Migration Studies*, vol. 27, no. 1.

Barber, B. (1995) *Jihad vs. MacWorld* (New York: Random House).

Barry, B. (1995) *Justice as Impartiality* (Oxford: Oxford University Press).

—— (2001a) 'The Muddles of Multiculturalism', *New Left Review*, no. 233.

—— (2001b) *Culture and Equality* (Cambridge: Polity).

Bayat, A. (2007) *Social Movements and the Post-Islamic Turn* (Stanford, Calif.: Stanford University Press).

Beitz, C. (1979) *Political Theory and International Relations* (Princeton, NJ: Princeton University Press).

Benhabib, S. (2002) *The Claims of Culture: Equality and Diversity in the Global Era* (Princeton, NJ: Princeton University Press).

Benyon, J. and Dunkerley, D. (eds) (2000) *Globalisation: The Reader* (London: Athlone Press).

Berger, P. L. and Huntington, S. P. (eds) (2002) *Many Globalizations: Cultural Diversity in the Contemporary World* (Oxford: Oxford University Press).

Berki, R. N. and Parekh, B. (eds) (1972) *The Morality of Politics* (London: Allen & Unwin).

Berlin, I. (1980) *Personal Impressions* (Harmondsworth: Penguin).

Binder, L. (1988) *Islamic Liberalism: A Critique of Development Ideologies* (Chicago: Chicago University Press).

Bowen, J. R. (2007) *Why the French Don't Like Headscarves: Islam, the State and Public Space* (Princeton, NJ: Princeton University Press).

Brown, C. (1992) *International Theory: New Normative Approaches* (Hemel Hempstead: Harvester Wheatsheaf).

Brubaker, R. and Cooper, F. (2000) 'Beyond Identity', *Theory and Society*, vol. 29.

Bryant, C. G. A. (2006) *The Nations of Britain* (Oxford: Oxford University Press).

Butt, H. (2005) 'An Interview', *Prospect*, July.

Cairns, A. C. (1991) *Charter versus Federalism: The Dilemmas of Constitutional Reform Options for a New Canada* (Toronto: University of Toronto Press).

Calhoun, C. (ed.) (1994) *Social Theory and the Politics of Identity* (Cambridge, Mass.: Blackwell).

Caplan, L. (1987) *Studies in Religious Fundamentalism* (London: Macmillan).

Carens, J. (1996) 'Dimensions of Citizenship and National Identity in Canada', *The Philosophical Forum*, vol. xxvii, nos. 1 and 2.

Casey, J. (1982) 'One Nation: The Politics of Race', *The Salisbury Review*, vol. 1.

Chandler, D. (2006) 'Back to the Future? The Limits of Neo-Wilsonian Ideals of Exporting Democracy', *Review of International Studies*, vol. 32.

Choueiri, M. (1990) *Islamic Fundamentalism* (London: Pinter).

Clark, S. (1977) *The Moral Status of Animals* (Oxford: Oxford University Press).

Cliteur, P. (2005) 'Cast Your Discomfort Aside', *The Times Education Supplement*, 18 February.

Cohn-Sherbok (ed.) (1997) *Islam in a World of Diverse Faiths* (London: Macmillan).

Colley, L. (1992) *Britons: Forging the Nation 1707–1837* (New Haven, Conn.: Yale University Press).

Cowen, T. (2002) *Creative Destruction* (Princeton, NJ: Princeton University Press).

Cowling, M. (ed.) (1978) *Conservative Essays* (London: Cassell).

Creppell, I. (2003) *Toleration and Identity* (New York: Routledge).

Crowther, I. (1983) 'Mrs Thatcher's Idea of Good Society', *The Salisbury Review*, vol. 2.

Cvekovich, A. and Kellner, D. (eds) (1997) *Articulating the Global and the Local* (Boulder, Col.: Westview Press).

Dallmayr, F. (1989) *Margins of Political Discourse* (Albany, NY: State University of New York Press).

—— (1998) *Alternative Visions: Paths in the Global Village* (Lanham, Md.: Rowman & Littlefield).

—— (ed.) (1999) *Border Crossings: Toward a Comparative Political Theory* (Lanham, Md.: Lexington Books).

Darling-Smith, B. (ed.) (2007) *Responsibility* (Lanham, Md.: Lexington Books).

Du Bois, W. E. B. (1989) *The Souls of Black Folk* (Harmondsworth: Penguin).

Dunn, J. (2005) *Setting the People Free: The Story of Democracy* (London: Atlantic Books).

Dworkin, R. M. (1981) 'What Is Equality? Part 2: Equality of Resources', *Philosophy and Public Affairs*, vol. 4.

Ellison, R. (1952) *The Invisible Man* (New York: Random House).

Erikson, E. (1968) *Identity: Youth and Crisis* (New York: W. W. Norton).

Esposito, J. (1996) *Islam and Democracy* (Oxford: Oxford University Press).

Esposito, J. and Burgat, F. (eds) (2003) *Modernising Islam* (London: Hurst & Company).

Fanon, F. (1952) *Black Skin, White Masks* (London: Pluto Press).

Fay, M. (1993) *Children and Religion: Making Choices in a Secular Age* (New York: Simon & Schuster).

Featherstone, M., Lash, S. and Robertson, R. (eds) (1996) *Global Modernities* (London: Sage Publications).

Figueredo, D. S. (2001) 'Democratic Governability in Latin America: Limits and Possibilities in the Context of Neoliberal Domination', *Critical Sociology*, vol. 32, issue 1.

Forst, R. (1994) *Contexts of Justice: Political Philosophy beyond Liberalism and Communitarianism* (Berkeley, Calif.: University of California Press).

—— (1997) 'Functions of a Theory of Multicultural Justice', *Constellations*, April, vol. 4, no. 1.

Fraser, N. (1995a) 'From Redistribution to Recognition? Dilemmas of Justice in a "Post-Socialist" Age', *New Left Review*, no. 212.

—— (1995b) 'Recognition and Redistribution: A Critical Reading of Iris Young's Justice and Politics of Difference', *Journal of Political Philosophy*, vol. 3, no. 2.

—— (1997) *Justice Interruptus: Rethinking Key Concepts of a Post-Socialist Age* (London: Routledge).

Friedman, L. (1999) *Identity's Architect: A Biography of Erik Erikson* (Cambridge, Mass.: Harvard University Press).

Fuller, G. E. (2003) *The Future of Political Islam* (Basingstoke: Palgrave Macmillan).

Fuller, T. (2000) 'Globalisation Brings New Cultural Traits to India', *International Herald Tribune*, 14 September.

Gewirth, A. (1988) 'Ethical Universalism and Particularism', *Journal of Philosophy,* vol. 85.

Giddens, A. (1990) *The Consequences of Modernity* (Cambridge: Polity Press).

—— (1991) *Modernity and Self-Identity* (Cambridge: Polity Press).

Gilbert, P. (2003) *New Terror, New Wars* (Edinburgh: Edinburgh University Press).

Glazer, N. (1993) 'Is Assimilation Dead?', *The Annals of the Academy of Political and Social Science*.

Gleason, P. (1983) 'Identifying Identity', *The Journal of American History*, March, vol. 69, no. 4.

Goddard, F. (1993) 'Gatt Real', *Television Business International,* November–December.

Goodhart, D. (2006) *Progressive Nationalism: Citizenship and the Left* (London: Demos).

Goodin, R. E. (1985) *Protecting the Vulnerable* (Chicago: Chicago University Press).

—— (1987) 'What Is so Special about our Fellow Countrymen?', *Ethics*, vol. 98, no. 4.

—— (2006) *What Is Wrong with Terrorism?* (Cambridge: Polity Press).

Gorringe, T. J. (2006) *Furthering Humanity: A Theology of Culture* (London: Ashgate).

Gray, J. (1995) *Enlightenment's Wake: Politics and Culture at the Close of the Modern Age* (London: Routledge).

Griffiths, L. and Potter, J. (2007) *World without End? Contours of a Post-Terrorism World* (Peterborough: Epworth).

Gutmann, A. (2003) *Identity in Democracy* (Princeton, NJ: Princeton University Press).

Haddad, Y. Y. and Smith, J. I., (2002) *Muslim Minorities in the West: Visible and Invisible* (Walnut Creek, Calif.: Alternative Press).

Haley, A. (1966) *The Autobiography of Malcolm X* (New York: Grove Park).

Harris, H. (ed.) *Identity* (Oxford: Clarendon Press).

Hayden, T. (2001) *Irish on the Inside: In Search of the Soul of Irish America* (London: Verso).

Hegel, G. (1961) *The Phenomenology of Mind*, trans. J. Baillie (London: George Allen & Unwin).

—— (1995) *Elements of the Philosophy of Right*, ed. by Allen Wood (Cambridge: Cambridge University Press).

Heimannsberg, B. and Schmidt, C. J. (eds) (1993) *The Collective Silence: German Identity and the Legacy of Shame* (London: Macmillan).

Held, D. (1995) *Democracy and the Global Order: From the Modern State to Cosmopolitan Governance* (Cambridge: Polity Press).

—— (1996) *Models of Democracy* (Cambridge: Polity Press).

Hill, C. (1989) 'History of Patriotism' in S. Raphael (ed.), *Patriotism: The Making and Unmaking of British National Identity*, vol. 1 (London: Routledge).

Hinton, T. (2002) 'Must Egalitarians Choose between Fairness and Respect', *Philosophy and Public Affairs*, vol. 30.

Hiro, D. (1988) *Islamic Fundamentalism* (London: Paladin).

Honderich, T. (2006) *Humanism, Terrorism, Terrorist War: Palestine, 9/11, Iraq, 7/7* (London: Continuum).

Hucku, E.M. (ed.) (1987) *The Democratic Tradition: Four German Constitutions* (Lemington Spa: Berg).

Huntington, S. (1996) *The Clash of Civilisations and the Remaking of the World Order* (New York: Simon & Schuster, 1996).

—— (2001) *Who Are We? The Challenge to America's National Identity* (New York: Simon & Schuster).

—— (2004a) 'Dead Souls: The Denationalisation of the American Elite', *The National Interest*, Spring.

—— (2004b) 'The Hispanic Challenge', *Foreign Policy*, March–April, vol. 141.

Hutber, P. (ed.) (1978) *What is Wrong with Britain?* (London: Sphere).

International Commission on Intervention and State Sovereignty (2001) *The Responsibility to Protect* (Ottawa: ICISS).

Jacks, J. (2002) *The Dignity of Difference* (London: Continuum).

Jackson, R. (1995) 'International Community Beyond the Cold War', in G. M. Lyons and M. M. Mastanduno (eds), *Beyond Westphalia: State Sovereignty and International Intervention* (Baltimore, Md.: Johns Hopkins University Press).

Jones, C. (1999) *Global Justice: Defending Cosmopolitanism* (Oxford: Oxford University Press).

Kandel, J. (n.d.) *Islam and Gessellschaft*, No. 2 (Berlin: Freidrich-Ebert Stiftung).

Kant, I. (1953) *Groundwork of the Metaphysics of Morals*, trans. Paton, H. J. as *The Moral Law* (London: Hutchinson).

Kaplan, W. (ed,) (1991) *Belonging: The Meaning and Future of Canadian Citizenship* (Montreal: McGill-Queen's University Press).

Karpat, K. H. (ed.) (1982) *Political and Social Thought in the Contemporary Middle East* (New York: Praeger).

Kastoryano, R. (2002) *Negotiating Identities* (Princeton, NJ: Princeton University Press).

Keane, J. (2003) *Global Civil Society?* (Cambridge: Cambridge University Press).

—— (2004) *Violence and Democracy* (Cambridge: Cambridge University Press).

Kedourie, E. (1960) *Nationalism* (London: Hutchinson).

—— (1990) *Islamic Revolution* (London: Salisbury Group), Paper No. 6.

Kiss, E. (1998) 'Saying We're Sorry: Liberal Democracy and Rhetoric of Collective Identity', *Constellations,* vol. 4, no. 3.

Klausen J. (2005) *The Islamic Challenge: Politics and Religion in Western Europe* (Oxford: Oxford University Press).

Knowlton, J. and Cates, T. (1993) *Forever in the Shadow of Hitler?* (New Jersey: Humanities Press).

Kourani, J. A. (ed.) (1998) *Philosophy in a Feminist Voice: Critiques and Reconstructions* (Princeton, NJ: Princeton University Press).

Kumar, K. (2003) *The Making of English National Identity* (Cambridge: Cambridge University Press).

Küng, H. and Kuschel, K. J. (1993) *A Global Ethic: The Declaration of the Parliament of the World's Religions* (London: SCM Press).

Kymlicka, W. and Opalski, M. (eds) (2001) *Can Liberal Pluralism Be Exported? Western Political Theory and Ethnic Relations in Eastern Europe* (New York: Oxford University Press).

—— (2003) 'Being Canadian', *Government and Opposition*, vol. 38.

Lännström, A. (2003) *Promise and Peril: The Paradox of Religion as Resource and Threat* (Notre Dame, Ind.: University of Notre Dame Press).

—— (ed.) (2004) *The Stranger's Religion: Fascination and Fear* (Notre Dame: University of Notre Dame).

Lerner, M. (1957) *America as a Civilisation* (New York: Simon & Schuster).

Lewis, R. (1979) *Enoch Powell* (London: Cassell).

Lyons, G. M. and Mastanduno M.M. (eds) (1995) *Beyond Westphalia? State Sovereignty and International Intervention* (Baltimore: Johns Hopkins University Press).

MacIntyre, A. (1984) *Is Patriotism a Virtue?*, Lindley Lecture (University of Kansas Philosophy Department).

Marty, M. E. and Appleby, R. Scott (1991–3) *Fundamentalism Observed* (Chicago: The University of Chicago Press).

Maslow, A. H. (1971) *The Farther Reaches of Human Nature* (Harmondsworth: Penguin).

Mason, A. (2000) *Community, Solidarity and Belonging* (Cambridge: Cambridge University Press).

May, S., Modood, T. and Squires, J. (eds) (2004) *Ethnicity, Nationalism and Minority Rights* (Cambridge: Cambridge University Press).

Midgley, M. (1986) *Animals and Why They Matter* (Athens, Ga.: University of Georgia Press).

Mill, J. S. (1989) *On Liberty*, ed. Stefan Collini (Cambridge: Cambridge University Press).

Miller, D. (1995) *On Nationality* (Oxford: Oxford University Press).

—— (2005) 'Against Global Egalitarianism', *Journal of Ethics*, vol. 9, no. 1.

Misra, A. (2004) *Identity and Religion: Foundations of Anti-Islamism in India* (New Delhi: Sage).

Mitra, S. (1999) *Culture and Rationality* (Delhi: Sage).

Modood, T. (2005) *Multicultural Politics: Racism, Ethnicity and Muslims in Britain* (Edinburgh: Edinburgh University Press).

—— (2007) *Multiculturalism* (Cambridge: Polity Press).

Mortimer, E. (1982) *Faith and Power* (London: Faber & Faber).

Nagel, T. (1991) *Equality and Partiality* (New York: Oxford University Press).

Nardin, T. (1983) *Law, Morality and the Relations of States* (Princeton, NJ: Princeton University Press).

Nasr, S. H. (1985) *Islamic Spirituality: Foundations* (London: SCM Press).

Nussbaum, M. (1996) 'Patriotism and Cosmopolitanism', in J. Cohen (ed.), *For Love of Country: Debating the Limits of Patriotism* (Boston, Mass.: Beacon Press).

Nye, J. S., Jr (2002) *The Paradox of American Power* (Oxford: Oxford University Press).

Oakeshott, M. (1962) *Rationalism in Politics and other Essays* (London: Methuen).

O'Neill, O. (1986) *Faces of Hunger: An Essay on Poverty, Justice and Development* (London: Allen & Unwin).

Parekh, B. (1981) *Hannah Arendt and the Search for a Political Philosophy* (London: Macmillan).

—— (1982) *Marx's Theory of Ideology* (London: Croom Helm).

—— (1990) (ed.) *Free Speech* (London: Commission for Racial Equality).

—— (1991) 'Nehru and the National Philosophy of India', *Economic and Political Weekly*, vol. 26.

—— (1993) 'The Cultural Particularity of Liberal Democracy', in D. Held (ed.), *Prospects for Democracy* (Cambridge: Polity Press).

—— (1994a) 'Three Theories of Immigration', in Spencer, S. (ed.), *Strangers and Citizens* (London: Rivers Oram Press).

—— (1994b) 'Discourses on National Identity', *Political Studies*, vol. 42, no. 3.

—— (1997) 'Rethinking Humanitarian Intervention', *International Political Science Review*, vol. 18, no. 1.

—— (1999) 'Non-ethnocentric Universalism', in T. Dunne and N. J. Wheeler (eds), *Human Rights in Global Politics* (Cambridge: Cambridge University Press).

—— (2000a) 'Defining British National Identity, *Political Quarterly*, vol. 71, no. 1.

—— (2000b) 'Theorising Political Theory', in N. O'Sullivan (ed.), *Political Theory in Transition* (London: Routledge).

—— (2002) 'Terrorism or Intercultural Dialogue', in K. Booth and T. Dunn (eds), *World in Collision: Terror and the Future of Global Order* (Basingstoke: Palgrave Macmillan).

—— (2003a) 'Cosmopolitanism and Global Citizenship', *Review of International Studies*, vol. 29.

—— (2003b) *Reimagining India* (The Sixth Lakdawala Memorial Lecture) (Delhi: Institute of Social Science).

—— (2004a) 'Redistribution and Recognition? A Misguided Debate', in S. May, T. Modood and J. Squires (eds), *Ethnicity, Nationalism and Minority Rights* (Cambridge: Cambridge University Press).

—— (2004b) 'Mahatma Gandhi and Osama bin Laden: An Imaginary Dialogue', in Anna Lännström (ed.), *The Stranger's Religion: Fascination and Fear* (Notre Dame, Ind.: University of Notre Dame Press).

—— (2004c) 'Conversations in International Relations: Interview with Bhikhu Parekh', *International Relations*, vol. 18, no. 3.

—— (2004d) 'Globalisation for a Multicultural World', in K. Horton and H. Patapan (eds), *Globalisation and Equality* (London: Routledge).

—— (2005a) 'Principles of a Global Ethic', in J. Eade and D. O'Byrne (eds), *Global Ethics and Civil Society* (Aldershot: Ashgate).

—— (2005b) 'Dialogue between Cultures', in R. Maiz and F. Requejo (eds), *Democracy, Nationalism and Multiculturalism* (London: Routledge).

—— (2006a) 'Defining India's Identity', *India International Quarterly*, Summer.

—— (2006b) *'Rethinking Multiculturalism*, 2nd edn (Basingstoke: Palgrave Macmillan).

—— (2006c) 'European Liberalism and the Muslim Question', in T. Modood, A. Triandafyllidou and R. Zapata-Barrero (eds), *Multiculturalism, Muslims and Citizenship: A European Approach* (London: Routledge).

—— (2006d) 'Liberal Contribution to a Universal Ethic', in R. Tinnevelt and G. Verschraegen (eds), *Between Cosmopolitan Ideals and State Sovereignty: Studies in Global Justice* (Basingstoke: Palgrave Macmillan).

—— (2006e) 'Finding a Proper Place for Human Rights', in K. Tunstall (ed.), *Displacement, Asylum, Migration: The Oxford Amnesty Lectures 2004* (Oxford: Oxford University Press).

—— (2007a) Interview, in J. Baggini and J. Strangroom (eds), *What More Philosophers Think* (London: Continuum).

—— (2007b) 'Moral Responsibility in a Democratic State', in B. Darling-Smith (ed.), *Responsibility* (Lanham, Md.: Lexington Books).

—— (2007c) 'Composite Culture and Multicultural Society', in B. Chandra and S. Mahajan (eds), *Composite Culture in a Multicultural Society* (New Delhi: Pearson Longman).

Paton, H. J. (1947) *The Moral Law* (London: Hutchinson).

Phillips, A. (1993) *Democracy and Difference* (Philadelphia, Pa.: Pennsylvania University Press).

—— (1995) *The Politics of Presence: Issues in Democracy and Group Representation* (Oxford: Clarendon Press).

—— (2007) *Multiculturalism without Culture* (Princeton, NJ: Princeton University Press).

Pieterse, J. N. (ed.) (1998) *World Orders in the Making: Humanitarian Intervention and Beyond* (London: Macmillan).

—— (2003) *Globalisation and Culture* (Boulder, Col.: Rowman & Littlefield).

—— (2007) *Ethnicities and Global Culture: Pants for an Octopus* (Lanham, Md.: Rowman & Littlefield).

Piscatori, J. (1984) *Islam in Political Process* (Cambridge: Cambridge University Press).

Popper, K. (1945) *The Open Society and its Enemies* (London: Routledge).

Prunier, G. (1996) *The Rwanda Crisis – 1959–1994: History of a Genocide* (London: Hurst and Company).

Ramadan, T. (2004) *Western Muslims and the Future of Islam* (Oxford: Oxford University Press).

Rawls, J. (1971) *A Theory of Justice* (Cambridge, Mass.: Harvard University Press).

—— (1999) *The Law of Peoples* (with 'The Idea of Public Reason Revisited') (Cambridge, Mass.: Harvard University Press).

Regan, T. (1983) *The Case for Animal Rights* (London: Routledge).

Resnick, P. (2005) *The European Roots of Canadian Identity* (Plymouth: Broadview Press).

Richards, D. J. A. (1991) *A Theory of Reasons for Action* (Oxford: Oxford University Press).

Rorty, A. (1976) *The Identity of Persons* (Berkeley: University of California Press).

Rousseau, J.-J. (1979) *Emile*, translated and introduced by Allan Bloom (New York: Basil Books).

Roy, O. (1986) *Islam and Resistance in Afghanistan* (Cambridge: Cambridge University Press).

—— (2005) 'Britain, Home-grown Terror', *Le Monde Diplomatique*, 5 August.

Runnymede Trust Commission (2000) *The Future of Multi-Ethnic Britain* (London: Profile Books).

Sachedina, A. (2006) 'The Role of Islam in the Public Square: Guidance on Governance?', ISIM Paper 5 (Amsterdam: Amsterdam University Press).

Saggar, S. (2003) 'Immigration and the Politics of Public Opinion', *Political Quarterly*, vol. 74.

Schaffer, F. (1988) *Democracy in Translation: Understanding Politics in an Unfamiliar Culture* (Ithaca, NY: Cornell University Press).

Scheffler, T. (2002) *Boundaries and Allegiances: Problems of Justice and Responsibility in Liberal Thought* (Oxford: Oxford University Press).

Scholte, J.-A. (2000) *Globalisation: A Critical Introduction* (London: Macmillan).

Sen, A. (1999) *Development as Freedom* (New York: Alfred A. Knopf).

—— (2006) *Identity and Violence: The Illusion of Destiny* (London: Penguin).

Shapiro, I. and Hacker-Cordón, C. (eds) (1999) *Democracy's Value* (Cambridge: Cambridge University Press).

Shariati, Ali (1979) *Red Shi'ism* (Tehran: Hamdani Publishers).

Sheth, D. L. and Nandy, A. (eds) (1996) *The Multiverse of Democracy* (New Delhi: Sage).

Skidelsky, R. (ed.) (1989) *Thatcherism* (Oxford: Basil Blackwell).

Smith, A. (1991) *National Identity* (Harmondsworth: Penguin).

Smith, M. J. (1989) 'Humanitarian Intervention: An Overview of the Ethical Issues', *Ethics and International Affairs*, vol. 3.

Spencer, S. (ed.) (1994) *Strangers and Citizens* (London: Rivers Oram Press).

Taylor, C. (1989) *Sources of the Self* (Cambridge: Cambridge University Press).

—— (1993) *Reconciling the Solitudes: Essays on Canadian Federalism and Nationalism* (Montreal: McGill–Queen's University Press).

Thatcher, M. (1988) Speech in Bruges (London: Conservative Political Centre).

Thompson, K. (ed.) (1997) *Media and Cultural Regulation* (London: Sage Publication).

Tibi, B. (2005) *Islam between Culture and Politics*, 2nd edn (Basingstoke: Palgrave Macmillan).

Tomlinson, J. (1999) *Globalisation and Culture* (Cambridge: Polity).

Tournabouni, J. (1995) 'European Cinema is Dying', *Guardian*, 2 March.

Tully, J. (1992) 'Multirow Federalism and the Charter', in P. Bryden, S. Douis and J. Russell, (eds), *The Charter – Ten Years After* (Toronto: Toronto University Press).

—— (2000) 'Struggles over Recognition and Distribution', *Constellations*, vol. 7, no. 4.

Vasagar, J. (2006) 'Welcome to Nollywood', *Guardian*, 18 March.

Vertovec, S. (ed.) (1999) *Migration and Social Cohesion* (Cheltenham: Edward Elgar).

Walker, R. B. T. and Mendlouitz, S. (eds) (1990) *Contending Sovereignties: Redefining Political Communities* (Boulder, Col.: Lynne Rienner).

Walsh, W. H. (1972) 'Open and Closed Morality', in R. Berki and B. Parekh (eds), *The Morality of Politics* (London: Allen & Unwin).

Walzer, M. (1977) *Just and Unjust Wars* (New York: Basic Books).

—— (1992) *What It Means to Be an American* (New York: Marsilio).

—— (1998) 'The Politics of Rescue', *Dissent*, vol. 42, no. 1.

Wheeler, N. J. (2000) *Saving Strangers, Humanitarian Intervention in International Society* (Oxford: Oxford University Press).

Willett, C. (ed.) (1998) *Theorising Multiculturalism: A Guide to the Current Debate* (Oxford: Basil Blackwell).

Williams, B. (1995) 'Identity and Identities' in H. Harris (ed.), *Identity* (Oxford: Clarendon Press).

Wolff, J. (1988) 'Fairness, Respect and the Egalitarian Ethos', *Philosophy and Public Affairs*, vol. 2.

Young, I. M. (1990) *Justice and the Politics of Difference* (Princeton, NJ: Princeton University Press).

Youngs, R. (2004) *The European Union and the Promotion of Democracy* (Oxford: Oxford University Press).

Index